MW00998032

Second Edition

An Easy Introduction to Financial Accounting:

A Self-Study Guide

Professor V.G. Narayanan
Harvard Business School

© 2019 by V.G. Narayanan.

All rights reserved. This book is protected under the copyright laws of the United States of America. Any reproduction or unauthorized use of the material or artwork herein is prohibited without the express written permission of the author.

ISBN-13: 978-0-9978936-1-8

ISBN-10: 0-9978936-1-3

http://www.hbs.edu/faculty/Pages/profile.aspx?facId=6520

First Edition: 2016

Second Edition: May 2019.

Dedication

I would like to dedicate this book to my parents V. D. Gopal and G. Sakunthala. They unconditionally supported my choices and celebrated even the smallest of my accomplishments from the time I was a young child. My father had suggested to me numerous times that I should write a book. This book is the result of his encouragement.

Acknowledgements

I would like to acknowledge with deep gratitude the assistance of several people in writing this book, which is based on the script that I wrote for the accounting course that forms part of HBX CORe. In turn, the script for HBX CORe was prepared with the assistance of Cason Graff, Emma Fernandez, and Valerie Funk. I am deeply indebted to all three of them for their help, patience, and humor in editing countless versions of the script for the HBX course. Ashley Hartman helped convert the script from HBX CORe into this book. The examples and cases I use in this book are different from those in HBX CORe, so that it may be used as a standalone book independent of the HBX course. Ashley did all the heavy lifting in coming up with these examples and review questions. She also handled all the technology aspects of writing this book. I am extremely grateful to my colleagues, Jan Hammond and Bharat Anand, for their friendship and guidance as the three of us created HBX CORe. Without their support and encouragement, I would not have completed this book. Thank you in advance for any feedback you have on the book; please send it to vgtext2016@gmail.com.

I would also like to acknowledge the support of my lovely wife and sons during the last three years as I assumed the additional responsibility of developing a new online course and this book over and above my regular teaching and administrative responsibilities at Harvard Business School. I hope to spend more time with them and make up for missed family time.

Table of Contents

1

Intro to Financial Accounting

Sections

Section 1
Accounting Equation Components

Concepts

1. Introduction to Assets, Liabilities, and Owners' Equity

2. The Accounting Equation

1.1.1   Introduction to Assets, Liabilities and Owners' Equity

In order to know how a business is performing, it's essential to understand the business' financial statements. The equation **Assets = Liabilities + Owners' Equity** is fundamental to all of accounting, and it's a crucial tool for understanding how a business is doing. This chapter will provide an overview of the **accounting equation** and its components, discuss some typical **transactions** and their effects on the accounting equation, and go over some general principles of accounting.

Assets

The first part of the accounting equation is assets. What is an asset?

In the world of accounting, assets are resources owned or controlled by a business that the business believes will produce economic benefits in the future. Examples of assets include cash, **inventory**, and equipment that are owned or controlled by a business or organization. Cash can be used to invest in projects or maintain equipment. Inventory can be sold for cash, and equipment can be used to make products that customers will purchase, which benefit a company in the future.

Liabilities + Owners' Equity

The other side of the **accounting equation** – liabilities plus owners' equity – shows how a business obtained its assets or resources.

Liabilities

Businesses typically need to raise money in order to acquire assets. One method a business might use is taking out a loan to borrow money from a bank or lending institution. Another method is purchasing assets and services on credit from its suppliers, creating **accounts payable**, an obligation to be paid later. The loans from banks and accounts payable to suppliers are examples of liabilities. Thus, liabilities represent claims on the assets of the company by third parties (i.e. outsiders who are not owners of the business). You can also think of liabilities as a business' obligations to pay a third party for the resources provided to the business.

Owners' Equity

Another way a business may fund its resources is through investments in the business by its owners. When an owner contributes capital to a business, he is making an equity investment, and this investment is recorded in the owners' equity section of the balance sheet. Owners' equity contains both the capital contributed by owners and the profits earned by the business. How does this source of money differ from liabilities?

First of all, the owners of the business control it and have a say in how the business is run. Lenders and suppliers do not normally have the ability to make decisions about how the business operates. Secondly, the business is obligated to pay back lenders, but payments to owners are discretionary. Owners typically do not expect their initial investment to be paid back; they expect to make money from their initial investment through dividends. A dividend is a portion of a company's profits that is distributed to shareholders. As a business grows, it becomes more valuable and has the ability to distribute all or part of its earnings as dividends. Earnings not distributed as dividends also belong to the owner of the business.

Also, in the case where a business fails, the owners might not receive anything. Owners are thus residual claimants, only paid back after all the liabilities have been repaid. Liabilities are not discretionary, and businesses must fulfill their obligations, such as making payments to suppliers and banks.

Assets = Liabilities + Owners' Equity

Returning to the accounting equation, all the assets of a business belong either to its creditors (liabilities) or its owners (equity).

1.1.2   The Accounting Equation

It's helpful to look at examples from companies when studying the accounting equation. The three companies we will focus on are The Coca-Cola Company, a well-known international beverage company; Acorns Bakery, a local sandwich and baked goods shop; and Netflix, Inc., an internet television network that offers streaming television and movie rentals.

The Coca-Cola Company is a global player in the beverage industry, offering hundreds of brands of non-alcoholic beverages, including soft drinks, juices, and sports drinks. Its headquarters are based in Atlanta, Georgia. It's likely that you're very familiar with Coca-Cola products, but let's take a look at Coca-Cola's financial reports to understand the company better.

There are three major statements in financial reports: the **balance sheet**, the **income statement**, and the **statement of cash flows**. These statements have various line items that link them together. It's important to study all three statements to truly understand a business because the information conveyed on one statement is not necessarily shown on another. The balance sheet is basically an expanded representation of the accounting equation, Assets = Liabilities + Owners' Equity.

Coca-Cola's balance sheet shows the financial status of the company as of September 27, 2013 (see Figure 1.1).

FIGURE 1.1

THE COCA-COLA COMPANY AND SUBSIDIARIES
CONDENSED CONSOLIDATED BALANCE SHEETS
(in millions except par value)

	Sept. 27 2013	Dec. 31 2012
ASSETS		
CURRENT ASSETS		
Cash and cash equivalents	$ 11,118	$ 8,442
Short-term investments Marketable securities	6,139	5,017
TOTAL CASH, CASH EQUIVALENTS AND SHORT-TERM INVESTMENTS	17,257	13,549
Marketable Securities	3,202	3,092
Trade accounts receivable, less allowances of $57 and $53, respectively	5,116	4,759
Inventories	3,321	3,264
Prepaid expenses and other assets	2,680	2,781
Assets held for sale	-	2,973
TOTAL CURRENT ASSETS	31,576	30,328
EQUITY METHOD INVESTMENTS	10,385	9,216
OTHER INVESTMENTS, PRINCIPALLY BOTTLING COMPANIES	1,150	1,232
OTHER ASSETS	4,270	3,585
PROPERTY, PLANT AND EQUIPMENT, less accumulated depreciation of $9,853 and $9,010, respectively	14,548	14,476
TRADEMARKS WITH INDEFINITE LIVES	6,608	6,527
BOTTLERS' FRANCHISE RIGHTS WITH INDEFINITE LIVES	7,426	7,405
GOODWILL	12,412	12,255
OTHER INTANGIBLE ASSETS	1,057	1,150
TOTAL ASSETS	$ 89,432	$ 86,174
LIABILITIES AND EQUITY		
CURRENT LIABILITIES		
Accounts payable and accrued expenses	$ 10,590	$ 8,680
Loans and notes payable	18,840	16,297
Current maturities of long-term debt	3,194	1,577
Accrued income taxes	418	471
Liabilities held for sale	-	796
TOTAL CURRENT LIABILITIES	33,042	27,821
LONG-TERM DEBT	14,173	14,736
OTHER LIABILITIES	4,445	5,468
DEFERRED INCOME TAXES	5,307	4,981
THE COCA-COLA COMPANY SHAREOWNERS' EQUITY		
Common stock, $0.25 par value; Authorized — 11,200 shares; Issued — 7,040 and 7,040 shares, respectively	1,760	1,760
Capital surplus	12,122	11,379
Reinvested earnings	61,187	58,045
Accumulated other comprehensive income (loss)	(4,699)	(3,385)
Treasury stock, at cost — 2,624 and 2,571 shares, respectively	(38,238)	(35,009)
EQUITY ATTRIBUTABLE TO SHAREOWNERS OF COCA-COLA CO.	32,132	32,790
EQUITY ATTRIBUTABLE TO NONCONTROLLING INTERESTS	333	378
TOTAL EQUITY	32,465	33,168
TOTAL LIABILITIES AND EQUITY	$ 89,432	$ 86,174

Balance sheets show the status of a company at a certain point in time (typically at the close of business as of the balance sheet date); they are snapshots of a company's resources (assets) and how the resources were financed (liabilities and owners' equity). The balance sheet is an excellent source of information for investors to determine how a company is doing.

Most businesses, including large ones such as Coca-Cola and small bakeries like Acorns, use this report to document their financial status. The term "balance sheet" stems from the fact that the two sides of the accounting equation must balance. At any point in time, the value of the company's assets should be equal to the sum of the company's liabilities and owners' equity.

In Figure 1.2, we see the balance sheet for Acorns. This small, family-owned business tracks its financial position through the balance sheet and the accounting equation, just like Coca-Cola. Even if a company is not required to publish its statements for investors to see, it is important to keep track of the data so the company can know its own progress year-over-year.

The balance sheet for Netflix (Figure 1.3) displays the same type of information that is on Coca-Cola's and Acorns' balance sheets.

FIGURE 1.2

Acorns Balance Sheet As of September 30, 2013

Assets	
Cash	$ 6,550
Accounts Receivable	2,480
Inventory	2,410
Prepaid Expenses	1,055
Other Current Assets	6,840
Total Current Assets	19,335
Property, Plant & Equipment	87,850
Accumulated Depreciation	(4,290)
Net Property, Plant & Equipment	83,560
Total Assets	102,895
Liabilities	
Accounts Payable	28,040
Current Portion of Long-term Debt	1,000
Taxes Payable	2,000
Accrued Expenses	1,032
Total Current Liabilities	32,072
Long-term Debt	2,050
Total Liabilities	34,122
Owners' Equity	
Common Stock and Paid-in Capital	65,773
Retained Earnings	3,000
Total Owners' Equity	68,773
Total Liabilities and Equity	102,895

FIGURE 1.3

Netflix, Inc.
Consolidated Balance Sheets
(in thousands)

	As of December 31,	
	2012	2011
Assets		
Current assets:		
Cash and cash equivalents	$ 290,291	$ 508,053
Short-term investments	457,787	289,758
Current content library, net	1,368,162	919,709
Prepaid content	59,929	56,007
Other current assets	64,622	57,330
Total current assets	2,240,791	1,830,857
Non-current content library, net	1,506,008	1,046,934
Property and equipment, net	131,681	136,353
Other non-current assets	89,410	55,052
Total assets	$ 3,967,890	$ 3,069,196
Liabilities and Stockholders' Equity		
Current liabilities:		
Current content liabilities	$ 1,366,847	$ 935,036
Accounts payable	86,468	86,992
Accrued expenses	53,139	54,231
Deferred revenue	169,472	148,796
Total current liabilities	1,675,926	1,225,055
Non-current content liabilities	1,076,622	739,628
Long-term debt	200,000	200,000
Long-term debt due to related party	200,000	200,000
Other non-current liabilities	70,669	61,703
Total liabilities	3,223,217	2,426,386
Stockholders' equity:		
Common stock	56	55
Additional paid-in capital	301,616	219,119
Accumulated other comprehensive income (loss)	2,919	706
Retained earnings	440,082	422,930
Total stockholders' equity	744,673	642,810
Total liabilities and stockholders' equity	$ 3,967,890	$ 3,069,196

Let's go over some examples of assets, liabilities and equity for each of the companies. While a company may have all of these accounts, each one doesn't necessarily need to be listed individually on the balance sheet.

Coca-Cola

Assets: cash, inventory, **accounts receivable**, and buildings

Liabilities: loans payable, long-term debt, and **wages payable**

Owners' Equity: contributed capital, and retained earnings

Acorns

Assets: cash, furniture, equipment, and pre-paid expenses

Liabilities: accounts payable, **salaries payable**, and gift certificates

Owners' Equity: paid-in capital, and retained earnings

Netflix

Assets: cash, content library, and pre-paid content

Liabilities:notes payable, **accrued expenses**, and long-term debt

Owners' Equity: common stock, preferred stock, and retained earnings

Some of these account names are straightforward while others might not be very clear. The balance sheet, and its respective accounts, will be covered in more depth in Chapter 3.

You also may have noticed that some of the balance sheets previously shown did not list owners' equity. This section can go by several different names, such as shareowners' equity or stockholders' equity if the company has shareholders or owner's equity if there is just one owner. The different names for this section of the balance sheet will also be covered in Chapter 3.

Accounting is a tool people use to evaluate how a business is performing. The financial reports communicate important information to owners, business managers, investors, employees and other stakeholders. Without these reports, it would be very challenging to understand what is going on within a business and see how the business compares to others in its industry or to itself at a different point in time.

Assets = Liabilities + Owners' Equity

After exploring each component of the accounting equation in depth, it's easier to understand why the equation must always be equal and balance. The assets represent the company's resources, whereas the other side of the equation, liabilities + owners' equity, represents how those resources were funded. What doesn't belong to outsiders in the form of Liabilities must belong to the owners in the form of Owner's Equity.

For answers to the following questions, please see the end of Chapter 1.

Review 1.1 Question 1

Which of the following is an example of an asset? Please select all that apply.

    a.   Cash
    b.   Property, plant, & equipment
    c.   Accounts payable
    d.   Retained earnings
    e.   Accounts receivable

Review 1.1 Question 2

Which of the following is an example of a liability? Please select all that apply.

    a.   Accounts receivable
    b.   Equipment
    c.   Accounts payable
    d.   Inventory
    e.   Notes payable

Review 1.1 Question 3

Which of the following is an example of owners' equity? Please select all that apply.

    a.   Retained earnings
    b.   Cash
    c.   Common stock
    d.   Paid-in capital
    e.   Notes payable

Section 2

Basic Transactions and the Accounting Equation

Concepts

1. Starting a Business

2. Running a Business

3. Buying on Credit

4. Selling on Credit

5. Receiving Payments in Advance

6. Making Prepayments

7. Tricky Transactions

1.2.1   Starting a Business

Transactions

Transactions are defined as events that impact the financial position of a business. Some examples of transactions are sales, purchases, or loans.

Analyzing transactions is a critical aspect of accounting because transactions impact one or more parts of the accounting equation. In this section, we will see how various components of the accounting equation are affected by transactions. It is important to note that all accounting transactions, even the small ones, affect the balance sheet equation.

The owner of Acorns Bakery, Jennifer Costello, first opened her shop in 2005. Imagine that Costello's initial investment was $100,000. Acorns originally had no assets, no liabilities, and no owner's equity. After Costello's investment, Acorns had $100,000 in assets (cash) and $100,000 in owner's equity, which represents the owner's stake in the business. Clearly, the equation is balanced.

In accounting, "cash" does not necessarily mean physical currency; it can refer to money in a bank account. Even transactions such as writing checks or making electronic transfers from bank accounts are considered cash transactions. When a business buys or sells goods on credit, meaning that payment isn't required immediately, it is an example of a non-cash transaction. There are many other words that are used differently in accounting than in everyday language, and we will highlight other examples throughout this book.

Besides initial investments, there are other necessary transactions to get a business started, such as purchasing property and supplies. When Acorns first started its bakery, it needed to purchase a lot of equipment so it could make its goods to sell to customers. Suppose Acorns bought two ovens for $5,000 each. How would this transaction affect the accounting equation? In this case, assets (cash) would decrease by $10,000, and assets (equipment) would increase by $10,000. Transactions affect multiple accounts, but the accounts can both be from the same side of the accounting equation. Assets both increases and decreases by $10,000, so the equation is still balanced.

Cash by   Equipment
$10,000   by $10,000

For answers to the following questions, please see the end of Chapter 1.

Review 1.2 Question 1

Jennifer Costello made an initial investment of $100,000 in Acorns Bakery. Additionally, Costello's family loaned Acorns $50,000 to help get her business started. How would the loan impact the accounting equation of Acorns? Please select all that apply.

    a.   Increase cash by $50,000
    b.   Increase accounts receivable by $50,000
    c.   Increase loans payable by $50,000
    d.   Increase owners' equity by $50,000

Review 1.2 Question 2

Suppose Jennifer's top baker wanted to invest in Acorns and offered to contribute $25,000. How would this contribution impact the accounting equation? Please select all that apply.

    a.   Increase owners' equity by $25,000
    b.   Increase loans payable by $25,000
    c.   Increase cash by $25,000
    d.   Increase inventory by $25,000

Review 1.2 Question 3

Suppose Acorns needed more mixing machines in its kitchen. It bought two mixing machines for a total of $1,400 in cash. How would this impact the accounting equation? Please select all that apply.

    a.   Increase cash by $1,400
    b.   Increase Property, Plant & Equipment (PP&E) by $1,400
    c.   Decrease cash by $1,400
    d.   Increase owner's equity by $1,400

Review 1.2 Question 4

BB Bookstore purchased 200 copies of a book from a publisher for $2,000, and it paid cash to complete the transaction. How will this transaction impact the accounting equation? Please select all that apply.

    a.   Increase inventory by $2,000
    b.   Increase owners' equity by $2,000
    c.   Decrease cash by $2,000
    d.   Decrease accounts payable by $2,000

1.2.2   Running a Business

Revenue

In order to earn money, a business sells products or services to customers. The balance sheet is a great tool for tracking the amount of assets, such as inventory, that will be sold. But businesses need a way to know how much they are earning. Revenue is defined as the money a business receives from its ordinary activities, such as providing goods or services to a customer.

It can be further broken down into operating revenues, the revenues earned from the main activity of the business, and non-operating revenues, those earned from secondary activities. Suppose Acorns loaned money to other companies; interest on those loans would be an example of non-operating revenue. Sometimes companies report **net revenue** on their income statements; this would be the company's revenue less sales returns or discounts on items.

For a company to be profitable, it is essential that, over the long run, the costs of running the business are not higher than the actual revenues of the business.

Revenue is not an asset; it represents an increase in owners' equity and is a description of why a business received an asset. Suppose Acorns sells a croissant to a customer. What **adjustments** should be made to the accounting equation to record this sale? The money received by Acorns is cash, which is an asset, and cash increases as a result of the sale. Simultaneously, the owners' claims on the assets of the company increase by the amount of the revenue recognized. Hence owners' equity also increases. The associated decrease to inventory and expense of selling a product will be covered in the next section.

Owners' equity has several components, and the account that increases when a company recognizes revenue is called **retained earnings**. Retained earnings is the amount of resources a business generates by running its operations and keeps for internal purposes (instead of distributing to owners). Eventually, say at the end of the year, the business may decide to distribute some of its earnings to its owners, which would reduce the retained earnings account.

There are many ways for a business to earn revenue. If a customer pays Acorns cash to buy a muffin, Acorns earns revenue. If Coca-Cola delivers 10 boxes of Coke to a grocery store that pays on credit, Coca-Cola earns revenue. However, a business does not necessarily have to sell assets to earn revenue; it can also provide services. Netflix, gyms, and tour guide companies are all examples of businesses that provide services to earn revenue.

For the answer to the following question, please see the end of Chapter 1.

Review 1.3 Question 1

Suppose DSW sells a pair of boots to a customer for $75.00. How would the cash inflow and revenue from this sale impact the accounting equation? Please select all that apply.

    a.   Cash increases by $75
    b.   Owners' equity increases by $75
    c.   Accounts payable increases by $75
    d.   Cash decreases by $75

Expenses

A business sells assets or provides services in order to generate revenue. The costs of the resources used by the company to provide goods or services to a customer are called **expenses**. They represent a decrease in owners' equity because the resources are no longer available to the business.

Cost of goods sold (COGS) is the cost of the products sold to the customers. It consists of the cost of the items plus other expenses needed to get the items ready for sale and placed in inventory.

Suppose Acorns sells chocolate bars made by a local chocolate shop, Choc Full of It (CHO). These chocolate bars are part of Acorns' inventory. Acorns purchases each bar for $2.00 and sells each one for $3.00. When Acorns sells a chocolate bar, assets would decrease by $2.00 because it no longer owns the asset. The other side of the equation must also reflect a change; owner's equity decreases by the same amount ($2.00) to indicate the use of an asset.

Not all expenses are directly linked to using up an asset. Businesses also incur other expenses, such as paying wages or taxes, in order to run the business and provide goods and services to customers.

For answers to the following questions, please see the end of Chapter 1.

Review 1.4 Question 1

Acorns purchases boxes of truffles for $15.00 from CHO and then sells them to its customers. How would the transfer of inventory to the customer and the expense of the sale impact the accounting equation? Please select all that apply.

    a.   Inventory decreases by $15
    b.   Owner's equity increases by $15 to recognize revenue
    c.   Cash increases by $15
    d.   Owner's equity decreases by $15 to recognize COGS

Review 1.4 Question 2

Suppose the boots DSW sold to the customer for $75 were purchased from DSW's supplier for $30 in cash and recorded as inventory. How would the cost of the boots sold impact the accounting equation? Please select all that apply.

    a.   Inventory decreases by $75
    b.   Inventory decreases by $30
    c.   Cash decreases by $30
    d.   Cash decreases by $75
    e.   Retained earnings decreases by $30
    f.   Retained earnings decreases by $75

Review 1.4 Question 3

Suppose BB Bookstore bought 20 history books from a teacher for $1,000 in cash and sold them for $1,500 in cash to a community center. What is the net impact of these transactions on Borders' accounting equation? Please select all that apply.

    a.   Inventory increases by $500
    b.   Cash increases by $500
    c.   COGS decreases by $1,000
    d.   Retained earnings decreases by $1,000
    e.   Retained earnings increases by $500

It makes sense that revenues and expenses are recorded through owners' equity because owners own the business and get to enjoy the benefits of all the revenues earned less the expenses spent to generate those revenues. Although revenues and expenses play a large role in running a business, not all transactions relate to revenues and expenses. As we showed in the previous section, a company can make purchases, such as buying Property, Plant & Equipment (PP&E) or supplies to run its business, without affecting revenue or expenses.

1.2.3 Buying on Credit

In the previous examples, it was assumed that customers paid in cash at the time of the purchase, or that businesses received cash at the time of the sale. However, it is possible to use other forms of payment that don't require an immediate transfer of money. Purchasing merchandise without paying immediately is called buying on credit, and companies establish **credit terms**, which are agreements between two or more companies that specify when the payment for the goods or services purchased is due. Most businesses have credit terms of 30, 60, or 90 days. Buying on credit affects the accounting equation in the same way that borrowing money from a bank affects the equation. A liability called **accounts payable** is created to represent the obligation to pay the supplier in the future.

For answers to the following questions, please see the end of Chapter 1.

Review 1.5 Question 1

Suppose Coca-Cola bought 10,000 mangos for $20K from a farmer on 1/1/14. Coca-Cola had 30 days to pay the farmer. How would this transaction affect Coca-Cola's accounting equation on 1/1/14?

    a.   Accounts receivable increases by $20K
    b.   Accounts payable increases by $20K
    c.   Owners' equity decreases by $20K
    d.   Inventory increases by $20K
    e.   Inventory decreases by $20K

Review 1.5 Question 2

Suppose Coca-Cola bought 10,000 mangos for $20K from a farmer on 1/1/14. Coca-Cola had 30 days to pay the farmer. It paid the farmer on 1/31/14. How would this payment affect Coca-Cola's accounting equation on 1/31/14?

    a.   Accounts payable increases by $20K
    b.   Accounts payable decreases by $20K
    c.   Cash increases by $20K
    d.   Cash decreases by $20K
    e.   Owners' equity decreases by $20K

Review 1.5 Question 3

Suppose Coca-Cola bought a new bottling machine for $9,000 on 3/1/14. It paid the manufacturer on 4/30/14. How would this payment affect Coca-Cola's accounting equation on 3/1/14?

a. Accounts receivable increases by $9,000
b. Accounts payable increases by $9,000
c. Inventory increases by $9,000
d. Cash increases by $9,000
e. Equipment increases by $9,000

Review 1.5 Question 4

Suppose Coca-Cola bought a new bottling machine for $9,000 on 3/1/14. It paid the manufacturer on 4/30/14. How would this payment affect Coca-Cola's accounting equation on 4/30/14?

a. Accounts payable decreases by $9,000
b. Equipment decreases by $9,000
c. Cash decreases by $9,000
d. Expense increases by $9,000

Let's consider Acorns Bakery again. When Acorns buys chocolate from CHO to sell in its store, it doesn't need to pay cash immediately. Acorns and Choc Full of It worked out the credit terms, and from the time Acorns receives the chocolate from its supplier, it has 30 days to pay for the purchase.

When Acorns records the purchase of the chocolate in its financials, Acorns records an increase in assets (because inventory is an asset and inventory increases) on the day the inventory is received. Acorns also receives an **invoice** from its supplier, and it must record the obligation to pay the invoice (**accounts payable**) under liabilities. Once Acorns pays the invoice for the chocolate, it records a decrease in cash (because it uses cash to pay the supplier) and a decrease in liabilities (because it no longer has the obligation to pay the invoice).

1.2.4   Selling on Credit

In addition to buying on credit, companies can also sell on credit. When a company sells on credit, it must have a good relationship with its clients because it is trusting the clients to pay down the road.

Suppose that Acorns supplies cookies to a school to sell in its cafeteria during lunch. Acorns has worked with the school for many years, and because of their strong relationship, Acorns doesn't require immediate payment for the cookies. But when should Acorns recognize revenue from the transaction? A few options come to mind: recognizing the revenue when Acorns receives the order, when the cookies are delivered, or when Acorns ultimately receives the payment for the cookies.

The correct choice for when the revenue should be recognized actually depends on the method of accounting used. The primary accounting methods for keeping track of a business' revenue and expenses are the cash and **accrual** methods. The methods differ only in the timing of when transactions are recorded.

The cash method is most commonly used in very small businesses. The method is straightforward: income is recorded when the cash is received, and expenses are recorded when they are paid. The only time transactions are recorded is when cash changes hands.

In this book, we will focus on the **accrual accounting method**, which is what the majority of companies use. Under this method, revenue is recognized when it is earned through the delivery of goods or services, and payment is assured. Expenses are treated similarly; they are recorded when they are incurred, or when the business used some resource, even if the expenses haven't been paid for yet. Accrual accounting is particularly useful because it shows underlying business transactions, not just those where cash changes hands.

Some transactions are quite straightforward, with delivery and payment happening at the same time, but others involve buying or selling on credit. The accounting method is particularly important when we consider **accounting periods**. The timing of when revenues and expenses are recognized can have a major effect on the perceived financial performance of a company. An accounting period is the time frame for which results are being reported; common accounting periods are a month, a quarter or a year.

When a company receives cash before a good has been delivered or a service has been provided, it creates an account called **unearned revenue** or **deferred revenue**. This account is a liability because the company has an obligation to deliver the good or provide the service in the future. You can think of the customer prepaying for goods or services he will receive in the future. Once the good or service has been delivered, the unearned revenue is converted into revenue.

Consider the other case where merchandise is sold to a customer in one period, but the payment isn't received until the next period. The decision of when to recognize the revenue could have a big impact on the company's results for each period.

The **realization principle** states that revenues are recognized when they are earned and realizable. This does not necessarily have to be when cash changes hands. If a business has performed the work, and it is likely to receive cash from the customer, the business can recognize the revenue.

If a business is not confident about the customer's ability to pay, then revenue would not be recognized until cash collection is more certain. The business would also wait to recognize revenue if it delivered merchandise (or performed services) that the customer hadn't agreed to pay for.

Suppose Acorns sold 10 pounds of coffee for $200 to Pete's Party Planning Committee (PPPC). Acorns didn't receive cash at the time of the purchase because it had a good relationship with PPPC. Acorns had bought the coffee from a local grower for $150. How would Acorns' accounting equation be impacted, both at the time of the sale and when the cash is collected?

First, revenue should be recognized at the time of the sale, increasing assets and owner's equity by $200. However, instead of increasing the asset cash, we increase the asset **accounts receivable**, which is the expected receipt of cash.

In order to record the expense of the sale, we must record both a decrease in assets (inventory) and a decrease in owner's equity. The 10 pounds of coffee is no longer in Acorns' inventory, and owner's equity must decrease because the expected benefit associated with the resource has also decreased.

Since the coffee was listed under Acorns' inventory at $150, the amount that Acorns paid the grower for the coffee, inventory and owner's equity will decrease by $150. Thus, on net, there is a $50 increase in accounts receivable and a $50 increase in owner's equity.

This example follows the **matching principle**, which states that expenses should be recognized in the period in which the revenues they helped generate are recognized. Since revenues are typically recognized when inventory is sold, expenses are generally recognized at the same time.

Whenever the cash is actually received from the sale, there needs to be two adjustments to assets, one positive and one negative. Assets (cash) increase because the company received cash, but assets (accounts receivable) also decrease because the company no longer has the right to receive cash from the customer. The two changes even out, so, on net, there is no change in overall assets, and there is no change in owners' equity.

For answers to the following questions, please see the end of Chapter 1.

Review 1.6 Question 1

Suppose Acorns sold five truffle boxes to a customer for $25 each. The boxes were purchased from CHO for $15 each and were held in inventory. The customer has 30 days to pay for the order after receiving it. How will the recognition of the receivable and revenue for the transaction impact the accounting equation at the time of the sale to the customer? Please select all that apply.

    a.   Accounts receivable increases by $125
    b.   Owner's equity increases by $75
    c.   Accounts receivable increases by $75
    d.   Owner's equity increases by $125

Review 1.6 Question 2

Acorns needs to recognize an expense for the cost of goods sold for $75 ($15*5). How will that recognition impact the accounting equation? Please select all that apply.

    a.   Inventory decreases by $75
    b.   Inventory increases by $75
    c.   Accounts payable increases by $75
    d.   Owner's equity decreases by $75

Review 1.6 Question 3

Acorns receives payment from the customer 20 days after the initial purchase. How would the accounting equation be impacted when the payment is received? Please select all that apply.

    a.   Accounts receivable increases by $125
    b.   Cash increases by $125
    c.   Owner's equity increases by $125
    d.   Accounts receivable decreases by $125

1.2.5   Receiving Payments in Advance

We've already discussed how selling on credit affects the accounting equation. Let's consider the case where a company gets paid in advance.

A customer can pay in advance for different spans of time; for example a customer can prepay for a month of unlimited train travel, for 6 months of farmers' market deliveries, or for several years of magazine subscriptions.

At Spartan Gym (SG), members can sign up for a year-long membership. Customers pay $1,800 in advance to go to the gym throughout the year. How should SG treat that transaction? Should it account for the $1,800 as revenue when the cash is received, evenly throughout the year, or at the end of the year?

Following the **accrual method of accounting**, SG should recognize the revenue evenly throughout the year because it recognizes revenue as the services are performed. When the advance payment is received, both assets and liabilities increase. Assets increase to reflect the cash received, and liabilities increase to reflect the obligation to provide services to the customers in the future.

For the yearly membership case, assets (cash) increase by $1,800 when SG receives the cash. But SG cannot recognize the revenue immediately because the customer hasn't actually gone to the gym yet. So, SG records an obligation to provide services to the customer in the future, and liabilities (unearned revenue) increase by $1,800.

Over time, as SG fulfills its obligation by providing gym access and other services to the customer, SG recognizes revenues by increasing owners' equity and decreasing the liability (unearned revenue) by the same amount. The membership fee provides unlimited monthly access to basic gym services, so revenue will be recognized over time.

SG could divide the $1,800 by 365 to recognize a portion of the revenue each day, but it's unlikely that SG updates its financial statements daily. SG would most likely just recognize the revenue at the end of each month.Suppose SG offers pilates equipment classes for an additional fee on top of the gym membership. One customer chooses to buy a 10 class punch card and prepays $100 for it. Assets would increase by $100 when SG receives the cash, and an obligation to provide the classes in the future would increase the liabilities by $100. In this case, revenue is recognized each time the customer takes a class. If the customer took 2 classes in a month, revenues would increase owners' equity by $20 and liabilities would decrease by $20. If the customer took 3 classes the next month, there would be a $30 increase in owners' equity and $30 decrease in liabilities.

For answers to the following questions, please see the end of Chapter 1.

Review 1.7 Question 1

SG offers personal training sessions for its members. It costs $125 for 5 sessions. Suppose a member prepaid for the personal training sessions in January and had 6 months to use them. The member didn't start his sessions in January and met with the personal trainer twice in February. How would this be recorded on the financial statements of SG? Please select all that apply.

a.   January: Assets increase by $125
b.   January: Liabilities increase by $125
c.   January: Owners' equity increases by $125
d.   February: Owners' equity increases by $50
e.   February: Liabilities decrease by $50
f.   February: Owners' equity increases by $125

Review 1.7 Question 2

SG's 10-class punch card expires 6 months after the first class was taken. Suppose Estelle bought the $100 card in March and took 8 classes that month. In April, she broke her leg and stopped working out. When should SG recognize the revenue?

a.   Recognize $16.66 ($100 / 6) of revenue at the end of each month from March until August.
b.   Recognize $80 of revenue at the end of March and $20 of revenue at the end of August.
c.   Recognize $100 of revenue at the end of March.
d.   Recognize $100 of revenue at the end of August.

Review 1.7 Question 3

Suppose Acorns sells a $50 gift card to a customer. How will this affect the accounting equation at the time of the sale? Please select all that apply.

    a.   Increase inventory by $50

    b.   Increase cash by $50

    c.   Increase owner's equity by $50

    d.   Increase liabilities by $50

Review 1.7 Question 4

Two months later, the customer purchases $25 of baked goods from Acorns using the gift card. It cost Acorns $10 to make these goods. What will be the impact of the sale and the expense on the accounting equation for Acorns? Please select all that apply.

    a.   Cash decreases by $25

    b.   Owner's equity increases by $25 to recognize revenue

    c.   Obligation to provide goods decreases by $25

    d.   Cash increases by $25

    e.   Inventory decreases by $10

    f.   Owner's equity decreases by $10 to recognize COGS

1.2.6   Making Prepayments

Sometimes businesses choose to prepay for goods or services that will provide a benefit in the future. In this case, the prepayment is initially recorded as an asset called **prepaid expenses**. Then that asset is reduced and an expense is recognized over time as the benefit is received.

Insurance is a typical example of a prepaid expense. Sometimes businesses choose to be more specific and list out the name of the prepaid expense, such as prepaid insurance, instead of lumping all prepaid expenses together.

Acorns is a member of the Retail Bakers of America (RBA), an association that provides networking opportunities, training programs, and bakery research. Dues are paid on an annual basis, and Acorns paid $300 this year. When Acorns pays for its membership, it records a decrease in assets (cash) of $300 and an increase in assets (prepaid membership) of $300. The prepaid membership reflects the right to receive the perks of the RBA membership for the next 12 months.

At the end of each month, Acorns will recognize $25 of expense ($300/12), which will decrease owner's equity. In addition, assets (prepaid membership) will decrease by $25 to show that a month's worth of benefits has been used.

Insurance is another common prepaid expense. Suppose Spartan Gym prepaid $12,000 for 1 year of property insurance on its gym. At the time of prepayment, SG recorded a decrease in cash of $12,000 and an increase in prepaid insurance of $12,000. Assets both increased and decreased by the same amount, so the accounting equation still balanced.

SG prepaid for the benefit of having property insurance for 12 months. So, SG must recognize an expense of $1,000 ($12,000/12) at the end of each month, decreasing owners' equity by $1,000. It also decreases the asset prepaid insurance by $1,000 to reflect that it used up a month of insurance.

A more uncommon prepaid example is prepaid subscription rights. Netflix likely has agreements with various TV networks to have the right to play popular TV shows on Netflix's website. Netflix and the TV network agree to a contract where Netflix prepays for the ability to play a show for a certain period of time, such as a year. As the year goes on, Netflix would decrease the asset prepaid subscription rights and decrease owners' equity to reflect the use of the asset.

For answers to the following questions, please see the end of Chapter 1.

Review 1.8 Question 1

Suppose Coca-Cola purchased insurance on a fleet of delivery trucks. It paid $30K on 1/1/14 for a year of insurance. How would this transaction impact Coca-Cola's accounting equation? Please select all that apply.

a.   Decrease cash by $30K
b.   Decrease accounts receivable by $30K
c.   Increase prepaid insurance by $30K
d.   Decrease owners' equity by $30K

Review 1.8 Question 2

What will be the impact on the accounting equation each month, when the prepaid insurance expense is recognized? Please select all that apply.

a.   Decrease cash by $2.5K
b.   Decrease owners' equity by $2.5K
c.   Decrease prepaid insurance by $2.5K
d.   Increase prepaid insurance by $2.5K

1.2.7　Tricky Transactions

It's important to note that transactions are not always straightforward, and it's possible for two reasonable people to identify different ways to account for a transaction. If a gift card expires, when is it appropriate to recognize revenue? If a company paints its building, is that an improvement to one of its assets or simply an expense? What about the money a business spends on research and development (R&D)? Should the costs be capitalized because the research will provide a future benefit to the business or expensed because we don't know when, or even if, there will be a future benefit? What if a flood soaked a factory's machines; do you recognize an **impairment** loss? Or suppose there is a big lawsuit between your company and a competitor. You are reasonably assured that you will win the lawsuit, but your competitor is very convinced it will win. Do you record an expected gain or loss from the lawsuit? Or neither?

There are many possible answers to the questions surrounding these tricky transactions, and several may seem reasonable. As a result, there needs to be a set of rules and standards to guide companies to make similar decisions in similar situations. The next section will discuss many of these accounting standards.

Section 3
Accounting Principles and Rules

Concepts

1.3.1   Introduction

In the past few sections, we've discussed how to record a transaction. We also reviewed some tricky transactions. Many different approaches seem reasonable, but there are certain accounting standards that mandate a specific way to record transactions and report information. Accounting standards vary by region, and there are many bodies around the world that develop them. The body in the United States is the Financial Accounting Standards Board (**FASB**). It has developed the Generally Accepted Accounting Principles (**GAAP**), a set of standards followed by most U.S. companies. The International Accounting Standards Board (**IASB**) is the largest standard-setting body outside the United States. The majority of public companies in Europe follow the standards set by the IASB, which are called the International Financial Reporting Standards (**IFRS**). In addition, Australia, Canada, China, India, Russia, and South Africa have adopted the International Financial Reporting Standards set by the IASB.

Many of the rules are quite similar between the two sets of standards, but there are some key differences that we will point out throughout the book. IASB and FASB have been working together to converge the standards, but it is a lengthy process. Typically, GAAP standards are more rules based, and there are specific rules and cutoff points for specific situations. The IFRS are more principles based, allowing businesses more discretion to make specific reporting decisions.

Accounting standards are extremely important because they create guidelines and rules so that different companies record similar transactions in a similar manner. Transactions can be very complex, so it's essential to have these guidelines. The purpose behind accounting standards is to ensure that users of the financial reports have access to high-quality, reliable information prepared across firms in a consistent manner.

Although these standards are defined by the major accounting boards, the principles behind these standards have been followed by businesses for hundreds of years because they are good practices. The principles we will cover include: **conservatism**, **relevance** and **reliability**, the **historical cost** principle, **consistency**, **materiality**, the **entity concept**, the **money measurement principle**, and the **going concern** concept. While it would be ideal to follow all of the principles, this is not always possible, and tradeoffs are inevitable. We will discuss some conflicts that might arise and cover the best approach for different situations.

Suppose Acorns sold a lot of gift cards during the holidays, but it knows from historical data that 20% of customers will never redeem their gift cards. When should Acorns recognize the revenue? What about the case where Microsoft sells its Windows operating system but then promises to give its customers free software updates? Should it recognize all the revenue from the Windows sale or wait because it will be providing some services in the future? Or imagine that Coca-Cola bought a manufacturing facility that is now worth twice what it paid several years ago. Even though it was originally recorded **on the books** (the financial records, **ledgers** or journals in which accounts are recorded) at the purchase price, should Coca-Cola change the books to reflect the increased value of the facility?

There are so many accounting standards that exist, and it's unrealistic to master them all in an introductory course. Once you master the guiding principles behind the standards, you'll understand how to apply them in various situations.

1.3.2   Conservatism

Your company has an item that cost $30 and is listed in inventory at $30. However, advances in technology have made that item much cheaper, and it can now be replaced for $20. Should the item be reflected in your books at $20 or $30?

The conservatism principle says you should record it at $20 and recognize a loss of $10.

One of the most fundamental principles in accounting is conservatism. This principle keeps business owners from exaggerating financial reports and prevents them from being overly optimistic. Business owners have a tendency to be very confident about their businesses, but a significant number of businesses fail, so that confidence isn't always justified. Investors and lenders look closely at financial reports, and overly optimistic ones can influence them to make decisions that might not be in their best interests.

In general, accounting standards require that businesses choose measurement methods that anticipate and record future losses but not future gains. An unrealized gain is an increase in the value of an investment, whereas an unrealized loss is a decrease in the value of an investment. A realized gain can occur when a company is able to sell an asset for more than it bought it for. Recording future losses but not future gains is conservative accounting, and it results in lower net income, assets, and owners' equity in earlier periods.

For answers to the following questions, please see the end of Chapter 1.

Review 1.9 Question 1

Suppose your company is involved in a lawsuit, and your lawyers predict you will most likely lose the case and have to pay $1 million to another party. The court decision has not been made yet, but should your business record a liability for $1 million?

a. Yes, because businesses should anticipate and record future losses, but not gains.

b. Yes, to set aside money in case the company loses the lawsuit.

c. No, because it isn't certain that the company will lose the case.

d. No, because it would reduce income for the period.

Review 1.9 Question 2

Suppose your company is suing another company for damages and your lawyers believe you will most likely win the case and be awarded $1 million. Should you record an increase in assets for the expected cash flow?

a. Yes, because it's likely the company will win.

b. Yes, because it will increase income for the period.

c. No, because businesses should anticipate and record future losses but not gains.

d. No, because it's not certain the company will win.

Review 1.9 Question 3

Which of the following demonstrate the principle of conservatism? Please select all that apply.

a. Computer Repair Center (CRC) has been fixing computers for 25 years and has a very good reputation. CRC wants to reflect the value of its reputation on its books and include it as an asset worth $150,000, which the company feels is a conservative estimate.

b. Apple produces iPods and iPhones and keeps stocks of finished-goods inventory for both. Suppose that demand for iPhones has increased significantly, increasing the price at which Apple can sell them. But demand for iPods has decreased because they're seen as obsolete. Apple lowers the asset value of its iPod inventory but doesn't increase the value of its iPhone inventory.

Which of the following demonstrate the principle of conservatism? Please select all that apply.

a.   One of Acorns' customers, Harry's, is having financial trouble and is likely to go out of business soon. Harry's owes Acorns $2,000 for purchases it made last month, but Acorns doesn't think it will receive the money, so it writes off the $2,000 in its accounts receivable account.

b.   Tom's Tools has a $500,000 investment in Harvey's Hardware, and Tom expects he will double his investment after Harvey's IPO next week. Tom's Tools wants to record the investment as $1M in his statements.

1.3.3   Relevance and Reliability

Information about businesses comes from a variety of sources and in varying degrees of quality. If Oliver's Oranges reads in a prominent newspaper that a competitor is coming out with sweeter, juicier oranges that are going to be much more popular than Oliver's oranges, should Oliver record a loss for the decline in the value of his groves?

When evaluating what information can be used when recording a transaction, relevance and reliability are very important. Information must be relevant, meaning it is useful to those looking at the financial information when making decisions. If information would influence the outcome of a given situation, it is considered relevant. The information in the previous example is relevant because if it is true, it could cause a big loss for Oliver's Oranges.

It is also very important for the information to be reliable. The information must be objective and unbiased, and it should accurately convey the reality of the situation. For financial information to be useful, it must reflect relevant facts and faithfully reflect the reality of what it aims to represent. The reliability principle is also known as faithful representation. There are many different levels of reliability, and while completely reliable information is best, it can be both time and cost intensive to verify the accuracy of information.

The information in the previous example would not be very reliable if it was simply a rumor or the opinion of a few people. Therefore, Oliver's Oranges should not write down the value of the inventory based on the news article. The information is too hard to verify, making it unreliable.

For answers to the following questions, please see the end of Chapter 1.

Review 1.10 Question 1

Suppose many research analysts are discussing how Apple is going to release a new phone that will dominate the market and reduce BlackBerry sales. Should BlackBerry record a loss for inventory that it won't be able to sell?

    a.   Yes, because BlackBerry won't be able to sell its inventory.

    b.   Yes, but only if the company is convinced that the information is true.

    c.   No, because it probably can still sell its inventory.

    d.   No, because research analysts aren't reliable enough.

Review 1.10 Question 2

Suppose a company wants to sell one of its subsidiaries, and it is close to closing the transaction, but the deal is not certain. Should it record the transaction on its books?

    a.   Yes, because the deal is likely to happen.

    b.   No, because the deal is not certain.

Review 1.10 Question 3

Which of the following would be considered relevant to disclose separately in the financial statements for Fred's Factory? Please select all that apply.

    a.   Fred's Factory is engaged in a lawsuit with another firm, and an unfavorable decision would result in financial instability for the company.

    b.   Fred's has net assets worth $10 million, and it expects one of its customers who owes Fred's $2,000 to default.

    c.   Fred's Factory prepared its balance sheet as of 12/31/2014, but on 1/2/2015, a fire burned down half of its inventory.

1.3.4   The Historical Cost Principle

A major principle in accounting that demonstrates how accounting standards encourage the use of reliable information is the historical cost principle. It states that transactions should be recorded at the actual price paid at the time of the transaction. This is a very reliable number because it is the actual amount that changed hands. Suppose Whole Foods receives a large supply of oranges from Florida to sell in its store. Shortly after, a huge hurricane hits Florida and wipes out the orange groves. Whole Foods thinks it no longer needs to offer discounts or 2 for 1 deals to sell its entire inventory because the storm has decreased the supply of oranges. Clearly the value of inventory at Whole Foods has increased. Although Whole Foods can increase its orange prices or stop offering discounts, it should still keep the value of the inventory on its balance sheet at the original price paid because that is the reliable value of the inventory. If businesses could adjust the value of their assets based on assumptions that are unverifiable and not actual transactions, there would be a greater risk of overstating assets in financial statements. This would be detrimental to the users of the financial statements.

However, ensuring that information is reliable can potentially lead to less relevant information if values have actually changed since the time of the transaction. A good example is an asset such as land. Generally, land appreciates in value. It is initially recorded at historical cost, and land reported many years ago could currently be much more valuable than the amount recorded on the books (a company's financial records). Another party may even offer to purchase the assets, giving a good estimate of the current value. However, unless the transaction actually takes place, the value of the assets on the books typically does not change.

The historical cost principle has been followed for hundreds of years, but in the recent past, accounting principles have transitioned away from historical costs and shifted in other directions. For certain assets, accounting standards allow values to be marked to market, which means they are changed to reflect their current market value. **Mark to market** is an accounting act that occurs when a company writes the value of an asset up or down to its current market value, instead of its book value, even if the transaction does not take place. This type of accounting is also known as fair value accounting.

Financial institutions are required to mark certain investment portfolios to the current market value. The balance sheets of financial institutions look quite different from the balance sheets of other companies. Their primary assets do not include items such as PP&E but instead include items such as investments. Investment portfolios are classified into three categories: trading securities, available-for-sale, and held-to-maturity. Accounting standards state that trading securities should be marked to market (and unrealized gains and losses are included in earnings), those available-for-sale should be marked to market (and unrealized gains and losses should be reported separately, not in earnings), and those held-to-maturity should not be marked to market (i.e. they should be kept at historical cost). However, the majority of transactions for the majority of businesses still follow the historical cost principle, and we will explain the exceptions.

Suppose your business bought two paintings, one by Renoir and one by Picasso, for $1M each; the Renoir painting has permanently appreciated in value and is now worth $1.5M, while the Picasso painting has permanently declined in value to $800,000.

Under U.S. GAAP, and applying conservatism and the historical cost principles, how would you account for the change in value of the two paintings?

Leave both paintings at $1M each on the books.

Leave the Renoir painting at $1M and adjust the Picasso painting down to $800,000.

Adjust the Renoir painting to $1.5M and the Picasso painting to $800,000

Adjust the Renoir painting to $1.5M and leave the Picasso painting at $1M.

Under U.S. GAAP, the Renoir painting would likely remain at $1M and the Picasso painting would be written down to $800,000. This is a good representation of both conservatism and the historical cost principle. However, the answer depends on the accounting standards that are being followed. Under IFRS, there is a greater possibility that each painting could be adjusted to its current value.

For the answer to the following question, please see the end of Chapter 1.

Review 1.11 Question 1

Which of the following demonstrates the historical cost principle? Please select all that apply.

    a.   John is wondering which method of accounting for inventory in his bike shop would be most appropriate. He decides that he should use the same method that he has been using for the last few years, since his business has been operating essentially the same way.

    b.   Harvey's Hardware bought 100 hammers a month ago for $8 per hammer. Now the price is $10 per hammer. Harvey's records the hammers on the balance sheet at $800.

    c.   Planet Fitness receives a one-year membership fee of $600 from a customer, and it records $50 as revenue each month.

    d.   Annie's Chairs wants to buy a La-Z-Boy chair that costs $400 at Jordan's Furniture, and the charming Annie is able to negotiate paying $350. Annie's records the cost of the chair on the balance sheet as $350.

1.3.5   Consistency

Sometimes accounting guidelines allow businesses to use discretion in the way they record transactions. The choices a business makes can have a major impact on its financial statements. One area of accounting that is flexible is **depreciation**. Typically, a business estimates how long a piece of equipment will last and records an expense to reflect the decrease in value of the equipment over its useful life. This expense is called depreciation. When a company has a long useful life for a piece of equipment, the business has lower expenses and higher income in the current period. Accounting standards require consistency, doing things in the same way from one period to the next. A business cannot change its assumptions from year to year unless it has a justifiable reason. Managers could manipulate financial statements to make them look better if changes were allowed on an ad hoc basis, and this could mislead investors who rely on the statements.

For answers to the following questions, please see the end of Chapter 1.

Review 1.12 Question 1

Suppose that prior to 2013, The Wine Emporium (TWE) recognized revenue on on-line sales when goods were shipped and recognized revenue on local credit sales when the goods were delivered. In 2013, TWE recognized revenue for both online sales and local credit sales when goods were delivered.

    a.   TWE's accounting prior to 2013 violated the consistency principle.

    b.   TWE's accounting in 2013 violated the consistency principle.

    c.   TWE's accounting did not violate the consistency principle before or during 2013.

    d.   TWE's accounting both before and during 2013 violated the consistency principle.

Review 1.12 Question 2

Suppose that Tom's Tools has a grinding machine that cost $2,000 and has a useful life of 10 years. Tom's has been using the straight line depreciation method, depreciating the machine by $200 per year. But Tom wants to switch to accelerated depreciation to report less profits.

    a.   If Tom's switches to the accelerated depreciation method, he will violate the consistency principle.

    b.   Tom's can switch without violating the consistency principle.

    c.   Tom's can only switch without violating the consistency principle if he switches the depreciation method for all other items.

1.3.6   Materiality

Consider the following two situations which will help explain the materiality concept.

Suppose Acorns, a business with $1,000,000 in annual sales last year, spent $1,500 on office supplies one month because it bought a new computer. How would Acorns report the $1,500 expense?

- Office supplies would be reported individually on the financial statements.

- Office supplies would be grouped with other expenses when reported on the financial statements.

- Office supplies would not be reported on the financial statements.

Suppose Coca-Cola spent $250,000 on a marketing event to introduce a new flavor of Coke. How would Coca-Cola report the $250,000 expense?

- Coca-Cola would report this event cost individually.

- Coca-Cola would report this cost combined with other marketing costs during the period.

- Coca-Cola would report this cost combined with sales, general, and administration (SG&A) costs during the year.

- The event cost would not be reported.

Why is it that a $1,500 charge might be reported separately for Acorns while a $250,000 charge might be lumped in with other similar expenses for Coca-Cola?

Materiality, which helps determine what has to be reported in detail, is another important concept in accounting. A transaction is considered material if it is reasonably likely to influence the decision making of people using the accounting data or the financial reports. It is only necessary to do detailed record keeping and reporting for material items. As we saw in the previous example, materiality is relative to the size and circumstances of individual businesses.

Suppose Yogurtland wanted to encourage customers to try a new kind of frozen yogurt made with Greek yogurt, and it offered those who bought the Greek yogurt free stickers as a souvenir. Although Yogurtland had to pay for the stickers, which was a cost of providing goods to the customer, the cost was small and nonrecurring, so it wouldn't make sense for Yogurtland to track those expenses separately and apply them to cost of goods sold. Yogurtland would not ignore the expenses, it just would not track them separately. The stickers would most likely be expensed when they were purchased as an operating expense.

The level of detail required in financial statements varies from business to business, and it is important to look at expenses in the context of a business' financial statements. For a large company like Coca-Cola, a $250,000 charge might not be material, so it would not be broken out separately in the financial statements. For a smaller business like Acorns, small charges could be material and would need to be reported separately.

Maintaining accurate and detailed accounting data requires time and money, so there is a certain point at which it doesn't make sense to track items on an individual basis.

For answers to the following questions, please see the end of Chapter 1.

Review 1.13 Question 1

Joe is reviewing his small pizza shop's financial information at the end of the year, and he realizes that no information was recorded throughout the year about the new light bulbs used to replace old ones. He knows that two light bulbs were replaced. Should he report the expense?

a. Yes, he should find out the cost and disclose the expense separately

b. Yes, he should find out the cost and lump it with other expenses.

c. No, the lightbulbs are a small expense and not necessary to record.

Review 1.13 Question 2

Yogurtland spent $15,000 to develop a new advertising campaign for its new Greek yogurt flavors. Should Yogurtland show the $15,000 charge separately on the income statement even it represents a trivial fraction of the total expenses of the business?

a. Yes, it's important to break out all expenses.

b. No, it does not need to report the expense separately.

Review 1.13 Question 3

Mark buys a trashcan for $20 and expects it to have a useful life of 10 years. Should he record depreciation expense of $2 per year?

a. Yes, he should record the depreciation expense.

b. No, it is not necessary to record the depreciation expense. Instead, he should write off the entire amount in one year as an expense.

Review 1.13 Question 4

Alice's small family business just settled a lawsuit and owes $1 million to the plaintiff. She isn't expecting any lawsuits next year, so it won't be a recurring cost. Should she disclose it separately in the financial statements?

a. Yes, it is a significant cost.

b. No, it won't be a recurring cost.

1.3.7   The Entity Concept

Suppose a company rents an apartment building for extra office space for $6,000 per month. Two of the floors in the building are used as offices, but the other two floors are being used by the business owner for storage while his house is being redone. How should the company record the rent expense on the company's books?

- It should record $6,000 per month as rent expense.

- It should record $3,000 per month as rent expense.

- It shouldn't record any rent expense.

The correct answer to this question is that the company should record $3,000 per month as rent expense. The books of a business must be kept separately from the books of individuals, even if there is only one owner of the company. This principle is known as the **entity concept** in accounting. In the previous example, the owner cannot expense the total rent cost to the business because half of the building is being used by the owner for personal use. A business is a distinct, separately identifiable entity, and only transactions of the business entity should be recorded on the books of the business.

Sometimes, companies abuse the entity concept rule and may try to portray a separate entity status when there really is none in order to take advantage of certain benefits. This allows the company to hide transactions from its own financial statements and shift them to the other entity. Enron used special purpose entities to avoid showing liabilities on its financial statements. A special purpose entity, also known as a special purpose vehicle, is an entity created to fulfill specific or temporary objectives. Large companies with subsidiaries can have entities within entities, but the financial reporting is most relevant at the consolidated level of the parent company. Subsidiaries must keep their own financial records in order to manage their business and prepare tax returns. There are a number of accounting issues surrounding the separate legal entity status of subsidiaries, such as transfer pricing, tax planning, and consolidation accounting. This book will not cover these issues in detail, but they are the result of the entity concept.

For answers to the following questions, please see the end of Chapter 1.

Review 1.14 Question 1

Which of the following transactions would be recorded on the books of the respective business entities? Please select all that apply.

    a.   Charlie is on a business trip in NYC and decides to spend an extra night in the hotel so he can visit his family the next day. The hotel costs $200 per night.

    b.   Sophie has some accounting books she doesn't want anymore and brings them to her accounting firm to sell them. The accounting firm pays her $400 for the books.

    c.   Maria, the owner of Spartan Gym, received a new $200 stereo for her birthday. She decides to use it occasionally at Spartan Gym for the classes she teaches.

    d.   The owner of a local bank receives a speeding ticket during her normal commute to work and will have to pay a $50 fine.

Review 1.14 Question 2

Suppose Annie's Art Gallery loaned Annie $20,000 to purchase an automobile, which she will use for personal transportation and to travel back and forth to work. How will this be reflected on the books of Annie's Art Gallery?

    a.   The asset cash will decrease by $20,000 and the asset loan will increase by $20,000.

    b.   The asset cash will decrease by $20,000 and the asset car will increase by $20,000.

    c.   The asset cash will decrease by $20,000 and the liability loan will increase by $20,000.

    d.   The transaction will have no impact on the books of Annie's Art Gallery.

1.3.8　Money Measurement

The money measurement principle states that accounting records only keep track of transactions that can be measured in monetary terms. This principle is also related to the reliability and the historical cost principle. Businesses only record events or circumstances that could have a financial impact on the business if they can be reliably measured in monetary terms and they relate to an actual historical transaction that has occurred. Events that cannot be assigned a monetary value on a historical transaction are not recorded.

For answers to the following questions, please see the end of Chapter 1.

Review 1.15 Question 1

Iggy's Inventions just won a new patent for one of the products that it developed and believes is worth millions. Should Iggy's record the worth of this patent on its balance sheet?

    a.   Yes
    b.   No

Review 1.15 Question 2

Mark just received his MBA and is a lot more valuable to his company. Can Mark's company record his increase in skill level on its financial statements?

    a.   Yes
    b.   No

1.3.9   Going Concern

In accounting, it is typically assumed that a business will continue to operate for the foreseeable future unless there is significant evidence that suggests otherwise. This is known as the **going concern** concept. A business that isn't a going concern is at risk of selling off its assets in the near future in a distress sale, possibly realizing a value that is lower than what it would be worth if it continued its operations. Many asset values take into account the future benefit they will generate, so the going concern concept is fundamental in accounting.

For answers to the following questions, please see the end of Chapter 1.

Review 1.16 Question 1

Suppose Cambridge Bikes Company is in the process of being liquidated (selling its assets) because it was unable to repay all of its liabilities. Should the financial statements of Cambridge Bikes Company be prepared under the going-concern assumption?

    a.   Yes
    b.   No

Review 1.16 Question 2

Continuing with the previous question, should the financial statements for Cambridge Bikes Company be prepared

    a.   As before, assuming that the company will be able to repay all its liabilities?

    b.   Assuming that the company will not be able to repay all its liabilities?

Review 1.16 Question 3

Suppose Bob's Paper and Packaging Company has two major customers that provide 90% of its revenue, and both just declared they will be filing for bankruptcy. Bob's isn't sure it will be able to make enough money from its remaining customers to stay afloat. Should Bob's financial statements be prepared under the going-concern concept?

    a.   Yes

    b.   No

Section 4
Formal Definitions of Accounting Terms

Concepts

1. Introduction

2. Assets

3. Liabilities

4. Equity

5. Revenues

6. Expenses

1.4.1   Introduction

After learning some basic accounting principles and concepts in the past few sections, it will be helpful to formally define key terms such as assets, liabilities, equity, revenues and expenses. Although U.S. GAAP and IFRS use slightly different language when defining the terms, the important components are the same. The definitions presented in this book combine aspects from both sets of standards.

1.4.2   Assets

There are many things that could potentially be considered an asset, but accounting standards strictly define what companies can record as an asset on their books.

These standards state that to be considered an asset, an item must:

- Be purchased at a cost that is measurable

- Produce probable economic benefit in the future

- Result from a past event

- Be owned or controlled by the entity

It's important to understand the formal definition because some items that appear to be assets might not meet all the criteria and therefore will not be recorded as an asset for the business.

As we already discussed, some typical assets for Acorns include equipment and furniture. These clearly satisfy the definition of an asset, as they were purchased at a cost that is measurable, produce benefits to the company because they will help create the bakery's inventory, result from a past event that involved a transaction with a separate entity, and are owned by Acorns.

The definition of an asset closely relates to many of the principles we have already covered. For example, assets need to be purchased at a cost that is measurable, and the money measurement principle and historical cost principle emphasize the importance of having a measurable cost.

For the answer to the following question, please see the end of Chapter 1.

Review 1.17 Question 1

Which of the following is an example of an asset that could be listed on a bottling factory's balance sheet? Please select all that apply.

    a.   Manufacturing facility
    b.   Bottling machine
    c.   Delivery truck
    d.   CEO's personal car
    e.   Cash

1.4.3   Liabilities

There are also stricter definitions for what qualifies as a liability. Typically, a liability must satisfy the following:

- It must impose a probable economic obligation on economic resources in the future

- The obligation has to be to another entity

- The event that created the obligation must have occurred in the past

As we already discussed, some typical liabilities for Acorns include gift cards and long-term debt. These create an obligation for Acorns to pay money or deliver goods in the future to another party.

For the answer to the following question, please see the end of Chapter 1.

Review 1.18 Question 1

Which of the following is an example of a liability that could be listed on a bottling factory's balance sheet? Please select all that apply.

    a.   Accounts payable
    b.   Wages payable
    c.   Long-term borrowings
    d.   CEO's home mortgage

1.4.4   Equity

Equity has a relatively simple formal definition; it is "the residual interest in the assets of an entity that remains after deducting its liabilities" according to the accounting standards board for the U.S. (see FASB Concepts Statement No. 6). This translates to owners' equity equals assets less liabilities.

As the previous chapters have shown, adjustments to equity typically take place when a transaction is recorded in the form of revenues and expenses, gains and losses, or contributions by owners. A different type of transaction is when a company makes a distribution to its owners. An example is when a public company buys back some of its stock that was previously issued, reducing the total amount of equity outstanding.

Equity is basically the resources of the business that belong to the owners. The total resources of the business (the assets) less the claims that others have against those assets results in the amount left for the owners (equity).

The terms owners' equity, stockholders' equity and shareholders' equity all refer to the same section on the balance sheet. The different names are simply used for different types of businesses. Sole proprietorships (small businesses with a single owner) use the term owners' equity whereas large corporations that sell shares of stock use the term stockholders' or shareholders' equity.

For the answer to the following question, please see the end of Chapter 1.

Review 1.19 Question 1

Which of the following is an example of owners' equity? Please select all that apply.

    a.   Common stock
    b.   Preferred stock
    c.   Retained earnings
    d.   Pensions owed to former employees
    e.   Land
    f.   Cash

1.4.5 Revenues

In the United States, the official definition for revenues is "inflows or other enhancements of assets of an entity or settlements of its liabilities (or a combination of both) from delivering or producing goods, rendering services, or other activities that constitute the entity's ongoing major or central operations," according to FASB Concepts Statement No. 6. The wording varies under IFRS standards, but it is the same concept.

While this definition may seem complicated, it follows our earlier description of revenue as "the money or the right to receive money from providing goods or services to a customer." However, the official definition stipulates that the goods or services must be related to the entity's central operations. If a toy factory sells a building that it no longer needs, and realizes a gain on the sale, the gain could not be counted as revenue because it is not related to the business' central operations. As we will discuss in later chapters, the gain would be reported as a gain on the sale of an asset, listed separately on the income statement. Separating the primary business from non-core operations allows users of financial reports to see how well the core business is doing.

There are other requirements that need to be satisfied in order for a business to be able to recognize revenue. The company must have earned the revenue, meaning that it provided the service or delivered the good to the customer, and it must have either received the cash or be confident that the customer will pay. In order for a company to be "confident" that the customer will pay, there must be a specific arrangement with the customer that states the amount that will be transferred for the good or service.

For the answer to the following question, please see the end of Chapter 1.

Review 1.20 Question 1

Which of the following is an example of revenue for a bottling factory? Please select all that apply.

    a.   Cash from sales of bottled beverages
    b.   Gains on sale of old machinery
    c.   Interest income

1.4.6 Expenses

In the United States, the official definition for expenses is "outflows or other using up of assets or incurrence of liabilities (or a combination of both) from delivering or producing goods, rendering services, or carrying out other activities that constitute the entity's ongoing major or central operations," according to FASB Concepts Statement No. 6. This is similar to our earlier definition of expenses as "the costs associated with providing goods or services to a customer." Expenses are typically recognized during the same period in which the revenues that they help generate are recognized, under the accrual method of accounting.

Expenses are costs associated with the central operations of the business. The outflows of money and assets on other items not related to the core operations are recorded as losses rather than expenses. If the toy factory suffered a loss on the sale of the building, the loss would be reported as a separate line item on the income statement.

For the answer to the following question, please see the end of Chapter 1.

Review 1.21 Question 1

Which of the following is an example of an expense for a bottling factory? Please select all that apply.

    a.   Cost of glass bottles used

    b.   CEO's speeding ticket

    c.   Wages

    d.   Manufacturing building rental costs

    e.   New machinery purchase

    f.   Accounts payable for materials purchased

Section 5
Review

Accounting allows us to understand how a business is performing.

Assets = Liabilities + Owners' Equity

- The accounting equation is fundamental to all of accounting.

- All transactions affect the accounting equation.

- The accounting equation must always balance.

Transactions: events that impact the financial position of a business

Examples of transactions:

- Sale of goods or services

- Purchase of inventory

- Loan

- Payment of rent

- Equity investment

The **accrual accounting method**, the method that the majority of companies use, recognizes revenue when it is earned through the delivery of goods or services and payment is assured.

The major accounting boards are the Financial Accounting Standards Board (**FASB**), which developed the Generally Accepted Accounting Principles (**GAAP**), and the International Accounting Standards Board (**IASB**), which developed the International Financial Reporting Standards (**IFRS**).

Accounting is based on principles and rules. Major **accounting principles** include conservatism, relevance and reliability, the historical cost principle, consistency, materiality, the entity concept, the money measurement principle, and the going concern concept.

General Definitions of Key Accounting Terms

- **Assets**: resources owned or controlled by a business that the business believes will produce economic benefits in the future.

- **Liabilities:** claims on the assets of the company by third parties (i.e. outsiders who are not owners of the business)

- **Owners' Equity:** the capital contributed by owners and the profits earned by the business

- **Revenues:** the money a business receives from its ordinary activities, such as providing goods or services to a customer

- **Expenses**: the costs of the resources used by the company to provide goods or services to a customer

Section 6
Review Questions

For answers to the following questions, please see the end of Chapter 1.

Review 1.22 Question 1

The fundamental equation of accounting is:

a.   Assets + Owners' Equity = Liabilities

b.   Assets + Liabilities = Owners' Equity

c.   Assets = Liabilities + Owners' Equity

Review 1.22 Question 2

The balance sheet

a.   shows a snapshot of a company's assets, liabilities and equity at a certain point in time

b.   shows revenues and expenses over a period of time

c.   shows the cash flows of a company over a period of time

Review 1.22 Question 3

All businesses are required to have a balance sheet, income statement, and statement of cash flows.

a.   True

b.   False

Review 1.22 Question 4

Who uses financial reports?

a.   Owners

b.   Investors

c.   Business Managers

d.   Banks

e.   All of the above

Review 1.22 Question 5

Which of the following is NOT an example of a liability?

    a.   Accounts Payable

    b.   Loans

    c.   Property used to secure a bank loan

    d.   Notes Payable

Review 1.22 Question 6

Which of the following is an example of a transaction? Please select all that apply.

    a.   Jennifer Costello invested $100,000 in her bakery.

    b.   Fred's Factory purchased three new machines.

    c.   Doug received his CFA, so his company can now charge more for his services.

Review 1.22 Question 7

Suppose a retail store earns revenues from renting out an extra building that it owns. Those revenues would be classified as:

    a.   assets

    b.   operating revenues

    c.   non-operating revenues

Review 1.22 Question 8

Suppose Fred's cousin wanted to invest in Fred's Factory Inc. and offered to contribute $50,000 to own part of the company. How would this contribution impact the accounting equation? Please select all that apply.

    a.   Increase loans payable by $50,000

    b.   Increase owners' equity by $50,000

    c.   Increase cash by $50,000

    d.   Increase accounts receivable by $50,000

Review 1.22 Question 9

Suppose a customer walked into The Boat Shop and purchased a boat for $75,000. He had 30 days to pay for it after receiving it. How would this transaction impact the accounting equation of The Boat Shop at the time of the sale to the customer? Please select all that apply.

a. Cash increases by $75,000
b. Inventory decreases by $75,000
c. Accounts receivable increases by $75,000
d. Owner's equity increases by $75,000
e. Owner's equity decreases by $75,000

Review 1.22 Question 10

Suppose a customer walked into The Boat Shop and purchased a boat for $75,000. That boat was actually purchased by The Boat Shop for $60,000 from a used boat dealer. The Boat Shop needs to recognize the cost of goods sold. How would the expense recognition affect The Boat Shop's accounting equation? Please select all that apply.

a. Cash decreases by $60,000
b. Cash increases by $75,000
c. Inventory decreases by $60,000
d. Inventory decreases by $75,000
e. Owner's equity decreases by $60,000
f. Owner's equity decreases by $75,000

Review 1.22 Question 11

Suppose Choc Full of It sells a $25 gift certificate to a customer. How will this affect the accounting equation at the time of the sale? Please select all that apply.

a. Increase cash by $25
b. Increase owners' equity by $25
c. Increase accounts receivable by $25
d. Increase accounts payable by $25
e. Increase the obligation to provide goods by $25

Review 1.22 Question 12

Six months later, the customer purchases $25 of chocolate from Choc Full of It using the gift card. What will be the impact on the accounting equation for Choc Full of It? Please select all that apply.

    a.   Owners' equity increases by $25
    b.   Cash decreases by $25
    c.   Obligation to provide goods decreases by $25
    d.   Cash increases by $25

Review 1.22 Question 13

Suppose a company wants to spin-off one of its divisions, and it has many different companies who have offered to purchase it. Should it record the transaction on its books?

    a.   Yes, because it's likely the deal will happen.
    b.   No, because the deal is not certain.

Review 1.22 Question 14

The Boat Shop bought 2 boats for $40,000 each in December 2012 and recorded them on its balance sheet at that price. Ever since Snoop Lion used the same type of boat in his music videos, they have been selling for $80,000 each. The Boat Shop changes the price of the boats on the balance sheet to reflect their increase in value.

    a.   This is a violation of the historical cost principle.
    b.   This is a violation of the reliability principle.
    c.   This is a violation of the consistency principle.
    d.   This does not violate any accounting principles.

Review 1.22 Question 15

Suppose Jennifer Costello, the owner of Acorns, took out a loan of $100,000 to help purchase a new house that costs $300,000. How will this transaction be reflected on Acorns books?

    a.   Assets and liabilities will increase by $100,000.
    b.   Assets and liabilities will increase by $300,000.
    c.   The transaction will have no impact on Acorns' books.

Review 1.22 Question 16

Suppose one of Fred's Factory's major customers is going bankrupt. Fred's Factory is confident that it will be able to earn 80% of last year's revenue and still earn a profit. Should Fred's Factory's financial statements be prepared under the going-concern concept?

    a.   Yes

    b.   No

Review 1.22 Question 17

Which of the following is an example of an asset that could be listed on a chocolate shop's balance sheet? Please select all that apply.

    a.   Baking and cooking equipment

    b.   Wages payable

    c.   Cash

    d.   Notes payable

Review 1.22 Question 18

Which of the following is an example of a liability that could be listed on a chocolate shop's balance sheet? Please select all that apply.

    a.   CEO's personal car

    b.   Long-term debt

    c.   Accounts receivable

    d.   Notes payable

Review 1.22 Question 19

Which of the following is an example of operating revenue for a chocolate shop? Please select all that apply.

    a.   Cash from chocolate sales

    b.   Income earned from renting out buildings

    c.   Dividends from investments

Which of the following is an example of an expense for a chocolate shop? Please select all that apply.

    a.   Cost of boxes to package chocolate

    b.   CEO's mortgage payments

    c.   Salaries

    d.   New equipment purchase

Section 7

Answer Key

Review 1.1 Explanations

Question 1

Answer: A,B,E

Cash and Property, Plant and Equipment (PP&E) are assets because they are resources that provide economic benefits to the company. Accounts receivable, which represents a company's right to receive cash in the future from its customers, is also an asset that will provide an economic benefit to the company. Accounts payable refers to payments the company will have to make in the future, so it is a liability, not an asset. Retained earnings is not an asset; it is an account under owners' equity.

Question 2

Answer: C,E

Accounts payable and notes payable are liabilities. Accounts payable represents a company's obligation to pay others in the future for services or goods previously received. Notes payable represents a company's obligation to pay back lenders in the future. Accounts receivable, equipment, and inventory are not liabilities; they are assets because they will all provide economic benefits to the company. Accounts receivable represents a company's right to receive cash in the future.

Question 3

Answer: A,C,D

Retained earnings, common stock, and paid-in capital are examples of owners' equity. Retained earnings is the earnings a company generates and decides to keep for internal purposes. Common stock is a form of capital contributed by owners of the company. Paid-in capital is the sum of a company's preferred stock, common stock, and additional paid-in capital. Cash is not an example of owners' equity; it is an asset that provides an economic benefit to a company. Notes payable is not an example of owners' equity; it is a liability because it represents a company's obligation to pay back lenders in the future.

Review 1.2 Explanations

Question 1

Answer: A, C

The loan would increase cash by $50,000 and would increase loans payable by $50,000 to reflect Acorns' obligation to pay back the loan in the future. The loan would not increase accounts receivable by $50,000 because the loan payment would be immediate and in cash. The loan would not increase owners' equity by $50,000 because Costello's family is lending money, not making an investment in the company.

Question 2

Answer: A, C

The contribution would increase cash by $25,000 and also increase owners' equity by $25,000 because the baker is making an investment in the company. The contribution would not increase loans payable by $25,000 because the baker did not lend money to the company. The contribution would not increase inventory by $25,000 because the baker made a cash contribution to the company and did not affect the inventory account.

Question 3

Answer: B, C

This purchase would increase PP&E by $1,400 because Acorns now has owns additional equipment. It would also decrease cash by $1,400 because Acorns spent cash to buy the equipment.

Question 4

Answer: A, C

This transaction will increase inventory by $2,000 to reflect the additional books that Borders owns and can sell in the future. It will also decrease cash by $2,000 because Borders used cash to purchase the books. This transaction will not affect owners' equity because no one is making a contribution to the business. This transaction will not decrease accounts payable because the question stated that Borders used cash to purchase the books.

Review 1.3 Explanations

Question 1

Answer: A, B

Cash increases by $75 because the customer paid cash to DSW to purchase the boots. Owners' equity increases by $75 because DSW earned revenue from the purchase. Accounts payable was not affected by this transaction. DSW does not owe additional money to any party as a result of this transaction.

Review 1.4 Explanations

Question 1

Answer: A, D

Inventory decreases by $15 because Acorns sold the truffles to its customer and no longer has the inventory. It decreases only by $15 because that is the amount Acorns paid CHO to purchase the inventory. Owners' equity also decreases by $15 to reflect the cost of the inventory sold. Owners' equity would not increase by $15 to recognize revenue. It would increase by $25 to reflect the revenue earned and decrease by $15 to reflect the inventory expense.Cash would not increase by $15 because the customer paid Acorns $25 for the box of truffles.

Question 2

Answer: B, E

Inventory would decrease by $30 (the amount DSW paid to purchase the boots) to show that DSW sold the boots and they are no longer in inventory. Inventory would not decrease by $75 because DSW only paid $30 to purchase the boots for inventory. Retained earnings would also decrease by $30 (not $75) to reflect COGS. Cash would not decrease. Cash should increase because a customer purchased boots and paid DSW in cash.

Question 3

Answer: B, E

Cash would increase by $500. Borders would have decreased cash by $1,000 to purchase the books and then increased cash by $1,500 when the community center paid for the books. $1,500 - $1,000 = $500. Retained earnings would increase by $500. Retained earnings would decrease by $1,000 to reflect COGS, but it would also increase by $1,500 to reflect revenue. $1,500 - $1,000 = $500. Inventory would not increase by $500. There would be no net impact on inventory because Borders bought the books and then sold them. (Inventory would increase by $1,000 and then decrease by $1,000.) COGS would not decrease by $1,000. Since Borders sold the books, COGS would increase by $1,000.

Review 1.5 Explanations

Question 1

Answer: B, D

Accounts payable would increase by $20K. When Coca-Cola bought the mangos from the farmer, Coca-Cola agreed to pay for them later. Inventory increases by $20K to reflect the $20K of mangos Coca-Cola added to inventory. Owners' equity would not decrease by $20K because Coca-Cola has not yet recognized an expense for the purchase. Inventory would not decrease by $20K because Coca-Cola did not sell its inventory. Accounts receivable would not increase by $20K. Coca-Cola owes the farmer money and would not expect to receive cash in the future from the farmer.

Question 2

Answer: B, D

Accounts payable would decrease by $20K. On 1/31/14, Coca-Cola would pay the $20K in cash that it owed the farmer, decreasing its obligation to pay at a later date (accounts payable). Cash would decrease by $20K. On 1/31/14, Coca-Cola would pay the cash it owed to the farmer. Owners' equity would not decrease by $20K because it is not affected by the transaction where Coca-Cola pays the farmer for the mangos.

Question 3

Answer: B, E

Accounts payable would increase by $9,000 on 3/1/14 because Coca-Cola agreed to pay the manufacture $9,000 in the future. Equipment would increase by $9,000 because Coca-Cola bought a new bottling machine, which is a piece of equipment. Inventory would not increase by $9,000 because Coca-Cola purchased equipment, not inventory. Accounts receivable would not increase by $9,000. Coca-Cola would not expect to receive cash in the future as a direct result of purchasing a bottling machine. Cash would not increase by $9,000 because Coca-Cola did not receive cash from the manufacturer. Coca-Cola agreed to pay the manufacturer later for the equipment it bought.

Question 4

Answer: A, C

Accounts payable would decrease by $9,000. On 4/30/14, Coca-Cola would reduce its accounts payable because it paid the manufacturer and no longer has the obligation to pay the manufacturer in the future. Cash would decrease by $9,000. On 4/30/14, Coca-Cola would pay cash to the manufacturer for the equipment it had purchased earlier. Equipment would not decrease by $9,000 because Coca-Cola still has the equipment and is not selling the asset. Expenses would not increase by $9,000. Coca-Cola purchased an asset, and this purchase does not affect expenses, which are the costs of bringing in revenues.

Review 1.6 Explanations

Question 1

Answer: A, D

Accounts receivable would increase by $125 to reflect that the customer will pay Acorns $125 (5 * $25) for the truffle boxes at some point in the future. Owner's equity would increase by $125 (5 * $25) to recognize the revenue for the transaction. The recognition of the receivable and revenue would not affect inventory.

Question 2

Answer: A, D

Inventory would decrease by $75 because Acorns sold the inventory to a customer. Inventory decreases by the amount Acorns originally paid to obtain the inventory (5 * $15). Inventory would not increase because Acorns sold the inventory; it did not purchase additional inventory. Owner's equity would decrease by $75 to reflect the expense for the COGS. Accounts payable would not increase by $75 because Acorns does not owe anyone cash in the future as a result of this transaction.

Question 3

Answer: B, D

Cash would increase by $125 because the customer paid $125 in cash to Acorns. Accounts receivable would decrease by $125 to reflect that the customer no longer has an obligation to pay Acorns. Owner's equity would not increase by $125. Acorns already recognized revenue earlier, when it had shipped the goods, so it would not recognize revenue as a result of receiving cash.

Review 1.7 Explanations

Question 1

Answer: A, B, D, E

Assets would increase by $125 to reflect the cash SG received as a prepayment for its services. Liabilities would also increase by $125 to reflect the obligation to provide 5 personal training sessions. Owners' equity would increase by $50 in February because SG would recognize revenue for the two personal training sessions the member has completed. Liabilities would decrease by $50 (2* $25) in February because SG performed two personal training sessions and no longer has that obligation. Owners' equity would not increase by $125 in January because SG should not recognize revenue for a personal training session until the member has completed it. Owners' equity would not increase by $125 in February because SG should not recognize revenue for a personal training session until the member has completed it, and the member only completed $50 of sessions in February.

Question 2

Answer: B

SG should recognize $80 (8 * $10) of revenue at the end of March because Estelle took 8 classes in March. SG should wait until the expiration of the class card in August to recognize the remaining revenue for the classes Estelle won't use. SG should recognize revenue when it is earned, which is after Estelle takes a class. It should not be recognized evenly over time.

Question 3

Answer: B, D

The gift card sale would increase cash by $50 because the customer paid Acorns $50 to purchase the gift card. Acorns should also increase the obligation to provide goods by $50. Acorns has not earned the revenue yet, so a liability account that shows the obligation to provide goods needs to increase. The gift card sale would not increase inventory by $50. Acorns did not buy any products for its inventory; it only received cash in exchange for selling a gift card. The gift card sale would not increase owner's equity by $50. Acorns should wait until the gift card is redeemed to recognize the revenue.

Question 4

Answer: B, C, E, F

Owner's equity would increase by $25 to recognize revenue. The customer redeemed half his gift card. The obligation to provide goods would decrease by $25 because half the gift card was redeemed and Acorns no longer has to provide $25 of goods. Inventory would decrease by $10 to reflect that Acorns sold some goods that were listed at $10 in inventory. Owner's equity would decrease by $10 to recognize the expense of the cost of goods sold. Cash would neither increase nor decrease by $25 because the customer used a gift card, not cash, for the purchase.

Review 1.8 Explanations

Question 1

Answer: A, C

The insurance purchase would decrease cash by $30K because Coca-Cola paid $30K immediately for a year of insurance. The asset prepaid insurance would increase by $30K because Coca-Cola now has the right to receive insurance for the next year. The asset accounts receivable would not decrease by $30K. Accounts receivable is the expected receipt of cash. Coca-Cola paid cash for insurance and would not expect to receive cash in the future as a result of this transaction. Owners' equity would not decrease by $30K. Coca-Cola should recognize the expense for the insurance as it is used up, not immediately.

Question 2

Answer: B, C

Owners' equity would decrease by $2.5K ($30K/12) each month to recognize the prepaid insurance expense. Prepaid insurance would decrease by $2.5K ($30/12) each month to reflect that one month of prepaid insurance was used up. Cash would not decrease by $2.5K ($30K/12). Coca-Cola already prepaid for the insurance, so there would be no decrease in cash as the insurance is used up throughout the year. Prepaid insurance would not increase by $2.5K ($30K/12). Prepaid insurance is an asset that will be decreased over time as the insurance is used up.

Review 1.9 Explanations

Question 1

Answer: A

The conservatism principle states that companies should anticipate and record future losses but not gains. Since it is very likely the company will lose the case, the company should record a liability for $1 million. The company does not need to record a liability to set aside money for the potential loss; the conservatism principle is what drives a company to record a liability for $1 million. The company should not make a decision about how to account for the potential loss based on how it would negatively affect net income. That decision would not follow accounting principles and would make financial statements inaccurate and less transparent.

Question 2

Answer: C

The conservatism principle states that companies should anticipate and record future losses but not gains. Even though it is likely the company will win the case, the company should not record an increase in assets. The company should not make a decision about how to account for the potential loss based on how it would positively affect net income. That decision would not follow accounting principles and would make financial statements inaccurate and less transparent.

Question 3

Answer: B

The conservatism principle states that companies should anticipate and record future losses but not gains. Since it looks like Apple won't be able to sell its iPod inventory, it should follow the conservatism principle and lower the asset value of its iPod inventory. Although it seems likely that Apple can sell its iPhones at a higher price, Apple should follow the conservatism principle and not increase the value of its iPhones. The conservatism principle does not give any guidance about how to reflect the value of a company's reputation on its books.

Question 4

Answer: A

The conservatism principle states that companies should anticipate and record future losses but not gains. It is correct for Acorns to write off the $2,000 because it seems unlikely that Acorns will receive the money. It is incorrect for Tom's Tools to increase the value of its investment in Harvey's because Tom's should not record future gains.

Review 1.10 Explanations

Question 1

Answer: B

The reliability principle states that information must be objective and unbiased and accurately convey the reality of the situation. The fact that Apple will release a new phone that could reduce BlackBerry's sales is relevant information that users of financial statements would find useful. BlackBerry should verify the information is accurate instead of simply assuming it's true before recording a loss.

Question 2

Answer: B

The reliability principle states that information must accurately convey the reality of the situation. Since the deal is not certain, the company should not record the transaction on its books.

Question 3

Answer: A, C

The lawsuit that could cause financial instability is relevant information that users of the financial statements would find useful. Fred's Factory is a relatively large company; the loss of $2,000 in accounts receivable would not significantly impact the relevance or reliability of the company's financial statements. A fire that destroyed half of the company's inventory would be relevant information. As a result, the company may encounter difficulty delivering on customer orders, thereby impacting the revenue generating capability of the firm.

Review 1.11 Explanations

Question 1

Answer: B, D

The historical cost principle states that transactions should be recorded at the actual price paid at the time of the transaction. Answer B, recording hammers at $8 per hammer, the actual price paid for the hammers, instead of the current price of the hammers is an application of the historical cost principle. Answer D, recording the chair on the balance sheet at the price Annie paid for it ($350) instead of what the chair was worth ($400) is correct. The decision to record revenue at the end of the month for a year-long membership is related to the revenue recognition principle, not the historical cost principle. Using the same inventory accounting method from year to year is related to the consistency principle, not the historical cost principle.

Review 1.12 Explanations

Question 1

Answer: B

The consistency principle states that a company should record transactions the same way from one period to the next. In 2013, TWE switched the way it recognized revenue, which violated the consistency principle. TWE's accounting prior to 2013 did not violate the consistency principle because it always recognized revenue the same way.

Question 2

Answer: A

The consistency principle states that a company should record transactions the same way from one period to the next. If Tom's switches its depreciation method, it will violate the consistency principle. Even if Tom's switches to the accelerated depreciation method for all other items, it will still violate the consistency principle because it used the straight line method in previous periods.

Review 1.13 Explanations

Question 1

Answer: B

The cost of the two light bulbs should be expensed. Even for a small pizza shop, the cost of two light bulbs is probably not material enough to disclose separately as a separate line item. So the cost of the two light bulbs should be lumped with other expenses.

Question 2

Answer: B

Since the advertising campaign is a trivial fraction of the total expenses of the business, it is not necessary to report the advertising expense separately. This follows the materiality concept, which states that it is only necessary to do detailed record keeping and reporting for material items.

Question 3

Answer: B

The materiality concept states that it is only necessary to do detailed record keeping and reporting for material items. Depreciation of $2 per year is not a significant expense and does not need to be recorded.

Question 4

Answer: A

The materiality concept states that it is necessary to do detailed record keeping and reporting for material items. Alice's family business is small, and a $1 million settlement payment is a significant cost, so it should be recorded.

Review 1.14 Explanations

Question 1

Answer: B

The accounting firm paid Sophie for accounting books it could use at the accounting firm, so this is a business transaction that should be recorded on the books of the business. The entity concept states that the books of a business should be kept separately from the books of individuals. Charlie's extra night in a hotel to visit his family the next day is a personal expense and should not be recorded on the books of the business. Maria received a personal stereo that she occasionally brings to work. This is an asset owned by Maria and should not be recorded on the books of the business according to the entity concept. The owner received a speeding ticket during her commute to work. The ticket is a personal expense, not an expense of the business, so it should not be recorded on the books of the business.

Question 2

Answer: A

The entity concept states that the books of a business should be kept separately from the books of individuals. Annie bought a car for personal transportation, so it should not be recorded on the books of Annie's Art Gallery. Annie's Art Gallery (the entity) loaned Annie (the person) money to buy the car, so the gallery is entitled to receive the loaned money back from Annie in the future. That makes the loan to Annie an asset on the financial statements of the gallery.

Review 1.15 Explanations

Question 1

Answer:B

The money measurement principle states that companies should only record transactions that can be measured in monetary terms. The patent cannot actually be measured in monetary terms, so it should not be recorded on the balance sheet.

Question 2

Answer: B

The money measurement principle states that companies should only record transactions that can be measured in monetary terms. The increase in skill level cannot actually be measured in monetary terms, so it should not be recorded on the balance sheet.

Review 1.16 Explanations

Question 1

Answer: B

A business is a going concern if it is likely to continue to operate for the foreseeable future. Since Cambridge Bikes Company is being liquidated, it is not a going concern.

Question 2

Answer: B

Since Cambridge Bikes Company is not a going concern, it should not prepare its financial statements the same way as before. To be conservative, CBC should prepare its statements differently, assuming it will not be able to repay its liabilities.

Question 3

Answer: B

A business is a going concern if it is likely to continue to operate for the foreseeable future. Bob's lost its major customers and is unsure it will be able to stay afloat, so it is not a going concern.

Review 1.17 Explanations

Question 1

Answer: A, B, C, E

Assets must be purchased at a cost that is measurable, produce benefits to the company in the future, result from a past event, and be owned by the entity. A manufacturing facility, a bottling machine, a delivery truck, and cash all fit the criteria of assets for a bottling factory. The CEO's personal car does not fit all of the criteria of an asset. The CEO owns the car, and it will not provide benefits to the company in the future.

Review 1.18 Explanations

Question 1

Answer: A, B, C

Liabilities must impose an obligation on a company's resources in the future, the obligation has to be to another entity, and the event that created the obligation must have occurred in the past. Accounts payable satisfies all the criteria of a liability for a bottling factory. Accounts payable is the obligation to pay another entity for goods or services received in the past. Wages payable (the obligation to pay wages to employees for services provided in the past) also satisfies all the criteria of a liability for a bottling factory. Another liability for a bottling factory is long-term borrowings. The liability was created when the factory borrowed money from a bank and promised to repay it in the future. A home mortgage is not a liability for a bottling factory. It is not an obligation on a company's resources; it's an obligation on the home owner's resources.

Review 1.19 Explanations

Question 1

Answer: A, B, C

Equity is essentially the resources of the business that belong to the owners. Common stock and preferred stock are types of securities that represent ownership in a company. Retained earnings is the amount of resources a business generates by running its operations and keeps for internal purposes and is a type of equity. Pensions owed to former employees are liabilities, not equity, because they represent an obligation owed to another party for services performed in the past. Land is an example of an asset, not equity. It was purchased at a measurable cost, will produce benefits to the company in the future, resulted from a past event, and is owned by the company.

Review 1.20 Explanations

Question 1

Answer: A

Cash from the sale of bottles is an example of revenue for a bottling factory. It's the money received from providing goods to customers. The gains on the sale of old machinery is not an example of revenue for a bottling factory because selling old machinery is not core to the factory's central operations. Interest income is not an example of revenue for a bottling factory because earning interest is not core to the factory's central operations.

Review 1.21 Explanations

Question 1

Answer: A, C, D

The cost of glass used to make bottles is an example of an expense for a bottling factory because it is a cost associated with providing goods to customers. Wages are an example of an expense for a bottling factory because they are costs associated with providing goods to customers. Manufacturing building rental costs are expenses for a bottling factory because they are costs associated with providing goods to customers. The CEO's speeding ticket is not an example of an expense for a bottling factory because it is not related to the company's central operations. A new machinery purchase is not an expense for a bottling factory because it is not an outflow of cash related to providing goods to customers. A machinery purchase would be an asset, and the company would calculate depreciation expense for the asset each year.

Chapter Review 1.22 Explanations

Question 1

Answer: C

The fundamental equation of accounting is Assets = Liabilities + Owners' Equity. Assets are the resources owned or controlled by a business, and they are funded by liabilities and owners' equity.

Question 2

Answer: A

The balance sheet is a snapshot of a company's resources (assets) and how the resources were financed (liabilities and owners' equity). The income statement shows revenues and expenses over a period of time. The cash flow statement shows the cash flows of a company over a period of time.

Question 3

Answer: B

Many companies have a balance sheet, an income statement, and a statement of cash flows, but it is not required. However, all publicly traded companies are required to publish quarterly financial statements.

Question 4

Answer: E

Financial reports are used for different purposes by many parties, including owners, investors, business managers, and banks. Owners could use financial statements to see how well their business is performing, investors could use them to determine whether a company is a good investment, managers could use them to identify areas of improvement, and banks could use them to determine if they should extend credit to a company.

Question 5

Answer: C

Property is an asset, not a liability. Property will provide an economic benefit to a company in the future. Accounts payable, the obligation to pay another party for services or goods received in the past, is a liability. Loans are liabilities because they represent the obligation to pay back the lender for money borrowed in the past. Notes payable, the obligation to pay creditors for money borrowed in the past, is a liability.

Question 6

Answer: A, B

A transaction is an event that impacts the financial position of a business. An investment in a bakery is an example of a transaction because it will increase cash and owners' equity, affecting the financial position of the business. The purchase of new machines is also an example of a transaction because it will decrease cash and increase equipment, affecting the financial position of the business. Doug receiving his CFA is not an example of a transaction because it won't affect the financial position of the business. The charges billed to customers for Doug's services would be an example of a transaction though.

Question 7

Answer: C

Operating revenues are revenues earned from the main activity of a business. Renting out an extra building is a secondary activity, not one of the main activities of a retail store, so the revenue earned from that activity would be classified as non-operating revenues. Assets are resources owned or controlled by a company that will provide an economic benefit to the company in the future. Revenues earned from renting out a building are not assets.

Question 8

Answer: B, C

Fred's cousin made a contribution to the company, so this transaction increased owners' equity by $50,000. Fred's cousin now owns part of the company. The contribution by Fred's cousin also increased the company's cash by $50,000. The contribution by Fred's cousin did not increase accounts receivable, which represents the right to receive cash in the future for goods or services provided in the past. Fred's cousin made a contribution to the company, not a loan, so loans payable would not increase as a result of this transaction.

Question 9

Answer: C, D

Accounts receivable would increase by $75,000 to reflect The Boat Shop's right to receive cash in the future for the boat that was sold to the customer. Owner's equity would increase by $75,000 to recognize the revenue earned from selling the boat. Cash would not increase by $75,000 at the time of the transaction because the customer did not pay cash. He had 30 days to pay for the boat. Inventory would not decrease by $75,000. Even though the boat was sold for $75,000, it was likely listed in inventory at a lower price, the price that it cost The Boat Shop to make the boat.

Question 10

Answer: C, E

Inventory would decrease by $60,000. The boat was listed in inventory at its original cost, $60,000. Owner's equity would decrease by $60,000 to reflect the expense cost of the goods sold. Inventory would not decrease by $75,000. It was listed in inventory at the price The Boat Shop paid for it, not the price The Boat Shop sold it for. Cash is not affected by the expense recognition.

Question 11

Answer: A, E

The sale of the gift certificate will increase cash by $25 because the customer paid $25 cash in exchange for the gift certificate. The sale of the gift certificate will also increase the obligation to provide goods by $25. Choc Full of It must provide the goods when the customer redeems the gift certificate. The sale of the gift certificate will not increase owners' equity by $25 because Choc Full of It will not recognize revenue until it provides the goods or services. The sale of the gift certificate will not increase accounts receivable by $25. Accounts receivable is the right to receive cash in the future for goods or services provided in the past. The sale of the gift certificate will not increase accounts payable by $25. Accounts payable is the obligation to pay cash in the future for goods or services received in the past.

Question 12

Answer: A, C

When the customer uses the gift card to purchase chocolates, the transaction would increase owners' equity by $25 to recognize the revenue earned from selling chocolates. It would also decrease the obligation to provide goods by $25 because the gift card was redeemed and Choc Full of It no longer has the obligation. Cash is not affected by this transaction; cash exchanged hands at an earlier date when the gift card was purchased.

Question 13

Answer: B

The company should follow the reliability and historical cost principles and should not record the spin-off transaction until it is certain. The transaction should eventually be recorded at the actual price paid at the time of the transaction, not an estimate.

Question 14

Answer: A

Changing the price of the boats from $40,000 to $80,000 is a violation of the historical cost principle. The historical cost principle states that transactions should be recorded at the actual price paid at the time of the transaction. The reliability principle and consistency principles are also important but not directly related to this transaction. The reliability principle states that information should be objective and unbiased and accurately convey the reality of the situation. The consistency principle states that businesses should record transactions in the same manner from one period to the next.

Question 15

Answer: C

The entity concept states that the books of a business must be kept separately from the books of individuals. So, even though the owner of Acorns took out a loan, the loan was used for personal purposes, not for Acorns. Therefore, the transaction should have no impact on Acorns' books.

Question 16

Answer: A

If a company is a going concern, it means that the company is likely to continue to operate for the foreseeable future. Since Fred's Factory is confident it can continue to operate despite the bankruptcy of one of its customers, it should be prepared under the going-concern concept.

Question 17

Answer:A, C

Baking and cooking equipment and cash are all examples of assets for a chocolate shop. These items are owned by the company and will provide an economic benefit to the company in the future. On the other hand, wages payable and notes payable are not assets; they are liabilities. They are obligations to pay others in the future for services or loans received in the past.

Question 18

Answer: B, D

Long-term debt and notes payable are examples of liabilities for a chocolate shop. They are obligations to pay others in the future for cash borrowed in the past. In contrast, accounts receivable is an asset that represents the right to receive cash in the future for goods provided in the past. The CEO's personal car should not show up on the chocolate shop's balance sheet. This is a personal item, and the entity concept states that the car should remain off of the books of the business.

Question 19

Answer: A

Operating revenue is revenue earned from the main activities of a business. The main activity of a chocolate shop is selling chocolates, so cash from chocolate sales is an example of operating revenue. Renting out buildings and investing in securities are not the main activities of the chocolate shop, so any income earned from those activities would be examples of non-operating revenues.

Question 20

Answer: A, C

The cost of boxes to package chocolates and salaries are examples of expenses for a chocolate shop. These are cash outflows incurred by carrying out activities related to the company's central operations. The CEO's mortgage payments are personal expenses and should not be on the books of the chocolate shop, according to the entity concept. Purchasing new equipment is not an expense; the equipment should be recorded as an asset, and the company will record depreciation expense over time.

2

Recording Transactions

Sections

Section 1
Journal Entries and T-Accounts

Concepts

1. Financial Statement Accounts

2. Debits and Credits

3. Journal Entries

4. T-Accounts

5. Journal Entries and the Accounting Equation

2.1.1   Financial Statement Accounts

In Chapter 1, we discussed accounting transactions and learned how they affect the financial position of a business. It was easy to see their impact on a business by looking at how they changed the accounting equation. The next step to focus on is how to record the transactions. It is important to learn how to properly record business transactions because they are the basis for forming financial statements.

While the accounting equation may be useful to gain a basic understanding of transactions and their effects, it isn't reasonable to use only the equation to analyze a business. Creating accounts, or groupings of similar transactions, will allow us to gain a better understanding of a business.

Accounts such as cash, accounts receivable, equipment, and property are listed under the category assets. On the other side of the equation, there is liabilities and owners' equity. Accounts such as long-term debt, wages payable, and interest payable are listed under liabilities. Common stock, paid-in capital, and retained earnings are examples of equity accounts.

Although many businesses have similar accounts, each business is free to determine the account name that best fits the nature of their business. In order to see what account names are used for a business, we can refer to the "**chart of accounts**," which lists all the accounts of a business. For Acorns, the chart of accounts would include items such as **wages payable**, inventory, and accounts payable. Companies could be extremely detailed and list every possible account, but that would make the financial statements too complex. On the other hand, too few accounts could leave out important details, so it is essential to achieve the right balance of accounts.

Let's discuss the definitions of some common accounts that you might see.

Assets

Receivables: money owed to a business by others; assets

Some examples of common receivables accounts include:

- **Accounts receivable**: money owed to a business by its customers for goods or services provided on credit

- **Notes receivable**: money owed to a business from debtors based on a formal written document stipulating the terms of the contract

Fixed assets: assets with a long-term useful life that a business uses in its operations; also known as **tangible assets** or property, plant and equipment (PP&E)

Inventory: goods and materials held by a business that are ready, or will be ready, for sale; assets

Goodwill: an **intangible asset** that arises during an acquisition; the amount the acquirer pays for the target firm less the target's fair market value of net assets

Liabilities

Payables: money owed by a business to others; liabilities

Some examples of common payables accounts include:

- **Accounts payable**: money owed to vendors or suppliers for products or services purchased on credit

- **Wages payable**: money owed to employees for hours previously worked. Similar to **accrued payroll**.

- **Notes payable**: money owed to banks or other creditors based on a formal written document stipulating the terms of the contract

Equity

Common stock: shares that represent ownership of a business

Preferred stock: shares that represent ownership of a business and rank above common stock, preferred shares have a claim on earnings (and assets in the event of **liquidation**) before common stockholders

Contributed capital: money that an investor paid to buy stock directly from a company, also known as paid-in capital. Consists of the stated value (par value or face value) of the shares plus additional paid-in capital, the amount over and above the par value paid to a company.

Additional paid-in capital: shareholder contributions that exceed a share's par value

In order to record transactions, we need to establish which accounts will be affected and by how much. The following sections will show different methods to record transactions and how these methods help us create the financial statements.

For answers to the following questions, please see the end of Chapter 2.

Review 2.1 Question 1

For each question, match the account name to the correct section of the accounting equation.

Assets = Liabilities + Owners' Equity

Account names: Accounts Payable, Common Stock, Cash

Review 2.1 Question 2

For each question, match the account name to the correct section of the accounting equation.

Assets = Liabilities + Owners' Equity

Account names: Accrued Expenses, Preferred Stock, Short-term Investments

---

Review 2.1 Question 3

For each question, match the account name to the correct section of the accounting equation.

Assets = Liabilities + Owners' Equity

Account names: Retained Earnings, Accounts Receivable, Income Tax Payable

---

Review 2.1 Question 4

For each question, match the account name to the correct section of the accounting equation.

Assets = Liabilities + Owners' Equity

Account names: Land, Paid-in Capital, Long-term Debt

2.1.2   Debits and Credits

In the last section, we discussed common accounts that most businesses use. In order to record transactions in those accounts, we need to understand the terms **debit** and **credit**.

The terms debit and credit are sometimes used in everyday context, and people typically assume debit is bad and credit is good. Those meanings are confusing and don't apply in accounting, so it is better to think of the formal accounting definitions.

A debit is an accounting entry that increases asset balances. Debits are always on the left-hand side of an account. If you want to increase an asset account, you debit that account. As you know, the opposite half of the accounting equation contains liabilities + equity. If we debit a liability or equity account, we will decrease the balance in that account. In summary, debits increase asset accounts and decrease liabilities and equity accounts. Expense and loss accounts are equity accounts. Hence, debits to expense and loss accounts, while increasing these accounts, decrease owner's equity.

The other half of an accounting entry is a credit. In order to increase the account balance for a liability, equity, revenue, or gain account, we credit that account. A credit can also be used to decrease the balance in an asset or expense account. Credits are always on the right-hand side of an account.

Table 2.1 summarizes the important aspects of debits and credits.

TABLE 2.1

Debits	Credits
Increase assets, expenses, and losses	Increase liabilities, equity, revenues, and gains
Decrease liabilities, equity, and revenues	Decrease assets and expenses
Left side	Right side

The debits and credits system can actually be traced back to Italy during the 13th and 14th centuries. Originally, merchants kept track of money received or paid using a single column. It was possible to sort out the accounts and determine the value of a business, but it wasn't easy. Eventually, the double column system was developed, and trading companies could keep track of all the increases on one side of an account and the decreases on the other. With debits and credits in separate columns, it was much easier to add up the increases and decreases to get the net balance in an account.

Figure 2.1 shows the debits and credits for a couple of common accounts, cash and accounts payable.

FIGURE 2.1

Cash (asset)	Debit	Credit
Received cash from customers	$$ (cash increases)	
Paid for materials and supplies		$$ (cash decreases)
Paid wages		$$ (cash decreases)
Received cash from bank	$$ (cash increases)	
Total	$$ (cash inflows)	$$ (cash outflows)

Accounts Payable (liability)	Debit	Credit
Paid money owed to vendor	$$ (AP decreases)	
Bought inventory on credit		$$ (AP increases)
Bought supplies on credit		$$ (AP increases)
Paid money owed for equipment repair	$$ (AP decreases)	
Total	$$ (decreases)	$$ (increases)

For answers to the following questions, please see the end of Chapter 2.

Review 2.2 Question 1

State whether you would debit or credit the account to achieve the following result.

Increase cash

a. Debit
b. Credit

Review 2.2 Question 2

State whether you would debit or credit the account to achieve the following result.

Decrease inventory

a. Debit
b. Credit

Review 2.2 Question 3

State whether you would debit or credit the account to achieve the following result.

Increase accounts receivable

a.   Debit
b.   Credit

Review 2.2 Question 4

State whether you would debit or credit the account to achieve the following result.

Increase accounts payable

a.   Debit
b.   Credit

Review 2.2 Question 5

State whether you would debit or credit the account to achieve the following result.

Decrease retained earnings

a.   Debit
b.   Credit

Review 2.2 Question 6

State whether you would debit or credit the account to achieve the following result.

Increase revenue

a.   Debit
b.   Credit

Review 2.2 Question 7

State whether you would debit or credit the account to achieve the following result.

Decrease rent expense

a. Debit
b. Credit

Review 2.2 Question 8

State whether you would debit or credit the account to achieve the following result.

Increase depreciation

a. Debit
b. Credit

2.1.3 Journal Entries

On 1/1/14, Acorns bought 10 boxes of truffles as inventory from Choc Full of It for a total price of $150 and paid in cash.

One way to record a transaction is by making a **journal entry**. A journal entry lists the date, the account name that is debited, and the amount by which it is debited. The next line lists the account to be credited and the corresponding amount. At least two lines are affected in a journal entry, and the entries are listed sequentially in the company's journal.

The journal entry to record the transaction for Acorns would look like this:

Date	Account Name	Debit	Credit
January 1, 2014	Inventory	$150.00	
	Cash		$150.00

In the journal entry, Acorns increases its assets by $150 to reflect the increase in inventory and decreases assets by $150 to reflect the reduction in cash.

In journal entries, the names of the accounts are important. In this example, inventory and cash are the accounts that are impacted. There are two columns, debits on the left and credits on the right. These columns indicate whether the account should be increased or decreased, and as we discussed before, debits increase asset and expense accounts and decrease liability, equity, and revenue accounts. Credits affect the accounts in the opposite way; credits increase liability, equity, and revenue accounts and decrease asset and expense accounts.

Both cash and inventory are assets, and in the example above, inventory increased with a debit and cash decreased with a credit.

Debits and credits always offset each other, so if we add up all the debits, it must equal the sum of all the credits. This principle guarantees that the fundamental equation in accounting is always satisfied.

Key Facts About Journal Entries:

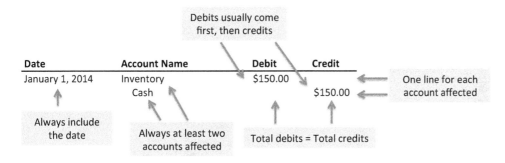

For answers to the following questions, please see the end of Chapter 2.

Review 2.3 Question 1

On January 1, 2014, Acorns purchased 20 jars of jam as inventory from its supplier for $100. Select the correct account and amount to be debited as a result of this transaction.

Date	Account Name	Debit	Credit
January 1, 2014	??	??	
	XX		XX

a.   Inventory
b.   Cash
c. $100
d. $20

On January 1, 2014, Acorns purchased 20 jars of jam as inventory from its supplier for $100. Select the correct account and amount to be credited as a result of this transaction.

Date	Account Name	Debit	Credit
January 1, 2014	Inventory	$100.00	
	??		??

a. Inventory
b. Cash
c. Accounts Payable
d. $100.00

2.1.4   T-Accounts

It is important for a business to track its transactions, but a list in the form of journal entries is not a useful way to summarize them. The next step in recording transactions, and ultimately creating the financial statements, is posting the journal entries to **t-accounts**. Posting refers to the act of transferring a journal entry to a specific account in the **ledger**.

T-accounts are a different way to visualize transactions. The name t-account is based on its shape, which looks like the letter T. A t-account lists all of the transactions that affect a particular account, and it provides a quick way to see changes made to an account over time. The t-account shows the beginning balance, the debits and credits made to the account during that period, and the ending balance in the account.

The chart of accounts contains all the accounts used by a business, and each one can be shown as its own t-account. Debits are always shown on the left, and credits are on the right, just as they are in the journal entries.

Since assets typically have debit balances, the beginning and ending balances are usually on the left. Liabilities and owners' equity generally have credit balances, so the beginning and ending balances would be on the right. In order to calculate the ending balance for a t-account, you take the beginning balance, add the transactions that impact the same side of the t-account and subtract the transactions that affect the other side.

The t-accounts for cash and inventory are shown below for the transaction in Question 1, where Acorns purchased $100 of inventory with cash.

Cash

| | $100.00 | 1/1/14 |

```
          Inventory
1/1/14     $100
```

Instead of a single journal entry that lists both accounts, this transaction is separated into two different t-accounts. This format makes it easier to see the overall impact on an account over a certain time period.

Examples of how t-accounts might look after a month are shown below. As you can see, they start with the beginning balance, show the transactions that occurred over the month, and end with the ending balance. Each individual transaction also has a date listed next to it, which makes it easy to link back to its journal entry.

Asset t-account for January 2014

```
                 Cash
Beg Bal  $51,789
                      22,340   1/11/14
                       2,659   1/15/14
1/28/14   30,000
End Bal  $56,790
```

Liability t-account for January 2014

```
            Accounts Payable
                      $4,520   Beg Bal
                       1,300   1/3/14
1/18/14    850
1/19/14  2,400
                      $2,570   End Bal
```

Use the following journal entry to determine the answer to Review Question 2.4.

On December 1, 2013, Acorns purchased 20 jars of jam to sell in its store. It purchased this inventory from its supplier for $100. The following journal entry was recorded:

Date	Account Name	Debit	Credit
June 1, 2014	Inventory	$100.00	
	Cash		$100.00

For the answer to the following question, please see the end of Chapter 2.

Review 2.4 Question 1

How would you post this transaction to the t-accounts? Please select all that apply.

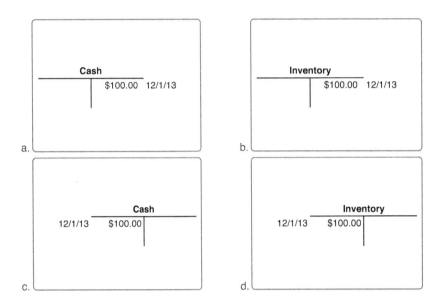

2.1.5   Journal Entries and the Accounting Equation

Now that we have learned how to record transactions with journal entries and t-accounts, let's study how they affect the accounting equation.

For answers to the following questions, please see the end of Chapter 2.

Review 2.5 Question 1

On September 1, 2013, Acorns bought a new mixer for $1,600 and paid in cash. Indicate whether the accounts that will be affected by the transaction are assets, liabilities or owner's equity.

a.   Mixer, Asset
b.   Mixer, Owner's Equity
c.   Cash, Asset
d.   Cash, Owner's Equity

Review 2.5 Question 2

On September 1, 2013, Acorns bought a new mixer for $1,600 and paid in cash. Select the correct account and amount to be debited as a result of this transaction.

Date	Account Name	Debit	Credit
September 1, 2013	??	??	
	XX		XX

a. Cash
b. Mixer
c. Inventory
d. $1,600

Review 2.5 Question 3

On September 1, 2013, Acorns bought a new mixer for $1,600 and paid in cash. Select the correct account and amount to be credited as a result of this transaction.

Date	Account Name	Debit	Credit
September 1, 2013	Mixer	$1,600	
	??		??

a. Cash
b. Accounts Payable
c. Inventory
d. $1,600

Review 2.5 Question 4

On September 1, 2013, Acorns bought a new mixer for $1,600 and paid in cash. Select the correct t-accounts for the transaction.

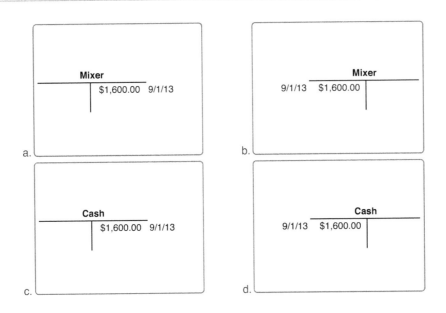

Review 2.5 Question 5

On September 1, 2013, Acorns bought a new mixer for $1,600 and paid in cash. How was the accounting equation affected? Please select all that apply.

a.   Assets increased by $1,600 to record mixer purchase
b.   Owner's equity decreased by $1,600 to record mixer expense
c.   Assets decreased by $1,600 to record cash payment
d.   Liabilities increased by $1,600 to record obligation to pay

Section 2
Advanced Journal Entries

Concepts

1. Accrual Journal Entries

2. Revenues and Expenses

3. Payments in Advance

4. Prepayments

2.2.1   Accrual Journal Entries

In the first chapter, we discussed accrual accounting, the method where businesses recognize events even if cash hasn't been exchanged yet. In this section, we will learn how to record **accruals** in journal entries. It might be helpful to go back and review debits and credits to reinforce which one is used to increase or decrease various accounts.

Suppose Spartan Gym (SG) has maintenance performed on its treadmills on November 1, 2014, but it typically pays the invoice 30 days later. When SG receives the maintenance service, it recognizes an expense immediately, even though the cash has not been paid yet. Since SG doesn't pay immediately, it records a liability to show its obligation to pay.

Date	Account Name	Debit	Credit
November 1, 2013	Equipment Maintenance	$400.00	
	Accounts Payable		$400.00

As you can see in the journal entry above, there is a debit to equipment maintenance expense, which increases expenses, and a credit to accounts payable, which increases the liability account. Expense accounts are equity accounts. Hence when equipment maintenance is debited, we are reducing owner's equity. As a result, the balance sheet equation remains in balance.

When the cash is actually paid, Acorns will record this journal entry:

Date	Account Name	Debit	Credit
November 30, 2013	Accounts Payable	$400.00	
	Cash		$400.00

There is no expense in this second journal entry because it was already incurred in the first transaction. In this transaction, Acorns is only paying its bill, not incurring an expense.

As the journal entry shows, cash is decreased through a credit because Acorns is paying $400 to the vendor. The liability, accounts payable, is debited by $400 because the obligation to pay the vendor is being fulfilled. Since an asset account is decreased and a liability account is also decreased, the balance sheet equation continues to remain in balance.

For answers to the following questions, please see the end of Chapter 2.

Review 2.6 Question 1

On 1/1/14, Acorns bought 10 boxes of chocolate from its supplier for $150. Acorns paid for the chocolate on 1/31/14. What would the entry for the initial purchase on 1/1/14 look like? Select the correct account and amount to be debited.

Date	Account Name	Debit	Credit
January 1, 2014	??	??	
	XX		XX

a. Inventory
b. Accounts payable
c. Accounts receivable
d. $150.00

Review 2.6 Question 2

On 1/1/14, Acorns bought 10 boxes of chocolate from its supplier for $150. Acorns paid for the chocolate on 1/31/14. What would the entry for the initial purchase on 1/1/14 look like? Select the correct account and amount to be credited.

Date	Account Name	Debit	Credit
January 1, 2014	Inventory	$150.00	
	??		??

a. Accounts receivable
b. Cash
c. Accounts payable
d. $150.00

Review 2.6 Question 3

On 1/1/14, Acorns bought 10 boxes of chocolate from its supplier for $150. Acorns paid for the chocolate on 1/31/14. What would the entry on 1/31/14 look like? Select the correct account and amount to be debited.

Date	Account Name	Debit	Credit
January 31, 2014	??	??	
	XX		XX

a. Cash
b. Accounts payable
c. Inventory
d. $150.00

Review 2.6 Question 4

On 1/1/14, Acorns bought 10 boxes of chocolate from its supplier for $150. Acorns paid for the chocolate on 1/31/14. What would the entry on 1/31/14 look like? Select the correct account and amount to be credited.

Date	Account Name	Debit	Credit
January 31, 2014	Accounts Payable	$150.00	
	??		??

a. Cash
b. Inventory
c. Expenses
d. $150.00

Review 2.6 Question 5

Indicate whether the accounts that will be affected by the transaction are assets, liabilities, or owners' equity. On 9/1/13, Acorns purchased an order of almond paste from its supplier for $80. It paid for the almond paste on 9/30/13.

a. Supplies, Owner's Equity
b. Accounts Payable, Liability
c. Supplies, Asset
d. Accounts Payable, Asset

Review 2.6 Question 6

On 9/1/13, Acorns purchased an order of almond paste from its supplier for $80. It paid for the almond paste on 9/30/13. How would the initial purchase be posted to the t-accounts? Please select all that apply.

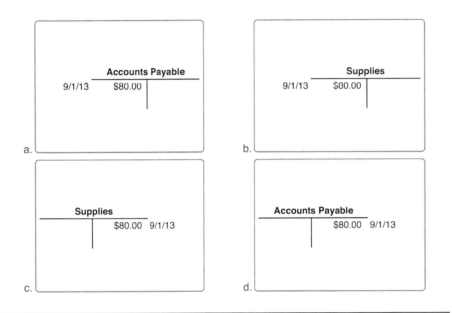

a.

Accounts Payable
9/1/13 $80.00

b.

Supplies
9/1/13 $80.00

c.

Supplies
            $80.00 9/1/13

d.

Accounts Payable
            $80.00 9/1/13

Review 2.6 Question 7

On 9/1/13, Acorns purchased an order of almond paste from its supplier for $80. It paid for the almond paste on 9/30/13. How would the payment on 9/30/13 be posted to the t-accounts? Please select all that apply.

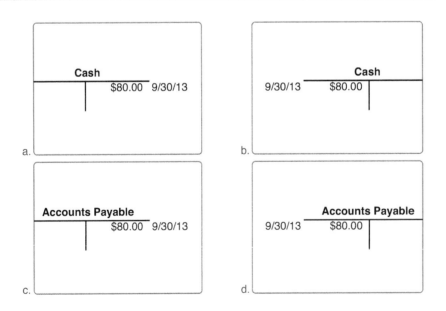

a.

Cash
            $80.00 9/30/13

b.

Cash
9/30/13 $80.00

c.

Accounts Payable
            $80.00 9/30/13

d.

Accounts Payable
9/30/13 $80.00

2.2.2   Revenues and Expenses

In the previous chapter, we studied how revenues and expenses impact the accounting equation. These transactions are also recorded in journal entries and can be summarized as t-accounts.

Suppose that SG sold a pair of sweatpants for $30 in its small gym store. SG originally bought the sweatpants for $20 from its supplier. What entry would be made to record the sale?

It's helpful to break the transaction into smaller parts to figure out the entries. SG received cash for the purchase, so we need to increase the cash account. Cash falls under the asset category, so it is increased with a debit. SG received the cash because it provided a good to a customer, so it is recorded as revenue. Since SG sold a product, it would record the revenue under the account called sales.

SG also sold some of its inventory, so the inventory account needs to be decreased. Inventory would be decreased with a credit of $20, the price SG paid its supplier for the sweatpants. Since the inventory was used up, we need to record an expense to show what it was used for. Debits increase expense accounts, so we would record a debit under the expense account.

What is the best account to record the sweatpants expense? Many businesses have a specific account called cost of goods sold (COGS) to record the cost of inventory that is sold. This is a good example of the matching principle; the expenses for the transaction are recognized at the same time as the revenues are recognized.

There are also other **operating expenses** that companies can incur and pay for later. A common example is utilities expense. SG uses electricity throughout a month and then pays for it at the end of the month. How would this transaction be recorded?

At the end of the month, SG would record a transaction that increases the expense account called utility expense. Since expenses are increased with debits, we would debit the utility expense account. SG also has to record an increase accounts payable to reflect the need to pay the utility vendor later. Accounts payable is a liability account, so it is increased with a credit.

When paying its bill, say the following month, SG would decrease the liability accounts payable with a debit and decrease the asset cash with a credit.

In terms of the balance sheet equation, it's helpful to think of revenue, gains, expenses, and losses as owner's equity accounts. Thus we credit revenues to increase owner's equity and debit expenses to reduce owner's equity.

For answers to the following questions, please see the end of Chapter 2.

Review 2.7 Question 1

On 1/1/14, SG sold two t-shirts to a gym member for $40 total. SG had previously pur-chased the t-shirts for $25 and recorded it as inventory. What would be the journal entry to record this sale? Please select all that apply.

Date	Account Name	Debit	Credit
January 1, 2014	1) ??	$40.00	
	2) ??		$40.00

a.   1) Cash
b.   1) COGS
c.   1) Revenue
d.   2) Cash
e.   2) COGS
f.   2) Revenue

Review 2.7 Question 2

On 1/1/14, SG sold two t-shirts to a gym member for $40 total. SG had previously pur-chased the t-shirts for $25 and recorded it as inventory. What would be the journal entry to record the expense associated with this sale? Please select all that apply.

Date	Account Name	Debit	Credit
January 1, 2014	Cash	$40.00	
	Revenue		$40.00
January 1, 2014	1) ??	$25.00	
	2) ??		$25.00

a.   1) Inventory
b.   1) COGS
c.   2) Inventory
d.   2) COGS

Review 2.7 Question 3

Suppose on 11/1/13, The Cheese Shop (TCS) sold 1 wheel of brie to Whole Foods for $120. TCS had originally bought the brie from France for $80. Whole Foods doesn't have to pay until 11/30/13. Select the correct account and amount for TCS to debit to record this transaction on 11/1/13.

Date	Account Name	Debit	Credit
November 1, 2013	??	??	
	XX		XX

a.   Revenue, $80.00
b.   Revenue, $120.00
c.   Accounts Receivable, $80.00
d.   Accounts Receivable, $120.00

Review 2.7 Question 4

Suppose on 11/1/13, The Cheese Shop (TCS) sold 1 wheel of brie to Whole Foods for $120. TCS had originally bought the brie from France for $80. Whole Foods doesn't have to pay until 11/30/13. Select the correct account and amount for TCS to credit to record this transaction on 11/1/13.

Date	Account Name	Debit	Credit
November 1, 2013	Accounts Receivable	$120.00	
	??		??

a.   Revenue, $80.00
b.   Revenue, $120.00
c.   COGS, $80.00
d.   COGS, $120.00

Review 2.7 Question 5

Suppose on 11/1/13, The Cheese Shop (TCS) sold 1 wheel of brie to Whole Foods for $120. TCS had originally bought the brie from France for $80. Whole Foods doesn't have to pay until 11/30/13. What would the ?? in the journal entry for TCS look like to record this transaction on 11/1/13? Please select all that apply.

Date	Account Name	Debit	Credit
November 1, 2013	Accounts Receivable	$120.00	
	Revenue		$120.00
November 1, 2013	1) ??	$80.00	
	2) ??		$80.00

a. 1) COGS
b. 1) Inventory
c. 2) COGS
d. 2) Inventory

Review 2.7 Question 6

Suppose on 11/1/13, The Cheese Shop (TCS) sold 1 wheel of brie to Whole Foods for $120. TCS had originally bought the brie from France for $80. Whole Foods paid on 11/30/13. What would the ?? in the journal entry for TCS look like to record this transaction on 11/30/13? Please select all that apply.

Date	Account Name	Debit	Credit
November 30, 2013	1) ??	$120.00	
	2) ??		$120.00

a. 1) Accounts Receivable
b. 1) Cash
c. 2) Accounts Receivable
d. 2) Cash

Review 2.7 Question 7

On 6/1/13, Acorns paid $150 for 10 boxes of tea. Then one of Acorns customers bought the 10 boxes for $200 and promised to send a check within 30 days. What would the ?? in the journal entry look like? Please select all that apply.

Date	Account Name	Debit	Credit
June 1, 2013	1) ??	$200.00	
	2) ??		$200.00

   a.   1) Accounts Receivable

   b.   1) Revenue

   c.   1) Cash

   d.   2) Accounts Receivable

   e.   2) Revenue

   f.   2) Cash

Review 2.7 Question 8

On 6/1/13, Acorns paid $150 for 10 boxes of tea. Then one of Acorns customers bought the 10 boxes for $200 and promised to send a check within 30 days. What would the ?? in the journal entry look like? Please select all that apply.

Date	Account Name	Debit	Credit
June 1, 2013	Accounts Receivable	$200.00	
	Revenue		$200.00
June 1, 2013	1) ??	$150.00	
	2) ??		$150.00

   a.   1) COGS

   b.   1) Inventory

   c.   2) COGS

   d.   2) Inventory

Review 2.8 Question 1

On 12/1/13, Acorns sold 2 bags of coffee to the Parent-Teacher Association (PTA) for $30. The PTA will pay for the coffee at the end of the month. Acorns bought the coffee for $20. How would the sale being made on 12/1/13 and the corresponding expense be posted to the t-accounts? Please select all that apply.

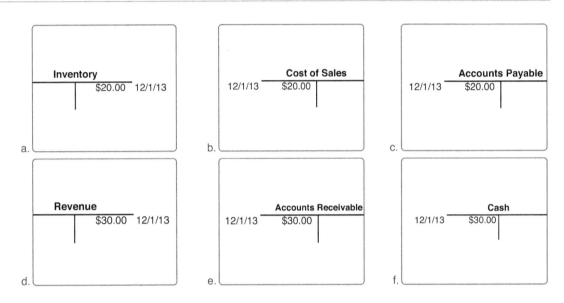

On 12/1/13, Acorns sold 2 bags of coffee to the Parent-Teacher Association (PTA) for $30. The PTA will pay for the coffee at the end of the month. Acorns bought the coffee for $20. How would the payment being received on 12/31/13 be posted to the t-accounts? Please select all that apply.

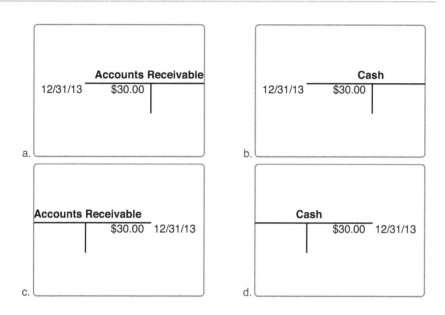

2.2.3   Payments in Advance

Sometimes customers will pay in advance for goods and services. A good example of this is gift cards – people pay immediately and use the gift card later. Making advance payments increases both assets (cash) and liabilities (obligation to provide services). Businesses often use an account titled **unearned revenue** or **deferred revenue** to record the obligation. **Deferred revenue is not a revenue account; it is a liability account**. Over time, the account is reduced as the product or service is delivered and the revenue is earned.

Suppose Acorns sold a $50 gift certificate to a customer on June 1, 2013. To record the receipt of cash, we would debit the cash account. We would also credit the liability account deferred revenue to accrue the obligation. The journal entry to record the receipt of payment of $50 by Acorns would look like this:

Date	Account Name	Debit	Credit
June 1, 2013	Cash	$50.00	
	Deferred Revenue		$50.00

When the customer redeems the gift card two weeks later, Acorns will record an entry to reduce the deferred revenue liability (debit deferred revenue) and recognize revenue (credit revenue) for the sale. That entry would look like this:

Date	Account Name	Debit	Credit
June 15, 2013	Deferred Revenue	$50.00	
	Revenue		$50.00

There are only three different types of **revenue recognition** journal entries that are possible:

1. Cash was collected from the customer, and revenue was earned. The journal entry would look like this:

Account Name	Debit	Credit
Cash	XX	
Revenue		XX

2.   Cash was not collected from the customer yet, but revenue was earned. The journal entry would look like this at the time of the transaction:

Account Name	Debit	Credit
Accounts Receivable	XX	
Revenue		XX

This entry assumes that the revenue is realizable and the customer is likely to pay in the future. When the cash is ultimately received by the business, the entry would look like this:

Account Name	Debit	Credit
Cash	XX	
Accounts Receivable		XX

3. Cash was collected from the customer, but the revenue was not earned yet.

The product or service was not delivered yet in this case, and the journal entry would look like this:

Account Name	Debit	Credit
Cash	XX	
Deferred Revenue		XX

Later, after the company delivered the good or service, the entry would look like this:

Account Name	Debit	Credit
Deferred Revenue	XX	
Revenue		XX

For answers to the following questions, please see the end of Chapter 2.

Review 2.9 Question 1

Suppose Spartan Gym sold a 3-month unlimited pilates class to one of its customers who paid $300 in cash on 1/1/14. What would the journal entry look like to record this transaction on 1/1/14? Please select all that apply.

Date	Account Name	Debit	Credit
January 1, 2014	1) ??	$300.00	
	2) ??		$300.00

a. 1) Cash
b. 1) Accounts Receivable
c. 2) Revenue
d. 2) Deferred Revenue

Review 2.9 Question 2

Suppose Spartan Gym sold a 3-month unlimited pilates class to one of its customers who paid $300 in cash on 1/1/14. What would the journal entry look like to record this transaction on 1/31/14? Please select all that apply.

Date	Account Name	Debit	Credit
January 31, 2014	1) ??	$100.00	
	2) ??		$100.00

a. 1) Revenue
b. 1) Deferred Revenue
c. 2) Revenue
d. 2) Deferred Revenue

2.2.4   Prepayments

Customers aren't the only ones who can make prepayments; businesses can also make prepayments to their suppliers. To record this transaction, we usually use an account that begins with the word "prepaid." They can fall under the general category prepaid expenses or have more specific titles. **Prepaid expenses are not expense accounts; they are assets.** For example, if a business paid in advance for an insurance policy on its building, the account prepaid insurance would be used to record the amount paid up-front. The journal entry to record one year of prepaid insurance for the business would look like this:

Date	Account Name	Debit	Credit
XX/XX/XXXX	Pre-paid Insurance	$4,000.00	
	Cash		$4,000.00

As the year goes on, the business recognizes the insurance expense. When the expense is incurred, the business would debit the insurance expense account to recognize that some of the insurance policy was used up. The business would also credit the prepaid insurance account, decreasing the asset prepaid insurance.

Date	Account Name	Debit	Credit
XX/XX/XXXX	Insurance Expense	$333.33	
	Prepaid Insurance		$333.33

For answers to the following questions, please see the end of Chapter 2.

Review 2.10 Question 1

Suppose The Candy Shop prepays a television network 3 months of advertising spots. Suppose it paid $30,000 on 6/1/13. What would the journal entry look like on 6/1/13? Please select all that apply.

Date	Account Name	Debit	Credit
June 1, 2013	1) ??	$30,000.00	
	2) ??		$30,000.00

a. 1) Cash
b. 1) Pre-paid Advertising
c. 2) Cash
d. 2) Pre-paid Advertising

Acorns has a membership in the Bakers Association of America and pays $150 for the year. If Acorns makes the payment on 1/1/14 and considers the fees paid as assets, how would this transaction be posted to the t-accounts? Select all that apply.

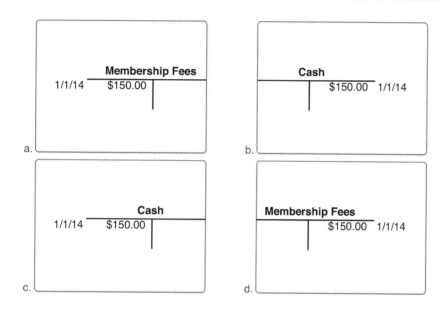

a.
Membership Fees
1/1/14 $150.00

b.
Cash
$150.00   1/1/14

c.
Cash
1/1/14 $150.00

d.
Membership Fees
$150.00   1/1/14

Section 3
Trial Balance

Concepts

1. Building a Trial Balance

2.3.1   Building a Trial Balance

Journal entries are recorded over the course of business, and as the entries are posted to the t-accounts, we can easily see the ending balance and know the amount in each account. This information is then used to produce financial statements.

In order to create the income statement and the balance sheet, we need to prepare a **trial balance**. Trial balances are as of a certain date, and they list the titles of all the t-accounts that have balances at that time and the ending balance in each account. A trial balance is a good way to verify account balances and make sure that all the debits equal the credits.

Typically, balance sheet accounts are listed first, starting with the assets, then the liabilities and then the equity accounts. Revenue and expense accounts are listed last. As we know, for each journal entry, the debits always equal the credits. The t-accounts list all the journal entries, and the total of all the debit balance accounts also equals the total of all the credit balance accounts.

An example of a trial balance is shown in Figure 2.2.

FIGURE 2.2

Crush Boutique's Trial Balance as of December 31, 2013

Balance Sheet Accounts	Debit	Credit
Cash	$200,000	
Inventory	5,000	
Accounts Receivable	5,000	
Prepaid Rent	18,000	
Accounts Payable		30,000
Notes Payable		60,000
Common Stock		100,000
Income Statement Accounts		
Cost of Goods Sold	30,000	
Revenues		68,000
Total	$258,000	$258,000

The trial balance lists each account from the ledger. The ending balance from each account appears in either the debit or credit column of the trial balance. Usually, asset and expense accounts are in the debit column while liability, equity and revenue accounts show credit balances.

For answers to the following questions, please see the end of Chapter 2.

Review 2.11 Question 1

Crush Boutique made 3 years of lease rental payments at the beginning of the year. How does Crush adjust the accounts to show that 1/3 of the asset prepaid rent was used up? Please select all that apply.

---

    a.   Debit Prepaid Rent
    b.   Credit Prepaid Rent
    c.   Debit Rent Expense
    d.   Credit Rent Expense

Review 2.11 Question 2

Crush Boutique made 3 years of lease rental payments at the beginning of the year. What should the balances in the accounts, "Prepaid Rent" and "Rent Expense" be on 12/31/13? Please select the correct account and corresponding amount to appear in the trial balance below.

Balance Sheet Accounts	Debit	Credit
Cash	$200,000	
Inventory	5,000	
Accounts Receivable	5,000	
Prepaid Rent	??	
Accounts Payable		30,000
Notes Payable		60,000
Common Stock		100,000
Income Statement Accounts		
Cost of Goods Sold	30,000	
Revenues		68,000
Rent Expense	??	
Total	**$258,000**	**$258,000**

a. 12,000

b. 6,000

Figure 2.3 shows the changes in the trial balance for the previous question.

FIGURE 2.3

Crush Boutique's Trial Balance as of December 31, 2013

Balance Sheet Accounts	Debit	Credit	Change in Dr	Change in Cr	Final Debit
Cash	$200,000				
Inventory	5,000				
Accounts Receivable	5,000				
Prepaid Rent	18,000			6,000	12,000
Accounts Payable		30,000			
Notes Payable		60,000			
Common Stock		100,000			
Income Statement Accounts					
Cost of Goods Sold	30,000				
Revenues		68,000			
Rent Expense			6,000		6,000
Total	$258,000	$258,000			

Suppose Crush Boutique must pay 5% interest to the bank on its notes payable, but it is going to make the payment at the beginning of 2014. How would this transaction change the trial balance?

As shown in the trial balance below, we would credit accrued interest liability by $3,000 ($60,000 * 5%) and debit interest expense by $3,000.

Balance Sheet Accounts	Debit	Credit	Change in Dr	Change in Cr	Final Debit	Final Credit
Cash	$200,000				$200,000	
Inventory	5,000				5,000	
Accounts Receivable	5,000				5,000	
Prepaid Rent	12,000				12,000	
Accounts Payable		30,000				30,000
Notes Payable		60,000				60,000
Accrued Interest Liability				3,000		3,000
Common Stock		100,000				100,000
Income Statement Accounts						
Cost of Goods Sold	30,000				30,000	
Revenues		68,000				68,000
Rent Expense	6,000				6,000	
Interest Expense			3,000		3,000	
Total	**$258,000**	**$258,000**			**$261,000**	**$261,000**

Section 4
Review

Accounts: groupings of similar transactions

Examples of Assets, Liabilities and Owners' Equity Accounts

Assets	Liabilities	Owners' Equity
Cash	Bank Loan	Common Stock
Inventory	Rent Payable	Preferred Stock
Accounts Receivable	Accounts Payable	Retained Earnings
Property, Plant and Equipment	Taxes Payable	
Land	Long-term Debt	

Receivables: money owed to a business by others; assets

Payables: money owed by a business to others; liabilities

Double entry accounting uses **debits** and **credits** to record transactions. Debits are on the left and credits are on the right. Debits and credits represent increases and decreases, depending on the account being affected.

Debits	Credits
Increase assets, expenses, and losses	Increase liabilities, equity, revenues, and gains
Decrease liabilities, equity, and revenues	Decrease assets and expenses
Left side	Right side

Journal entries are ways to record transactions.

Key Facts About Journal Entries

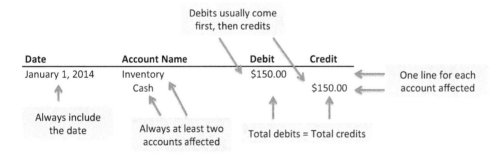

In order to summarize transactions, the journal entries can be posted to **t-accounts**. The t-account shows the beginning balance of an account, the debits and credits made to the account during that period, and the ending balance in the account.

The **trial balance** summarizes all the t-accounts, listing the balance in each account as of a certain date in either the debit or credit column. In the trial balance, the total debits of all the t-accounts equals the total credits of all the t-accounts.

Accounts that typically have…

Debit Balances	Credit Balances
Assets	Liabilities
Expenses	Equity
	Revenues

Account	Normal Balance	Debit	Credit
Assets	Debit	Increase	Decrease
Liabilities	Credit	Decrease	Increase
Owners' equity	Credit	Decrease	Increase
Revenues	Credit	Decrease	Increase
Expenses	Debit	Increase	Decrease
Gains	Credit	Decrease	Increase
Losses	Debit	Increase	Decrease

Debit	Credit
Increase cash	Decrease cash
Increase equipment	Decrease equipment
Increase office supplies	Decrease office supplies
Increase accounts receivable	Decrease accounts receivable
Increase rent expense	Decrease rent expense
Increase loss on sale of asset	Increase gain on sale of asset
Decrease accounts payable	Increase accounts payable
Decrease long-term debt	Increase long-term debt
Decrease deferred revenue	Increase deferred revenue
Decrease wages payable	Increase wages payable
Decrease common stock	Increase common stock
Decrease retained earnings	Increase retained earnings

Transaction	Potential Accounts Affected	Debits	Credits
Sold goods to customer on account	Increase accounts receivable (asset)	Dr accounts receivable	
	Increase revenue (revenue)		Cr revenue
Paid rent	Increase rent expense (expense)	Dr rent expense	
	Decrease cash (asset)		Cr cash
Purchased supplies on credit	Increase supplies (asset)	Dr supplies	
	Increase accounts payable (liability)		Cr accounts payable
Declared dividends	Decrease retained earnings (equity)	Dr retained earnings	
	Increase dividends payable (liability)		Cr dividends payable
Borrowed cash from bank	Increase cash (asset)	Dr cash	
	Increase notes payable (liability)		Cr notes payable

Section 5
Review Questions

For answers to the following questions, please see the end of Chapter 2.

Review 2.12 Question 1

For each question, match the account name to the correct section of the accounting equation.

Assets = Liabilities + Owners' Equity

Account names: Accounts Receivable, Accounts Payable, Retained Earnings

Review 2.12 Question 2

For each question, match the account name to the correct section of the accounting equation.

Assets = Liabilities + Owners' Equity

Account names: Notes Payable, Property, Common Stock

Review 2.12 Question 3

State whether you would debit or credit the account to achieve the following result.

Increase equipment

a. Debit
b. Credit

Review 2.12 Question 4

State whether you would debit or credit the account to achieve the following result.

Decrease revenue

a.   Debit
b.   Credit

Review 2.12 Question 5

State whether you would debit or credit the account to achieve the following result.

Increase notes payable

a.   Debit
b.   Credit

Review 2.12 Question 6

State whether you would debit or credit the account to achieve the following result.

Decrease accounts receivable

a.   Debit
b.   Credit

Review 2.12 Question 7

Debits...
Please select all that apply.

a.   Increase assets
b.   Decrease assets
c.   Increase expenses
d.   Decrease liabilities
e.   Increase equity

Review 2.12 Question 8

Credits...

Please select all that apply.

a. Increase expenses
b. Decrease assets
c. Increase revenues
d. Decrease equity
e. Increase liabilities

Review 2.12 Question 9

Suppose Coca-Cola sold 50 cases of Coke to a convenience store for $1,000 on 10/1/2013. The store paid cash. It had cost Coca-Cola $600 to make the 50 cases. Which of Coca-Cola's journal accounts would be affected? Please select all that apply.

a. Cash
b. Accounts receivable
c. Sales
d. Inventory
e. COGS
f. Accounts payable

Review 2.12 Question 10

Suppose Coca-Cola sold 50 cases of Coke to a convenience store for $1,000 on 10/1/2013. The store paid cash. It had cost Coca-Cola $600 to make the 50 cases. How would the various accounts be affected to reflect the revenues and expenses associated with this sale? Please select all that apply.

a. Debit cash
b. Debit inventory
c. Debit COGS
d. Credit cash
e. Credit inventory
f. Credit sales

Review 2.12 Question 11

Suppose Coca-Cola sold 50 cases of Coke to a convenience store for $1,000 on 10/1/2013. The store paid cash. It had cost Coca-Cola $600 to make the 50 cases. Select the correct account and amount to be credited.

Date	Account Name	Debit	Credit
October 1, 2013	Cash	$1,000	
	??		??

a.   Sales
b.   COGS
c.   Inventory
d. $600
e. $1,000

Review 2.12 Question 12

Suppose Coca-Cola sold 50 cases of Coke to a convenience store for $1,000 on 10/1/2013. The store paid cash. It had cost Coca-Cola $600 to make the 50 cases. Select the correct account and amount to be debited.

Date	Account Name	Debit	Credit
October 1, 2013	??	??	
	Inventory		$600

a.   Sales
b.   COGS
c.   Inventory
d. $600
e. $1,000

Review 2.12 Question 13

Suppose Coca-Cola sold 50 cases of Coke to a convenience store for $1,000 on 10/1/2013. The store paid cash. It had cost Coca-Cola $600 to make the 50 cases. How much revenue did Coca-Cola earn on this sale?

    a. $1,000
    b. $600
    c. $400
    d. $0

Review 2.12 Question 14

Suppose Coca-Cola sold 50 cases of Coke to a convenience store for $1,000 on 10/1/2013. The store paid cash. It had cost Coca-Cola $600 to make the 50 cases. How would the sale be posted to the t-accounts? Please select all that apply.

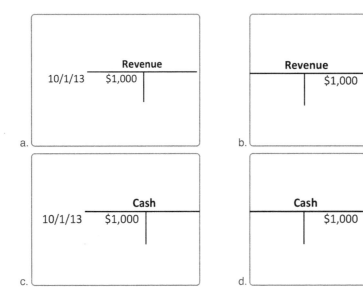

Review 2.12 Question 15

Suppose Coca-Cola sold 50 cases of Coke to a convenience store for $1,000 on 10/1/2013. The store paid cash. It had cost Coca-Cola $600 to make the 50 cases. How would the expense associated with this sale be posted to the t-accounts? Please select all that apply.

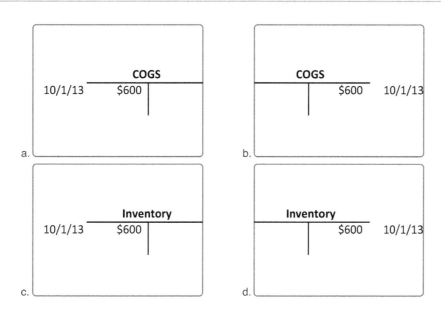

a.

b.

c.

d.

Review 2.12 Question 16

Suppose that, on 1/1/13, Coca-Cola signed an agreement with Pineapple Farms to buy a 1-year supply of pineapple juice for $60,000. Pineapple Farms delivered the juice at the beginning of the month and expected payment at the end of the month. Which account(s) should Coca-Cola DEBIT on 1/1/13?

   a.   Cash
   b.   Accounts Payable
   c.   Inventory
   d.   COGS

Review 2.12 Question 17

Suppose that, on 1/1/13, Coca-Cola signed an agreement with Pineapple Farms to buy a 1-year supply of pineapple juice for $60,000. Pineapple Farms delivered the juice at the beginning of the month and expected payment at the end of the month. Which account(s) should Coca-Cola CREDIT on 1/1/13?

    a.   Cash
    b.   Accounts Payable
    c.   Inventory
    d.   COGS

Review 2.12 Question 18

Suppose that, on 1/1/13, Coca-Cola signed an agreement with Pineapple Farms to buy a 1-year supply of pineapple juice for $60,000. Pineapple Farms delivered the juice at the beginning of the month and expected payment at the end of the month. Which account(s) should Coca-Cola DEBIT on 1/31/13 when payment is made to Pineapple Farms?

    a.   Cash
    b.   Accounts Payable
    c.   Inventory
    d.   COGS

Review 2.12 Question 19

Suppose that, on 1/1/13, Coca-Cola signed an agreement with Pineapple Farms to buy a 1-year supply of pineapple juice for $60,000. Pineapple Farms delivered the juice at the beginning of the month and expected payment at the end of the month. Which account(s) should Coca-Cola CREDIT on 1/31/13 when payment is made to Pineapple Farms?

    a.   Cash
    b.   Accounts Payable
    c.   Inventory
    d.   COGS

Review 2.12 Question 20

Suppose that, on 1/1/13, Coca-Cola signed an agreement with Pineapple Farms to buy a 1-year supply of pineapple juice for $60,000. Pineapple Farms delivered the juice at the beginning of the month and expected payment at the end of the month. Coca-Cola has yet to bottle the juice as of 1/31/13. What is the expense recognized by Coca-Cola on 1/31/13?

a. $60,000
b. $12,000
c. $5,000
d. $0

Section 6

Answer Key

Review 2.1 Explanations

Question 1

Answer: Cash (assets), Accounts payable (liabilities), Common stock (equity)

Cash is owned by the company and will provide an economic benefit to the company in future, so it is an asset. Accounts payable represents the obligation to pay others for services or goods received in the past, so it is a liability. Common stock is a type of ownership in a company, so it is equity.

Question 2

Answer: Short-term investments (assets), Accrued expenses (liabilities), Preferred stock (equity)

Short-term investments are owned by the company and will provide an economic benefit to the company in the future, so they are assets. Accrued expenses represent the obligation to pay for expenses incurred in the past, so they are liabilities. Preferred stock is type of ownership in a company, so it is equity.

Question 3

Answer: Accounts receivables (assets), Income tax payable (liabilities), Retained earnings (equity)

Accounts receivable represents the right to receive cash for goods or services provided in the past. They will provide economic benefits to a company in the future, so they are assets. Income tax payable is the obligation to pay taxes in the future for taxes incurred in the past, so it is a liability. Retained earnings are the earnings kept by a company instead of being distributed to others, and they are classified as equity.

Question 4

Answer: Land (assets), Long-term debt (liabilities), Paid-in capital (equity)

Land is owned by the company and will provide an economic benefit to the company in the future, so it is an asset. Long-term debt is an obligation to pay back lenders for money borrowed in the past, so it is a liability. Paid-in capital is the capital contributed to a company through the purchase of stock from the company, so it is equity.

Review 2.2 Explanations

Question 1

Answer: Increase cash (debit)

Debits increase assets, so in order to increase cash, we would debit the account.

Question 2

Answer: Decrease inventory (credit)

Credits decrease assets, so in order to decrease inventory, we would credit the account.

Question 3

Answer: Increase accounts receivable (debit)

Debits increase assets, so in order to increase accounts receivable, we would debit the account.

Question 4

Answer: Increase accounts payable (credit)

Credits increase liabilities, so in order to increase accounts payable, we would credit the account.

Question 5

Answer: Decrease retained earnings (debit)

Debits decrease equity, so in order to decrease retained earnings, we would debit the account.

Question 6

Answer: Increase revenue (credit)

Credits increase revenues.

Question 7

Answer: Decrease rent expense (credit)

Credits decrease expenses.

Question 8

Answer: Increase depreciation (debit)

Debits increase expenses, so in order to increase depreciation, we would debit the account.

Review 2.3 Explanations

Question 1

Answer: A, C

This transaction increased Acorns' inventory by $100. So, in order to increase the asset inventory, we would debit the inventory account for $100.

Question 2

Answer: B, D

This transaction decreased Acorns' cash by $100. So, in order to decrease the asset cash, we would credit the cash account for $100.

Review 2.4 Explanations

Question 1

Answer: A, D

Inventory should be debited for $100, and cash should be credited for $100. Debits are on the left and credits are on the right. So, the t-accounts shown in A and D are correct.

Review 2.5 Explanations

Question 1

Answer: A, C

Both cash and mixers are assets because they are owned by the company and will provide economic benefits to the company in the future.

Question 2

Answer: B, D

This transaction increased the mixer account by $1,600. So, in order to increase the asset mixer, we would debit the mixer account for $1,600. The mixer is not classified as inventory because Acorns plans to use it to make products, not sell the mixer to others.

Question 3

Answer: A, D

This transaction decreased the cash account by $1,600. So, in order to decrease the asset cash, we would credit the cash account for $1,600. Accounts payable is not affected because Acorns used cash to pay for the purchase.

Question 4

Answer: B, C

The mixer should be debited for $1,600, and cash should be credited for $1,600. Debits are on the left and credits are on the right. So, the t-accounts shown in B and C are correct.

Question 5

Answer: A, C

This transaction caused the asset mixer to increase by $1,600 and the asset cash to decrease by $1,600. The mixer purchase was not an expense; it was a purchase of an asset that will be depreciated over time. So, owner's equity was not affected. Liabilities were not affected because there was no obligation to pay at a future date; Acorns paid cash immediately.

Review 2.6 Explanations

Question 1

Answer: A, D

On 1/1/14, this transaction increased the inventory account by $150. So, in order to increase the asset inventory, we would debit the inventory account for $150. Accounts payable is affected by this transaction, but it should be credited, not debited.

Question 2

Answer: C, D

On 1/1/14, this transaction increased the accounts payable account by $150. So, in order to increase the liability accounts payable, we would credit the accounts payable account for $150. Accounts receivable, the right to receive cash in the future for goods already provided, is not affected by this transaction. Acorns chose to pay for the chocolates at a later date, so cash is not affected either.

Question 3

Answer: B, D

On 1/31/14, Acorns paid its supplier the money it owed for the chocolates. This transaction decreased the accounts payable account by $150. So, in order to decrease the liability accounts payable, we would debit the account for $150. Cash is affected by this transaction, but it should be credited, not debited.

Question 4

Answer: A, D

On 1/31/14, Acorns paid its supplier the money it owed for the chocolates. This transaction decreased the cash account by $150. So, in order to decrease the asset cash, we would credit the cash account for $150.

Question 5

Answer: B, C

This transaction would affect accounts payable, the obligation to pay for goods received at a later date, because Acorns did not pay for the supplies until 30 days after it had received them. Accounts payable is a liability. The transaction would also affect supplies, which is an asset that will provide a future economic benefit to Acorns because it'll be used to make products that Acorns can sell.

Question 6

Answer: B, D

On 9/1/13, Acorns needs to increase the asset supplies by $80. So, it should debit the account, and since debits are on the left, answer B is correct. On 9/1/13, Acorns also needs to increase the liability accounts payable by $80. In order to increase the account, Acorns should credit it, and since credits are on the right, answer D is correct.

Question 7

Answer: A, D

On 9/30/13, Acorns needs to decrease the asset cash by $80. So, it should credit the account, and since credits are on the right, answer A is correct. On 9/30/13, Acorns also needs to decrease the liability accounts payable by $80 to reflect that Acorns no longer has that obligation. In order to decrease the account, Acorns should debit it, and since debits are on the left, answer D is correct.

Review 2.7 Explanations

Question 1

Answer: A, F

As a result of this transaction, SG increased its cash account and recognized revenue. In order to increase the asset cash, we would debit the cash account for $40, the amount the customer paid SG for the t-shirts. In order to recognize revenue, we would credit the revenue account for $40.

Question 2

Answer: B, C

As a result of this transaction, SG decreased its inventory account and recognized an expense for the cost of the items sold. In order to decrease the asset inventory, we would credit the account for $25, the amount SG paid its supplier to purchase the t-shirts. In order to recognize an expense for COGS, we would debit the COGS account for $25.

Question 3

Answer: D

On 11/1/13, The Cheese Shop should record a journal entry to increase the accounts receivable account. In order to increase the asset accounts receivable, we should debit the account for $120, the amount Whole Foods will eventually pay The Cheese Shop. The Cheese Shop should also recognize revenue, but the revenue account should be credited, not debited.

Question 4

Answer: B

On 11/1/13, The Cheese Shop should recognize revenue for the sale of the brie. In order to increase revenue, we should credit the account for $120, the amount Whole Foods paid to The Cheese Shop. The Cheese Shop also needs to recognize an expense for the COGS, but the account should be debited, not credited.

Question 5

Answer: A, D

On 11/1/13, The Cheese Shop decreased is inventory account and recognized an expense for the cost of the goods sold. In order to decrease the asset inventory, we should credit inventory for $80, the amount that The Cheese Shop paid to purchase the cheese from France. In order to recognize an expense for COGS, we should debit the COGS account for $80.

Question 6

Answer: B, C

On 11/30/13, The Cheese Shop should increase its cash account and decrease its accounts receivable account. In order to increase the asset cash, we should debit cash for $120, the amount Whole Foods will pay to The Cheese Shop. We should also decrease the asset accounts receivable by crediting it for $120.

Question 7

Answer: A, E

On 6/1/13, Acorns should increase its accounts receivable and recognize revenue from the sale of the tea. The customer chose to pay later instead of paying in cash. In order to increase the asset accounts receivable, we should debit the account for $200, the amount the customer will pay Acorns. In order to recognize revenue, we should credit the revenue account for $200.

Question 8

Answer: A, D

On 6/1/13, Acorns should decrease its inventory and recognize an expense for the cost of goods sold. In order to decrease the asset inventory, we should credit inventory for $150, the amount Acorns paid to purchase the inventory. We should also increase the COGS account by debiting it for $150.

Review 2.8 Explanations

Question 1

Answer: A, B, D, E

On 12/1/13, there are 4 journal entries that should be made and posted to the t-accounts. Acorns needs to increase its accounts receivable, recognize revenue, decrease its inventory, and recognize an expense for the COGS. In order to increase the asset accounts receivable, Acorns should debit accounts receivable for $30, the amount the PTA will pay Acorns. In order to recognize revenue, Acorns should credit revenue for $30. In order to decrease the asset inventory, Acorns should credit inventory for $20, the amount Acorns had paid to obtain the inventory. Acorns also needs to recognize an expense for the COGS, so it should debit the cost of sales account for $20. Debits are on the left and credits are on the right, so the t-accounts shown in A, B, D, and E are correct.

Question 2

Answer: B, C

On 12/31/13, Acorns needs to increase its cash account and decrease its account receivable to reflect the payment by the PTA. In order to increase the asset cash, we would debit the account for $30, the amount the PTA owed Acorns. In order to decrease the asset accounts receivable, we would credit the account for $30. Debits are on the left and credits are on the right, so the t-accounts shown in B and C are correct.

Review 2.9 Explanations

Question 1

Answer: A, D

On 1/1/14, Spartan Gym needs to increase its cash account and increase its deferred revenue account. In order to increase the asset cash, SG would debit the account for $300. The account deferred revenue is a liability, so in order to increase the liability, we would credit it for $300. Spartan Gym will recognize revenue and decrease deferred revenue over time as the 3-month membership is used up.

Question 2

Answer: B, C

On 1/31/14, 1 month of the 3-month membership will be used up. So, Spartan Gym should recognize $100 ($300/3) of revenue and decrease deferred revenue by $100. In order to decrease the liability deferred revenue, we would debit the account for $100. In order to recognize revenue, we would credit the revenue account.

Review 2.10 Explanations

Question 1

Answer: B, C

On 6/1/13, The Candy Shop paid $30,000 in cash for prepaid advertising. The Candy Shop needs to decrease its cash and increase the account prepaid advertising. So, in order to increase the asset prepaid advertising, we would debit the account for $30,000. In order to decrease the asset cash, we would need to credit cash for $30,000.

Question 2

Answer: A, B

On 1/1/14, Acorns would need to decrease the cash account and increase the membership fees account. In order to increase the asset membership fees, we would debit the account for $150. In order to decrease the asset cash, we would credit cash for $150. Debits are on the left and credits are on the right, so the t-accounts shown in A and B are correct.

Review 2.11 Explanations

Question 1

Answer: B, C

Crush needs to adjust its accounts to show that 1/3 of the asset prepaid rent was used up. In order to recognize rent expense, Crush needs to debit rent expense. Crush also needs to decrease the asset prepaid rent, so it should credit the asset prepaid rent.

Question 2

Answer: $12,000 in prepaid rent, $6,000 in rent expense

Crush needs to recognize $6,000 ($18,000 / 3) in rent expense, so the trial balance should show a debit for $6,000 in rent expense. After Crush credits the prepaid rent account for $6,000, the prepaid rent account would reflect a balance of $12,000 ($18,000 - $6,000) in the debit column.

Chapter Review 2.12 Explanations

Question 1

Answer: Accounts Receivable (Asset), Accounts Payable (Liability), Retained Earnings (Equity)

Accounts receivable, the right to receive cash for goods or services provided in the past, is an asset. Accounts payable represents the obligation to pay others for services or goods received in the past, so it is a liability. Retained earnings are the earnings kept by a company instead of being distributed to others, and they are equity.

Question 2

Answer: Property (Asset), Notes Payable (Liability), Common Stock (Equity)

Property is controlled by a company and will provide an economic benefit to the company in the future, so it is an asset. Notes payable is the obligation to pay back lenders for cash borrowed in the past, so it is a liability. Common stock is a type of ownership in a company, so it is equity.

Question 3

Answer: Increase equipment (debit)

Debits increase assets, so, in order to increase equipment, we would debit the account.

Question 4

Answer: Decrease revenue (debit)

Debits decrease revenue, so, in order to decrease revenue, we would debit the account.

Question 5

Answer: Increase notes payable (credit)

Credits increase liabilities, so, in order to increase notes payable, we would credit the account.

Question 6

Answer: Decrease accounts receivable (credit)

Credits decrease assets, so, in order to decrease accounts receivable, we would credit the account.

Question 7

Answer: A, C, D

Debits increase assets, increase expenses, and decrease liabilities. Credits decrease assets and increase equity.

Question 8

Answer: B, C, E

Credits increase revenues, increase liabilities, and decrease assets. Debits increase expenses and decrease equity.

Question 9

Answer: A, C, D, E

This transaction would affect 4 accounts: cash, sales, inventory, and COGS. Coca-Cola would receive cash and recognize revenue as a result of the sale. It would also decrease its inventory and recognize an expense for the COGS.

Question 10

Answer: A, C, E, F

This transaction would cause Coca-Cola to increase its cash and increase its revenue. In order to increase the asset cash, we would debit the cash account, and in order to increase revenue, we would credit the sales account. The transaction would also cause Coca-Cola to decrease its inventory and recognize an expense. In order to decrease the asset inventory, we would credit the inventory account, and in order to increase expense, we would debit the COGS account.

Question 11

Answer: A, E

On 10/1/13, cash is debited by $1,000, and sales are credited by $1,000, the amount that the convenience store paid to Coca-Cola. COGS should be debited, not credited.

Question 12

Answer: B, D

On 10/1/13, inventory was credited for $600, and the corresponding entry should be to debit COGS for $600, the amount it cost Coca-Cola to make the 50 cases of Coke. Sales and cash are also affected by this transaction, as shown in question 11. Although cash is debited for $1,000, it does not make sense to have it paired with the credit to inventory for $600 because the accounting equation would not balance.

Question 13

Answer: A

As a result of the sale, Coca-Cola earned $1,000 in revenue. Coca-Cola only earned $400 ($1,000 revenue - $600 expense) in profits.

Question 14

Answer: B, C

As a result of the transaction, cash was debited for $1,000 and revenue was credited for $1,000. Debits are on the left and credits are on the right, so the t-accounts shown in B and C are correct.

Question 15

Answer: A, D

As a result of this transaction, COGS were debited for $600 and inventory was credited for $600. Debits are on the left and credits are on the right, so the t-accounts shown in A and D are correct.

Question 16

Answer: C

On 1/1/13, Coca-Cola should debit the inventory account in order to increase it. Cash is not affected because Coca-Cola signed an agreement to pay at a later date. Accounts payable is affected, but it is a liability that should be credited, not debited. COGS will be affected at a later date when Coca-Cola sells its products to others and recognizes an expense.

Question 17

Answer: B

On 1/1/13, Coca-Cola should credit the accounts payable account in order to increase it. Accounts payable is a liability, and crediting the account increases the liability and reflects the obligation to pay Pineapple Farms at a later date. Cash is not affected at this time because Coca-Cola signed an agreement to pay at a later date. Inventory should be debited, not credited. COGS will be affected at a later date when Coca-Cola sells its products to others and recognizes an expense.

Question 18

Answer: B

On 1/31/13, Coca-Cola should debit accounts payable. As stated in the agreement, Coca-Cola will pay cash to Pineapple Farms and decrease the amount that it owes Pineapple Farms (accounts payable). Cash should be credited, not debited. Inventory is delivered at the beginning of the month and will not be affected on 1/31/13. COGS will be affected at a later date when Coca-Cola sells its products to others and recognizes an expense.

Question 19

Answer: A

On 1/31/13, Coca-Cola should credit cash. Coca-Cola will pay cash to Pineapple Farms, decreasing the asset cash. Accounts payable should be debited, not credited. Inventory is delivered at the beginning of the month and will not be affected on 1/31/13. COGS will be affected at a later date when Coca-Cola sells its products to others and recognizes an expense.

Question 20

Answer: D

Coca-Cola should recognize $0 in expenses on 1/31/13. Coca-Cola will recognize an expense at a later date when it sells its products.

3

Financial Statements

Sections

Section 1

Introduction

Concepts

1. Permanent and Temporary Accounts

3.1.1 Permanent and Temporary Accounts

Learning how to record transactions and create trial balances is an essential part of financial accounting. This process was covered in depth in Chapter 2, and we will now build on it by using the trial balance to prepare actual financial reports, the primary output used in financial accounting. These reports are extremely important because they allow investors, managers and other stakeholders to determine how well a business is performing.

The balance sheet and the income statement, two of the three main financial statements, can be prepared by using only the information in the trial balance. Details about how to create the third main financial statement, the statement of cash flows, will be discussed in Chapter 5.

In Chapter 1, we showed examples of balance sheets from Coca-Cola, Netflix, and Acorns. We will now learn more about the balance sheet and income statement in the context of Black Ink, a general store with a focus on paper and stamp products, and Hayden Bank, a local bank.

A business needs to be well-informed of its financial position and its performance over time in order to run its business successfully. If a business tracks this information, it can quickly highlight any red flags or areas for improvement and easily show others how well it is doing. The easiest way to keep track of its position and performance is to take the information it gathers in the journal entries and organize it into financial reports.

The trial balance is a fundamental tool to use when preparing the balance sheet and the income statement because it contains all the information about a business' account balances in one place. As we have discussed before, the sum of the debits in the trial balance always equals the sum of the credits. It balances, just as its name suggests.

The accounts listed on the trial balance can be divided into two groups: **permanent accounts** and **temporary accounts**.

Permanent accounts, also known as real accounts, are reported on the balance sheet, and they are continuous accounts that have a cumulative balance over time. Accounts such as cash, accounts receivable, and inventory are examples of Black Ink's permanent accounts. All asset, liability, and owner's equity accounts are permanent accounts. Permanent accounts are also called stock measures because they're measured at a certain point in time.

The other type of accounts, temporary accounts or nominal accounts, are listed on the income statement. These accounts only show activity for a certain period of time, and they reset to zero at the beginning of a new accounting period. General and administrative expenses, sales, and tax expense are examples of nominal accounts for Black Ink. All income statement accounts, including revenues, expenses, gains, and losses, are temporary accounts. These accounts are sometimes referred to as flow measures because they measure the flow of transactions over a period of time.

The temporary account called tax expense reflects the taxes for a given accounting period, not the cumulative taxes a business has ever paid. However, accounts receivable is a permanent account, and it will most likely have receivables that have not yet been collected at the end of the year. This account carries over to the next year and is still kept on the balance sheet as an asset because the receivables will be collected later.

Figure 3.1 is an example of a trial balance as of the end of the **fiscal year.** It begins with the asset accounts, such as cash and inventory, which have debit balances. Next, the liabilities are listed. This includes accounts such as bank loans and wages payable, and these accounts have credit balances. Equity accounts follow the liabilities, and these accounts also typically have credit balances. At the end of the trial balance, the revenue, expense, gain and loss accounts are listed, with revenues having credit balances and expenses having debit balances.

The retained earnings account has a balance as of the beginning of the year, even though all the other accounts reflect the balance as of the end of the year. Why does the retained earnings account have a balance as of the beginning of the year? We already learned that retained earnings are increased and decreased over time by revenues, expenses, losses, and gains. But during an accounting period, revenues and expenses are stored in temporary (nominal) accounts instead of being put directly into owners' equity.

FIGURE 3.1

Trial Balance as of 12/31/2013

Accounts	Debit	Credit
Balance sheet accounts		
Cash	$ 164,000	
Accounts receivable	7,500	
Inventory	7,500	
Prepaid rent	4,500	
Desks	750	
Accumulated depreciation		$ 185
Bank loan		37,500
Accounts payable		18,750
Wages payable		4,525
Accrued utilities liability		675
Accrued interest liability		3,750
Share capital		75,000
Retained earnings		10,000
Income statement accounts		
Cost of goods sold	30,000	
Utilities expense	2,700	
Rent expense	4,500	
Interest expense	3,750	
Depreciation expense	185	
Revenues		75,000
Total	$ 225,385	$ 225,385

Nominal accounts allow us to see owners' equity in more detail. At the end of the fiscal year, the net effect of the nominal accounts is transferred to retained earnings. This is known as the closing process, and it resets the nominal accounts back to zero and updates the retained earnings balance to the current point in time. This will be discussed in more depth later in this chapter.

For answers to the following questions, please see the end of Chapter 3.

Review 3.1 Question 1

Match each account listed to either the permanent or temporary section below.

Permanent   Temporary

Account names: Cash, Tax Expense

Review 3.1 Question 2

Match each account listed to either the permanent or temporary section below.

    Permanent   Temporary

Account names: Sales, Accounts Receivable

Review 3.1 Question 3

Match each account listed to either the permanent or temporary section below.

    Permanent   Temporary

Account names: Rent Expense, Prepaid Rent

Review 3.1 Question 4

Match each account listed to either the permanent or temporary section below.

    Permanent   Temporary

Account names: Inventory, Interest Expense

Section 2
The Balance Sheet

Concepts

1. Introduction

2. Assets

3. Liabilities

4. Equity

5. Review

3.2.1   Introduction

The first financial statement that we will look at in depth is the balance sheet. As you know, the trial balance shows the balances of all of a business' accounts at a certain point in time, and it's a helpful tool for creating the balance sheet. Let's look at the trial balances of various companies and show the changes made throughout a typical accounting period.

In the previous section, we showed Figure 3.1, a trial balance for Rosa's Tailor Shop as of the end of the fiscal year 2013. Figure 3.2 shows the trial balance for Rosa's Tailor Shop on the first day of their fiscal year, January 1, 2013. How do these two trial balances differ?

FIGURE 3.2

Trial Balance for Rosa's Tailor Shop
January 1, 2013

Accounts	Debit	Credit
Balance sheet accounts		
Cash	$ 145,308	
Accounts receivable	6,740	
Inventory	9,302	
Prepaid rent	4,500	
Desks	250	
Accumulated depreciation		$ 25
Bank loan		45,000
Accounts payable		23,200
Wages payable		8,875
Accrued utilities liability		850
Accrued interest liability		3,150
Share capital		75,000
Retained earnings		10,000
Total	$ 166,100	$ 166,100

In Figure 3.2, there are no nominal accounts because the business hasn't had any revenues or expenses yet for the period; they were all reset to zero at the end of the last accounting period. This trial balance only shows real accounts: the assets, liabilities and owners' equity accounts.

The balance sheet basically contains all the real, permanent accounts from the trial balance, organized in a standard format so it can be easily understood. A balance sheet, also called the statement of financial position, is a snapshot of the business at a certain point in time. The accounts show the financial position of the firm as of a certain date.

3.2.2   Assets

Balance sheets can be organized differently, and the format depends on the company and the set of standards (IFRS or US GAAP) it chooses to follow. We will highlight many of the differences as we discuss the balance sheet in detail. One of the most common types of formats is the classified balance sheet, which classifies accounts into different groups. Within these groups, the organization can also be slightly different.

Typically, assets are listed first on the balance sheet. There are two types of assets: current and non-current. When an asset will be used within one year, it is classified as a **current asset**. The technical definition of a current asset states that it must be used within one year or one operating cycle, whichever is longer. An **operating cycle** is the amount of time it takes a business to produce its goods, sell the goods, and receive the cash from its customers. Since most businesses have operating cycles of less than one year, you can effectively think of current assets as those that are used up in a year or less. Accounts such as cash, inventory, and accounts receivable are examples of current assets.

The other category of assets is **non-current assets**. All assets that will be held for more than a year are classified as non-current. Long-term assets, such as buildings or equipment, are examples of non-current assets, and they will likely be useful to the business for a long time. Non-current assets also includes **leasehold improvements,** which are long-lived changes made by a tenant to a leased property in order to enhance the property.

An asset can actually be broken out into two different sections. If a company has a long-term notes receivable, it will likely collect payments at different points in time. The amount that it will receive within a year will be listed in the current assets section under an account name such as current portion of notes receivable. The rest of the note will be listed under non-current assets. A liability can also be separated out and listed under current and non-current liabilities.

In the US, the accounts are ordered according to their **liquidity**, or how quickly and easily they can be converted to cash. So, under GAAP, cash is always listed first under current assets. Next, there is short-term investments, if the company has any, because these can quickly be sold for cash. Following short-term investments, there is accounts receivables. Accounts receivable is listed before inventory because it would take longer to turn inventory into cash than it would take to collect the receivables. Accounts receivable is just one step away from being cash; the company has already made the sale and is just waiting to receive the cash from the customer. Inventory needs to be sold, and then the company needs to wait to receive the cash, so it is less liquid than accounts receivable. Lastly, there are any pre-payments the company has made for expenses it has paid for in advance. The order of the accounts starts with the most liquid items and ends with the least liquid ones.

For non-current assets, a company's long-term investments are generally listed first. Then there are a company's fixed assets, followed by a company's **intangible assets**.

The main subcategories for current assets and non-current assets are typically listed in the manner previously described. However, within each subcategory, there is some room for debate about which asset is the most liquid. For example, perhaps the brand-new mixers Acorns owns would be much easier to sell than the ovens that Acorns has owned for 20 years. You would need to know more details about a company's assets to correctly place them in the right order.

However, under international standards, the least liquid items are listed first and the other items follow in order of increasing liquidity. This means that the asset section of the balance sheet starts with non-current assets, listing intangibles first, then fixed assets, and lastly long-term investments. The current assets section follows, with the least liquid accounts coming first and cash at the very end.

In Figure 3.2, you might have noticed an account under fixed assets called **accumulated depreciation**. Depreciation is the decrease in value of an asset that occurs over time, and accumulated depreciation is the sum of all the depreciation recognized over the life of the asset. Since assets have debit balances, and depreciation decreases the value of an asset, it's listed under the credit column. Depreciation is known as a **contra account** because its balance is the opposite of normal asset account balances.

Many balance sheets include an "other assets" section, which consolidates small, immaterial items or includes items that don't clearly fit into a category. This could include accounts such as the cost of buildings still under construction, money set aside for a special purpose, or **employee advances**, which are funds given to employees before they earn them.

For answers to the following questions, please see the end of Chapter 3.

Review 3.2 Question 1

Which is the correct order of the assets section of the balance sheet for Java & Juice according to **US GAAP**?

Current Assets
Inventory
Short-term investments
Accounts receivable
Cash and cash equivalents
Non-current Assets
Property, plant & equipment
Accounts payable
Goodwill

a.

Current Assets
Cash and cash equivalents
Short-term investments
Accounts receivable
Inventory
Non-current Assets
Long-term investments
Property, plant & equipment
Goodwill

b.

Current Assets
Cash and cash equivalents
Long-term investments
Inventory
Accounts receivable
Non-current Assets
Short-term investments
Goodwill
Property, plant & equipment

c.

Current Assets
Inventory
Property, plant & equipment
Short-term investments
Cash and cash equivalents
Non-current Assets
Goodwill
Accounts receivable
Long-term investments

d.

Review 3.2 Question 2

Which is the correct order of the assets section of the balance sheet for Java & Juice according to **IFRS**?

a.
Non-current Assets
Long-term investments
PP&E
Goodwill
Current Assets
Cash and cash equivalents
Short-term investments
Accounts receivable
Inventory

b.
Non-current Assets
Long-term investments
PP&E
Goodwill
Current Assets
Short-term investments
Accounts payable
Inventory
Cash and cash equivalents

c.
Non-current Assets
PP&E
Goodwill
Short-term investments
Current Assets
Inventory
Cash and cash equivalents
Long-term investments
Accounts receivable

d.
Non-current Assets
Goodwill
PP&E
Long-term investments
Current Assets
Inventory
Accounts receivable
Short-term investments
Cash and cash equivalents

3.2.3   Liabilities

Liabilities follow a similar pattern to assets on the balance sheet. **Current liabilities** are those that will be due within one year, and **non-current liabilities** come due in more than one year.

For companies that follow US GAAP, current liabilities are listed first and non-current ones second. Within the sections, liabilities that are likely to be paid soonest are listed first. In contrast, current liabilities are listed second under IFRS, and the liabilities that are likely to be paid soonest are placed last.

In terms of current liabilities, accounts payable, notes payable due in a few weeks, and **accrued expenses** are likely to be paid quickly, so they could be listed first under US GAAP. Accrued expenses are expenses that have been recognized on the income statement but are not yet due. These accounts are liabilities because the company owes this money to others and will have to pay them in the future. There are many types of accrued expenses, such as accrued wages, accrued interest expense, or accrued income taxes.

The account that would be paid next could be the current portion of long-term debt, followed by say accrued income taxes.

When a company takes out a loan, it usually repays the loan over many years, and the current portion of long-term debt is the portion of the principal that the company will pay during that year. The interest payments on the loan are reported separately under the interest payable account.

For answers to the following questions, see the end of Chapter 3.

Review 3.3 Question 1

In 2003, Black Ink issued a 10 year **bond**, a common form of long-term debt, to raise additional capital. The bond will come due in September 2013. When preparing the balance sheet as of 12/31/2012, where should Black Ink place the bond?

a. Current assets
b. Non-current assets
c. Current liabilities
d. Non-current liabilities

Review 3.3 Question 2

Which is the correct order of the liabilities section of the balance sheet for Java & Juice according to **US GAAP** if Notes and loans payable are due in less than a month?

a.
Current Liabilities
Notes and loans payable
Long-term debt
Accounts payable
Non-current Liabilities
Deferred income taxes
Current portion of LTD

b.
Current Liabilities
Notes and loans payable
Accounts payable
Inventory
Non-current Liabilities
Current portion of LTD
Deferred income taxes

c.
Current Liabilities
Accounts receivable
Current portion of LTD
Notes and loans payable
Non-current Liabilities
Long-term debt
Goodwill

d.
Current Liabilities
Accounts payable
Notes and loans payable
Current portion of LTD
Non-current Liabilities
Long-term debt
Deferred income taxes

Review 3.3 Question 3

Which is the correct order of the liabilities section of the balance sheet for Java & Juice according to **IFRS?**

a.
Non-current Liabilities
Deferred income taxes
Long-term debt
Current Liabilities
Accounts payable
Current portion of LTD
Notes and loans payable

b.
Non-current Liabilities
Current portion of LTD
Deferred income taxes
Current Liabilities
Notes and loans payable
Long-term debt
Accounts payable

c.
Non-current Liabilities
Long-term debt
Deferred income taxes
Current Liabilities
Inventory
Accounts payable
Notes and loans payable

d.
Non-current Liabilities
Deferred income taxes
Long-term debt
Current Liabilities
Notes and loans payable
Accounts receivable
Current portion of LTD

Review 3.3 Question 4

For each question, match the accounts to the correct section of the balance sheet.

	Asset	Liability
Current	??	??
Non-current	??	??

a.   Cash
b.   Plant & Equipment
c.   Current Portion of LTD
d.   10-yr Bond Due in 9 Years

Review 3.3 Question 5

For each question, match the accounts to the correct section of the balance sheet.

	Asset	Liability
Current	??	??
Non-current	??	??

a. Short-term Investment
b. Mortgage Payable Due in 3 to 5 years
c. Notes Payable Due in 6 Months
d. Patent

Review 3.3 Question 6

For each question, match the accounts to the correct section of the balance sheet.

	Asset	Liability
Current	??	??
Non-current	??	??

a. Land
b. Wages Payable
c. Accounts Receivable
d. Pension Payable

3.2.4 Equity

The final section of the balance sheet is owners' equity. This section tracks both the contributions made into a business and the earnings a business has generated and decided to reinvest to fund future operations. When there are many shareholders, owners' equity is typically called stockholders' equity or shareholders' equity, but these terms are interchangeable.

The equity section for Black Ink looks like this:

Stockholders' Equity	
Preferred Stock	20,000
Common Stock	90,000
Retained Earnings	220,000
Total Stockholders' Equity	$ 330,000

There are many names for capital stock, the cash contributions that owners make to a business. Shares of stock issued to the public are often called common stock or preferred stock, contributions made by owners in a partnership are called partner capital, and sole proprietorships use the term contributed capital.

Under US GAAP, the stockholders' equity section is placed last whereas under IFRS, it is generally placed before the liabilities section.

Within the equity section, the components are typically listed in the following order:

Preferred Stock
Common Stock
Additional Paid-in Capital
Retained Earnings
Accumulated Other Comprehensive Income
Treasury Stock

Both IFRS and US GAAP list the components of their equity sections in the same order.

We have already covered basic definitions for preferred stock, common stock, additional paid-in capital, and retained earnings. Contributed capital, also known as **paid-in capital**, is the sum of a company's preferred stock, common stock, and additional paid-in capital.

Accumulated other comprehensive income consists of unrealized gains or losses, such as those from investments held by the firm or foreign currency transactions. Unrealized gains or losses are those that haven't been settled yet. Once they are realized, the company would earn income (or suffer a loss) on the transaction, and the amount would be shifted to retained earnings. **Treasury stock** is stock that is repurchased by the issuing company, effectively reducing the amount of stock available on the open market. Eventually, the company might retire the stock or resell it sometime in the future.

For the answer to the following question, please see the end of Chapter 3.

Review 3.4 Question 1

Organize the following accounts to build the shareholders' equity section of the balance sheet for Java & Juice according to US GAAP.

1. ??
2. ??
3. ??
4. ??

a. Paid-in Capital
b. Common Stock
c. Preferred Stock
d. Retained Earnings

3.2.5　Review

The complete balance sheet consists of all three sections: assets, liabilities, and owners' equity. The balance sheet shows a snapshot of a company's financial position at a point in time, which is why it is also called the statement of financial position. The balance sheet is extremely useful because it easily shows a company's resources and how they were obtained.

Figure 3.3 shows Black Ink's complete classified balance sheet.

FIGURE 3.3

Balance Sheet as of December 31, 2013

ASSETS	
Current Assets:	
Cash	$ 345,000
Accounts receivable	91,000
Inventory	76,600
Prepaid rent	4,500
Total Current Assets	$ 517,100
Long-term Assets:	
Stock investments	15,000
Equipment	5,500
Less: accumulated depreciation	(800)
Total Long-term Assets	$　19,700
Total Assets	$ 536,800
LIABILITIES	
Current Liabilities:	
Current portion of long-term debt	15,000
Accounts payable	22,000
Wages payable	13,000
Accrued utilities liability	2,200
Accrued interest liability	4,600
Total Current Liabilities	$　56,800
Long-term Liabilities	
Long-term debt	150,000
Total Long-term Liabilities	$ 150,000
Total Liabilities	$ 206,800
STOCKHOLDERS' EQUITY	
Preferred stock	20,000
Common stock	90,000
Retained earnings	220,000
Total Stockholders' Equity	$ 330,000
Total Liabilities and Stockholders' Equity	$ 536,800

This section has covered the format of the balance sheet and some common types of assets, liabilities and equity. But it's important to remember that balance sheets can look very different depending on the industry that you're studying.

For example, the trial balance for Hayden Bank is shown in Figure 3.4. We typically think of loans as liabilities, but for a bank, loans are assets because banks lend out their money to others and receive interest payments on them.

FIGURE 3.4

Trial Balance as of January 1, 2013

Accounts	Debit	Credit
Cash	$ 39,704	
Short-term investments	56,906	
Investment securities available for sale, at fair value	541,068	
Residential mortgage loans	837,684	
Commercial real estate loans	811,463	
Property and equipment	35,769	
Deposits		$ 1,898,320
Borrowings		130,137
Repurchase agreements		40,027
Accrued interest payable		540
Accrued expenses and other liabilities		19,318
Undistributed earnings		234,252
Total	$ 2,322,594	$ 2,322,594

Figure 3.5 shows the balance sheet for Hayden Bank, which was created using the trial balance.

FIGURE 3.5

Hayden Bank
Statement of Financial Position

January 1, 2013
($ in thousands)

ASSETS
Current Assets

Cash	$ 39,704
Short-term investments	56,906
Total Current Assets	96,610

Long-term Assets

Investment securities available for sale, at fair value	541,068
Residential mortgage loans	837,684
Commercial real estate loans	811,463
Property and equipment	35,769
Total Long-term Assets	2,225,984
Total Assets	2,322,594

LIABILITIES AND EQUITY CAPITAL
Liabilities

Deposits	1,898,320
Borrowings	130,137
Repurchase agreements	40,027
Accrued interest payable	540
Accrued expenses and other liabilities	19,318
Total Liabilities	2,088,342

Equity Capital

Undistributed earnings	234,252
Total Equity Capital	234,252
Total Liabilities and Equity Capital	$2,322,594

For the following questions, use the trial balance shown in Figure 3.6 and the facts listed below to create the balance sheet.

FIGURE 3.6

Accounts	Debit	Credit
Cash	$ 134,000	
Accounts receivable	7,500	
Inventory	7,500	
Prepaid rent	4,500	
Desks	750	
Accumulated depreciation		$ 185
Bank loan		37,500
Accounts payable		18,750
Wages payable		8,390
Accrued utilities liability		675
Accrued interest liability		3,750
Share capital		75,000
Retained earnings		10,000
Total	154,250	154,250

• Accrued interest and accrued utilities are due in 30 days.

• Wages and accounts payable are due in 2 months.

• The bank loan is due in 2 years.

For the answers to the following questions, please see the end of Chapter 3.

Review 3.5 Question 1

Use the trial balance shown in Figure 3.6 to create the asset section of the balance sheet according to US GAAP.

Assets

Cash	$134,000
Accounts receivable	7,500
Inventory	7,500
Prepaid rent	4,500
Desks	565
Total Assets	**154,065**

a.

Assets

Desks	$750
Accumulated depreciation	(185)
Prepaid rent	4,500
Inventory	7,500
Accounts receivable	7,500
Cash	134,000
Total Assets	**154,065**

b.

Assets

Cash	$134,000
Accounts receivable	7,500
Inventory	7,500
Prepaid rent	4,500
Desks	750
Accumulated depreciation	(185)
Total Assets	**154,065**

c.

Assets

Desks	$565
Prepaid rent	4,500
Inventory	7,500
Accounts receivable	7,500
Cash	134,000
Total Assets	**154,065**

d.

Review 3.5 Question 2

Use the trial balance shown in Figure 3.6 to create the liability section of the balance sheet according to US GAAP.

a.

Liabilities	
Accrued interest	3,750
Accrued utilities	675
Wages payable	8,390
Accounts payable	18,750
Bank loan	37,500
Total liabilities	69,065

b.

Liabilities	
Accrued interest	3,750
Accrued utilities	675
Wages payable	8,390
Accounts payable	18,750
Current portion of LTD	37,500
Accumulated depreciation	185
Total liabilities	69,250

c.

Liabilities	
Bank loan	37,500
Accounts payable	18,750
Wages payable	8,390
Accrued utilities	675
Accrued rent	3,750
Total liabilities	69,065

d.

Liabilities	
Accumulated Depreciation	185
Bank Loan	37,500
Long-term debt	18,750
Wages payable	8,390
Accrued utilities	675
Retained earnings	3,750
Total liabilities	69,250

Use the trial balance shown in Figure 3.6 to create the stockholders' equity section of the balance sheet.

Stockholders' Equity	
Share capital	75,000
Retained earnings	10,000
Total Stockholders' Equity	85,000

a.

Stockholders' Equity	
Retained earnings	10,000
Share capital	75,000
Total Stockholders' Equity	85,000

b.

Figure 3.7 shows the complete balance sheet for the trial balance shown in Figure 3.6.

FIGURE 3.7 BALANCE SHEET

Assets		
Cash	$	134,000
Accounts receivable		7,500
Inventory		7,500
Prepaid rent		4,500
Desks		750
Accumulated depreciation		(185)
Total Assets	$	154,065
Liabilities		
Accrued interest liability		3,750
Accrued utilities liability		675
Wages payable		8,390
Accounts payable		18,750
Bank loan		37,500
Total Liabilities	$	69,065
Stockholders' Equity		
Share capital		75,000
Retained earnings		10,000
Total Stockholders' Equity	$	85,000
Total Liabilities and Stockholders' Equity	$	154,065

Section 3

The Income Statement

Concepts

3.3.1   Introduction

It's possible to look at the balance sheet after every transaction to determine how it changed a company's financial position. But there is an easier way to see how a business is performing; the income statement shows changes over a given period.

As we know, balances accumulate in the temporary accounts of a business throughout the year, due to the revenues, expenses, losses, and gains that are being recognized. The income statement shows these accounts and how they change over time; it's the story of a company's operating activities. The income statement is an easy way to see the revenues a company has earned and the resources used to earn those revenues. Losses and gains from non-operating activities are also reflected in the income statement.

The income statement and balance sheet are both very important financial statements that show different aspects of a company, but they are linked together by the retained earnings account. The income statement lists all the changes that affect retained earnings, which is a component of owners' equity. **Net income** (loss), one of the most important lines on the income statement, is calculated by subtracting the expenses and losses from the revenues and gains. The net income increases (or decreases) retained earnings. Net income is also known as the bottom line because it is the last line of the income statement. Other names for net income include **net earnings** or **net profit**.

Figure 3.8 shows Black Ink's trial balance at the end of the period, after posting all the transactions for the year.

FIGURE 3.8

Trial Balance as of December 31, 2013

Accounts	Debit		Credit
Balance sheet accounts			
Cash	$	82,100	
Accounts receivable		3,850	
Inventory		3,750	
Prepaid rent		2,350	
Desks		475	
Accumulated depreciation			$ 193
Bank loan			18,850
Accounts payable			9,475
Wages payable			2,363
Accrued utilities liability			438
Accrued interest liability			1,975
Share capital			37,600
Retained earnings			5,100
Income statement accounts			
Cost of goods sold		15,100	
Utilities expense		1,450	
Rent expense		2,350	
Interest expense		1,975	
Depreciation expense		193	
Revenues			37,600
Total	$	113,593	$ 113,593

The trial balance contains all the information we need to create an income statement. The typical format is called the multi-step income statement format, and it shows multiple calculations before arriving at the net income or net loss. This format provides more information and is more useful than the single-step income statement. On the income statement, there are two categories for revenues: operating and non-operating revenues, and there are several categories for expenses: cost of good sold, operating expenses, other expenses, and tax expenses. This format leads to key metrics, such as **gross profit** and **operating income**, that analysts find useful to monitor over time and examine in an industry context.

Figure 3.9 shows the income statement for Black Ink based off its trial balance.

FIGURE 3.9

Income Statement for the year ending December 31, 2013

Revenues	$ 37,600
Cost of goods sold	(15,100)
Gross profit	$ 22,500
Utilities expense	(1,450)
Rent expense	(2,350)
Depreciation expense	(193)
Operating profit	$ 18,508
Interest expense	(1,975)
Net income	$ 16,533

3.3.2   Gross Profit

In the multi-step income statement, the first section calculates the gross profit for the business. Gross profit is calculated by subtracting the cost of goods sold (COGS) from sales. Gross profit shows how successful a business is – it is essential for the business to make a profit by selling inventory or providing services for more than it costs to deliver them. For Black Ink, a retail store, gross profit is the amount customers paid for inventory, less the amount the business paid for the inventory. It doesn't include any selling expenses. For a company that produces products, such as a factory, COGS includes items such as raw material costs, factory depreciation, and the wages tied directly to the factory workers who made the products.

Many companies that provide services instead of goods don't show gross profit because they don't have a production process and don't have COGS. Some service industry companies choose to report gross profit as the revenue received from customers for services minus the costs of providing the services.

Gross Profit = Sales - COGS

For answers to the following questions, please see the end of Chapter 3.

Review 3.6 Question 1

Which of the following expenses for a factory would be categorized under COGS?

    a.   Cost of the raw materials used

    b.   Cost of storing the finished products in inventory before being sold

    c.   Pension benefits of the factory workers

    d.   Salary of the CEO

    e.   Rent paid for the factory space

Review 3.6 Question 2

For the year 2013, Acorns had revenues of $2,000,000. Their income statement shows that gross profit was $1,200,000 and other expenses were $500,000. What was Acorns cost of goods sold (COGS)?

    a. $800,000

    b. $1,700,000

    c. $500,000

    d. $700,000

3.3.3   Operating Income

The next section of the multi-step income statement leads to operating income. This section contains all the operating expenses incurred by the business in order to fund its operations (but not costs directly associated with production). Examples of operating expenses include items such as wages, pension contributions, rent, depreciation, utilities expenses and selling expenses. Many companies combine these expenses into a single category titled **Sales, General, and Administrative expenses** (SG&A). This provides the important information to investors without giving away too many details about expenses to competitors. Another common operating expense category is Research & Development (R&D). There is no standard order for listing operating expenses if company chooses to break them out.

After the list of operating expenses, the multi-step income statement shows the total of them, and then the total is subtracted from gross profit to get operating income. This figure can tell us whether the business makes enough money to pay for its operating expenses. Operating income is also known as **Operating Profit** and **Earnings Before Interest and Taxes** (**EBIT**).

> **Operating Income** = Gross Profit - Operating Expenses

For answers to the following questions, please see the end of Chapter 3.

Review 3.7 Question 1

Which of the following would be considered operating expenses?

   a. Rent
   b. Research costs
   c. Costs of raw materials
   d. Advertising expenses
   e. Shipping costs of products sold

Review 3.7 Question 2

For 2013, Acorns had gross profit of $1,200,000 and the expenses listed below. Cost of goods sold (COGS) for the year was 800,000. What was Acorn's operating income for 2013?

Salaries & Wages Expense	($300,000)
Building & Utilities Expense	($100,000)
Other Operating Expenses	($40,000)
Interest Expense	($25,000)
Income Tax Expense	($35,000)

   a. $460,000
   b. $400,000
   c. $760,000
   d. $300,000

3.3.4   Other Income and Expenses

Sometimes a business earns money from activities other than normal business operations. It is typically not a significant source of income compared to income generated from a company's core operations. For example, a business could own a building and rent out the space it doesn't use to someone else. This activity generates rental income, and even though it isn't part of the main operations of the business, it is still accounted for on the income statement under other income. Foreign transaction gains and late fees are some other examples of other income. In addition to earning revenue from non-core operations, a business can also generate expenses from non-core operations. These would also be included in the other income and expense section so they can be clearly separated from the main operations of a business.

There is also a section on the income statement for interest income and expense, and it is usually shown as the net of interest received and paid.

Another way for a company to earn non-operating income is through a gain on the sale of an asset or a subsidiary. If the company sells an asset for more than its worth, it realizes a gain on the sale of the asset. Of course, a company might have to sell it for less than its worth, realizing a loss on the sale of the asset. Gains and losses are included in the other income / expense section because they are not part of a company's core operations.

The term income instead of revenue is used in this section of the income statement because the figures are net figures; they have been adjusted by subtracting the expenses from the revenues. There might be both positive and negative numbers in this section; the positive ones reflect revenues and the negative numbers reflect expenses. Income before taxes, also known as profit before taxes, is equal to operating income adjusted for other income or expenses.

Income Before Taxes = Operating Income + Other Income - Other Expenses

For answers to the following questions, please see the end of Chapter 3.

Review 3.8 Question 1

Which of the following could be considered an item that would fall under the Other Income / Expense category?

- a. Foreign transaction gains
- b. Loss on the sale of an asset
- c. Salary of the CEO
- d. Shipping costs

Review 3.8 Question 2

Black Ink's operating income for 2013 was $1,640,000. They also had the following income and expenses during the year. What was Black Ink's income before taxes for 2013?

Selling, Gen. & Admin	($1,822,000)
Interest Income	$2,000
Income Taxes	($574,000)
Depreciation Expense	($250,000)

- a. $(182,000)
- b. $1,638,000
- c. $2,214,000
- d. $1,642,000

3.3.5   Net Income

The final section includes tax expenses, which are subtracted from operating profit to calculate net income. Determining a business' income taxes is complex and will not be discussed in this introductory accounting book. A common way to approximate a business' taxes is to take a percentage (such as 40%) of its income before taxes.

Net income is the amount of revenue remaining after all a business' expenses have been deducted. It is a very important number that is frequently used in ratio analysis and financial statement analysis. However, the bottom line does not measure how much cash a company earned over a period of time because the income statement includes non-cash expenses. We need to look at a company's cash flow statement in order to examine its cash.

Net Income	=	Income Before Taxes - Taxes

For the answer to the following question, please see the end of Chapter 3.

Review 3.9 Question 1

Black Ink had net income of $1,200,000 for the year 2012. They also had the following income and expenses. What was Black Ink's operating income for the year 2012?

COGS	($6,000,000)
SG&A	($1,900,000)
Other Income	$200,000
Interest Income	$25,000
Depreciation Expense	($440,000)
Income Tax Expense	($570,000)

- a. $1,770,000
- b. $1,545,000
- c. $1,570,000
- d. $1,995,000

3.3.6   Review

The income statement is extremely useful because it contains essential information about a business' performance over time. Outside investors need to carefully analyze the information to determine whether a company is a good investment, and management also needs to study its results to determine ways to improve the business.

Although there are many rules and guidelines about reporting information on the income statement, companies can still exert some discretion. The order of accounts within subcategories can vary, and companies can choose the level of detail they report by how they group accounts.

IFRS and US GAAP also have some differences regarding the income statement. US GAAP income statements classify expenses by function and always have a COGS or cost of sales line that directly ties expenses to revenues. Under IFRS, companies are permitted to classify expenses by function (SG&A, **cost of sales**) or by type (**raw materials**, wages), and it is not necessary to report cost of sales. The majority of companies choose to classify expenses by function.

Figures 3.10, 3.11, and 3.12 show the different ways to organize income statements under US GAAP and IFRS.

FIGURE 3.10

US GAAP INCOME STATEMENT

Cracker Barrel Old Country Store, Inc.
Consolidated Statement of Income
(In thousands)

	August 1, 2014
Total revenue	$ 2,683,677
Cost of goods sold	(872,758)
Gross profit	1,810,919
Labor and other related expenses	(966,593)
Other store operating expenses	(506,533)
Store operating income	337,793
General and administrative expenses	(129,387)
Operating income	208,406
Interest expense	(17,557)
Income before income taxes	190,849
Provision for income taxes	(58,721)
Net income	$ 132,128

FIGURE 3.11

IFRS INCOME STATEMENT, EXPENSE BY FUNCTION

Henkel
Consolidated Statement of Income
(in million euros)

	Dec. 31, 2014
Sales	€ 16,428
Cost of sales	(8,712)
Gross profit	7,716
Marketing, selling and distribution expenses	(4,151)
Research and development expenses	(413)
Administrative expenses	(852)
Other operating income	109
Other operating charges	(165)
Operating profit (EBIT)	2,244
Interest income	39
Interest expense	(48)
Other financial result	(46)
Investment result	6
Financial result	(49)
Income before tax	2,195
Taxes on income	(533)
Net income	€ 1,662

FIGURE 3.12

IFRS INCOME STATEMENT, EXPENSE BY TYPE

GDF Suez
Income Statement
(In millions of euros)

	Dec. 31, 2013
Revenues	€ 89,300
Purchases	(51,216)
Personnel costs	(11,704)
Depreciation, amortization and provisions	(6,600)
Other operating expenses	(14,058)
Other operating income	2,107
Current operating income	7,828
Mark-to-market on commodity contracts other than trading instruments	(226)
Impairment losses	(14,943)
Restructuring costs	(305)
Changes in scope of consolidation	406
Other non-recurring items	545
Income/(loss) from operating activities	(6,695)
Financial expenses	(2,487)
Financial income	510
Net financial income/(loss)	(1,977)
Income tax expense	(727)
Share in net income of associates	490
Net income/(loss)	€ (8,909)

The multi-step income statement is a useful format because it organizes the statement in a logical manner and breaks out many key metrics. It's easier to read and analyze than the simple format of just listing revenues and expenses because the multi-step format has useful subtotals. The names and calculations for the main ones are summarized below.

Gross Profit = Gross Income = Gross Margin = Revenue - COGS

Operating Income = Operating Profit = Gross Profit – Operating Expenses

Income before Taxes = Profit before Taxes = Earnings before Taxes = EBT = Operating Income – Other Income / Expenses

Net Income = Bottom Line = Income before Taxes – Taxes

Although companies may choose to organize or aggregate their income statements in slightly different ways, Figure 3.13 shows a skeleton of a typical multi-step income statement.

FIGURE 3.13

Revenue
   COGS
Gross Profit

Operating Expenses
   List Individual Accounts
Total Operating Expenses

Operating Income

Other Revenue and (Expenses)
   List Individual Accounts
Total Other Revenue and (Expenses)

Income Before Tax
   Income Tax
Net Income

Use the trial balance in Figure 3.14 for the questions that follow.

FIGURE 3.14

Trial Balance as of December 31, 2013

Accounts	Debit		Credit	
Balance sheet accounts				
Cash	$	41,050		
Accounts receivable		1,925		
Inventory		1,875		
Prepaid rent		1,175		
Desks		238		
Accumulated depreciation			$	100
Bank loan				9,425
Accounts payable				4,738
Wages payable				1,181
Accrued utilities liability				219
Accrued interest liability				988
Share capital				18,800
Retained earnings				2,550
Income statement accounts				
Cost of goods sold		7,550		
Utilities expense		725		
Pension expense		1,500		
Rent expense		1,175		
Interest expense		988		
Tax expense		3,200		
Depreciation expense		100		
Revenues				22,000
Other income				1,500
Total	$	61,500	$	61,500

For answers to the following questions, please see the end of Chapter 3.

Review 3.10 Question 1

Use the trial balance in Figure 3.14 to create the first part of the income statement
that calculates gross profit.

Income Statement for the Year Ending December 31, 2013

_ _ _ _ _ _ $_ _ _ _ _ _

_ _ _ _ _ _ $_ _ _ _ _ _

_____

_ _ _ _ _ _ $_ _ _ _ _ _

a.   Revenue
b.   Gross Profit
c.   COGS
d.   14,450
e.   22,000
f.   7,550

Review 3.10 Question 2

Match the label to the correct area of the income statement to calculate operating
expenses for 2013.

_ _ _ _ _ _ $ 725
_ _ _ _ _ _ $1,500
_ _ _ _ _ _ $1,175
_ _ _ _ _ _ $ 100
_ _ _ _ _ _ $3,500

Account Names: Pension Expense, Utilities Expense, Rent Expense, Depreciation Expense, Operating Expenses

Review 3.10 Question 3

Match the label to the correct area of the income statement to calculate operating profit for 2013.

_ _ _ _ _ _	$14,450
_ _ _ _ _ _	$ (3,500)
_ _ _ _ _ _	$10,950

Account Names: Gross Profit, Operating Expenses, Operating Profit

Review 3.10 Question 4

Use the trial balance in Figure 3.14 to calculate income before taxes.

_ _ _ _ _ _	$_ _ _ _ _ _
_ _ _ _ _ _	$_ _ _ _ _ _
_ _ _ _ _ _	$_ _ _ _ _ _

a.   Other Income
b.   Interest Expense
c.   Income before Taxes
d.   1,500
e.   988
f.   11,462

Review 3.10 Question 5

Use the trial balance in Figure 3.14 to calculate net income.

_ _ _ _ _ _	$_ _ _ _ _ _
_ _ _ _ _ _	$_ _ _ _ _ _
_ _ _ _ _ _	$_ _ _ _ _ _

a.   Income before Taxes
b.   Tax Expense
c.   Net Income
d.   11,462
e.   (3,200)
f.   8,262

Review 3.10 Question 6

Diamonds Are Forever had net income of $2,500,000 for the year 2013. It also had the following income and expenses. What was Diamonds Are Forever's operating income for the year 2013?

COGS	($6,000,000)
SG&A	($2,200,000)
Other Income	$400,000
Interest Income	$45,000
Depreciation Expense for Office Equipment	($375,000)
Income Tax Expense	($900,000)

a. $3,400,000
b. $3,000,000
c. $2,955,000
d. $2,200,000

Review 3.10 Question 7

Diamonds Are Forever's operating income for the year 2013 was $2,955,000. It also had the following income and expenses. What was Diamonds Are Forever's gross profit for the year 2013?

COGS	($6,000,000)
SG&A	($2,200,000)
Other Income	$400,000
Interest Income	$45,000
Depreciation Expense for Office Equipment	($375,000)
Income Tax Expense	($900,000)

a. $5,530,000
b. $5,975,000
c. $11,575,000
d. $8,500,000

Section 4

Trial Balances and Accounting Periods

Concepts

1. Simplifying the Trial Balance

2. An Accounting Period

3.4.1   Simplifying the Trial Balance

In order to create the balance sheet and income statements, we only need to use a company's trial balance. However, the trial balance contains information about all of a business' accounts, and it isn't important to include the information for every single account in the financial statements. We only need to include the information that is material and relevant for the people using the financial statements. Too much information obscures the overall picture, so the very detailed trial balance will be simplified into more general accounts.

For example, Netflix earns revenues from its membership fees for streaming content and its membership fees for DVDs by mail. These two accounts are combined into one line item on Netflix's consolidated income statement: Revenues. Each company has the flexibility to determine how detailed its reporting should be.

Sometimes companies report general account information on their consolidated statements and report details about certain accounts in their notes to the financial statements. For example, companies might report detailed information about their segments or their operations in different countries.

For answers to the following questions, please see the end of Chapter 3.

Review 3.11 Question 1

Crazy Coffee has 6 different notes payables with different terms. Should it list each one separately on the balance sheet?

    a.   Yes

    b.   No

Review 3.11 Question 2

Crazy Coffee has sales accounts for its coffee sales, its pastry sales, and its merchandise sales. Should it report each one separately on its income statement?

    a.   Yes

    b.   No

Review 3.11 Question 3

Some investors invested in preferred shares and others in common stock issued by the public company Party Favors. Should Party Favors report the investments separately?

    a.   Yes

    b.   No

3.4.2   An Accounting Period

Nearly all businesses prepare annual financial statements, but many also prepare statements more regularly, such as on a quarterly or monthly basis. The length of time over which a business evaluates its financial performance is called an accounting period. Publicly traded companies are required to publish quarterly financial statements, and they likely prepare income statements and trial balances at the end of every month for internal use.

In order to see the financial performance of a company over a period of time, we only need the trial balance at the end of the period. The changes in owners' equity are posted to revenue and expense accounts, not directly to owners' equity. The balances in those temporary accounts will be moved to owners' equity at the end of the year.

However, if a statement is prepared for a period of time that is less than a year, the balances in the revenue and expense accounts need to be transferred to owners' equity so that the balance sheet will balance.

It's important to use both the balance sheet and the income statement when analyzing a company because the income statement gives us more insight into a company's performance, and the balance sheet gives information about a company's financial position at a point in time.

Section 5

Review

Two types of accounts on trial balances: **Permanent Accounts** and **Temporary Accounts**

Permanent Accounts	Temporary Accounts
Real Accounts	Nominal Accounts
Stock Measures	Flow Measures
Listed on the Balance Sheet	Listed on the Income Statement
Assets, Liabilities, Owner's Equity	Revenues, Expenses, Gains and Losses
Continuous accounts with a cumulative balance	Reset to zero at new accounting periods

Examples of Permanent Accounts	Examples of Temporary Accounts
Cash	Sales
Property, Plant, and Equipment	Cost of Goods Sold
Inventory	General and Administrative Expenses
Accounts Payable	Operating Expenses
Accounts Receivable	Interest Expense
Land	Rent Expense
Notes Payable	Advertising Expense
Notes Receivable	Research and Development Expense
Goodwill	Wage Expense
Deferred Revenue	Impairment Loss
Prepaid Expenses	Marketing Expenses
Long-term debt	Interest Income
Common Stock	Gain on Sale of Long-term Asset
Additional Paid-in Capital	Loss on Lawsuit

Closing process - at the end of an accounting period, the net effect of the temporary accounts is transferred to retained earnings. This resets the temporary accounts back to zero and updates the retained earnings balance to the current point in time.

Trial balance accounts are generally consolidated into groups to list on the balance sheet and income statement.

Balance Sheet

The balance sheet, also called the statement of financial position, is a **snapshot of the business at a certain point in time**. The asset, liability, and owners' equity accounts show the financial position of the firm as of a certain date.

Classified balance sheets separate their assets and liabilities into current assets (will be used within one year or one operating cycle) and non-current assets (will be held for more than one year or operating cycle) and current liabilities (will be due within one year) and non-current liabilities (will come due in more than one year).

There are different formats for the balance sheet under IFRS and US GAAP. Generally, IFRS presents the least liquid items first and US GAAP presents the most liquid items first.

General Order of Balance Sheet Accounts:

IFRS

Non-current assets

Current assets

Owners' equity

Non-current liabilities

Current liabilities

US GAAP

Current assets

Non-current assets

Current liabilities

Non-current liabilities

Owners' equity

Income Statement

The income statement, also called the statement of operations or the profit and loss statement, **shows a company's operating performance over a period of time**. It shows the revenues, expenses, losses, and gains that are being recognized during an accounting period.

The income statement is often shown in a multi-step format, which contains multiple calculations before arriving at net income or net loss. These include:

Gross profit = sales – COGS

Operating Income = Gross Profit – Operating Expenses

Income Before Taxes = Operating Income – Non-operating Expenses

Net Income = Income Before Taxes - Taxes

Section 6
Review Questions

For answers to the following questions, please see the end of Chapter 3.

Review 3.12 Question 1

Which of the following categories would you find on a balance sheet?

    a.   Revenues
    b.   Liabilities
    c.   Losses
    d.   Gains

Review 3.12 Question 2

Which of the following would not be a current asset?

    a.   Accounts Payable
    b.   Inventory
    c.   Accounts Receivable
    d.   Short-term investments

Review 3.12 Question 3

The income statement is shown

    a.   As of a certain date
    b.   For a period of time

Review 3.12 Question 4

Which of the following would be a current liability? Please select all that apply.

- a.   Prepaid Rent
- b.   Accounts Receivable
- c.   Notes Payable Due in 3 years
- d.   Deferred Revenue
- e.   Wages Payable

Review 3.12 Question 5

Flow measures is another term for

- a.   Real accounts
- b.   Nominal accounts

Review 3.12 Question 6

Real accounts are found on the

- a.   Balance sheet
- b.   Income statement

Review 3.12 Question 7

At the beginning of a fiscal year, the trial balance shows

- a.   Only real accounts
- b.   Only nominal accounts
- c.   Both real and nominal accounts

Review 3.12 Question 8

A balance sheet...
(Please select all that apply)

- a.   is also called a statement of financial position.
- b.   Contains nominal accounts
- c.   Is a snapshot of a business at a certain point in time
- d.   Shows changes in a business over a period of time

Review 3.12 Question 9

Under US GAAP, balance sheet accounts

    a.   are ordered from the most liquid to the least liquid

    b.   are ordered from the least liquid to the most liquid

    c.   can be ordered however the company chooses, as long as it is consistent in its choice

Review 3.12 Question 10

Suppose Spartan Gym took out a short-term loan from a bank that is due in 9 months. Where should Spartan Gym place the note on its balance sheet?

    a.   Current assets

    b.   Current liabilities

    c.   Non-current assets

    d.   Non-current liabilities

Review 3.12 Question 11

Accounting standards require that companies break out revenues from different countries on the income statement.

    a.   True

    b.   False

Review 3.12 Question 12

Calculate operating income based on the following information.

Revenue	$800
COGS	($300)
Operating Expenses	($200)
Interest Expenses	($50)

    a. $250

    b. $300

    c. $450

    d. $500

Review 3.12 Question 13

Calculate gross profit based on the following information.

Revenue	$900
COGS	($300)
Operating Expenses	($150)
Interest Expenses	($75)

    a. $375

    b. $450

    c. $600

    d. $750

Review 3.12 Question 14

Calculate EBT based on the following information.

Revenue	$700
COGS	($300)
Operating Income	$325
Interest Expenses	($100)
Non-operating Income/(Expense)	$50
Taxes	($60)

    a. $115

    b. $175

    c. $225

    d. $275

Review 3.12 Question 15

Calculate net income based on the following information.

Revenue	$700
COGS	($300)
Operating Income	$325
Interest Expenses	($100)
Non-operating Income/(Expense)	$50
Taxes	($60)

a. $100
b. $165
c. $190
d. $215

Section 7

Answer Key

Review 3.1 Explanations

Question 1

Answer: Cash (permanent), Tax expense (temporary)

Cash is a permanent account. It is reported on the balance sheet, and it is a continuous account that has a cumulative balance over time. Tax expense is a temporary account. Tax expense is reported on the income statement and shows activity over a period of time, resetting to zero at the beginning of a new accounting period.

Question 2

Answer: Accounts receivable (permanent), Sales (temporary)

Accounts receivable is a permanent account. It is reported on the balance sheet, and it is a continuous account that has a cumulative balance over time. Sales is a temporary account. Sales is reported on the income statement and shows activity over a period of time, resetting to zero at the beginning of a new accounting period.

Question 3

Answer: Prepaid rent (permanent), Rent expense (temporary)

Prepaid rent is a permanent account. It is reported on the balance sheet, and it is a continuous account that has a cumulative balance over time. Rent expense is a temporary account. Rent expense is reported on the income statement and shows activity over a period of time, resetting to zero at the beginning of a new accounting period.

Question 4

Answer: Inventory (permanent), Interest expense (temporary)

Inventory is a permanent account. It is reported on the balance sheet, and it is a continuous account that has a cumulative balance over time. Interest expense is a temporary account. Interest expense is reported on the income statement and shows activity over a period of time, resetting to zero at the beginning of a new accounting period.

Review 3.2 Explanations

Question 1

Answer: B

According to US GAAP, assets should be ordered according to their liquidity, or how quickly and easily they can be converted to cash. For current assets, cash and cash equivalents are the most liquid, then short-term investments, then accounts receivable and then inventory. For non-current assets, long-term investments are listed first, then fixed assets, and lastly intangible assets. So, the correct order would be long-term assets, then property, plant & equipment, and lastly goodwill.

Question 2

Answer: D

Under IFRS, the least liquid items are listed first and then the other items follow in order of increasing liquidity. An item is very liquid if it can be quickly and easily converted to cash. So, the non-current assets would be listed at the beginning of the asset section, with intangibles coming first, then fixed assets, and lastly long-term investments. The correct order would be goodwill, then PP&E, then long-term investments. Next, there would be the current assets section. The least liquid item, inventory would be listed first. Then there would be accounts receivable, then short-term investments, and lastly cash and cash equivalents.

Review 3.3 Explanations

Question 1

Answer: C

The bond should be placed in the current liabilities section. A current liability is a liability that will be due within one year. Since we are creating the balance sheet as of 12/31/2012, and the bond will be due in 9 months (September 2013), it is a current liability.

Question 2

Answer: D

According to US GAAP, the liabilities that are likely to be paid soonest should be listed first. So, the current liabilities section is at the beginning, and notes and loans payable comes first because they will be paid the quickest. Next, there is the current portion of long-term debt, and lastly accounts payable. The next section is non-current liabilities, and long-term debt would be listed first before deferred income taxes.

Question 3

Answer: A

According to IFRS, the liabilities that are likely to be paid soonest should be listed last. So, the non-current liabilities section comes first, with deferred income taxes at the beginning and long-term debt listed second. The next section is current liabilities. Within current liabilities, accounts payable is listed first, current portion of long-term debt is second and notes and loans payable is listed last.

Question 4

Answer: Cash (Current asset), Plant and equipment (Non-current asset), Current portion of long-term debt (Current liability), 10-year bond (Non-current liability)

Cash is a current asset because it will be used within one year. Plant and equipment are non-current assets because they will be held for over one year and likely be useful to the business for a long time. The current portion of long-term debt is a current liability because it is the part of debt that is due within one year. A 10-year bond is a non-current liability because it will come due in more than one year.

Question 5

Answer: Patent (Non-current asset), Short-term investment (Current asset), Notes payable due in 6 months (Current liability), Mortgage payable due in 3 to 5 years (Non-current liability)

A patent is a non-current asset because it will be held for more than a year and be useful to the business for a long time. Short-term investments are current assets because they are investments that will be held by the company under a year, perhaps being sold to others or converted into cash. Notes payable due in 6 months is a current liability because it is money a company borrowed but needs to repay within a year. Mortgage payable due in 3 to 5 years is a non-current liability because it will come due in more than one year; payments are likely spread out over many years.

Question 6

Answer: Land (Non-current asset), Accounts receivable (Current asset), Wages payable (Current liability), Pension payable (Non-current liability)

Land is a non-current asset that will be held for more than a year. Accounts receivable is a current asset that will be held by the company for less than a year. Oftentimes companies require those paying on account to pay within 30, 60, or 90 days. Wages payable is a current liability that will be due within one year. Many companies pay wages each month. Pension payable is a non-current liability that will come due in more than one year.

Review 3.4 Explanations

Question 1

Answer: Preferred stock, Common stock, Paid-in-capital, Retained earnings

According to US GAAP, preferred stock is listed first, then common stock, then paid-in capital and lastly retained earnings.

Review 3.5 Explanations

Question 1

Answer: C

According to US GAAP, assets should be ordered according to their liquidity, or how quickly and easily they can be converted to cash. So, cash should be listed first, then accounts receivable, then inventory, then prepaid rent, then desks, and lastly accumulated depreciation. Depreciation is negative because it is a contra-asset account that is netted against the assets it depreciates.

Question 2

Answer: A

According to US GAAP, the liabilities that are likely to be paid soonest should be listed first. So accrued interest and accrued utilities, which are due in 30 days would be listed first. Wages payable and accounts payable, which are due in 2 months will be listed next, followed by Accounts payable. Bank loan that's due in 2 years should be listed last.

Question 3

Answer: A

The stockholder section of the balance sheet, which is similar under US GAAP and IFRS, should list share capital before retained earnings.

Review 3.6 Explanations

Question 1

Answer: A, B, C, E

Costs directly related to producing goods are categorized under COGS, so the cost of raw materials used, the cost of storing the products in inventory before being sold, the pension benefits of the factory workers, and the rent paid for the factory space would be categorized under COGS. The salary of the CEO would not be a cost directly related to producing goods, so it would not categorized under COGS.

Question 2

Answer: A

We know that gross profit = sales − COGS, so COGS = sales − gross profit = $2,000,000 - $1,200,000 = $800,000.

Review 3.7 Explanations

Question 1

Answer: A, B, D

Rent, research costs, and advertising expenses would be considered operating expenses. The costs of raw materials and the shipping costs of products sold would be categorized under COGS.

Question 2

Answer: C

Operating income is calculated by the formula: Operating Income = Gross Profit − Operating Expenses. For Acorns, operating expenses include salaries and wages expense, building and utilities expense, and other operating expenses.

So, operating expenses = $300,000 + $100,000 + $40,000 = $440,000. So, operating income = $1,200,000 - $440,000 = $760,000.

Review 3.8 Explanations

Question 1

Answer: A, B

Foreign transaction gains and the loss on the sale of an asset would fall under the Other Income / Expense category because those are expenses that are not related to normal business operations. Shipping costs would be classified as COGS.

Question 2

Answer: D

Income before taxes is calculated by the formula: Income before Taxes = Operating Income – Other Income/Expenses. For Black Ink, other income / expenses is $2,000 in interest income. SG&A and depreciation were expenses that were already subtracted to calculate operating income, so they should not be subtracted again here. Income taxes is subtracted later. So, Income before Taxes = $1,640,000 + $2,000 = $1,642,000.

Review 3.9 Explanations

Question 1

Answer: B

Net income is calculated by the formula: Net Income = Income before Taxes – Taxes.

So, Income before Taxes = Net Income + Taxes = $1,200,000 + $570,000 = $1,770,000.

We also know that Income before Taxes = Operating Income + Other Income - Other Expenses, so Operating Income = Income before Taxes - Other Income + Other Expenses. Other Income/Expenses include other revenues and interest revenue.

So, working backwards, Operating Income = $1770,000 - $200,000 - $25,000 = $1,545,000.

Review 3.10 Explanations

Question 1

Answer:

Revenue   22,000

COGS   7,550

Gross Profit 14,450

In order to calculate gross profit, we would subtract COGS from revenues. According to the trial balance, revenues are $22,000 and COGS are $7,550, so gross profit = $22,000 - $7,550 = $14,450.

Question 2

Answer:

Utilities Expense	725
Pension Expense	1,500
Rent Expense	1,175
Depreciation Expense	100
Operating Expenses	3,500

In order to calculate operating expenses, we need to add utilities expense ($725), pension expense ($1,500), rent expense ($1,175), and depreciation expense ($100). This results in operating expenses of $3,500.

Question 3

Answer:

Gross Profit	14,450
Operating Expenses	3,500
Operating Profit	10,950

In order to calculate operating profit, we must subtract operating expenses ($3,500) from gross profit ($14,450). This results in operating profit of $10,950.

Question 4

Answer:

Other Income	1,500
Interest Expense	988
Income before Taxes	11,462

In order to calculate income before taxes, we must add other income ($1,500) and subtract interest expense ($988) from operating profit. This results in income before taxes of $11,462.

Question 5

Answer:

Income before Taxes	11,462
Tax Expense	3,200
Net Income	8,262

In order to calculate net income, we must subtract tax expense ($3,200) from income before taxes ($11,462). This results in net income of $8,262.

Question 6

Answer: C

We know Net Income = Income before Taxes – Taxes. So, Income before Taxes = Net Income + Taxes = $2,500,000 + $900,000 = $3,400,000. We also know that Income before Taxes = Operating Income + Other Income / (Expenses). So, Operating Income = Income before Taxes - Other Income / (Expenses). Other Income / Expenses only includes Other Income and Interest Income. SG&A and depreciation are considered to be operating expenses. So, Operating Income = $3,400,000 -$400,000 - $45,000 = $2,955,000.

Question 7

Answer: A

We know that Operating Income = Gross Profit – Operating Expenses. So, Gross Profit = Operating Income + Operating Expenses. Operating Expenses include SG&A and office equipment depreciation. So, Gross Profit = $2,955,000+ $2,200,000 + $375,000 = $5,530,000.

Review 3.11 Explanations

Question 1

Answer: B

Crazy Coffee does not need to list each one separately; the notes payable can be combined into one line item on its balance sheet to simplify reporting.

Question 2

Answer: B

Crazy Coffee does not need to separate out information about the sales for coffee, pastries, and merchandise on its income statement; it could combine them all into one sales account. Crazy Coffee could include additional details about sales in the notes to the financial statements if it felt like the information would be very useful.

Question 3

Answer: A

Party Favors should report the different types of shares owned on its balance sheet. This information is material and relevant for users of the financial statements.

Chapter Review 3.12 Explanations

Question 1

Answer: B

The balance sheet contains information about a company's assets, liabilities, and owner's equity. Revenues, gains, and losses are shown on a company's income statement.

Question 2

Answer: A

Current assets are assets that will be used within one year or one operating cycle. Inventory, accounts receivable, and short-term investments are all examples of current assets. Accounts payable, the obligation to another party in the future for goods or services received in the past, is a liability.

Question 3

Answer: B

The income statement shows a company's financial performance over a period of time. The balance sheet shows a snapshot of a company's financial position as of a certain date.

Question 4

Answer: D, E

Unearned revenue, also known as deferred revenue, and wages payable are examples of current liabilities. Unearned revenue is an account that is created when a company receives payment before providing goods or services. The company has an obligation to provide it in the future. Wages payable is a liability because the company owes its employees for work they previously performed. Prepaid rent and accounts receivable are assets whereas notes payable due in 3 years is a non-current liability.

Question 5

Answer: B

A flow measure is another term for a nominal or temporary account. It is shown on the income statement and measures the flow of an account over a period of time. Real or permanent accounts are sometimes called stock measures because they're measured at a certain point in time.

Question 6

Answer: A

Permanent accounts, also known as real accounts, are found on the balance sheet. They are continuous accounts that have a cumulative balance over time. Temporary accounts are found on the income statement, and they reset to zero at the beginning of each new accounting period.

Question 7

Answer: A

At the beginning of a fiscal year, the trial balance only shows permanent, or real, accounts. The temporary accounts reset to zero at the beginning of a new accounting period.

Question 8

Answer: A, C

The balance sheet is a snapshot of a company's financial position at a certain point in time. It can also be called a statement of financial position. The income statement contains nominal, or temporary, accounts and shows changes in a business over a period of time.

Question 9

Answer: A

Under US GAAP, balance sheet accounts should be listed according to liquidity, starting with the most liquid accounts. Under IFRS, the least liquid accounts are listed first. Companies cannot choose to list balance sheet accounts in which-ever order they want.

Question 10

Answer: B

A short-term loan due in 9 months should be listed under current liabilities. Current liabilities are liabilities that will come due in under one year.

Question 11

Answer: B

Accounting standards do not require that companies break out revenues from different countries on the income state-ment. If companies want to provide additional detail, they can choose to disclose this information in the notes to the financial statements.

Question 12

Answer: B

Operating Income = Gross Profit − Operating Expenses = Revenue − COGS − Operating Expenses = $800 - $300 - $200 = $300. Interest expense is not considered an operating expense.

Question 13

Answer: C

Gross Profit = Revenue − COGS = $900 - $300 = $600.

Question 14

Answer: D

Earnings Before Taxes = EBT = Operating Income + Non-operating Income − Interest expense = $325+ $50 - $100 = $275.

Question 15

Answer: D

Net Income = Operating Income + Non-operating Income − Interest Expense − Taxes = $325+ $50 - $100 - $60 =$215.

4

Adjusting Journal Entries

Sections

Section 1

Introduction

---

1. Explicit vs. Implicit Transactions

4.1.1   Explicit vs. Implicit Transactions

The past few chapters have covered how to use accounting information from transactions and journal entries to create useful end products, such as financial reports.

This chapter will delve deeper into certain transactions and discuss some complex journal entries to record events that are not so straightforward.

The majority of the journal entries we have studied in the past have been caused by an event that "triggers" the transaction and the resulting journal entry. These are known as **explicit transactions** because there is a clear event that caused the transaction, and we can easily identify the amount and timing of the transaction. Oftentimes, the two participants in the transaction exchange resources, and there is usually some form of documentation about the exchange, such as an invoice or a purchase order.

Some examples of explicit transactions include when Acorns Bakery receives flour from its supplier and pays its supplier with cash, or Netflix sells a monthly subscription to a customer on credit. These transactions have invoices that explicitly state the amount, making it straightforward to record.

However, not all transactions are explicit. There are also **implicit transactions**, which do not have a "trigger" but still need to be tracked in journal entries. We record implicit transactions by adjusting journal entries. In general, the timing and the amount of the transaction are not clearly defined, so businesses need to use their best judgment when recording the transaction.

Adjusting entries are made at the end of the accounting cycle, after having recorded the explicit transactions. The accounting cycle includes identifying explicit transactions, recording them throughout the accounting period using t-accounts and journal entries, adjusting the journal entries, making a trial balance, and summarizing the information in financial reports.

Adjustments are challenging because there aren't clear triggers to identify them, but the principles of revenue recognition, expense matching, and conservatism can guide you on when to make adjustments. There are also some key characteristics that all adjustments have, which can help identify them. In particular, adjustments never involve cash, don't involve external parties and are only recorded internally, and are recorded at the end of an accounting period.

Examples of	
Explicit Transactions	**Implicit Transactions**
Purchasing machinery	Recognizing the use/consumption of pre-paid insurance
Selling goods or services	Recording an impairment loss
Paying wages	Recognizing depreciation of equipment
Paying rent	Recognizing amortization of a patent
Collecting receivables	Recording office supplies used
Recognizing a loss on the disposal of an asset	

The following example can help explain the concept of implicit transactions. Suppose Acorns bought a new oven for its bakery. The first part of this transaction is explicit; the company will record an asset and an expense. But there is an additional transaction, an implicit one, which occurs over time. The company needs a way to match the cost of the oven with the future revenues it will generate. It also needs to document how long the equipment will last and what its value will be at various points in time.

There are no triggers to recognize the decrease in asset value over time, which is why it is an implicit transaction. This chapter will describe how to record these transactions by adjusting journal entries.

Even though the new oven that Acorns bought might be losing value every day, it's not practical to constantly adjust the account and the balance sheet. Typically, companies just make an entry at the end of an accounting period to reflect the changed value over that time frame. Remember that accounting periods can vary in length across businesses, but are generally a month, a quarter, or a year. When recording the journal entry, accountants must adhere to the revenue recognition and matching principles, which were covered in the previous chapters.

An individual's judgment plays a larger role in adjustments for implicit transactions than it does in explicit transactions. It is possible that two people could arrive at different conclusions, but both could be correct. The leeway involved in accounting for implicit transactions presents opportunities for people to manipulate a company's books. Many accounting scandals relate to these types of entries and happen because people use their discretion and judgment to falsify financial statements.

The accounting entries can be divided into four general cases: Recognizing Expenses, Capitalizing Assets, Recognizing Revenues, and Accruing Liabilities. These will be discussed in detail in the following sections.

For answers to the following questions, please see the end of Chapter 4.

Review 4.1 Question 1

State whether the following transaction is implicit or explicit.

Paying 2 years of rent in advance

a. Implicit

b. Explicit

Review 4.1 Question 2

State whether the following transaction is implicit or explicit.

Purchasing equipment

    a.   Implicit

    b.   Explicit

Review 4.1 Question 3

State whether the following transaction is implicit or explicit.

Recording depreciation on equipment

    a.   Implicit

    b.   Explicit

Review 4.1 Question 4

State whether the following transaction is implicit or explicit.

Paying wages

    a.   Implicit

    b.   Explicit

Review 4.1 Question 5

State whether the following transaction is implicit or explicit.

Expiration of prepaid rent

    a.   Implicit

    b.   Explicit

Section 2

Common Adjustments and Recognizing Expenses

Concepts

4.2.1   Straight Line Depreciation

In previous chapters, we covered examples of different types of explicit transactions. We will now discuss common adjusting entries, starting with depreciation.

As we learned in Chapter 1, the matching principle states that a business must recognize an expense from a transaction in the same period in which it recognizes the revenue from the transaction. So when a business makes a purchase, it must also determine when it will receive the benefit from that purchase.

Not all purchases result in an immediate benefit, and some may produce a benefit over a long period of time. Certain expenses, such as travel costs, are expensed immediately because their benefit is immediate. Others, such as research and development or marketing costs, are expensed right away because the company is not sure when, or if, they will generate revenues. If the expense cannot be matched up to its corresponding revenue, it is expensed immediately. There are also purchases that are initially recorded as assets and are later expensed when they are used or the benefit from them no longer exists. These include items such as inventory or pre-paid rent.

There are other assets, such as buildings, equipment or **furniture and fixtures**, which produce revenues over an extended period of time. Since the benefit lasts a while, companies generally expense these assets over the longer time frame, making adjustments in multiple accounting periods. The expense for long-lived physical assets is called depreciation.

There are several ways to calculate depreciation for **long-lived assets**, and **straight line depreciation** is one of the most frequently used methods.

In order to use the straight line method, the company needs to know the original cost of the asset, the estimated useful life of the asset, and how much the asset will be worth at the end of its useful life. With this information, the company can split up the expense of the asset into equal amounts and recognize the expense over time.

When a company records an asset on its books, it is recorded as the price paid plus extra expenses, such as delivery, installation, or testing, necessary to prepare the asset for service in the business. This amount is known as the **original cost** or the **gross book value**. When recording the asset at this value, we are applying the historical cost principle.

Another important value for the calculation of depreciation is the expected **useful life** of an asset. Generally, it is not possible to directly observe the amount of the asset physically used in a given period, so management must make an estimate of how long the asset will provide a benefit to the company. The useful life is not based on how long the asset will last, it is based on how long the asset will be useful to the company. For example, cars may last 20 years, but rental car companies estimate a useful life of 2-3 years for their rental cars because that is how long they typically use them.

The last figure needed is the **salvage value**, which is the amount the business believes the asset could be sold for after its useful life to the business is over. Even though the company considers it completely used up, it could be sold as scrap to someone else.

The formula for the straight line depreciation method is the following:

$$\text{Depreciation Expense} = \frac{\text{Gross Book Value - Salvage Value}}{\text{Useful Life}}$$

The useful life should be measured in months or years, depending on the accounting period used for the financial reports.

There may be some situations where an asset has no salvage value, and when the asset is used up, the company will need to pay to dispose of it safely. In this case, the disposal costs should be spread out over the life of the asset. These costs are necessary for the asset to generate revenues, so the anticipated disposal costs should be depreciated as well.

Let's look at an example to fully understand the straight-line depreciation method.

Acorns wants to buy four new ovens for its bakery, and it expects the total cost to be $20,000, including the delivery and installation of the ovens. Acorns expects them to last 10 years, and it believes the salvage value of the ovens will be $500 each.

In order to determine the **depreciation expense** for each year, we take the amount the company paid for the asset ($20,000), subtract the amount that it will receive when it disposes of the asset ($500*4 = $2,000), and divide it by the estimated useful life (10 years).

So, we have:

Gross Book Value - Salvage Value = $20,000 - $2,000 = $18,000

Then we have:

$$\frac{\text{Depreciable Cost}}{\text{Useful Life}} = \frac{\$18,000}{10} = \$1,800$$

In order to record the annual depreciation expense of $1,800 as a journal entry, each year we must debit depreciation expense for $1,800 and credit **accumulated depreciation** for $1,800.

In the journal entries, we separate out the depreciation expense as a **contra-asset** account. It is called a contra-asset account because its balance is usually the opposite of typical asset accounts. All **contra accounts** generally have balances that are opposite of the typical account. In order to get the asset's net book value, the contra-asset account is netted against, or subtracted from, the original asset. If we had just credited the equipment account instead of accumulated depreciation, it would be hard to identify the amount of the depreciation expense.

This contra account, called Accumulated Depreciation, is listed directly below the asset that is being depreciated on a trial balance. Accumulated Depreciation is the sum of all the depreciation recognized over the life of the asset.

$$\text{Accumulated Depreciation} = \frac{\text{Depreciation}}{\text{Expense per Period}} * \frac{\text{Number of}}{\text{Periods}}$$

Assets typically have debit balances, but since depreciation is a contra-asset account, its balance is a credit balance. Contra-asset accounts increase with credits and decrease with debits. The original asset listed under PP&E can still be changed and decreased with a credit if it is sold or impaired. The **net book value** of the asset, also called the net asset value, is the original cost of the asset less the accumulated depreciation. It is recorded on the balance sheet, and it's a useful figure for determining gains or losses when selling long-term assets.

It is important to notice that depreciation expense and accumulated depreciation are not the same. The temporary account, depreciation expense, is shown on the income statement and only shows the expense for the income statement period. The permanent account, accumulated depreciation, consists of all the depreciation expense recognized against the asset. It is a cumulative figure.

If we simply decreased the asset by the depreciation instead of placing the depreciation expense in a separate account, the net value of the asset would be the same. However, having a separate account for accumulated depreciation is quite useful to readers of financial statements. It is easy to compare the original cost of the asset to its current cost and to get a sense of how old the assets of a business are by comparing the accumulated depreciation account to the gross value of the assets.

Although most long-lived physical assets are depreciated, land is an exception. Land is not depreciated because it generally doesn't decrease in value, and it is not "used up" by a business.

Let's consider the following situation.

Parma Pharmaceuticals recently bought a building that it will use for research and production. The building and land were purchased for $2,500,000 on 1/1/2013, and it was determined that the value of the land was $700,000.

Parma Pharma expects to use the land and the building for 20 years. It believes that it can sell them for $1,000,000 (the building for $300,000 and the land for $700,000) at that time.

What will the balance in the accumulated depreciation account be on 12/31/2023? How much depreciation expense will be recognized in 2023?

The calculations to perform to answer these questions include:

determining the building value:

$2,500,000 – $700,000 = $1,800,000

determining the yearly depreciation expense:

($1,800,000 – $300,000) / 20 = $75,000

and determining the accumulated depreciation on 12/31/2023: 10* $75,000 = $750,000

For answers to the following questions, please see the end of Chapter 4.

Review 4.2 Question 1

Accumulated depreciation generally has a debit balance.

 a. True
 b. False

Review 4.2 Question 2

Accumulated depreciation is shown on

 a. The balance sheet
 b. The income statement

Review 4.2 Question 3

Recording depreciation expense on the income statement is an application of

 a. The matching principle
 b. The historical cost principle

Review 4.2 Question 4

The cost of an asset minus the accumulated depreciation is called…
Please select all that apply.

 a. Book value
 b. Fair market value
 c. Carrying value

4.2.2   Other Depreciation Methods

Straight line depreciation is not the only way to record the depreciation of an asset. Some companies choose to use **accelerated depreciation** methods in order to deduct more depreciation expense in the early years of an asset's life and less in the later years. This method is the correct one to use if an asset generates more revenues in the early years of its life. The straight line method is more appropriate if the rate at which an asset's economic value decreases is relatively even over time.

With an accelerated depreciation method, the higher depreciation expense reduces a company's net income in the early years, but it also has the advantage of decreasing a company's tax expense in those years. Over the life of the asset, the same amount of depreciation will be recognized, but the timing of the depreciation expense will be different.

One accelerated depreciation method is called the **double declining balance method.** This method applies a constant rate of depreciation to the declining book value of an asset until the book value reaches the salvage value.

Consider an asset that cost $2,000,000 and has a salvage value of $250,000. It is expected to have a useful life of 10 years. The following graph shows the difference in annual depreciation expense using the straight line method versus the double declining balance method. The dark grey line shows the straight line method, which calculates a constant yearly depreciation expense of $175,000. The light grey line shows the double declining balance method, which calculates depreciation expense of $400,000 in year 1 and much lower depreciation expense in the later years.

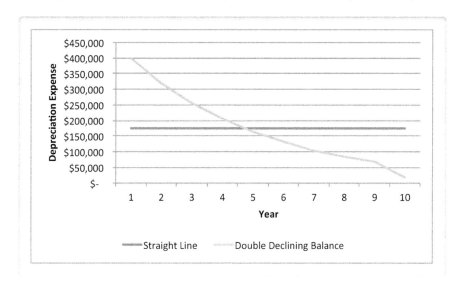

Although this textbook will not discuss the details of how to calculate depreciation expense using the double declining balance method, it should be clear how much of an impact it can have on the financial statements.

There is another depreciation method called units of measure depreciation. This method is for assets that have an expected fixed output, such as a machine that will be able to produce 500,000 products over its lifetime. With this information, we could calculate depreciation expense based on the proportionate number of products created.

For answers to the following questions, please see the end of Chapter 4.

Review 4.3 Question 1

Consider the methods listed below. Which one would result in **lower net income** in the **earlier years**?

    a.   Straight line method
    b.   Double declining balance method
    c.   Cannot be determined

Review 4.3 Question 2

Consider the methods listed below. Which one would result in **lower taxes** in the **earlier years**?

    a.   Straight line method
    b.   Double declining balance method
    c.   Cannot be determined

Review 4.3 Question 3

One business might depreciate its computers over a period of 2 years whereas another might depreciate the same computers over 5 years. Can they both be correct?

    a.   Yes
    b.   No

Review 4.3 Question 4

The double declining balance depreciation method recognizes more **total** depreciation expense than the straight line method over the life of the asset.

    a.   True
    b.   False

The double declining balance method recognizes more depreciation expense in the earlier years than the straight line method.

a. True
b. False

4.2.3 Asset Disposal

In order to calculate depreciation, management has to estimate the useful life and the salvage value of an asset. It's hard to make perfect estimates, and sometimes an asset is disposed of before the end of its predicted useful life. In this section, we will see how to remove retired or sold assets from the books and account for the differences in estimates.

Let's look at an example to understand how it works. Suppose The Construction Company (TCC) had originally bought a delivery truck for $85,000, and as of October 1,2013, the accumulated depreciation for the truck was $40,000.

On 10/1/13, the balance sheet line items related to the asset looked like this:

Delivery truck	$85,000
Accumulated depreciation	(40,000)

Gain on Sale

Suppose that TCC sold one of its delivery trucks on 10/1/13 for $50,000.

Let's look at the accounts and walk through how to record the transaction step-by-step.

First, we must remove the asset from the books. As we know, depreciation is a separate account, and the asset is recorded at its original cost on the books. So, in order to remove it, we simply credit the account for $85,000.

Next, we must remove the accumulated depreciation recorded for the asset. In this case, the accumulated depreciation for the delivery truck was $40,000. Since accumulated depreciation is a contra-asset account with a credit balance, we debit the account for $40,000. Accumulated depreciation is a contra-asset account, and it can only exist if the asset has a non-zero balance. So, if the asset has a balance of zero, which is the case when we remove the asset from the books, the accumulated depreciation account must also have a balance of zero.

Now we need to record the $50,000 we received for selling the truck.

The journal entries for the transaction just described look like this:

Date	Account Name	Debit	Credit
10/1/13	Accumulated depreciation	$40,000	
	Cash	50,000	
	Delivery truck		85,000

It's important to notice that the equation doesn't balance – the debits don't equal the credits because we sold the truck for $50,000, but the value on the books was only $45,000 ($85,000 truck - $40,000 accumulated depreciation). We need to account for this difference and make the debits equal the credits.

In order to account for this in the books, we recognize a gain on the sale of the asset. This is similar to revenues, and it will increase owner's equity, but it is reported separately because it is not recurring. This is a one-time event that is outside the business' normal operations. The complete entry looks like this:

Date	Account Name	Debit	Credit
10/1/13	Accumulated depreciation	$40,000	
	Cash	50,000	
	Delivery truck		85,000
	Gain on sale of truck		5,000

Why would we be able to sell an asset for more than its net book value? One explanation is that we depreciated the asset faster than necessary - it wasn't losing as much value as we expected it to lose.

Loss on Sale

What if we didn't make a gain on the sale of the asset, and we could only sell the truck for $30,000? The entry would be similar, but there would be a loss on the sale of the asset, and we would debit that account. It would decrease owner's equity. This is also considered a one-time event because selling trucks is not the focus of The Construction Company.

We would need to credit the delivery truck asset for $85,000 and debit the accumulated depreciation account for $40,000, just as we did in the previous example. However, we would debit the cash account by $30,000 and debit the loss on sale of truck account by $15,000. The complete entry to record the loss would look like this:

Date	Account Name	Debit	Credit
10/1/13	Accumulated depreciation	$40,000	
	Cash	30,000	
	Loss on sale of truck	15,000	
	Delivery truck		85,000

Impairment

Another possible situation could be that the value of the truck decreased to $24,000, perhaps because the manufacturer no longer produced it and stopped making spare parts. If The Construction Company planned to use it for several more years, it would be more costly to service it. In this situation, The Construction Company should record an impairment charge to decrease the value of the asset.

The net book value of the asset is $45,000 ($85,000 truck - $40,000 accumulated depreciation), and the loss on impairment is $21,000 ($45,000 book value - $24,000 market value). The loss on impairment is calculated as the difference between the net book value and the market value or fair value of the asset.

There are two methods to record the impairment. The first method is to debit the expense account "loss on impairment" for $21,000 and credit accumulated depreciation for $21,000. This method leaves the equipment on the books at its original cost and recognizes additional depreciation to reduce it to its carrying value. After posting this entry, the truck would have a carrying value of $24,000 ($85,000 truck - $40,000 accumulated depreciation - $21,000 accumulated depreciation).

The journal entry would look like this:

Date	Account Name	Debit	Credit
10/1/13	Loss on impairment	$21,000	
	Accumulated depreciation		21,000

The second method is to credit the $85,000 truck account for $61,000 to reduce it to its current value of $24,000. To complete the accounting entry, we would debit the accumulated depreciation account for $40,000, and recognize the actual impairment by debiting the "loss on impairment" account for the remaining $21,000. This method removes the accumulated depreciation already recorded, so it's essentially as though the company bought a new truck for $24,000.

The journal entry would look like this:

Date	Account Name	Debit	Credit
10/1/13	Accumulated depreciation	$40,000	
	Loss on impairment	21,000	
	Delivery truck		61,000

Both of these methods have the same net effect; they record a loss of $21,000 and ultimately end up with the truck's net book value of $24,000. The difference in the methods is how they treat the accumulated depreciation account. For both methods, the future depreciation expense would be based on the current value of $24,000.

For answers to the following questions, please see the end of Chapter 4.

Review 4.4 Question 1

Suppose a retail store had a book value of $50,000, historical cost of $55,000 and accumulated depreciation of $5,000. A tornado hit the town and damaged the building. The owner determined the market value decreased to $30,000.

The loss on impairment is:

a. $30,000
b. $25,000
c. $20,000

Review 4.4 Question 2

Suppose a retail store had a book value of $50,000, historical cost of $55,000 and accumulated depreciation of $5,000. A tornado hit the town and damaged the building. The owner determined the market value decreased to $30,000.

Select the journal entries that apply.

    a.   Debit loss on impairment for $20,000
    b.   Debit loss on impairment for $30,000
    c.   Credit accumulated depreciation for $20,000
    d.   Credit accumulated depreciation for $30,000

Review 4.4 Question 3

Suppose a retail store had a book value of $50,000, historical cost of $55,000 and accumulated depreciation of $5,000. A tornado hit the town and damaged the building. The owner determined the market value decreased to $30,000.

What will be the value of the building on the balance sheet?

    a. $50,000
    b. $30,000
    c. $20,000

Review 4.4 Question 4

After the impairment, the depreciation expense will be calculated using the asset's new value.

    a.   True
    b.   False

4.2.4   Amortization

Businesses have many different types of assets; in addition to long-lived physical assets, there are non-physical assets, such as pre-paid rent, pre-paid insurance, or **patents**. We just learned how to recognize expenses on physical assets by recording depreciation expenses. Similarly, we can record expenses for non-physical or intangible assets, which is called **amortization**.

Suppose that The Construction Company rents one of its storage facilities and paid $30,000 for a 1-year rental starting on January 1, 2013 and ending on December 31, 2013. TCC would first debit the account titled pre-paid rent by $30,000 and credit the cash account by the same amount. Throughout the year, the company will "use up" its pre-paid rent. So, after one month, TCC will record amortization by debiting pre-paid rent expense and crediting the pre-paid rent account by $2,500 ($30,000 / 12 months).

The journal entry will look like this:

Date	Account Name	Debit	Credit
1/31/13	Amortization expense	$2,500	
	Accumulated amortization		2,500

This is another application of the matching principle; it causes the expense for the asset to be recognized during the same period in which it provides the benefit.

For amortization, it's possible to directly reduce the asset instead of keeping amortization in a separate account. Businesses have the discretion to choose whether they would like to use a contra-asset account called accumulated amortization or deduct amortization from the asset directly. Patents are one type of assets that generally have an accumulated amortization account.

The previous journal entry could have also looked like this:

Date	Account Name	Debit	Credit
1/31/13	Amortization expense	$2,500	
	Pre-paid rent		2,500

Amortization is generally calculated using the straight line method, which is the same as the one used for depreciation. Intangible assets that don't have a defined life, such as goodwill, are not amortized and are instead regularly tested for impairment. If it is determined that they are impaired, the company recognizes an expense for the impairment.

For answers to the following questions, please see the end of Chapter 4.

Review 4.5 Question 1

Should the following accounts be amortized or depreciated or neither?

Building

---

    a.   Amortized

    b.   Depreciated

    c.   Neither

Review 4.5 Question 2

Should the following accounts be amortized or depreciated or neither?

Land

- a. Amortized
- b. Depreciated
- c. Neither

Review 4.5 Question 3

Should the following accounts be amortized or depreciated or neither?

Patent

- a. Amortized
- b. Depreciated
- c. Neither

Review 4.5 Question 4

Should the following accounts be amortized or depreciated or neither?

Pre-paid Insurance

- a. Amortized
- b. Depreciated
- c. Neither

Review 4.5 Question 5

Should the following accounts be amortized or depreciated or neither?

Equipment

- a. Amortized
- b. Depreciated
- c. Neither

Should the following accounts be amortized or depreciated or neither?

Goodwill

---

a. Amortized
b. Depreciated
c. Neither

4.2.5   Inventory

The past couple of topics have covered how to adjust assets for changes in their values at the end of an accounting period. Another asset that needs to be analyzed at the end of a period is inventory. It is important that reported inventory levels and cost of goods sold are accurate. **Service businesses**, which are those that provide a service, such as consulting, accounting, or electrical services, do not typically sell inventory. But **retail businesses**, which are companies that primarily purchase products and sell them to customers, often have a large inventory supply.

It is normal for a business, such as a retailer or wholesaler, to purchase a lot of inventory at a time and not sell all of it during an accounting period. Even though it will have some leftover inventory, the business may still purchase more inventory to make sure it has enough on hand. The sum of the leftover inventory plus the newly purchased inventory is the amount that is available for sale. It is allocated to both ending inventory, on the balance sheet, and cost of goods sold, an expense on the income statement.

In earlier chapters, we used the **perpetual inventory system** where we assumed that inventory was expensed at the time the inventory was sold. TCC uses this system: when it sells its inventory and ships it to a customer, TCC credits the inventory account and debits the cost of goods sold account. This is an explicit transaction and would not require an adjusting entry.

The perpetual inventory system is a relatively common method and a good way to track inventory. Other companies use a **periodic inventory system** in which they periodically determine the cost of goods sold by physically counting the inventory and subtracting it from the sum of the inventory it had at the beginning of the period and the inventory it purchased during that period. This system requires adjusting entries because it records inventory as implicit transactions.

> Beginning Inventory
> Add: Purchased Inventory
> Less: Ending Inventory
> _____
> COGS

The sum of beginning inventory and inventory purchased during an accounting period is called **goods available for sale**. During an accounting period, these goods will either remain in inventory or be sold. The cost of goods sold for an accounting period is simply calculated by subtracting ending inventory from goods available for sale.

Let's consider a case where a business had $500 of inventory at the beginning of the accounting period and bought $900 of inventory during the period. At the end of the period, the inventory on hand was $800.

In order to determine the cost of goods sold using the periodic inventory system, the business would add $500 to $900 and then subtract $800. This results in a cost of goods sold of $600. The business would increase the cost of goods sold account with a debit and decrease inventory with a credit.

Thus,

Beginning Inventory	
Add: Purchased Inventory	
Inventory Available For Sale	
Less: Ending Inventory	
COGS	

Periodic Inventory System

Beginning Inventory	$500
Add: Purchased Inventory	900
Less: Ending Inventory	(800)
COGS	$600

Physical inventory counts are still important to do once in a while, even if a business always uses a perpetual inventory system. The number from the physical count can be compared to the perpetual inventory number to ensure accuracy. Sometimes, there are events that were not accounted for, such as shoplifting, recording errors, or damaged goods.

When the company recognizes that there is a difference in the numbers, it records an entry in the books to reconcile them.

For answers to the following questions, please see the end of Chapter 4.

Review 4.6 Question 1

Suppose a company had $200 of inventory on hand on January 1, 2013. It bought $400 of inventory during the accounting period and had $500 on hand on March 31, 2013. What adjustments would the company make to its statements?

    a.   Debit cost of goods sold by $100
    b.   Credit cost of goods sold by $500
    c.   Debit cost of goods sold by $500
    d.   Credit cost of goods sold by $100
    e.   Debit inventory $500
    f.   Credit inventory $100

Suppose a company uses the perpetual inventory method and records that there is $500 of inventory on hand. But the physical count reveals $300 of inventory. What should the company record? Please select all that apply.

a.   An expense for $200
b.   A gain on assets of $200
c.   Debit inventory for $200
d.   Credit inventory for $200

Inventory valuation is not straightforward because prices change over time. Suppose a company has inventory on hand that it bought for $2.00 a piece and then it buys more inventory for $3.00 a piece during the accounting period. How do you know whether a customer bought the $3.00 piece or the $2.00 piece?

Some businesses choose to track inventory and costs on an item-by-item basis. However, this is not very practical or efficient, so most companies make some logical assumptions about how to determine the amount they paid for inventory and the cost of goods sold.

Let's look at an example to understand the common methods for inventory valuation. Suppose The Construction Company had 1,000 hammers in its inventory. 200 were purchased at the start of the year, and they cost $10 per hammer. 400 were purchased in the third quarter when it cost $12 per hammer. The last 400 were purchased in the last quarter, when there was a big spike in costs, so the cost of those hammers was $14 per hammer. If TCC sold 500 hammers, what cost per hammer should be used when determining cost of goods sold? Should they be $10, $12, or $14?

One of the main methods to determine the correct figure for COGS is known as First In, First Out, or FIFO. This method assumes that items that enter into inventory first are the ones that leave inventory first. These are the items that are expensed or entered into Cost of Goods Sold first. Once all the items in the first production are gone, we move to the next newest items and use them to calculate COGS.

In this situation, the $10 hammers would be the first to leave TCC. It is likely that this method reflects the actual flow of inventory, and this is especially true in industries that involve perishables, but it's not required to use the FIFO method.

Since TCC sold 500 hammers, it sold all 200 hammers that cost $10 (the ones that were purchased first) and 300 hammers that cost $12 per hammer (the ones that were purchased second). So, the cost of goods sold under the FIFO method for the 500 hammers was $5,600 (200*$10 + 300*$12).

Another common method is **LIFO**, or Last In, First Out, which assumes that the newest items are expensed first and used to calculate COGS.

Under the LIFO method, TCC sold the $14 hammers first because they were the newest items, and once it finished selling the $14 hammers, it moved to selling the next most recent items, the $12 hammers. Under the LIFO method, the cost of goods sold was $6,800 (400*$14 + 100*$12).

LIFO and FIFO are very common methods used to value inventory, but there is also the **weighted average method**, which uses the average cost of all the items in inventory to calculate COGS.

There are some businesses, such as car dealers, where it makes the most sense to track the cost of individual items. These businesses use the **specific identification** inventory valuation method, which records each item in the inventory account at its specific cost. A car dealer has particularly unique and expensive inventory, so the previous methods discussed could significantly change the financials of the company, and it is most accurate to use individual costs of items.

IFRS does not allow companies to use the LIFO method, but all inventory methods are allowed under US GAAP.

For answers to the following questions, please see the end of Chapter 4.

Review 4.8 Question 1

Beaches Be Crazy (BBC) sells swimsuits, and since they are a seasonal item, they sell them as soon as possible to avoid the decrease in price at the end of summer. Which method is the most appropriate to value BBC's inventory?

    a.   LIFO
    b.   FIFO

Review 4.8 Question 2

Mark owns a candle store. On January 1, he buys 300 candles for $5 each. On January 15, he buys 100 candles for $7 each. On January 18, he sells 200 candles for $10 each. Select the correct value(s) for the COGS.

    a.   COGS under LIFO is $1,000.
    b.   COGS under LIFO is $1,200.
    c.   COGS under LIFO is $2,000.
    d.   COGS under FIFO is $1,000.
    e.   COGS under FIFO is $1,200.
    f.   COGS under FIFO is $2,000.

4.2.6   Product Manufacturing

Manufacturing businesses track inventory in a slightly different way. They generally have two categories of costs: **product costs** and **period costs**. The costs of buying materials to produce a good, manufacturing the good, and ultimately distributing it to customers are known as product costs. In the past examples we have studied, the product cost was simply the amount paid for the inventory. Product costs are tied to the product, and they are recorded as inventory when purchased and expensed as cost of goods sold when the products are sold.

The other type of costs, period costs, consists of all the other costs a company incurs while doing business. These do not directly apply to the products, but they do play a role in the company being able to successfully sell them. Examples of period costs include sales team salaries, marketing expenses, and office rent.

The accounting treatment for these two types of costs is different. Product costs are recorded on the balance sheet as inventory and expensed at the time of sale, whereas period costs are expensed in the period that they are incurred.

Manufacturing companies often use the **standard cost** inventory valuation method. This method values inventory and COGS at a calculated standard cost based on costs such as material, labor and overhead. Sometimes assigning the actual costs of these items to a product is too complex, so companies simplify the process by assigning an expected or standard cost.

The process to determine product costs is a bit complex for manufacturing businesses. Since they create their own inventory, and don't purchase it from a supplier, there are more steps in the process and different types of costs are incurred.

Manufacturing companies carefully track the costs of the production process, generally splitting inventory into several categories: raw materials, **work in process (WIP)**, and **finished goods**. It is important for manufacturing businesses to track the costs to this level of detail so that they can allocate the correct cost to each individual item in finished goods and can also expense the item for the proper amount when it is sold. Retail companies might also have some manufacturing activities, such as grocery stores that create prepared meals on-site.

Raw materials are the items a business uses in the initial stages of production. It includes supplies such as wood and nails for a chair manufacturing business or flour, sugar, and butter for a bakery. Businesses generally keep a supply of these raw materials on hand.

After removing an item from raw materials and shifting it to the production process, it is now under the inventory category called work in process (WIP). These are no longer considered raw materials because some work has been started on them, but they are not quite finished goods. An item might fall under the WIP category for a very short time frame, or it could be there for months. It depends how complicated the manufacturing process is. There are other costs, such as labor and **overhead** costs, which are also added to work in process inventory. It makes sense that the labor costs, specifically the wages paid to factory workers, fall under this category because they are directly associated with making the product.

Overhead costs are the costs in the manufacturing process that aren't directly applicable to a specific product. Some examples include utilities expenses for the factory building and depreciation of manufacturing equipment. Businesses allocate these overhead costs to the items they help produce.

The last category is finished goods inventory, and as the name suggests, these items have gone through the complete manufacturing process and are ready to be sold to customers. All of the previous costs, including raw materials, labor costs, and factory overhead, are included in the cost of finished goods inventory.

Let's look at the manufacturing process for M&M's, the famous candy-coated chocolate. The raw materials for M&M's would consist of items such as sugar, milk, cocoa, and food coloring. These would all be stored under the raw materials category.

The next step in the process is to take the raw materials and produce the goods. As the raw materials are used in the production process, they become part of the work in process costs. There are a number of machines involved in making M&M's, such as the mixers to make the chocolate, the machines to shape the chocolate, and the conveyer belts to pass the chocolate down to the candy coating machine. These equipment-related costs contribute a lot to the WIP costs. The overhead costs, including the depreciation on the equipment and the salary of the factory workers, are also included here.

The ultimate step in the process is packaging the candy to prepare it for shipment. This is also added to the work in process costs.

After this is completed, the total expenses from WIP, which includes the costs from many steps of the production process, are transferred to finished goods inventory.

As the M&M's are sold, the total cost of the packages sold are expensed on the income statement under cost of goods sold, and the remaining inventory that hasn't been sold yet stays under inventory on the balance sheet.

For answers to the following questions, please see the end of Chapter 4.

Review 4.9 Question 1

Match the cost to the correct category.

Research and development
Material to produce goods

a. Period cost
b. Product cost

Review 4.9 Question 2

Match the cost to the correct category.

Wages of factory workers
Executive salaries

a. Period cost
b. Product cost

Section 3
Deferrals and Accruals

Concepts

1. Deferred Revenues

2. Deferred Expenses

3. Accruing Revenues

4. Accruing Expenses

4.3.1   Deferred Revenue

In Chapter 1, we learned about situations where customers prepay for a good or service and the business promises to provide it later. At the end of each accounting period, the business recognizes the revenue it has earned.

A **deferral** occurs when a company delays recognizing revenue or expenses until a later point in time; the transfer of cash happens before the recognition. **Deferred revenue**, or **unearned revenue**, occurs when a company receives cash before it recognizes revenue.

A good example is a gym membership, where a person pays for a year-long subscription and attends the gym throughout the year. The business will decrease the deferred revenue liability and recognize a part of the revenue at the end of each month.

Suppose that a customer paid $600 for a year-long gym membership on January 1, 2013. To record this transaction, the gym would increase the asset cash by debiting it for $600 and increase the liability deferred revenue by crediting it for $600. It has not yet earned the revenue because it still has to provide the gym services.

The journal entry would look like this:

Date	Account Name	Debit	Credit
1/1/13	Cash	$ 600	
	Deferred revenue		600

On March 31, 2013, a quarter of the membership (3 out of 12 months) has been used up. Therefore, the company should decrease the balance sheet account deferred revenue by debiting it for $150 (($600 * (3/12 months)) and recognize $150 of revenues on the income statement.

The journal entry would look like this:

Date	Account Name	Debit	Credit
3/31/13	Deferred revenue	$ 150	
	Revenue		150

The deferred revenue account now has a credit balance of $450 ($600 - $150) to reflect the remaining obligation to provide gym services for 9 more months.

4.3.2   Deferred Expenses

A **deferred expense** occurs when a company pays cash for an item that it will recognize as an expense in a later period.

An example of a deferred expense is prepaid rent. Suppose that the gym prepays its rent of $18,000 in December 2012 for 6 months. To record this transaction, the gym would increase the asset prepaid rent, which is the deferred expense, by debiting it for $12,000, and it would also decrease the asset cash by crediting it for $12,000. The journal entry would look like this:

Date	Account Name	Debit	Credit
12/31/12	Prepaid rent	$12,000	
	Cash		$12,000

On January 31, 2013, the gym would recognize that 1 month of prepaid rent was used up. It would increase expenses by debiting the account for $2,000 and decrease prepaid rent by crediting the account for $2,000 ($12,000 * (1/6 months)).

Date	Account Name	Debit	Credit
1/31/13	Rent expense	$ 2,000	
	Prepaid rent		2,000

Now, the deferred expense account called prepaid rent has a balance of $10,000 ($12,000 -$2,000) to reflect that there are 5 more months of prepaid rent.

It's important to note that deferred revenue is not a revenue account but a liability account while deferred expense is not an expense account but an asset account.

4.3.3   Accruing Revenues

An **accrual** occurs when a company recognizes revenues or expenses immediately, before the transfer of cash happens. **Accrued revenue** occurs when revenue is reported before the company receives cash.

Suppose a consulting company signs a 3-month contract on July 1, 2013 to provide services to a customer, and it will receive a $15,000 payment once it turns in its final report. Over the 3-month period, the consulting company is earning revenue because it is working on the project, but it will ultimately receive cash on September 30, 2013.

At the end of the first month, on July 31, 2013, the company accrued 1/3 of the revenue. So, we would increase the asset accounts receivable by debiting it for $5,000 ($15,000 / 3) and we would also credit revenue for $5,000.

The journal entry would look like this:

Date	Account Name	Debit	Credit
7/31/13	Accounts receivable	$ 5,000	
	Revenue		5,000

The increase in accounts receivable and accrued revenue would occur at the end of each month of the consulting project. This follows the matching principle, which states that companies should recognize revenues and expenses during the period in which they occur, not when cash is exchanged. On September 30, 2013, the balance of accounts receivable and revenue would be $15,000 ($5,000 revenue for July + $5,000 revenue for August + $5,000 revenue for September).

When the cash payment ultimately occurs on September 30, 2013, the company would debit cash for $15,000 and credit accounts receivable for $15,000.

Date	Account Name	Debit	Credit
9/30/13	Cash	$15,000	
	Accounts receivable		15,000

4.3.4   Accruing Expenses

A company can also incur an expense before it actually pays for it. An **accrued expense** occurs when a company recognizes an expense before it pays out cash. A good example is interest paid on loans. Businesses are continually accruing interest on their loans, but they do not generally prepay the interest. Businesses usually make payments in arrears, at the end of a period.

In order to follow the matching principle, the company needs to record the obligation to pay interest during the period in which it helped generate revenues, not when the company actually pays the interest in cash. If a company accrued interest in June 2013, but pays it in July 2013, it would just record an entry at the end of June 2013 for a liability that it will pay later. In the following period, the company would make an adjustment to record the decrease in accrued interest and decrease in cash.

Suppose that The Construction Company needs to make an interest payment of $50,000 on a loan by January 15, 2014, for the interest related to the year 2013. On December 31, 2013, TCC would record an **accrued liability** for the interest payment called accrued interest or interest payable. TCC would debit interest expense by $50,000 and credit accrued interest by $50,000.

The journal entry would look like this:

Date	Account Name	Debit	Credit
12/31/13	Interest expense	$50,000	
	Accrued interest		50,000

When TCC actually makes the payment on January 15, 2014, it would debit accrued interest by $50,000 and credit cash by $50,000.

The journal entry would look like this:

Date	Account Name	Debit	Credit
1/15/14	Accrued interest	$50,000	
	Cash		50,000

Some other examples of accrued expenses include wages payable, **taxes payable**, and accrued utilities expense.

It can be challenging to recognize these adjustments because there is no invoice or clear sign that draws attention to them. One method many companies use is looking at the invoices for the next period to check if there are some that relate to the previous period. Invoices for the last few weeks of December 2013 would come in during early January 2014. These can notify accountants of adjustments they may have to make to December financials.

Another way to know when to make these adjustments is by relying on the experience of the accountants. Many entries are repeated year after year, so the accounting personnel has a good idea of what to expect. For example, some companies do regular reviews of potential legal obligations and create an estimated accrual account to account for this exposure.

The four basic adjustments we covered in this section include:

- converting liabilities to revenues (deferred revenues)
- converting assets to expenses (deferred liabilities)
- accruing revenues not yet collected
- accruing expenses not yet paid for

Remember that deferrals occur when cash transfers happen before the recognition of revenues or expenses and that accruals occur when cash transfers happen after the recognition of revenues or expenses. Lastly, **accrued expenses** are not expenses. Rather, they are liabilities. Likewise, **accrued revenue** is not a revenue but rather an asset.

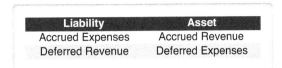

Liability	Asset
Accrued Expenses	Accrued Revenue
Deferred Revenue	Deferred Expenses

Adjusting entries can have a significant impact on a company's financial statements, so it is very important to account for them correctly. Adjustments are meant to capture all transactions, including those without clear triggers, so that readers of the financial statements have an accurate picture of the company.

For answers to the following questions, please see the end of Chapter 4.

Review 4.10 Question 1

Deferred revenues occur when a company

    a.   receives cash before recognizing revenues
    b.   pays out cash before recognizing revenues
    c.   receives cash after recognizing revenues
    d.   pays out cash after recognizing revenues

Review 4.10 Question 2

Suppose a company prepaid $60,000 on 1/1/13 for 1 year of insurance. This transaction would result in

    a.   deferred revenues
    b.   deferred expenses
    c.   accrued revenues
    d.   accrued expenses

Review 4.10 Question 3

Suppose a company prepaid $60,000 on 1/1/13 for 1 year of insurance. What journal entries would the company make **on 1/1/13**? Please select all that apply.

    a.   Debit deferred expenses by $60K
    b.   Credit accrued expenses by $60K
    c.   Debit cash by $60K
    d.   Credit cash by $60K

Review 4.10 Question 4

Suppose a company prepaid $60,000 on 1/1/13 for 1 year of insurance. What journal entries would the company make **on 3/31/13**? Please select all that apply.

    a.   Debit deferred expenses by $15K
    b.   Debit expenses by $15K
    c.   Credit deferred expenses by $15K
    d.   Credit expenses by $15K

Review 4.10 Question 5

Suppose a company prepaid $60,000 on 1/1/13 for 1 year of insurance. What would be the ending balance of the deferred expense account **on 3/31/13, after any adjustments**?

    a. $60K
    b. $45K
    c. $15K
    d. $0

Review 4.10 Question 6

The Ice Cream Shop (ICS) has a year end of December 31, 2013. Which of the following events will create an accrued revenue?

    a.   ICS pays rent for January 2014 in December 2013.
    b.   ICS pays its employees on December 31, 2013 for the previous two weeks.
    c.   ICS receives an invoice in January 2014 for delivery services it used in December 2013.
    d.   ICS loaned money to a customer at a 1% monthly interest rate. In January 2014, ICS receives the interest payment it was owed for December 2013.

Review 4.10 Question 7

The Ice Cream Shop (ICS) has a year end of December 31, 2013. Which of the following events will create an accrued expense?

    a.   ICS pays rent for January 2014 in December 2013.
    b.   ICS pays its employees on December 31, 2013 for the previous two weeks.
    c.   ICS receives an invoice in January 2014 for delivery services it used in December 2013.
    d.   ICS loaned money to a customer at a 1% monthly interest rate. In January 2014, ICS receives the interest payment it was owed for December 2013.

Section 4
Deferred Taxes

Concepts

4.4.1   Introduction

The past few lessons have discussed many adjusting accounting entries, and now we will learn about the adjustments required for tax entries.

There are many different factors that go into tax accounting entries, such as tax laws and tax codes for different states or countries and the **profitability** of the company. Although tax laws can be significantly different between countries, most countries impose taxes on for-profit companies, and the amount of taxes paid varies depending on the profitability of the company.

Tax-related accounts show up both on the income statement and the balance sheet. On the income statement, we have **income tax expense**, whereas on the balance sheet, we have deferred income taxes.

There are many places that you can find deferred income taxes on the balance sheet, including current or long-term assets, or current or long-term liabilities. For a company that recognizes revenue and depreciation at different times for financial reporting than it does for tax filings, the deferred income taxes could show up both as a short-term asset and a long-term liability.

Let's examine the details behind this accounting.

The majority of companies have two different sets of books: financial books and tax books. Although it sounds questionable to have two different books for the same company, it is legal and extremely common. The tax laws for a country don't necessarily line up with the country's financial reporting standards, so it is perfectly acceptable to use two different methods to report performance.

The people looking at the tax books and financial books have different perspectives. The tax authorities are looking at it from a tax collector and government policy maker perspective, and their rules about how to calculate taxable income can be different from how a business determines its income before taxes for financial reporting purposes.

Consider an example of these documents for a US company. The income statement and the income tax calculation document have some similarities, but the income before taxes is different from the taxable income.

On the tax return, there is the figure called **taxable income**. This is calculated by taking gross income and subtracting all of the company's **deductions**. Gross income is similar to gross profit, and it's calculated by taking a company's revenues and subtracting COGS. Deductions are a company's expenses that are legally allowed to be subtracted from gross income for tax calculation purposes. There are different tax codes for different regions, so it's important to check which deductions are allowed.

On the income statement, there is **income before taxes**, which is revenues and gains less all losses and expenses, except for tax expenses. The deductions on the tax return don't have to be equivalent to the expenses on the income statement. Even more, the gross income for the tax statement doesn't have to equal the gross profit for revenues for that matter from the income statement.

The next few lessons will show examples of the different calculations and identify how they affect the accounts. We will focus on situations where the differences are temporary and reverse over time, carefully walking through the changes in accounts.

4.4.2   Deferred Tax Liabilities

Depreciation is one item that can create a temporary timing difference between taxable income and income before taxes. Some companies may wish to record more depreciation in the early years on their tax statements so that they can pay fewer taxes. But they also want to show investors that they generated a lot of earnings, so they want a small depreciation expense on their income statement.

As we learned in the previous section, there are many ways to calculate depreciation, and long-lived assets can be depreciated using the straight line method for financial statements but the accelerated method for tax purposes. This would cause the company to have two different depreciation amounts – initially, a small depreciation expense in the financial records and a larger deduction for depreciation in the tax records. This also means that income before taxes, or **pretax income**, would be higher than taxable income. Since the company uses the lower taxable income to determine how much it owes in taxes, it pays less in taxes than if it had just used the pretax profit from the income statement to calculate its tax obligation.

However, this tax difference does not last forever. In future years, the tax depreciation will be lower than the book depreciation. This will cause the lower tax payment this year to be offset by a higher tax payment in a future year. Essentially, some of the taxes that will be due in the future will actually relate to income reported in the current period. This is recorded as a **Deferred Tax Liability**, and it reflects the obligation to pay taxes in the future on the income in the current period.

Let's look at an example to understand the journal entries. On 12/31/13, ABC company reports $40,000 in income before taxes, but its taxable income is only $15,000 because of differences in depreciation between the tax return and financial statements. If the income tax rate is 40%, ABC would have $16,000 ($40,000 * 40%) in income tax expense. However, it would only have $6,000 ($15,000 * 40%) of taxes on its tax return. The journal entries would look like this:

Date	Account Name	Debit	Credit
12/31/13	Income tax expense	$16,000	
	Income taxes payable		6,000
	Deferred tax liability		10,000

The main takeaway from this example is that a Deferred Tax Liability represents the obligation to pay taxes in the future on income reported in the current accounting period. As you can see, income tax expense is based on the income before taxes, and **taxes payable** is based on taxable income. In this situation, the difference between the two figures is reconciled with a deferred tax liability.

For answers to the following questions, please see the end of Chapter 4.

Review 4.11 Question 1

A deferred tax liability occurs when taxable income is temporarily smaller than reported income on the income statement.

- a. True
- b. False

Review 4.11 Question 2

Suppose a company has income before taxes of $20,000 and taxable income of $15,000. Its tax rate is 30%. What will its income tax expense be?

- a. $6,000
- b. $4,500
- c. $1,500

Review 4.11 Question 3

Suppose a company has income before taxes of $20,000 and taxable income of $15,000. Its tax rate is 30%. What will its taxes payable be?

- a. $6,000
- b. $4,500
- c. $1,500

$40k
-$4k
_____
$36k → $9k in Taxes
          @ 25% rate

$20k → $5k in taxes
          @ 25% rate

Suppose a company has income before taxes of $20,000 and taxable income of $15,000. Its tax rate is 30%. What would be the increase in deferred tax liability?

- a. $6,000
- b. $5,000
- c. $4,500
- d. $1,500

Over the life of a company, the balance of deferred tax asset and deferred tax liability accounts will go to zero.

- a. True
- b. False

4.4.3 Deferred Tax Assets

In addition to Deferred Tax Liabilities, there are also **Deferred Tax Assets.** These reflect that a company overpaid its taxes for the current period by prepaying taxes for income that will be reported in the future. Deferred tax assets are calculated by finding the difference between the higher taxes payable (based off of the taxable income found on the income tax report) and the lower income tax expense (based off of the income before taxes found on the financial report).

Deferred taxes can be split between current and non-current sections of the balance sheet, and the classification depends on when the company expects to resolve the timing differences between the financial statements and the tax returns. Consistent with our former definitions of current vs. non-current, the portion of the deferred tax that is expected to be resolved within one year is classified as current. Those amounts that will be resolved in over a year are listed under the non-current section.

Let's look at Spartan Gym, a business that often receives prepayments for its gym memberships. Since Spartan Gym files its taxes on a cash basis, and it receives cash in advance from customers, the cash is considered taxable income. When Spartan Gym files its financial statements, it defers the revenue and recognizes it over the year-long period of the membership. This timing difference results in a Deferred Tax Asset.

Suppose a company's income before taxes is $40,000 and its taxable income is $60,000. At a 40% tax rate, the income tax expense would be $16,000 ($40,000 * 40%) and the tax return would show taxes payable of $24,000 ($60,000 * 40%). This would result in a deferred tax asset of $8,000 ($24,000 - $16,000). The journal entry would look like this:

Date	Account Name	Debit	Credit
12/31/13	Income tax expense	$16,000	
	Deferred tax asset	8,000	
	Income taxes payable		24,000

Review 4.12 Question 1

Suppose a company has $40,000 in financial net income and $50,000 in taxable net income. This temporary timing difference would result in a:

    a.   Deferred tax asset

    b.   Deferred tax liability

Review 4.12 Question 2

Suppose a company has $10,000 in income tax expense and $8,000 in taxes payables. This would result in an:

    a.   Increase to a deferred tax asset

    b.   Increase to a deferred tax liability

Review 4.12 Question 3

Suppose a company has $20,000 in income before taxes and $30,000 in taxable income. Its tax rate is 40%. What would its income tax expense be?

    a. $12,000

    b. $8,000

    c. $4,000

Review 4.12 Question 4

Suppose a company has $20,000 in income before taxes and $30,000 in taxable income. Its tax rate is 40%. What would its taxes payable be?

    a. $12,000

    b. $8,000

    c. $4,000

Suppose a company has $20,000 in income before taxes and $30,000 in taxable income. Its tax rate is 40%. What would be the increase in deferred tax asset?

    a. $12,000
    b. $10,000
    c. $8,000
    d. $4,000

4.4.4   Review of DTLs and DTAs

As we have seen, different situations can lead to Deferred Tax Assets or Deferred Tax Liabilities. Deferred Tax Assets are recorded when the timing difference leads to higher taxable income than pretax income. When the timing difference causes pretax income to be higher than taxable income, a Deferred Tax Liability account is created to reflect the obligation to pay taxes in the future.

There are other situations in which deferred tax entries are recorded, but this book will not go into that level of detail. One important concept to remember is that the tax books, not the financial books, are used to determine tax payments. So, a change in accounting policies typically does not impact cash flows.

As we know, a company can use straight line depreciation for its financial books and accelerated deprecation for its tax books. If the company chooses to change its depreciation method and apply the accelerated depreciation method in both situations, the change would not affect the amount or timing of cash flows. There would no longer be a difference in the depreciation amounts, or a difference between the taxable income and the pretax income, so the deferred tax amount would be eliminated. But this would not change the actual cash flow, which is based on the tax books that have not changed.

4.4.5   Judgment Calls

It's clear that many transactions and adjustments to the financial statements require managerial judgment to determine the best way to account for a situation. Businesses use their assets in different ways, and it's impossible to create rules that would apply in every situation. For example, a graphic design company might depreciate its computers over 2 years because it needs to upgrade them frequently to have the best software, whereas an accounting firm can depreciate them over 5 years because the software doesn't change.

It's important for management to be honest when determining the amount and timing of adjustments, making sure that they reflect the operations of the business. This makes the financial statements relevant and useful to its users.

The flexibility in judgment creates windows of opportunity for individuals to manipulate the statements and report incorrect information. There have been many accounting scandals over the years, and the Enron case is particularly infamous. Enron hid billions of dollars of debt from the financial statements, which eventually led the company to file for bankruptcy. Even though just a few individuals were behind the scandal, it had significant consequences, and investors lost billions.

It is essential that you are ethical when exercising judgment and applying accounting principles. Many people rely on financial statements to provide reliable information, and they expect you to fairly represent the information.

Section 5
Review

Explicit transactions are caused by an event that "triggers" the transaction, and we can easily identify the amount and timing of the transaction

Implicit transactions do not have a "trigger" and in general, the timing and the amount of the transaction are not clearly defined. Implicit transactions are recorded by adjusting journal entries.

Adjustments

- never involve cash
- don't involve external parties
- are only recorded internally
- are recorded at the end of an accounting period

There are many different types of adjustments made during an accounting period, such as gains or losses on sales, impairments, depreciation and amortization expense, and recognizing inventory used.

Examples of	
Explicit Transactions	**Implicit Transactions**
Purchasing machinery	Recognizing the use/consumption of pre-paid insurance
Selling goods or services	Recording an impairment loss
Paying wages	Recognizing depreciation of equipment
Paying rent	Recognizing amortization of a patent
Collecting receivables	Recording office supplies used
Recognizing a loss on the disposal of an asset	

Depreciation

Straight line method splits up the depreciation expense of the asset into equal amounts and recognizes the expense over time.

Accelerated depreciation methods deduct more depreciation expense in the early years of an asset's life and less in the later years.

Depreciation expense is a contra-asset account, which means its balance is usually the opposite of typical asset accounts.

The temporary account, depreciation expense, is shown on the income statement and only shows the expense for the income statement period. The permanent account, accumulated depreciation, consists of all the depreciation expense recognized against the asset. It is a cumulative figure.

Straight line method:

$$\text{Depreciation Expense} = \frac{\text{Gross Book Value - Salvage Value}}{\text{Useful Life}}$$

$$\text{Accumulated Depreciation} = \frac{\text{Depreciation}}{\text{Expense per Period}} * \frac{\text{Number of}}{\text{Periods}}$$

Inventory

The **perpetual inventory system** expenses inventory when it is sold. It's an explicit transaction that doesn't require an adjustment.

The **periodic inventory system** is a system where companies periodically determine the cost of goods sold and requires adjusting entries because it records inventory as implicit transactions. It uses the formula:

```
  Beginning Inventory
     Add: Purchased Inventory
  Inventory Available For Sale
     Less: Ending Inventory
  COGS
```

Common Inventory Valuation Methods: FIFO, LIFO, Weighted Average, Specific Identification

FIFO (First In, First Out) is a method that assumes that items that enter into inventory first are the ones that leave inventory first. They are the items that are expensed or entered into Cost of Goods Sold first.

LIFO (Last In, First Out) is a method that assumes that the newest items are expensed first and used to calculate COGS. IFRS does not allow the LIFO method.

Product Manufacturing

Product costs are tied to the product (buying materials to produce a good, manufacture it and distribute it), and they are recorded as inventory when purchased and expensed as cost of goods sold when the products are sold.

Period costs are all the other costs a company incurs while doing business that do not directly apply to the products, such as marketing expenses and office rent.

Manufacturing companies typically have three steps to the production process used to track inventory: **raw materials, work in process (WIP), and finished goods**.

Deferrals and Accruals

A **deferral** occurs when a company **delays recognizing revenue or expenses until a later point in time**; the transfer of cash happens before the recognition.

Deferred revenue, or unearned revenue, occurs when a company receives cash before it recognizes revenue.

A deferred expense occurs when a company pays cash for an item that it will recognize as an expense in a later period.

Deferred revenue is not a revenue account but a liability account and deferred expense is not an expense account but an asset account.

An **accrual** occurs when a company **recognizes revenues or expenses immediately, before the transfer of cash happens.**

Accrued revenue occurs when revenue is reported before the company receives cash.

An accrued expense occurs when a company recognizes an expense before it pays out cash.

Accrued expense is not an expense account but a liability account and accrued revenue is not a revenue account but an asset account.

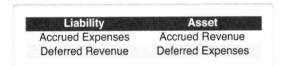

Liability	Asset
Accrued Expenses	Accrued Revenue
Deferred Revenue	Deferred Expenses

Taxes

Income tax expense appears on the income statement and **deferred income tax** appears on the balance sheet.

Taxable income, which is gross income less deductions, appears on the tax return.

Pretax income, which is revenues and gains less all losses and expenses, except for tax expenses, appears on the income statement.

A **deferred tax liability** represents the obligation to pay taxes in the future on income reported in the current accounting period. Deferred tax liabilities are calculated by finding the difference between the higher income tax expense (based off of the income before taxes found on the financial report) and the lower taxes payable (based off of the taxable income found on the income tax report).

A **deferred tax asset** reflects that a company overpaid its taxes for the current period by prepaying taxes for income that will be reported in the future. Deferred tax assets are calculated by finding the difference between the higher taxes payable (based off of the taxable income found on the income tax report) and the lower income tax expense (based off of the income before taxes found on the financial report).

Section 6
Review Questions

For answers to the following questions, please see the end of Chapter 1.

Review 4.13 Question 1

State whether the following transaction is implicit or explicit.

Prepaying two years of insurance

    a.   Implicit
    b.   Explicit

Review 4.13 Question 2

State whether the following transaction is implicit or explicit.

Purchasing a building

    a.   Implicit
    b.   Explicit

Review 4.13 Question 3

State whether the following transaction is implicit or explicit.

Recording depreciation on equipment

    a.   Implicit
    b.   Explicit

Review 4.13 Question 4

Accumulated depreciation is shown on the

    a.   Balance Sheet
    b.   Income Statement

Review 4.13 Question 5

Contra-asset accounts increase with credits and decrease with debits.

a. True
b. False

Review 4.13 Question 6

Consider the methods listed below. Which one would result in higher taxes in the earlier years?

a. Straight line method
b. Double declining balance method
c. Cannot be determined

Review 4.13 Question 7

Using a different depreciation method for financial statements and tax returns is deceitful.

a. True
b. False

Review 4.13 Question 8

Businesses should track each individual item so they can know when it is sold and have an accurate value for its inventory and COGs figures.

a. True
b. False

Review 4.13 Question 9

Product costs are...
Please select all that apply.

    a.   recorded on the balance sheet to the extent it pertains to unsold inventory

    b.   expensed at the time of sale

    c.   expensed in the period that they are incurred

Review 4.13 Question 10

ABC company has a year end of June 30, 2014. Which of the following events will create an accrued expense?

    a.   ABC buys a new machine on June 1, 2014.

    b.   ABC pays its employees on the 15th of every month.

    c.   ABC pays its insurance for the period January 1, 2014 – June 30, 2014 in December 2013.

Review 4.13 Question 11

Suppose a company has $12,000 in income tax expense and $6,000 in taxes payables. This temporary timing difference would result in a:

    a.   Deferred tax asset

    b.   Deferred tax liability

Review 4.13 Question 12

A deferred tax asset is created as the result of a temporary timing difference between taxable income and income before taxes.

    a.   True

    b.   False

Review 4.13 Question 13

A company can pay less total taxes on its tax returns if it uses deferred tax liabilities.

    a.   True
    b.   False

Review 4.13 Question 14

TCC bought a machine for $7,000 on 1/1/2014 and expects to sell it for $2,000 on 12/31/2018. Based on the straight line depreciation method, what would the depreciation listed on the income statement be for the year ended 12/31/2015?

    a. $1,000
    b. $1,250
    c. $2,000
    d. $2,500

Review 4.13 Question 15

TCC bought a machine for $7,000 on 1/1/2014 and expects to sell it for $2,000 on 12/31/2018. Based on the straight line depreciation method, what would the accumulated depreciation listed on the balance sheet be as of 12/31/2015?

    a. $1,000
    b. $1,250
    c. $2,000
    d. $2,500

Section 7

Answer Key

Review 4.1 Explanations

Question 1

Answer: B

Paying two years of rent in advance is an explicit transaction. There is a clear event that triggers the transaction, and the amount and timing of the transaction can be identified.

Question 2

Answer: B

Purchasing equipment is an explicit transaction. There is a clear event that triggers the transaction, and the amount and timing of the transaction can be identified.

Question 3

Answer: A

Recording depreciation on equipment is an implicit transaction. There is no clear event that triggers a journal entry, and the timing and amount are not clearly defined. Businesses need to use their best judgment when deciding how to record depreciation.

Question 4

Answer: B

Paying wages is an explicit transaction. There is a clear event that triggers the transaction, and the amount and timing of the transaction can be identified.

Question 5

Answer: A

Expiration of prepaid rent is an implicit transaction. There is no clear event that triggers a journal entry, and the timing and amount are not clearly defined.

Review 4.2 Explanations

Question 1

Answer: B

Accumulated depreciation, the sum of all the depreciation recognized over the life of an asset, generally has a credit, not a debit, balance. Assets generally have debit balances, but accumulated depreciation is a contra-asset account, so it has a credit balance.

Question 2

Answer: A

Accumulated depreciation is shown on the balance sheet as a contra-asset. Depreciation expense is shown on the income statement.

Question 3

Answer: A

Recording depreciation expense on the income statement is an application of the matching principle. The expense for the asset should be recognized during the same period in which it provides the benefit, and depreciation expense is recognized over time as the asset is used up. The historical cost principle states that transactions should be recorded at the actual price paid at the time of the transaction.

Question 4

Answer: A, C

The cost of an asset minus the accumulated depreciation can be called the book value, the net book value, the net asset value, or the carrying value.

Review 4.3 Explanations

Question 1

Answer: B

The double declining balance method would result in lower net income in the earlier years than the straight line method. The double declining balance method is an accelerated depreciation method that records more depreciation expense early on, which lowers net income. The units of measure method is used for assets that have a fixed output, and depreciation expense is recorded based on the number of products produced.

Question 2

Answer: B

The double declining balance method would result in lower taxes in the earlier years than the straight line method. The double declining balance method is an accelerated depreciation method that records more depreciation expense early on, which lowers net income. Since net income is lower, the company pays fewer taxes than it would have had to pay if it had used the straight line method. The units of measure method is used for assets that have a fixed output, and depreciation expense is recorded based on the number of products produced.

Question 3

Answer: A

It is possible for one business to depreciate its computers over a period of 2 years and another business to depreciate the same computers over 5 years. A business has the discretion to choose the depreciation method that is most appropriate for the business. For example, one company might need to replace its computers every two years because it needs the latest technology and another company can depreciate its computers over 5 years because they don't need to replace them as often.

Question 4

Answer: B

The double declining balance method does not recognize more total depreciation than the straight line method. The methods only vary in terms of the timing of the depreciation expense.

Question 5

Answer: A

The double declining balance method is an accelerated depreciation method that records more depreciation expense in the earlier years of an asset's life than the straight line method.

Review 4.4 Explanations

Question 1

Answer: C

Loss on impairment is calculated by subtracting the asset's market value from the book value. The net book value of the asset is $50,000 ($55,000 historical cost - $5,000 accumulated depreciation). The loss on impairment is $20,000 ($50,000 book value - $30,000 market value).

Question 2

Answer: A, C

Using the first method to record an impairment, we would debit Loss on Impairment for $20,000 and credit Accumulated Depreciation for $20,000 bringing the carrying value of the asset to $30,000. Using the second method, we would debit Loss on Impairment for $20,000, debit Accumulated Depreciation for $5,000, and credit the asset for $25,000. Of the options, only A and C show entries corresponding to the first method.

Question 3

Answer: B

The value of the building on the balance sheet will be $30,000, the market value of the building. $50,000 is the previous book value of the building, and $20,000 is the loss on impairment.

Question 4

Answer: A

The future depreciation expense should be calculated off of the new book value of the building.

Review 4.5 Explanations

Question 1

Answer: B

A building is a physical asset that should be depreciated over time.

Question 2

Answer: C

Land should never be depreciated or amortized.

Question 3

Answer: A

A patent is a non-physical asset that should be amortized over time.

Question 4

Answer: A

Pre-paid insurance is a non-physical asset that should be amortized over time.

Question 5

Answer: B

Equipment is a physical asset that should be depreciated over time.

Question 6

Answer: C

Goodwill should never be depreciated or amortized.

Review 4.6 Explanations

Question 1

Answer: A, F

The company had $200 on hand on January 1, 2013, bought $400 of inventory during the accounting period and had $500 on hand on March 31, 2013. We know that beginning inventory + purchased inventory − ending inventory = COGS. So, COGS = $200 + $400 − $500 = $100. The company should debit (increase) COGS by $100 and credit (decrease) inventory by $100 to reflect the inventory sold by the company.

Review 4.7 Explanations

Question 1

Answer: A, D

The company should credit (decrease) inventory for $200 and record an expense for $200.

Review 4.8 Explanations

Question 1

Answer: B

FIFO is the most appropriate method because it values inventory at a price that reflects what the product is currently worth. The LIFO method would likely value inventory at outdated prices (because the swimsuits are worth less after the swimsuit season is over) and could overstate the market value of the inventory.

Question 2

Answer: B, D

LIFO refers to last in, first out. Mark sold 200 candles on January 18th. The first candles he sold were the 100 candles that cost $7 each. The next candles he sold were from the 300 candle batch that cost $5 each. So, under LIFO, Mark's COGS was 100*$7 + 100*$5 =$1,200. FIFO refers to first in, first out. Mark sold 200 candles on January 18th. The candles he sold were all from the first batch of candles he bought, the 300 candles that cost $5 each. So, under FIFO, Mark's COGS was 200*$5 = $1,000.

Review 4.9 Explanations

Question 1

Answer: Research and development: period cost, material to produce goods: product cost

Research and development would be a period cost. It does not directly apply to a product, but it does play an indirect role in a company being able to sell its products. The material to produce goods would be a product cost because it is a cost that is directly tied to a product and is necessary to manufacture the product.

Question 2

Answer: Wages of factory workers: product cost, executive salaries: period cost

The wages of factory workers are product costs because they are directly tied to the manufacturing of a product. Executive salaries are period costs because they are not directly tied to a product, but they are still costs that are necessary to sell the products.

Review 4.10 Explanations

Question 1

Answer: A

Deferrals occur when the cash transfer happens before the recognition of revenues or expenses and accruals occur when the cash transfer happens after the recognition of revenues or expenses. So, deferred revenue occurs when a company receives cash before recognizing revenues.

Question 2

Answer: B

If a company prepaid $60,000 for 1 year of insurance, it results in an asset for the company that will be used up over the course of the year. The cash transfer happened before the recognition of the expense, so it is a deferred expense.

Question 3

Answers: A, D

Prepaying insurance on 1/1/13 results in a deferred expense because the cash transfer occurred before the recognition of the expense. On 1/1/13, we have to increase the asset deferred expense, so we would debit deferred expenses by $60K. We also need to decrease the asset cash by $60K, so we would credit cash by $60K.

Question 4

Answers: B, C

On 3/31/13, after one quarter of the year has passed and one quarter of the prepaid insurance has been used up, we need to decrease the asset deferred expense by $15K ($60K / 4). So, we credit deferred expenses by $15K. We also need to recognize the expense, and debits increase the expense account, so we debit expenses by $15K.

Question 5

Answer: B

On 3/31/13, we decrease the asset deferred expense by $15K ($60K / 4) to reflect that we have recognized insurance expense. After this adjustment, the balance of the deferred expense account is now $60K - $15K = $45K.

Question 6

Answer: D

If ICS pays in December 2013 for the rent it owes for January 2014, this transaction would increase the account pre-paid rent, which is an asset. If ICS pays its employees on December 31, 2013 for the work its employees' previously completed, this transaction would decrease the accrued expense wages payable. If ICS receives an invoice in January 2014 for services it previously received in December 2013, this transaction would create the accrued expense delivery services. If ICS was owed interest revenue in December 2013 but was not paid until January 2014, it would create the account accrued interest revenue. ICS recognized revenue in December before the transfer of cash happened.

Question 7

Answer: C

If ICS pays in December 2013 for the rent it owes for January 2014, this transaction would increase the account pre-paid rent, which is an asset. If ICS pays its employees on December 31, 2013 for the work its employees' previously completed, this transaction would decrease the accrued expense wages payable. If ICS receives an invoice in January 2014 for services it previously received in December 2013, this transaction would create the accrued expense delivery services.

Review 4.11 Explanations

Question 1

Answer: A

A deferred tax liability occurs when taxable income is smaller than reported income on the income statement. This will create the obligation to pay taxes in the future on the income reported in the current period.

Question 2

Answer: A

Income tax expense is a company's income before taxes multiplied by its tax rate. Since the company has a 30% tax rate and income before taxes of $20,000, the company's income tax expense would be $20,000 * 30% = $6,000.

Question 3

Answer: B

Taxes payable is equal to taxable income multiplied by a company's tax rate. Since the company has a 30% tax rate and taxable income of $15,000, the company's taxes payable would be $15,000 * 30% = $4,500.

Question 4

Answer: D

Deferred tax liabilities are calculated by finding the difference between the higher income tax expense (based off of the income before taxes found on the financial report) and the lower taxes payable (based off of the taxable income found on the income tax report). This company has income tax expense of $6,000 ($20,000 * 30%) and taxes payable of $4,500 ($15,000 * 40%), so the increase in deferred tax liability would be $6,000 - $4,500 = $1,500.

Question 5

Answer: A

Over the life of a company, the balance of deferred tax asset accounts and deferred tax liability accounts will go to zero. These accounts are temporary timing differences that will resolve over the life of a company.

Review 4.12 Explanations

Question1

Answer: A

Deferred tax assets arise when a company has higher taxable net income reported on its tax statement than it has in financial net income reported on its income statement. So, if a company has $40,000 in financial net income and $50,000 in taxable net income, it would create a deferred tax asset. The company will have to pay fewer taxes in the future.

Question 2

Answer: B

Deferred tax liabilities arise when a company has higher tax expense than taxes payable or when a company has higher financial net income than taxable net income. So, if a company has $10,000 in income tax expense and $8,000 in taxes payables, it would create a deferred tax liability. The company will have to pay more taxes in the future.

Question 3

Answer: B

Income tax expense is a company's income before taxes multiplied by its tax rate. Since the company has a 40% tax rate and income before taxes of $20,000, the company's income tax expense would be $20,000 * 40% = $8,000.

Question 4

Answer: A

Taxes payable is equal to taxable income multiplied by a company's tax rate. Since the company has a 40% tax rate and taxable income of $30,000, the company's taxes payable would be $30,000 * 40% = $12,000.

Question 5

Answer: D

Deferred tax assets are calculated by finding the difference between the higher taxes payable (based off of the taxable income found on the income tax report) and the lower income tax expense (based off of the income before taxes found on the financial report). This company has taxes payable of $12,000 ($30,000 * 40%) and income tax expense of $8,000 ($20,000 * 40%), so the increase in deferred tax asset would be $12,000 - $8,000 = $4,000.

Chapter Review 4.13 Explanations

Question 1

Answer: B

Prepaying two years of insurance is an explicit transaction. There is a clear event that triggers the transaction, and the amount and timing of the transaction can be identified.

Question 2

Answer: B

Purchasing a building is an explicit transaction. There is a clear event that triggers the transaction, and the amount and timing of the transaction can be identified.

Question 3

Answer: A

Recording depreciation on equipment is an implicit transaction. There is no clear event that triggers a journal entry, and the timing and amount are not clearly defined. Businesses need to use their best judgment when deciding how to record depreciation.

Question 4

Answer: A

Accumulated depreciation, the sum of all depreciation recognized over the life of an asset, is shown on the balance sheet.

Question 5

Answer: A

Contra-asset accounts have balances that are opposite those of normal asset accounts. Unlike asset accounts, contra-asset accounts increase with credits and decrease with debits.

Question 6

Answer: A

The straight line method would result in higher taxes in the earlier years than the double declining balance or units of measure methods. The double declining balance method is an accelerated depreciation method, and it depreciates an asset more quickly in the early years, resulting in lower net income and lower taxes in the earlier years than the straight line method.

Question 7

Answer: B

Using a different depreciation method for financial statements and tax returns is not manipulative. Eventually, the same amount of depreciation will be recognized.

Question 8

Answer: B

Businesses do not need to track the cost of each individual item to know when it is sold and have the correct inventory and COGS figures. It is not practical to track individual items, and most companies can use inventory valuation methods that closely approximate the cost of individual items.

Question 9

Answer: A, B

Product costs are directly tied to the product and are necessary costs in order to manufacture the product. These costs are recorded on the balance sheet as inventory and expensed at the time of sale. Period costs are costs incurred while doing business but not directly tied to a product. Period costs are expensed at the time they are incurred.

Question 10

Answer: B

If ABC Company pays its employees on the 15th of every month, it creates an accrued expense called wages payable, so the correct answer is B. The company recognized an expense before it actually paid the cash to its employees. If ABC Company buys a new machine on June 1, 2014, it will be a straightforward transaction where the company simply increases PP&E and decreases cash, not create an accrued expense, so answer A is incorrect. If ABC Company prepays its insurance in December 2013 for the period January 1, 2014 - June 30, 2014, it will create a deferred expense, so answer C is incorrect. The company prepaid cash for an expense it will recognize at a later period.

Question 11

Answer: B

If a company has higher income tax expense than taxes payable, it creates a deferred tax liability, and the company will have to pay more taxes in the future related to transactions that occurred in the past. So, if a company that has $12,000 in income tax expense and $6,000 in taxes payable, it will create a deferred tax liability.

Question 12

Answer: A

A deferred tax asset is a result of a temporary timing difference between taxable income and income before taxes. It will be reversed over time as the company recognizes more tax expense in its income statement and decreases the deferred tax asset.

Question 13

Answer: B

If a company has deferred tax liabilities, it will not pay less total taxes on its tax return. Deferred tax liabilities are temporary timing differences that are reversed over time.

Question 14

Answer: A

The depreciation expense listed on the income statement would be $1,000. The formula for calculating depreciation expense using the straight line method is (gross book value - salvage value) / useful life. The useful life of the asset is 5 years (1/1/14 to 12/31/18), so the depreciation expense each year would be ($7,000 - $2,000) / 5 years = $1,000.

Question 15

Answer: C

As of 12/31/2015, the accumulated depreciation would be the sum of two years of depreciation expense: $1,000 + $1,000 = $2,000. The formula for calculating depreciation expense using the straight line method is (gross book value - salvage value) / useful life. The useful life of the asset is 5 years (1/1/14 to 12/31/18), so the depreciation expense each year would be ($7,000 - $2,000) / 5 years = $1,000, and the accumulated depreciation as of 12/31/2015 would be $2,000.

5

Statement of Cash Flows

Sections

Section 1

Introduction

Concepts

1. Statement of Cash Flows

5.1.1   Statement of Cash Flows

In Chapter 3, we discussed two of the three major financial statements: the income statement and the balance sheet. This chapter will cover the remaining statement: the cash flow statement. We will learn how to build the statement and also how to analyze it in order to understand how a company is performing.

The cash flow statement tracks a company's cash flows throughout an accounting period. It shows what the total cash balances were at the beginning and the end of the period, where it received additional cash from, and how a company spent its cash. Users of the cash flow statement can gain a better idea of a company's **liquidity** and solvency because it's easy to see whether the company will have enough cash to buy resources or repay creditors.

The majority of companies use accrual accounting. This means that when revenues are earned, it does not necessarily imply that cash was received. It is possible for a company to accrue revenue and receive the cash at a later date. If a business reports $20,000 in net income, it does not mean that the business increased its cash by $20,000; it's possible that some of the income was due to a receivable or some cash was spent to purchase assets or pay down loans. If a business has positive net income, it does not always mean that it has positive cash flows.

The cash flow statement is used to determine whether a company is generating cash. Many people believe that cash flow from operations cannot be manipulated, but this belief is a misconception. It's possible for companies to engage in accounting tricks, such as misclassifying expenses, to boost their cash flow from operations. This is why it's so important to get a complete picture of a company by using the cash flow statement in conjunction with the income statement. It's great for a company to earn a lot of money, but if it is having cash flow issues, or not generating enough cash for shareholders, it may not be a good investment.

In order to evaluate a company's performance, investors often look at net income. However, it's also helpful to analyze a company's cash flows to determine where cash is generated and how it is being used. The financial statements should be used together to truly understand a company. The cash flow statement provides details about cash inflows and outflows that ultimately help us value a business and evaluate its liquidity.

There is lot of information that is necessary in order to create a cash flow statement. In particular, we need the income statement, the balance sheet information for the beginning and end of the accounting period, and some transactional data.

There are three separate sections of a cash flow statement: Operating Activities, Investing Activities, and Financing Activities. The organization of the statement varies depending on whether the company follows IFRS or US GAAP, and these variations will be pointed out throughout this chapter.

For answers to the following questions, please see the end of Chapter 5.

Review 5.1 Question 1

If a business has positive net income, it must have positive cash flows.

    a.   True
    b.   False

Review 5.1 Question 2

How would the following transaction impact the cash flow of a business?

Purchasing equipment on credit

    a.   Increase cash flow
    b.   Decrease cash flow
    c.   No impact

Review 5.1 Question 3

How would the following transaction impact the cash flow of a business?

Paying down a loan

    a.   Increase cash flow
    b.   Decrease cash flow
    c.   No impact

Review 5.1 Question 4

How would the following transaction impact the cash flow of a business?

Selling inventory on credit

    a.   Increase cash flow

    b.   Decrease cash flow

    c.   No impact

Section 2
Operating Activities: Direct Method

Concepts

1. Operating Activities

2. Direct Method

5.2.1   Operating Activities

The cash flow statement starts with the Operating Activities section. As the name suggests, this part shows all the cash flows relating to operating activities, or preparing and providing goods and services to customers. For Acorns Bakery, it includes cash used to purchase supplies and manufacture the products as well as the cash received from selling its products to customers.

For AMC Entertainment Holdings, Inc., a company that owns and operates movie theaters, operating activities would include cash earned from selling tickets to customers, expenses to operate the theaters, and wages paid to employees. Cash Flow from Operations also includes taxes paid and depreciation and amortization.

The operating section provides insight into the operating decisions that management makes, and it is probably the most helpful part of the cash flow statement. The cash flows that apply to current asset and current liability accounts are usually found in the operating section.

It's important to remember that the net income figure using the cash accounting method is different from net income using the accrual method. The operating section of the cash flow statement can be thought of as showing the net operating income figure under the cash accounting method by removing the income statement components that don't impact the cash account and don't relate to the company's operations.

If the company is following US GAAP, interest paid on borrowings will be included under operating activities. If the company follows IFRS, it can choose where it wants to place interest paid: the operating section or the financing section.

Another key difference between US GAAP and IFRS is the treatment of dividends paid. Under US GAAP, dividends paid are included in the financing section. But under IFRS, a company can choose whether dividends paid should be included in the operating section or the financing section.

The table below summarizes the correct sections for interest paid and dividends paid under different accounting guidelines.

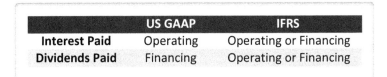

	US GAAP	IFRS
Interest Paid	Operating	Operating or Financing
Dividends Paid	Financing	Operating or Financing

There are two different methods used to create the operating activities section of the cash flow statement and to determine net cash flow from operating activities. These methods will be covered in the following sections.

For answers to the following questions, please see the end of Chapter 5.

Review 5.2 Question 1

Which of the following is considered an operating activity under US GAAP? Please select all that apply.

a. Interest paid
b. Dividends paid
c. Wages paid
d. Taxes paid

Review 5.2 Question 2

Which of the following could be considered an operating activity under IFRS? Select all that apply.

a. Interest paid
b. Depreciation
c. Purchase of property
d. Cash distributed to shareholders

5.2.2   Direct Method

A company that uses the direct method for the operating section of the statement of cash flows simply takes its operating inflows and subtracts its operating outflows to get the net cash flow from operating activities. Each operating cash flow activity is listed along with its respective amount. This is an intuitive method that is straightforward and easy to interpret.

The two main components of Cash Flow from Operations (CFO) under the direct method are cash collected from customers and cash paid to suppliers. Cash collected from customers includes items such as cash collected from current sales, cash collected from previous credit sales (accounts receivables), and cash collected from customers who prepaid for future goods or services. Cash paid to suppliers includes items such as cash purchases to produce goods or deliver services, cash paid for items and services previously received (accounts payable, wages payable), and cash paid for items that will be received in the future (prepaid rent, prepaid insurance).

An example of the operating section of cash flows prepared under the direct method is shown in Figure 5.1.

FIGURE 5.1

Cash Flow from Operating Activities Direct Method

Cash collections from customers	$	235,000
Other cash collections		15,000
Total cash collections		250,000
Cash paid for inventory		(120,000)
Cash paid for SG&A		(55,000)
Cash paid for salaries		(60,000)
Cash paid for prepaid rent		(2,000)
Total cash payments	$	(237,000)
Net cash provided by operating activities	$	13,000

Positive cash numbers represent an inflow to the company during the accounting period. It's important to recognize that the cash inflow number for sales does not necessarily equal the actual sales during a period – a company could have had additional revenue earned that has not yet been collected in cash, or it could have collected cash from customers that related to sales in previous periods.

Negative numbers, which are often shown in parenthesis, represent cash outflows during the period. This does not have to equal the expenses for the period; it is simply the cash paid out to others during the period.

It is most common for companies to list cash inflows before cash outflows, but it's not a requirement.

Section 3
Operating Activities: Indirect Method

Concepts

1. Indirect Method

2. Gains and Losses

3. Asset Accruals

4. Liability Accruals

5. Review

5.3.1   Indirect Method

The indirect method is another way to prepare the cash flow from operations section.

This method is better for showing the difference between the company's net income and net cash flow from operations for the accounting period. It starts with the net income amount and adjusts for differences between revenues and inflows as well as differences between expenses and outflows.

The accrual accounting method is the reason for the differences between revenues and expenses incurred and the inflows and outflows of cash. The indirect method basically adjusts net income to become actual cash flows by undoing the impact of accruals. This process is sometimes called "de-accruing" net income.

A good way to begin is to look at the income statement and find non-cash expenses for the accounting period. The main ones are depreciation and amortization.

Depreciation and amortization are recorded to match the expense of a long-lived asset with the revenues it generates. Even though expenses are recognized, cash isn't paid out because the cash outflow already happened when the asset was first purchased.

Suppose AMC bought a new movie theater and paid for it with cash. The payment is recorded as an asset under PP&E, and it is depreciated over the expected useful life of the theater.

Depreciation and amortization decrease net income on the income statement, so, in order to get cash flow from operations, we need to add back the depreciation and amortization for that period to net income.

Adjustments are made to guarantee that there are no net effects on CFO for items that did not involve operating cash inflows or outflows. Adding back depreciation doesn't increase CFO; it simply undoes the effect of depreciation expense on net income in order to get to operating cash flow.

For the answer to the following question, please see the end of Chapter 5.

Review 5.3 Question 1

If the income statement shows $10,000 of depreciation and $3,000 of amortization, in order to get closer to cash flow from operations, you should

a. Add $13,000 to net income.
b. Subtract $13,000 to net income.
c. Not adjust net income because depreciation and amortization are cash expenses.

5.3.2   Gains and Losses

Net income also includes non-operating gains and losses, and the operating section of the statement of cash flows needs to be adjusted to exclude non-operating and non-cash gains and losses so that it only includes cash flows from operations. A gain or loss can occur when a company disposes of an asset and the net book value of the asset differs from the amount actually received from the disposal.

These gains or losses often have an impact on cash, but they are not operating cash flows because they are generally one-time transactions that aren't a part of normal operations. To get cash flow from operating activities, gains need to be subtracted from net income and losses need to be added back to net income. Usually gains or losses are placed in the investing section, which will be covered next.

As we discussed earlier, it's possible to include interest paid in the operating section or in the financing section under IFRS. Interest paid on borrowings is included in net income, so if the company chooses to include interest in the financing section, it must be added back to net income to get the cash flow from operations.

5.3.3   Asset Accruals

There are also other adjustments that are necessary when preparing the statement of cash flows using the indirect method.

The balance sheet is an essential source for creating the statement of cash flows. The balance sheet shows the effects of accruals on a company's financials, and it is important to deaccrue net income in order to get operating cash flow.

Accounts receivable is an account on the balance sheet that increases when a company performs a service or delivers a good before it actually receives cash from the customer. The company recognizes revenue without receiving cash. Since this increase in revenue was recorded on the income statement, the increase in accounts receivable must be subtracted from net income to get to operating cash flow.

If accounts receivable decreases, it means that the company received cash that it had already recognized as revenue in a previous period. So, the cash inflow was not included in net income for the current period. This needs to be reflected on the statement of cash flows, so the decrease in accounts receivable would be added back to net income on the cash flow statement.

Similar adjustments need to be made for the other current asset accounts that relate to a company's operations. A company typically pays cash for assets, so when a current asset account increases, the cash decreases. If a company collects receivables or sells assets, which decreases its asset accounts, it usually receives cash. This increase in cash should be added back to net income.

Let's look at an example to understand how changes in inventory affect the statement of cash flows. The Construction Company (TCC) had $30,000 in inventory on December 31, 2012. One year later, TCC had $45,000 in inventory. The Construction Company's inventory increased by $15,000 during that time frame. The company paid cash to purchase the inventory, but it did not show up as an expense on the income statement. In order to adjust for this, the company decreases net income by $15,000 in the operating section of the statement of cash flows.

12/31/2012 Inventory: $30,000

12/31/2013 Inventory: $45,000

Adjustment: Decrease net income by $15,000

The following key points will help you remember how to adjust net income to get CFO using the indirect method:

- Increase in Current Assets: Subtract from Net Income

- Decrease in Current Assets: Add back to Net Income

For answers to the following questions, please see the end of Chapter 5.

Review 5.4 Question 1

If prepaid rent increased, this amount needs to be

    a.   Subtracted from net income in order to get to operating cash flow
    b.   Added to net income in order to get to operating cash flow.

If inventory decreased, this amount needs to be

    a.   Subtracted from net income in order to get to operating cash flow

    b.   Added to net income in order to get to operating cash flow.

Review 5.4 Question 3

If prepaid insurance increased, this amount needs to be

    a.   Subtracted from net income in order to get to operating cash flow

    b.   Added to net income in order to get to operating cash flow.

5.3.4   Liability Accruals

There are also adjustments made to the statement of cash flows for operating current liability accounts. The calculation is the opposite of the calculation for current assets: an increase in operating current liabilities is added to net income, and a decrease in operating current liabilities is subtracted from net income.

Accounts payable is an account on the balance sheet that increases if a company receives a benefit before paying cash for that benefit. The company must make an adjustment to net income, adding the increase in accounts payable, to get to operating cash flow. In this accounting period, the company essentially saved cash and postponed the cash outflow to a later date, spending less cash than it owed for the benefits received.

For The Construction Company, accounts payable was $12,000 as of December 31, 2012 and $15,000 as of December 31, 2013. Since accounts payable increased by $3,000, it means that the company received a benefit without paying cash for it. The statement of cash flows is adjusted by adding $3,000 to net income.

    12/31/2012 Accounts payable: $12,000

    12/31/2013 Accounts payable: $15,000

    Adjustment: Add $3,000 to net income

The following key points will help you remember how to adjust net income to get CFO using the indirect method:

- Increase in Operating Current Liabilities: Add back to Net Income

- Decrease in Operating Current Liabilities: Subtract from Net Income

Some companies have very complex transactions, such as acquisitions, that cause changes on the balance sheet that don't directly translate to the cash flow statement. For example, a company could fund an acquisition with a mix of equity, debt, and cash, but the cash flow statement would only show the cash payment made for the acquisition. These complex transactions will not be covered in this book. Figure 5.2 shows some adjustments made to the statement of cash flows for some common accounts and transactions.

FIGURE 5.2

Cash Flow from Operating Activities		
Net income (loss)	$	450
Depreciation and amortization		150
(Increase) / decrease in receivables		(230)
(Increase) / decrease in inventories		120
Increase / (decrease) in accounts payable		160
Increase / (decrease) in wages payable		50
Net cash provided by operating activities	$	700

The following rules will help you remember what type of adjustments to make to net income in order to calculate operating cash flow:

- Deduct all increases in operating current assets.

- Add all decreases in operating current assets.

- Add all increases in operating current liabilities.

- Deduct all decreases in operating current liabilities.

For answers to the following questions, please see the end of Chapter 5.

Review 5.5 Question 1

If accounts payable increased, this amount needs to be

    a.   Subtracted from net income in order to get to operating cash flow

    b.   Added to net income in order to get to operating cash flow.

Review 5.5 Question 2

If salaries payable increased, this amount needs to be

    a.   Subtracted from net income in order to get to operating cash flow

    b.   Added to net income in order to get to operating cash flow.

If notes payable decreased, this amount needs to be

    a.   Subtracted from net income in order to get to operating cash flow

    b.   Added to net income in order to get to operating cash flow.

5.3.5   Review

Ultimately, whether the company uses the direct method or the indirect method, it will get the same number for the cash flow from operations. The indirect method may look more complicated, but it clearly breaks out the adjustments necessary to reconcile net income and operating cash flows.

Both US GAAP and IFRS require that companies reconcile net income and operating cash flows, so even if a company chooses to report its operating cash flow section under the direct method, it needs to supplement this section with the reconciliation. This is why most businesses choose to use the indirect method. The indirect method also uses information from existing financial statements, as opposed to mainly transactional data. The direct method requires an inside knowledge of the cash inflows and outflows of a company, but anyone can build the statement of cash flows using the indirect method by pulling information from the other financial statements.

The following diagram is a good summary of how to calculate operating cash flow from net income.

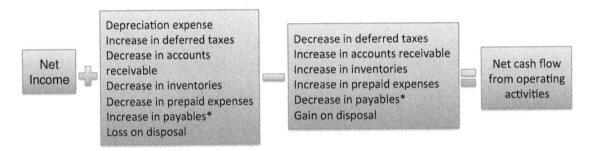

* Includes accounts payable, wages payable, interest payable, and taxes payable. Does not include notes payable, short-term borrowings, or current portion of long-term debt. Source: Anthony, Robert N., David Hawkins, and Kenneth Merchant. Accounting: Text and Cases. 11th ed. New York: McGraw-Hill/Irwin, 2003.

Section 4

Investing and Financing Activities

Concepts

1. Investing

2. Financing

5.4.1   Investing

The next section of the statement of cash flows is the investing section. Investing activities are those that are associated with long-lived assets, such as acquiring or divesting property, plant and equipment. These items are expected to provide benefits for more than one year, so they are not listed as current assets. They are expenditures that are recorded as assets instead of recognized as expenses immediately. Buying buildings and upgrading equipment are examples of items that would be listed as expenditures, or cash outflows, in the investing section. Selling long-term assets would create receipts, or cash inflows, that would be listed under investing activities. This section also includes long-term investments in securities that are not cash equivalents and loans a company might make to others (loans receivables).

To create this section of the cash flow statement, we first list the cash paid out to purchase long-lived assets and then the cash received through divesting the long-lived assets. Remember that positive numbers indicate cash inflows and negative numbers indicate cash outflows. An example of the cash flows from investing section is shown in Figure 5.3.

FIGURE 5.3

Cash Flow from Investing Activities	
Acquisition of plant and equipment	$(80,000)
Proceeds from disposal of plant and equipment	30,000
Purchase of investment securities	(20,000)
Proceeds from sales of investment securities	50,000
Net cash used by investing activities	**$(20,000)**

For answers to the following questions, please see the end of Chapter 5.

Review 5.6 Question 1

Will the following cash inflows and outflows belong in the investing activities section?

Purchasing a new building

    a.   Yes

    b.   No

Review 5.6 Question 2

Will the following cash inflows and outflows belong in the investing activities section?

Paying rent

    a.   Yes

    b.   No

Review 5.6 Question 3

Will the following cash inflows and outflows belong in the investing activities section?

Buying new machines for a factory

    a.   Yes

    b.   No

Review 5.6 Question 4

Will the following cash inflows and outflows belong in the investing activities section?

Purchasing new inventory

    a.   Yes

    b.   No

Suppose a company paid $50,000 for a new machine, recognized $25,000 of depreciation on it, and sold it for $35,000. These were the company's only investing activities for the period. What would be the net cash used by investing activities?

    a. $(15,000)

    b. $15,000

    c. $10,000

    d. $(10,000)

5.4.2   Financing

The final section of the statement of cash flows is the **financing section**. When a company borrows cash or issues securities, it is included in this section. Repaying borrowings, paying back investors, retiring stock, and repurchasing stock are other activities listed under the financing section. Under US GAAP, dividends paid are included in the financing section, but under IFRS, dividends paid can be in either the operating or the financing section. This section can also include interest paid under IFRS, but interest paid must be listed in the operating section under US GAAP.

Figure 5.4 is an example of the financing section of a cash flow statement. Remember that positive numbers indicate cash inflows and negative numbers indicate cash outflows.

FIGURE 5.4

Cash Flow from Financing Activities	
Short-term debt proceeds	$ 15,000
Short-term debt payments	(30,000)
Long-term debt proceeds	250,000
Long-term debt payments	(25,000)
Proceeds from stock issuance	60,000
Dividends paid	(40,000)
Net cash provided by financing activities	**$230,000**

For answers to the following questions, please see the end of Chapter 5.

Would the following cash inflows and outflows belong in the financing activities section under US GAAP?

Notes payable

    a.   Yes

    b.   No

Review 5.7 Question 2

Would the following cash inflows and outflows belong in the financing activities section under US GAAP?

Mortgages payable

    a.   Yes
    b.   No

Review 5.7 Question 3

Would the following cash inflows and outflows belong in the financing activities section under US GAAP?

Dividends paid

    a.   Yes
    b.   No

Review 5.7 Question 4

Would the following cash inflows and outflows belong in the financing activities section under US GAAP?

Accounts payable

    a.   Yes
    b.   No

Review 5.7 Question 5

Would the following cash inflows and outflows belong in the financing activities section under US GAAP?

Wages payable

    a.   Yes
    b.   No

Section 5
Classifications and Other Statements

Concepts

1. US GAAP vs. IFRS

2. Sources and Uses of Funds

5.5.1   US GAAP vs. IFRS

The past few sections have covered a few differences between IFRS and US GAAP requirements for the statement of cash flows. The treatment of interest and dividends is the major difference between the guidelines. IFRS has more flexible guidelines about the treatment of these items, allowing the company to choose the section that is more appropriate.

Interest paid or received on loans is classified as an operating activity under US GAAP. Under the indirect method, interest is already incorporated into net income, so it does not appear as a separate line item. Loans are a financing activity, so one might expect the interest paid or received to be under financing activities, but that is not the case for US GAAP. Under IFRS, the company can choose where transactions relating to interest should be classified. Interest paid can be under financing or operating activities, and interest received can be under operating or investing activities.

Under US GAAP, dividends paid are under the financing section, and under IFRS, the company can choose the most appropriate classification, either the financing or the operating section.

Dividends received are placed under the operating section for US GAAP, but under IFRS, the company can choose to place dividends received under either the operating or the investing section.

IFRS is more flexible in its classification requirements, but it does insist that companies are consistent from period to period.

For answers to the following questions, please see the end of Chapter 5.

Review 5.8 Question 1

If a company lists dividends paid and interest paid under the financing activities section, which accounting standards does it follow?

    a.   IFRS

    b.   GAAP

    c.   Cannot tell from the information provided

Review 5.8 Question 2

If a company lists dividends paid under the financing activities section and interest paid under the operating activities section, which accounting standards does it follow?

    a.   IFRS

    b.   GAAP

    c.   Cannot tell from the information provided

The following table summarizes the differences between US GAAP and IFRS in how interest and dividends are reflected in the cash flow statement.

Transaction	US GAAP Classification	IFRS Classification
Interest Received	Operating	Operating or Investing
Dividends Received	Operating	Operating or Investing
Interest Paid	Operating	Financing or Operating
Dividends Paid	Financing	Financing or Operating
Income Taxes	Operating	Operating unless specifically associated with financing or investing activity

The statement of cash flows shows the change in the cash balance over the accounting period. The equations in Figure 5.5 show how the accounting equation transitions into the change in cash balance.

FIGURE 5.5

Step 1

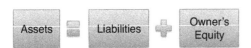

Step 2

Step 3

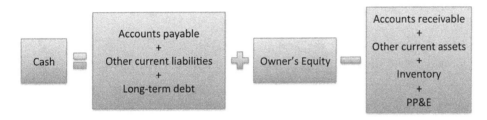

Step 4

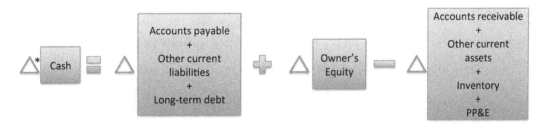

Step 5

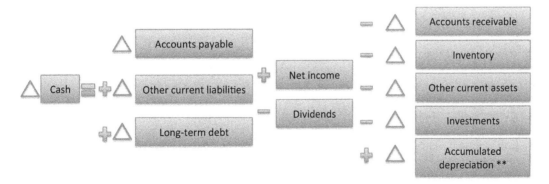

Step 6

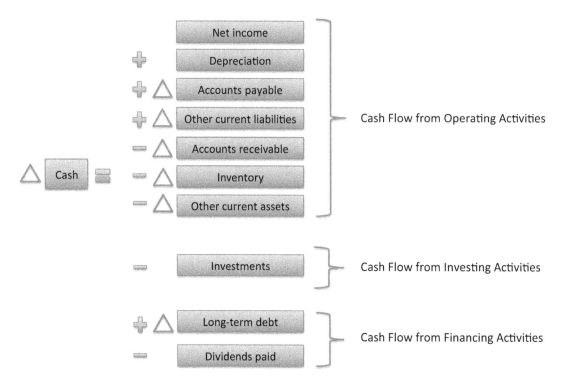

* △ = Change from the beginning of the period to the end of the period.

** = Change in accumulated depreciation is just the depreciation expense for the period if there are no asset disposals.

As you can see, the change in the cash balance is equal to the combined changes of the other components of the equation.

5.5.2   Sources and Uses of Funds

In addition to the statement of cash flows, there is another more informal statement that shows how a business manages its cash. The statement of sources and uses of funds is created by finding the differences between the balance sheet at the beginning of the period and the balance sheet at the end of the period. Each change in accounts is classified as either a source or a use of funds.

These statements are easily prepared, and they don't include separate sections (operating, investing, and financing). They also don't require the complicated de-accrual steps that are necessary in the operating section of the statement of cash flows. If an asset account decreases, it is a source of funds, whereas if an asset account increases, it is a use of funds. For example, if the asset account equipment decreases, the company likely sold the equipment, receiving cash for the sale. Thus, it's a source of funds for the company. If the equipment account increases, the company used its funds to purchase additional equipment.

For the opposite side of the equation, liabilities + owner's equity, a decrease in one of the accounts is a use of funds, while an increase is a source of funds. This also makes sense intuitively. A decrease in the liability accounts payable indicates that the company used its cash to pay a supplier and decrease accounts payable. If accounts payable increases, it's as though the company is saving cash, resulting in a source of funds. Figure 5.6 shows an example of a statement of sources and uses of funds.

FIGURE 5.6

Sources of Funds	Amount	Total
Increase in Equity Share Capital	$ 200,000	
Increase in Preferred Share Capital	100,000	
Increase in Long-term Liabilities	300,000	
Increase in Retained Earnings	100,000	
		700,000
Uses of Funds		
Increase in Fixed Assets	500,000	
		500,000
Change in working capital		$ 200,000

Section 6

Interpreting the Statement of Cash Flows

Concepts

1. Introduction

2. Startup / Fast Growing

3. Profitable / Growing

4. Mature / Steady State

5. In Decline

6. Cash Flow Manipulation

5.6.1   Introduction

The statement of cash flows divulges a lot of information that is useful for both managers and investors.

Both the investing and financing activities sections can help a company understand whether they are investing capital appropriately. Working capital is another metric that can be analyzed from the cash flow statement; a company needs to ensure that it has sufficient cash to cover its day to day operations. It's also important to determine whether cash flow is sufficient for long-term liability payments.

It's crucial to remember that the information from the cash flow statement needs to be analyzed in the overall context of a business' industry. It's also necessary to consider the phase of business a company is in because the statement can drastically change depending on the business stage. The cash flows are different for a fast-growing startup, a steady, mature company, and an unprofitable, declining company.

The next few sections will discuss cash flows at the different stages of a business lifecycle.

5.6.2   Startup / Fast Growing

For a startup, there are a lot of cash outflows and not that many inflows because the company is just getting started. Once it is more established, it can expect to earn money. The cash outflows include items such as inventory, supplies, new equipment, and office space. The company also has to focus on finding customers to earn money.

In terms of operating cash flows, startups generally have negative or extremely low cash flows. Some companies take years to achieve positive cash flow and move on from the startup / fast growing phase. When companies have to pay suppliers before they can collect cash from their customers, they could have negative cash flows from operations, even if they have positive gross profit and net income.

Startups are also likely to have negative investing cash flows. Startups need to spend a significant amount of money purchasing property and equipment, and they generally don't have equipment to sell in order to receive cash.

The financing section can vary widely for startups. As a startup, it can be difficult to obtain financing because the startup is a risky investment, and it's questionable whether banks would want to lend money to it. The company needs a way to fund its operations and investments, so it often raises the money through equity financing. This money can be raised through contributions by many people, and it's quite common for owners to invest and contribute a lot of the financing to the business. It's also possible for a business to raise a lot of money one year and use it over several years to fund its investments and operations.

Figure 5.7 is an example of a statement of cash flows for a startup.

Figure 5.7

Statement of Cash Flows

($ in 000s)	Year Ended December 31, 2013
Cash Flow from Operating Activities	
Net income (loss)	$ (150)
Depreciation and amortization	100
(Increase) / decrease in receivables	(70)
(Increase) / decrease in inventories	40
Increase / (decrease) in accounts payable	20
Changes in other current accounts	16
Net cash (used for)/provided by operating activities	$ (44)
Cash Flow from Investing Activities	
Capital Expenditures	(100)
Purchases of property, plant and equipment	(500)
Disposal of plant assets	25
Purchase of short-term investment	(80)
Net cash (used for)/provided by investing activities	$ (655)
Cash Flow from Financing Activities	
Issuance of debt	600
Payments of debt	(200)
Issuance of stock	100
Dividends paid	0
Net cash (used for)/provided by financing activities	$ 500
Increase (decrease) in cash	$ (199)

For answers to the following questions, please see the end of Chapter 5.

Review 5.9 Question 1

A startup typically has

    a.   Approximately equal cash inflows and outflows

    b.   Many cash outflows and not too many inflows

    c.   Many cash inflows and not too many outflows

Review 5.9 Question 2

A startup typically has

    a.   Negative investing cash flows

    b.   Positive investing cash flows

    c.   Positive operating cash flows

Review 5.9 Question 3

Startups can have negative CFO even if they have positive net income

    a.   True

    b.   False

5.6.3   Profitable / Growing

In the profitable / growing phase, the business moved on from the startup phase and is making money, but it is still trying to expand.

Operating cash flow will typically be positive because the company earns enough revenue, and grows at a slow enough pace, to cover operating expenses.

Since the company is continuing to grow, it still needs to invest in long-term assets. Oftentimes, cash flow from investing will be negative because the company spends more to purchase new equipment than it receives from selling its old equipment.

Cash flow from financing activities could be positive, neutral, or negative for a fast growing company; it depends on the growth rate and how much cash flow from operations the company generates. If the company generates a lot of cash flow from operations, it could use the cash to pay for investing activities and then use the remaining cash to pay down loans. This would cause financing cash flows to be negative. If the business is growing so fast that cash flow from operations cannot pay for investing activities, then the business will need to obtain money from investors and creditors, resulting in positive cash flow from financing activities. Financing cash flows could also be close to zero if the company can pay for its investments but not yet return cash to shareholders by paying dividends.

Figure 5.8 is an example of a statement of cash flows for a growing company.

FIGURE 5.8

Statement of Cash Flows

($ in 000s)	Year Ended December 31, 2013
Cash Flow from Operating Activities	
Net income (loss)	$ 225
Depreciation and amortization	75
(Increase) / decrease in receivables	(150)
(Increase) / decrease in inventories	65
Increase / (decrease) in accounts payable	90
Changes in other current accounts	28
Net cash (used for)/provided by operating activities	$ 333
Cash Flow from Investing Activities	
Capital Expenditures	(160)
Purchases of property, plant and equipment	(450)
Disposal of plant assets	145
Purchase of short-term investment	(100)
Net cash (used for)/provided by investing activities	$ (565)
Cash Flow from Financing Activities	
Issuance of debt	350
Payments of debt	(175)
Issuance of stock	125
Dividends paid	(50)
Net cash (used for)/provided by financing activities	$ 250
Increase (decrease) in cash	$ 18

For answers to the following questions, please see the end of Chapter 5.

Review 5.10 Question 1

A profitable and growing company

   a. Typically has positive cash flows from operating activities
   b. Does not need to purchase new assets
   c. Spends significantly more than it earns

Review 5.10 Question 2

If the company needs to obtain a lot of money from investors and lenders,

   a. Cash flow from financing will likely be negative
   b. Cash flow from financing will likely be positive
   c. Cash flow from investing will likely be positive
   d. Cash flow from investing will likely be negative

A profitable and growing company will likely have

    a.   Negative operating cash flow because it is spending money to expand

    b.   Positive operating cash flow because it receives enough money to cover its operating expenditures

5.6.4   Mature / Steady State

Well-established companies are often in a mature or steady state. They do not experience rapid growth but instead experience slower constant growth. Companies such as Coca-Cola or Starbucks are mature businesses.

Usually mature companies have positive operating cash flows that are consistent and steady because these companies are well-established in their markets.

Businesses in a steady state aren't focused on expanding. However, they are still purchasing new equipment to replace old equipment, so it's likely that cash flow from investing activities will be slightly negative.

For mature companies, cash flow from financing activities is usually negative. These companies have more than enough cash from operations to spend on investing activities, so they do not need to raise money through creditors or investors. The extra cash is often used to repay loans or return to shareholders in the form of dividends.

Figure 5.9 is an example of a statement of cash flows for a mature company.

FIGURE 5.9

Statement of Cash Flows

($ in 000s)	Year Ended December 31, 2013
Cash Flow from Operating Activities	
Net income (loss)	$ 550
Depreciation and amortization	230
(Increase) / decrease in receivables	(300)
(Increase) / decrease in inventories	160
Increase / (decrease) in accounts payable	(40)
Changes in other current accounts	50
Net cash (used for)/provided by operating activities	$ 650
Cash Flow from Investing Activities	
Capital Expenditures	(130)
Purchases of property, plant and equipment	(250)
Disposal of plant assets	340
Proceeds from notes receivable	16
Net cash (used for)/provided by investing activities	$ (24)
Cash Flow from Financing Activities	
Issuance of debt	100
Payments of debt	(180)
Issuance of stock	150
Dividends paid	(200)
Net cash (used for)/provided by financing activities	$ (130)
Increase (decrease) in cash	$ 496

For answers to the following questions, please see the end of Chapter 5.

Review 5.11 Question 1

An example of a mature / steady state company is:

    a.   Twitter

    b.   Proctor & Gamble

    c.   Delta Air Lines

Mature companies generally

a. Have consistent and steady revenue streams
b. Have consistently high growth
c. Have negative growth but still have positive revenues
d. Need to raise money from investors and creditors to support their investments

Review 5.11 Question 3

Mature companies often use extra cash

a. To repay loans
b. To pay dividends
c. Both
d. Neither

5.6.5   In Decline

A company can be in a state of decline for a variety of reasons, such as more competition, higher costs, or fewer customers. This state could eventually lead to bankruptcy.

The company will typically have negative operating cash flows because the business is not performing well under the environment's new conditions.

A company in a state of decline does not have to invest in new equipment because it has fewer customers and less revenue than it would at a more profitable stage. It could also sell off its older assets that are not necessary, increasing its cash flow. Both of these factors make it likely that its cash flow from investing activities is positive. Although positive investing cash flows increase a company's overall cash flow, it's not necessarily a good sign for the company. It's important to analyze the cash flow statement as a whole to truly understand a company's position.

Cash flow from financing activities could be either positive or negative. It might be challenging to obtain loans since the company has deteriorating business conditions, but it also isn't able to pay down its loans because it doesn't have excess cash flow.

Figure 5.10 is an example of a statement of cash flows for a company in decline.

FIGURE 5.10

Statement of Cash Flows

($ in 000s)	Year Ended December 31, 2013
Cash Flow from Operating Activities	
Net income (loss)	$ (160)
Depreciation and amortization	10
(Increase) / decrease in receivables	50
(Increase) / decrease in inventories	(80)
Increase / (decrease) in accounts payable	20
Changes in other current accounts	14
Net cash (used for)/provided by operating activities	$ (146)
Cash Flow from Investing Activities	
Capital Expenditures	(60)
Purchases of property, plant and equipment	(10)
Disposal of plant assets	170
Net cash (used for)/provided by investing activities	$ 100
Cash Flow from Financing Activities	
Issuance of debt	50
Payments of debt	(20)
Issuance of stock	0
Dividends paid	0
Net cash (used for)/provided by financing activities	$ 30
Increase (decrease) in cash	$ (16)

The chart below identifies some key aspects of the cash flow statement for various business states.

	Startup	Growing	Mature	In Decline
CFO	Negative or very low	Positive	Positive	Negative
CFI	Negative	Negative	Slightly negative	Positive
CFF	Varies	Varies	Typically negative	Varies

For answers to the following questions, please see the end of Chapter 5.

Review 5.12 Question 1

A company in a state of decline

a. Should invest in new equipment to bring in new customers
b. Generally has negative operating cash flow
c. Should pay down its loans with the extra cash on hand

264

Review 5.12 Question 2

For a company in a state of decline, cash flows from financing

- a.   Are typically positive
- b.   Are typically negative
- c.   Vary by company and can be either positive or negative

5.6.6   Cash Flow Manipulation

The statement of cash flows is a very useful tool to analyze how a business manages its cash. Even though it is created from actual cash flows, it can still be manipulated because a business can choose where to place its cash flows.

One famous example of a company manipulating its cash flows is WorldCom. This large telecommunications firm went bankrupt in the early 2000s after an accounting scandal became public knowledge. In this situation, management classified certain expenses, "line costs," as capital assets instead of as expenses.

This caused WorldCom's cash flow from operations to be artificially high. It looked like WorldCom was spending a lot of money on capital investments, but they were really just expenses. The incorrect classification increased net income and cash flow from operations, seriously misleading investors.

The fraud even caused one of WorldCom's major competitors to exit the business because it thought it could not compete with them. In reality, the two companies had similar operating expenses, and WorldCom was just engaging in fraud.

The statement of cash flows can lead to great insights for managers and investors when it is properly prepared. Fully understanding the various parts of the statement will allow you to analyze it correctly and derive useful conclusions.

Section 7

Review

The three major financial statements are the balance sheet, the income statement and the cash flow statement.

The **cash flow statement** tracks a company's cash flows throughout an accounting period, showing the total cash balances at the beginning and the end of the period, where the company received additional cash from, and how it spent its cash.

The cash flow statement is useful to better understand a company's liquidity and solvency because it's easy to see whether the company will have enough cash to buy resources or repay creditors.

There are three separate sections of a cash flow statement: Operating Activities, Investing Activities, and Financing Activities.

Operating Activities

Operating activities are cash flows related to preparing and providing goods and services to customers.

There are two methods to calculate cash flow from operations (CFO): the **direct method** and the **indirect method**. Ultimately, whether the company uses the direct method or the indirect method, it will get the same number for the cash flow from operations.

Direct method for the operating section of the statement of cash flows simply takes its operating inflows and subtracts its operating outflows to get the net cash flow from operating activities

Indirect method starts with the net income amount and adjusts for differences between revenues and inflows as well as differences between expenses and outflows. It basically adjusts net income to become actual cash flows by undoing the impact of accruals.

The following rules will help you remember what type of adjustments to make to net income in order to calculate operating cash flow under the indirect method:

- Deduct all increases in operating current assets.

- Add all decreases in operating current assets.

- Add all increases in operating current liabilities.

- Deduct all decreases in operating current liabilities.

Investing Activities

Investing activities are those that are associated with long-lived assets, such as acquiring or divesting property, plant and equipment.

Financing Activities

Financing activities are those associated with repaying borrowings, paying back investors, retiring stock, and repurchasing stock.

Examples of Different Activities

Transaction	Operating Activity	Investing Activity	Financing Activity
Cash paid to purchase land		X	
Cash received from customers	X		
Cash paid to buy new equipment		X	
Cash paid to repay loans			X
Cash proceeds from issuing stock			X
Cash paid to a supplier	X		
Cash paid for dividends			X
Cash paid to purchase a patent		X	
Cash paid to purchase inventory	X		
Cash received from selling property		X	
Cash paid for income taxes	X		
Cash paid to purchase new plant		X	
Cash paid to employees	X		
Cash received from borrowings			X

US GAAP vs. IFRS

Transaction	US GAAP Classification	IFRS Classification
Interest Received	Operating	Operating or Investing
Dividends Received	Operating	Operating or Investing
Interest Paid	Operating	Financing or Operating
Dividends Paid	Financing	Financing or Operating
Income Taxes	Operating	Operating unless specifically associated with financing or investing activity

The **statement of sources and uses of funds** is an informal statement that shows how a business manages its cash. It's created by finding the differences between the balance sheet at the beginning of the period and the balance sheet at the end of the period. Each change in accounts is classified as either a source or a use of funds.

Interpreting the Statement of Cash Flows

For a startup, there are a lot of cash outflows and not that many inflows because the company is just getting started.

In the profitable / growing phase, the business moved on from the startup phase and is making money, but it is still trying to expand.

Well-established companies are often in a mature or steady state and experience slower constant growth. Usually mature companies have positive operating cash flows that are consistent and steady because these companies are well-established in their markets.

A company in a state of decline is not performing well, and it could be for a variety of reasons, such as more competition, higher costs, or fewer customers.

	Startup	Growing	Mature	In Decline
CFO	Negative or very low	Positive	Positive	Negative
CFI	Negative	Negative	Slightly negative	Positive
CFF	Varies	Varies	Typically negative	Varies

Section 8

Review Questions

For answers to the following questions, please see the end of Chapter 1.

Review 5.13 Question 1

The indirect method

    a.   adjusts net income to become actual cash flows by undoing the impact of accruals

    b.   takes the operating inflows and subtracts the operating outflows to get the net cash flow from operating activities

Review 5.13 Question 2

If a business has positive net income,

    a.   It must have positive cash flows.

    b.   It must have positive cash flow from operations.

    c.   It likely has positive cash flow from operations.

    d.   Cash flows may be positive or negative.

Review 5.13 Question 3

How would the following transaction impact the cash flow of a business?

Purchasing land

    a.   Increase cash flow

    b.   Decrease cash flow

    c.   No impact

Review 5.13 Question 4

How would the following transaction impact the cash flow of a business?

Increasing inventory

    a.   Increase cash flow

    b.   Decrease cash flow

    c.   No impact

Review 5.13 Question 5

Which of the following could be considered an operating activity under IFRS? Select all that apply.

    a.   Issuing stock

    b.   Paying interest

    c.   Purchasing inventory

    d.   Purchasing equipment

Review 5.13 Question 6

Under the indirect method, if accounts payable decreased, this amount needs to be

    a.   Subtracted from net income in order to get to operating cash flow

    b.   Added to net income in order to get to operating cash flow.

Review 5.13 Question 7

If a company lists dividends received and interest received under the investing activities section, which accounting standards does it follow?

    a.   IFRS

    b.   GAAP

    c.   Cannot tell from the information provided

Review 5.13 Question 8

Suppose a company lists dividends paid under investing activities and interest received under financing activities. This is acceptable under

    a.   IFRS
    b.   GAAP
    c.   Neither IFRS nor GAAP
    d.   Both IFRS and GAAP

Review 5.13 Question 9

Select whether the following transaction should be an operating, investing or financing activity under US GAAP. ABC Company issued 50,000 shares of $10 par value stock for $700,000 cash.

    a.   Operating
    b.   Investing
    c.   Financing

Review 5.13 Question 10

Select whether the following transaction should be an operating, investing or financing activity under US GAAP. ABC Company purchased a new warehouse for its products for $600,000.

    a.   Operating
    b.   Investing
    c.   Financing

Review 5.13 Question 11

Select whether the following transaction should be an operating, investing or financing activity under US GAAP. ABC Company collected $35,000 for products it sold.

    a.   Operating
    b.   Investing
    c.   Financing

Review 5.13 Question 12

Select whether the following transaction should be an operating, investing or financing activity under US GAAP. ABC Company signed a 2-year note with 9% interest, borrowing $100,000 from a bank.

    a.   Operating
    b.   Investing
    c.   Financing

Review 5.13 Question 13

State whether you should add or deduct the change in account to convert net income to cash flow from operating activities.

    Increase in current asset account
    Decrease in current asset account

    a.   Add
    b.   Deduct

Review 5.13 Question 14

State whether you should add or deduct the change in account to convert net income to cash flow from operating activities.

    Increase in current liability account
    Decrease in current liability account

    a.   Add
    b.   Deduct

Review 5.13 Question 15

A company in a state of decline typically has

a. positive CFO and negative CFI
b. positive CFO and CFI that varies
c. negative CFO and CFI that varies
d. negative CFO and positive CFI

Review 5.13 Question 16

A growing company typically has

a. positive CFO and negative CFI
b. negative CFO and positive CFI
c. positive CFO and positive CFI
d. negative CFO and negative CFI

Review 5.13 Question 17

Startups typically have...
Please select all that apply.

a. Negative or very low CFO
b. Positive CFI because they purchase new equipment
c. Negative CFI because they purchase new equipment
d. Equal cash inflows and outflows

Review 5.13 Question 18

If a company has $400 in CFO, ($300) in CFI and $250 in CFF, it is likely a...
Please select all that apply.

a. startup
b. profitable / growing company
c. mature / steady state company
d. company in decline

Review 5.13 Question 19

PepsiCo is an example of a

    a.   startup

    b.   profitable / growing company

    c.   mature / steady state company

    d.   company in decline

Review 5.13 Question 20

The statement of cash flows cannot be manipulated because it is based on actual cash inflows and outflows.

    a.   True

    b.   False

Section 9

Answer Key

Review 5.1 Explanations

Question 1

Answer: B

If a business has positive net income, it does not have to have positive cash flows. Most businesses use accrual accounting, which means that when revenues are earned, it does not necessarily imply that cash was received. One situation that could cause positive net income and negative cash flows is when a company prepays for several years of insurance. Only a portion of that payment shows up as an expense on the income statement because it should be spread out over several years and expensed as the prepaid insurance is used up. However, the payment is a huge cash outflow during that accounting period.

Question 2

Answer: C

Purchasing equipment on credit affects accounts payable, not cash flow.

Question 3

Answer: B

Paying down a loan requires paying cash to the lender. This would decrease cash flow.

Question 4

Answer: C

Selling inventory on credit affects accounts receivable, not cash flow.

Review 5.2 Explanations

Question 1

Answers: A, C, D

Interest paid, wages paid, and taxes paid are all considered operating activities under US GAAP. Dividends paid is considered a financing activity under US GAAP.

Question 2

Answers: A, B, D

Depreciation is an operating activity under IFRS. Interest paid and cash distributed to shareholders (dividends paid) could be considered operating activities under IFRS. They could also be considered financing activities under IFRS. The purchase of property would be considered an investing activity under IFRS.

Review 5.3 Explanations

Question 1

Answer: A

In order to get closer to cash flow from operations, you should add $13,000 to net income. Depreciation and amortization were expenses that were subtracted from revenues in order to get to net income. Since they are non-cash expenses, they need to be added back to net income.

Review 5.4 Explanations

Question 1

Answer: A

Prepaid rent is an asset, and all increases in assets should be deducted from net income in order to get to operating cash flow. So, if prepaid rent increased, it should be subtracted from net income.

Question 2

Answer: B

Inventory is an asset, and all decreases in assets should be added to net income in order to get to operating cash flow. So, if inventory decreased, it should be added to net income.

Question 3

Answer: A

Prepaid insurance is an asset, and all increases in assets should be deducted from net income in order to get to operating cash flow. So, if prepaid insurance increased, it should be subtracted from net income.

Review 5.5 Explanations

Question 1

Answer: B

Accounts payable is a liability, and all increases in liabilities should be added to net income in order to get to operating cash flow.

Question 2

Answer: B

Salaries payable is a liability, and all increases in liabilities should be added to net income in order to get to operating cash flow.

Question 3

Answer: A

Notes payable is a liability, and all decreases in liabilities should be subtracted from net income in order to get to operating cash flow.

Review 5.6 Explanations

Question 1

Answer: A

Purchasing a new building is an investing activity. The building would be expected to provide benefits for more than one year and would not be classified as a current asset.

Question 2

Answer: B

Paying rent would be considered an operating activity, not an investing activity.

Question 3

Answer: A

Buying a new machine for a factory would be considered an investing activity. The machine would be expected to provide benefits for more than one year and would be classified as a long-term asset.

Question 4

Answer: B

Purchasing new inventory would be considered an operating activity, not an investing activity.

Question 5

Answer: A

In order to calculate net cash used by investing activity, we would subtract the cash outflows from investing activities from the cash inflows from investing activities. The company received $35,000 from selling the machine and paid $50,000 to buy the machine. So, $35,000 - $50,000 = $(15,000). Depreciation is a non-cash expense, so it is not included in cash flow from investing activities.

Review 5.7 Explanations

Question 1

Answer: A

Notes payable is considered a financing activity under both US GAAP and IFRS.

Question 2

Answer: A

Mortgages are considered financing activities under both US GAAP and IFRS.

Question 3

Answer: A

Dividends paid is considered a financing activity under US GAAP.

Question 4

Answer: B

Accounts payable is considered an operating activity, not a financing activity, under US GAAP.

Question 5

Answer: B

Wages payable is considered an operating activity, not a financing activity, under US GAAP.

Review 5.8 Explanations

Question 1

Answer: A

If a company lists dividends paid and interest paid under the financing activities section, it follows IFRS. Although dividends paid are listed under financing activities under US GAAP, interest paid must be listed under operating activities, not financing activities.

Question 2

Answer: C

If a company lists dividends paid under the financing activities section and interest paid under the operating activities section, it could follow IFRS or US GAAP. GAAP requires dividends paid to be listed under financing activities and interest paid to be listed under operating activities. IFRS allows those activities to be classified as operating or financing activities.

Review 5.9 Explanations

Question 1

Answer: B

A startup typically has many cash outflows and not too many inflows. Since it is just getting started, it must spend a lot of money buying items such as inventory, supplies, and equipment and also work to attract customers to earn money.

Question 2

Answer: A

Startups often have negative investing cash flows because they spend a lot of money to purchase property and equipment and they don't have long-term assets to sell in order to receive cash.

Question 3

Answer: A

Any company can have negative CFO but still have positive net income. Suppose the company sold an expensive long-term asset. This would have a positive impact on net income, and the sale would affect CFI, not CFO.

Review 5.10 Explanations

Question 1

Answer: A

A profitable and growing company typically earns enough money to cover its operating expenses and still make a profit. It usually does not spend significantly more than it earns. It might need to purchase new assets to keep running its operations and continue growing.

Question 2

Answer: B

Money from investors and lenders affects cash flow from financing. Cash flow from investing activities relates to activities where the company makes investments, such as purchasing new equipment or securities. If a company obtains a lot of money from investors and lenders, it will increase its cash flow from financing activities, and CFF will likely be positive.

Question 3

Answer: B

A profitable and growing company will likely have positive operating cash flow. Even though it might spend money to expand, a profitable and growing company usually earns enough money to cover operating expenses.

Review 5.11 Explanations

Question 1

Answer: B

Proctor & Gamble is an example of a mature / steady state company. Twitter would be an example of a startup and Delta Air Lines would be an example of a company in a state of decline.

Question 2

Answer: A

Mature companies generally have consistent and steady revenue streams. Mature companies don't experience rapid growth but instead experience slower constant growth. They generally have more than enough cash from operations to spend on investments, so they don't need to raise money from investors and creditors.

Question 3

Answer: C

Mature companies often use extra cash to repay loans and to pay dividends.

Review 5.12 Explanations

Question 1

Answer: B

A company in a state of decline generally has negative operating cash flow because the business is not performing well. It does not have to invest in new equipment because it has fewer customers and less revenue than it did in its more profitable stage. It doesn't have extra cash on hand and may have difficulty paying down its loans.

Question 2

Answer: C

For a company in a state of decline, cash flows from financing vary by company and can be either positive or negative. It could be negative because the company might be unable to obtain loans (resulting in a positive cash inflow). It could also be positive because the company might not have enough funds to pay down its loans (resulting in a negative cash outflow).

Chapter Review 5.13 Explanations

Question 1

Answer: A

The indirect method adjusts net income to become actual cash flows by undoing the impact of accruals. The direct method takes the operating inflows and subtracts the operating outflows to get the net cash flow from operating activities.

Question 2

Answer: D

If a business has positive net income, cash flows may be positive or negative. It's important to look at both the income statement and the statement of cash flows to truly understand how a company is doing. One situation that could cause positive net income and negative cash flows is when a company prepays for several years of insurance. Only a portion of that payment shows up as an expense on the income statement because it should be spread out over several years and expensed as the prepaid insurance is used up. However, the payment is a huge cash outflow during that accounting period.

Question 3

Answer: B

Purchasing land would decrease cash flow from investing activities. The company would spend cash to buy land.

Question 4

Answer: B

Increasing inventory would decrease cash flow from operating activities. The company would spend cash to buy inventory.

Question 5

Answers: B, C

Under IFRS, paying interest and purchasing inventory would both be considered operating activities. Issuing stock is a financing activity, and purchasing equipment is an investing activity.

Question 6

Answer: A

Under the indirect method, if accounts payable decreased, this amount needs to be subtracted from net income in order to get to operating cash flow. Accounts payable is a current liability, and all decreases in current liabilities should be subtracted from net income to get to CFO.

Question 7

Answer: A

If a company lists dividends received and interest received under the investing activities section, it must follow IFRS. Dividends received and interest received must be classified under the operating section under US GAAP.

Question 8

Answer: C

Listing dividends paid under investing activities and interest received under financing activities is not acceptable under any accounting standards. Dividends paid are classified under financing activities under US GAAP and can be under operating or financing activities under IFRS. Interest received can be under operating or investing activities under IFRS, but it must be classified as an operating activity under US GAAP.

Question 9

Answer: C

Issuing shares of stock is classified as a financing activity.

Question 10

Answer: B

Purchasing a new warehouse is an investing activity because the warehouse is an asset that will provide benefits to the company for many years.

Question 11

Answer: A

Collecting money for products sold is an operating activity because it is an activity related to the company's main activities, providing goods to customers.

Question 12

Answer: C

Signing a two-year note to borrow $100,000 from a bank is a financing activity.

Question 13

Answer: Increase in current asset account (Deduct), Decrease in current asset account (Add)

Under the indirect method, all increases in current asset accounts should be deducted from net income to get to cash flow from operations, and all decreases in current asset accounts should be added to net income to get to cash flow from operations.

Question 14

Answer: Increase in current liability account (Add), Decrease in current liability account (Deduct)

Under the indirect method, all increases in current liability accounts should be added to net income to get to cash flow from operations, and all decreases in current liability accounts should be deducted from net income to get to cash flow from operations.

Question 15

Answer: D

A company in a state of decline typically has negative CFO and positive CFI. The business is not performing well, which is why it has negative CFO, and it likely has positive CFI because there is no need to invest in new equipment and it can sell off its older assets because of the lack of business.

Question 16

Answer: A

A growing company typically has positive CFO and negative CFI. The company usually earns enough revenue and grows at a slow enough pace to cover its operating expenses, leading to positive CFO. It generally has negative CFI because the company spends more to purchase new equipment than it receives from selling old equipment.

Question 17

Answers: A, C

Startups generally have negative or very low CFO and negative CFI because they purchase new equipment. Startups usually spend a lot of money to get their operations running, and buying equipment is a cash outflow which leads to negative CFI.

Question 18

Answer: B

If a company has $400 in CFO, ($300) in CFI and $250 in CFF, it is likely a profitable / growing company. CFO is typically positive for a profitable / growing company because it earns enough revenue and grows at a slow enough pace to cover its operating expenses. A growing company typically has negative CFI because the company spends more to purchase new equipment than it receives from selling old equipment. CFF can vary depending on the growth of the company. In this situation, positive CFF might suggest that the company is growing so quickly that it cannot pay for investing activities, so it needs to obtain money from investors and lenders, which leads to positive CFF. The other company stages generally do not have positive CFO, negative CFI, and positive CFF.

Question 19

Answer: C

PepsiCo is an example of a mature / steady state company. It is well-established and grows at a constant rate.

Question 20

Answer: B

The statement of cash flows can be manipulated, even though it is based on actual cash inflows and outflows.

6

Financial Statement Analysis

Sections

Section 1
Introduction

___

Concepts

1. Introduction

2. The DuPont Framework

6.1.1   Introduction

The previous chapters have covered important accounting concepts and how to create financial statements. Many people use the financial statements to understand how a company is performing, and this chapter will show you the key aspects of financial statement analysis.

It's essential for both managers and investors to know how a business is performing in order to make strategic decisions, such as how to prepare for future challenges and whether or not to invest.

This chapter will cover the financial analysis process, mainly focusing on examples from Macy's Inc., a large, multinational department store.

The financial statements contain so much information that it may seem overwhelming to analyze them and draw conclusions. We will break down the key figures to focus on and explain the information that various metrics reveal. One major component of financial statement analysis is ratio analysis. With ratios, we are able to compare a company's performance to its peers or to its own past performance to determine how well it is doing. Ratios uncover relationships between items on the financial statements.

There are many different kinds of ratios, such as liquidity ratios, profitability ratios, and efficiency ratios. Each one shows a certain aspect of a business, and when viewed all together, they tell a comprehensive story about a business' performance.

When studying ratios, it's necessary to get an overall understanding of the company and its industry because ratios are used for comparisons. The more thoroughly the user understands the business, the easier it will be to identify problems or strategic advantages.

This chapter will only cover a few of the most common ratios, but there are many more to learn about. There are also some ratios that are specific to certain industries, so it is very important to immerse yourself in the industry and understand the typical ratios. It's also important to note that ratios can have multiple formulas and can be calculated in different ways, depending on the needs of the analysis. When comparing ratios, you need to make sure they are calculated the same way.

6.1.2   The DuPont Framework

One of the most useful ratios to analyze is a firm's return on equity, commonly abbreviated as ROE. This ratio is calculated by dividing net income by average total owners' equity, and it shows the return that a business earned during an accounting period on the equity invested by owners.

$$\text{ROE} = \frac{\text{Net Income}}{\text{Average Total Owners' Equity}}$$

ROE is closely followed by management and investors because it is a good indicator of how well a company's management creates value for its owners.

However, only looking at ROE can be misleading. If a company's ROE increases over time, it means the business is generating a higher rate of return on the equity invested by owners. ROE can also increase when a company decreases shareholder equity and increases its leverage. Although additional leverage may be beneficial, it also increases the risk profile of a company. Analyzing ROE at a high level can be helpful, but it would be ideal if we could understand what was driving the returns. This is why the **DuPont framework** is so useful.

The DuPont framework breaks down return on equity into three key components to identify exactly where the returns are being generated. This framework allows management to determine which areas of the company are strong and which are weak. DuPont analysis is also useful for comparing two companies; even if they have the same ROE, the components that contribute to their ROE may be quite different.

The three components are:

1.   **Profitability**

2.   **Operating Efficiency**

3.   **Financial Leverage**

Efficiency refers to how well a company uses its assets to generate revenue, and leverage refers to how a company uses debt to finance its assets. There are many different ratios to analyze profitability, efficiency, and leverage, but the DuPont framework incorporates three of them.

To analyze profitability, we study profit margin; to analyze operating efficiency, we look at asset turnover; and to analyze financial leverage, we use the ratio of assets to equity. These areas will be discussed in more detail as the chapter progresses.

$$\text{ROE} = \text{Profit Margin} * \text{Asset Turnover} * \text{Leverage}$$

$$\frac{\text{Net Income}}{\text{Avg Equity}} = \frac{\text{Net Income}}{\text{Sales}} * \frac{\text{Sales}}{\text{Avg Total Assets}} * \frac{\text{Avg Total Assets}}{\text{Avg Equity}} \quad **$$

**Another equally acceptable condition is to use beginning numbers rather than average numbers for the balance sheet items (total assets and equity).

Using the DuPont framework, management can identify which areas have favorable or unfavorable returns and determine what to focus on to improve the overall ROE. It can also help guide analysts on additional ratios to calculate to have an in-depth understanding of the financial statements.

In the following sections, we will look at the DuPont Framework for Macy's, a department store chain. Macy's ROE was 24% for fiscal year 2013, and we will identify how the different components affected the ROE.

In order to better understand how the ratios are calculated, you should familiarize yourself with Macy's income statement and balance sheet, shown below in Figures 6.1 and 6.2.

FIGURE 6.1

Macy's Inc
Consolidated Statements of Income (Unaudited)
(All amounts in millions)

	52 weeks ended February 1, 2014		52 weeks ended February 2, 2013	
Net sales	$	27,931	$	27,686
Cost of sales		16,725		16,538
Gross margin		11,206		11,148
Selling, general and administrative expenses		(8,440)		(8,482)
Impairments, store closing, and other costs		(88)		(5)
Operating income		2,678		2,661
Interest expense		(388)		(422)
Premium on early retirement of debt		-		(137)
Income before taxes		2,290		2,102
Federal, state and local income tax expense		(804)		(767)
Net income	$	1,486	$	1,335

FIGURE 6.2

Macy's Inc
Consolidated Balance Sheets (Unaudited)
(All amounts in millions)

	February 1, 2014		February 3, 2013	
ASSETS:				
Current Assets:				
Cash and cash equivalents	$	2,273	$	1,836
Receivables		438		371
Merchandise inventories		5,557		5,308
Prepaid expenses and other current assets		420		361
Total Current Assets		8,688		7,876
Property and Equipment – net		7,930		8,196
Goodwill		3,743		3,743
Other Intangible Assets – net		527		561
Other Assets		746		615
Total Assets	$	21,634	$	20,991
LIABILITIES AND SHAREHOLDERS' EQUITY:				
Current Liabilities:				
Short-term debt	$	463	$	124
Merchandise accounts payable		1,691		1,579
Accounts payable and accrued liabilities		2,810		2,610
Income taxes		362		355
Deferred income taxes		400		407
Total Current Liabilities		5,726		5,075
Long-Term Debt		6,728		6,806
Deferred Income Taxes		1,273		1,238
Other Liabilities		1,658		1,821
Shareholders' Equity		6,249		6,051
Total Liabilities and Shareholders' Equity	$	21,634	$	20,991

Section 2
Profitability

Concepts

1. Profit Margin

2. Gross Profit Margin

3. EBIAT

6.2.1   Profit Margin

Profit margin is the first component of the DuPont framework, and it tells us how much a company keeps in earnings for every dollar of sales after all the expenses have been subtracted.

The formula for profit margin is:

$$\text{Profit Margin} = \frac{\text{Net Income}}{\text{Total Sales}}$$

Figure 6.3 shows where to find the numbers to calculate Macy's profit margin.

FIGURE 6.3

Macy's Inc
Consolidated Statements of Income (Unaudited)
(All amounts in millions)

	52 weeks ended February 1, 2014
Net sales	$ 27,931
Cost of sales	16,725
Gross margin	11,206
Selling, general and administrative expenses	(8,440)
Impairments, store closing, and other costs	(88)
Operating income	2,678
Interest expense	(388)
Premium on early retirement of debt	-
Income before taxes	2,290
Federal, state and local income tax expense	(804)
Net income	$ 1,486

In 2013, the profit margin for Macy's was 5.32%. This means that Macy's earned $5.32 dollars for every $100 in sales.

$$\text{Profit Margin} = \frac{\text{Net Income}}{\text{Total Sales}} = \frac{1{,}486}{27{,}931} = 5.32\%$$

Profit margin is one of the most useful ratios to analyze, and it's particularly useful when comparing companies in similar industries. This type of analysis can show which company is best at controlling its costs and earning profits.

6.2.2   Gross Profit Margin

Another important profit ratio is the gross profit margin. This figure captures the percentage of revenue available to pay for a company's expenses after the cost of goods sold is subtracted. Recall that gross profit is calculated by subtracting the cost of goods sold from revenues.

The formula for the gross profit margin is:

$$\text{Gross Profit Margin} = \frac{\text{Gross Profit}}{\text{Sales}}$$

Figure 6.4 shows where to find the numbers to calculate Macy's gross profit margin.

FIGURE 6.4

Macy's Inc
Consolidated Statements of Income (Unaudited)
(All amounts in millions)

	52 weeks ended February 1, 2014
Net sales	$ 27,931
Cost of sales	16,725
Gross margin	11,206
Selling, general and administrative expenses	(8,440)
Impairments, store closing, and other costs	(88)
Operating income	2,678
Interest expense	(388)
Premium on early retirement of debt	-
Income before taxes	2,290
Federal, state and local income tax expense	(804)
Net income	$ 1,486

For Macy's, the gross profit margin is 40.12% for 2013.

Revenues	$ 27,931
Less COGS	16,725
Gross Profit	11,206
Sales	27,931

$$\text{Gross Profit Margin} = \frac{11,206}{27,931} = 40.12\%$$

Just because a company's profits are growing, it doesn't mean the company is doing really well. For example, a company could be expanding rapidly, and if its square footage is increasing faster than the profit per square foot is falling, the company's overall profitability is still going up, making it look attractive. However, this isn't a sustainable business model, and if an analyst digs into the underlying causes of ratio trends, he or she can discover the driving factors behind the changes and get a better picture of a company.

6.2.3   EBIAT

Earnings before interest after taxes, or EBIAT, is a good measure of a company's operating performance. It shows the earnings a company has generated without the effects of the company's capital structure, or the amount of debt to equity.

To calculate EBIAT, we must take income before taxes and add back interest expense, which gives us earnings before interest and taxes, or EBIT. Then, we subtract tax expense based on EBIT. This tax expense is calculated by applying the company's corporate tax rate to EBIT.

$$\text{EBIAT} = (\text{Income Before Taxes} + \text{Interest}) * \left(1 - \frac{\text{Tax expense}}{\text{Income before taxes}} \right)$$

$$\text{EBIAT} = \text{EBIT} * (1 - \text{Corporate tax rate})$$

Taxes are determined by the government and are not really a cost that the company can control; so many users like to look at EBIAT because it shows earnings after taxes. For Macy's, EBIAT was $1.9 billion.

Figure 6.5 shows where to find the figures needed to calculate Macy's income before interest and taxes.

FIGURE 6.5

Macy's Inc
Consolidated Statements of Income (Unaudited)
(All amounts in millions)

	52 weeks ended February 1, 2014
Net sales	$ 27,931
Cost of sales	16,725
Gross margin	11,206
Selling, general and administrative expenses	(8,440)
Impairments, store closing, and other costs	(88)
Operating income	2,678
Interest expense	(388)
Premium on early retirement of debt	-
Income before taxes	2,290
Federal, state and local income tax expense	(804)
Net income	$ 1,486

After determining income before interest and taxes, you can apply the tax rate to calculate EBIAT.

Income Before Taxes	$ 2,290
Plus Interest	388
	2,678
Less Taxes at 35.1% corporate tax rate	(940)
EBIAT	$ **1,738**

You should note that the purpose of adding back interest is not to increase EBIAT. We do it simply to undo the effect of subtracting interest expense in the first place. EBIAT ignores interest paid on debt so we can get a figure without the effects of a company's capital structure. EBIAT is sometimes referred to as Net Operating Profit After Taxes (NOPAT).

For answers to the following questions, please see the end of Chapter 6.

Review 6.1 Question 1

Suppose a company had sales of $50K, cost of goods sold of $30K, gross profit of $20K, and net income of $4K. What is the company's profit margin?

    a.   4%
    b.   8%
    c.   12.5%
    d.   20%

Review 6.1 Question 2

Suppose a company had sales of $50K, cost of goods sold of $30K, gross profit of $20K, and net income of $4K. What is the company's gross profit margin?

    a.   8%
    b.   20%
    c.   40%
    d.   66%

Section 3
Efficiency

Concepts

1. Asset Turnover

2. Inventory Turnover

3. Accounts Receivable Turnover

4. Accounts Payable Turnover

5. Cash Conversion Cycle

6.3.1   Asset Turnover

Asset turnover is the next component of the DuPont framework, and this ratio measures the efficiency with which a company uses its assets to generate revenues. When analyzing two companies, you might think that the one with more assets is better off. But it's important to look at how those assets are being used. The company that uses fewer assets to produce more sales operates better from an efficiency perspective.

The formula for asset turnover is:

$$\text{Asset Turnover} = \frac{\text{Revenues}}{\text{Average Total Assets}}$$

The asset turnover ratio uses items from both the income statement and the balance sheet. The income statement shows figures over the whole year, whereas the balance sheet just shows the figures at the beginning and the end of the year. A business can change significantly over the course of a year, so people often use the average of the beginning and ending balance sheet figures in the ratio calculation because it usually provides a more accurate picture than using the figure from the end of the year.

This book will typically use the average balance sheet figures when calculating a ratio that has both income statement and balance sheet items.

Figures 6.6 and 6.7 show where to find the numbers to calculate Macy's asset turnover.

FIGURE 6.6

Macy's Inc
Consolidated Statements of Income (Unaudited)
(All amounts in millions)

	52 weeks ended February 1, 2014
Net sales	$ 27,931
Cost of sales	16,725
Gross margin	11,206
Selling, general and administrative expenses	(8,440)
Impairments, store closing, and other costs	(88)
Operating income	2,678
Interest expense	(388)
Premium on early retirement of debt	-
Income before taxes	2,290
Federal, state and local income tax expense	(804)
Net income	$ 1,486

FIGURE 6.7

Macy's Inc
Consolidated Balance Sheets (Unaudited)
(All amounts in millions)

	February 1, 2014	February 3, 2013
ASSETS:		
Current Assets:		
Cash and cash equivalents	$ 2,273	$ 1,836
Receivables	438	371
Merchandise inventories	5,557	5,308
Prepaid expenses and other current assets	420	361
Total Current Assets	8,688	7,876
Property and Equipment – net	7,930	8,196
Goodwill	3,743	3,743
Other Intangible Assets – net	527	561
Other Assets	746	615
Total Assets	$ 21,634	$ 20,991

Macy's asset turnover for 2013 was 1.31x. This means that Macy's generated $1.31 of revenues for each dollar of assets.

$$\text{Revenues} \qquad \$\,27{,}931$$

Beginning Assets	20,991
Ending Assets	21,634
Average Total Assets	21,313

$$\textbf{Asset Turnover} \;=\; \frac{\text{Revenues}}{\text{Average Total Assets}} \;=\; \frac{27{,}931}{21{,}313} \;=\; \textbf{1.31x}$$

For the answer to the following question, please see the end of Chapter 6.

___

Review 6.2 Question 1

___

Suppose a company had revenues of $5K, gross profit of $2K, net income of $400, beginning assets of $3K and ending assets of $5K. What is the company's asset turnover?

    a.   0.5x
    b.   0.6x
    c.   1.0x
    d.   1.25x
    e.   1.67x

6.3.2   Inventory Turnover

___

Although the DuPont framework provides a good starting point to understanding a company's operating efficiency, there are other ratios that also reveal helpful information. Inventory turnover is a commonly used one.

Inventory turnover is an important ratio because it shows how fast a company is selling its inventory. It's defined as the number of times a company sells through and replaces its inventory during a year. More inventory for a given level of sales decreases efficiency because excess inventory uses resources and cash the company could use for other purposes. However, a company cannot decrease its inventory to an extremely low level to improve efficiency because it must maintain some inventory on hand to deliver quickly to customers.

The formula for calculating inventory turnover is:

$$\textbf{Inventory Turnover} \;=\; \frac{\text{COGS}}{\text{Average Inventory}}$$

The inventory turnover ratio uses income statement and balance sheet figures, so the average inventory is used in the denominator. This might not be so important if a company has relatively static inventory figures, but for a company that is growing quickly, inventory levels can be dramatically different. For a fast-growing company that had much more inventory towards the end of the year than the beginning, dividing COGS for the whole year by the ending balance for inventory would result in a low inventory turnover, inaccurately representing the efficiency of the company. It's possible to improve the accuracy of the ratio if quarterly or monthly inventory balances are averaged, but it's common to simply use beginning and ending balances.

It's also important to note that for manufacturing companies, there are additional costs in cost of goods sold, such as labor and overhead, which are not part of actual purchases. Thus, inventory turnover is not a perfect approximation of how fast a manufacturing company sells its inventory.

The inventory turnover ratio can be interpreted as the number of times a company sells through its inventory per year. If inventory turnover is 2, it means the company sells through its inventory every 6 months, or twice a year. When comparing inventory turnover figures, a higher ratio indicates more efficient inventory management.

Figures 6.8 and 6.9 show where to find the figures to calculate Macy's inventory turnover.

FIGURE 6.8

Macy's Inc
Consolidated Statements of Income (Unaudited)
(All amounts in millions)

	52 weeks ended February 1, 2014
Net sales	$ 27,931
Cost of sales	**16,725**
Gross margin	11,206
Selling, general and administrative expenses	(8,440)
Impairments, store closing, and other costs	(88)
Operating income	2,678
Interest expense	(388)
Premium on early retirement of debt	-
Income before taxes	2,290
Federal, state and local income tax expense	(804)
Net income	$ 1,486

FIGURE 6.9

Macy's Inc
Consolidated Balance Sheets (Unaudited)
(All amounts in millions)

	February 1, 2014		February 3, 2013	
ASSETS:				
Current Assets:				
Cash and cash equivalents	$	2,273	$	1,836
Receivables		438		371
Merchandise inventories		**5,557**		**5,308**
Prepaid expenses and other current assets		420		361
Total Current Assets		8,688		7,876
Property and Equipment – net		7,930		8,196
Goodwill		3,743		3,743
Other Intangible Assets – net		527		561
Other Assets		746		615
Total Assets	$	21,634	$	20,991

Macy's inventory turnover for fiscal year 2013 was 3.08x. So, Macy's sells through its inventory about 3 times per year.

COGS	$ 16,725
Beginning Inventory	5,557
Ending Inventory	5,308
Average Inventory	5,433

$$\textbf{Inventory Turnover} = \frac{COGS}{Average\ Inventory} = \frac{16,725}{5,433} = \textbf{3.08x}$$

Another ratio that is related to inventory turnover is days inventory, which is also called days of inventory on hand, days sales of inventory, or days inventory outstanding. The formula is:

$$\textbf{Days Inventory} = \frac{Average\ Inventory}{(COGS\ /\ 365)}$$

This ratio shows the average number of days that items sit in inventory before being sold. When analyzing inventory management, days inventory outstanding might seem more intuitive than inventory turnover because it is reported in days.

Another way to calculate days inventory is by taking the inverse of inventory turnover and multiplying it by 365. This calculation gives the same result as the previous one. The formula is:

$$\textbf{Days Inventory} = \frac{365}{Inventory\ Turnover}$$

Macy's days inventory for fiscal year 2013 was 118.5 days, so an item typically sat in inventory for 118.5 days before being sold.

$$\text{Days Inventory Outstanding} = \frac{365}{\text{Inventory Turnover}} = \frac{365}{3.08} = 118.5$$

For answers to the following questions, please see the end of Chapter 6.

Review 6.3 Question 1

Suppose a company had sales of $5K, COGS of $3K, and average inventory of $1K. What is the company's inventory turnover?

a. 0.2x
b. 0.3x
c. 0.5x
d. 3x
e. 5x

Review 6.3 Question 2

Suppose a company had sales of $5K, COGS of $3K, and average inventory of $1K. Approximately what is the company's days inventory?

a. 73 days
b. 122 days
c. 183 days

6.3.3   Accounts Receivable Turnover

Accounts receivable turnover, also known as AR turnover, is another ratio used to analyze a company's operating efficiency. This ratio shows how quickly a company collects payment from its customers. It can be thought of as the number of times a year the outstanding average receivable balance is fully collected. It's important to collect receivables fairly quickly so that the company can use the cash. A high AR turnover means a company is efficient at collecting receivables, and a low AR turnover means a company takes a while to collect its receivables. This could suggest that its customers are having trouble paying. If a company is too slow to collect its cash, it could lead to cash flow problems. The formula for AR turnover is:

$$\text{Accounts Receivable Turnover} = \frac{\text{Net Credit Sales}}{\text{Average Accounts Receivable Balance}}$$

Net credit sales is calculated by taking gross sales and subtracting cash sales and also subtracting sales returns and sales allowances that are related to credit sales. Some companies don't break out cash and credit sales in their financial reports, so net sales can be used as a substitute for net credit sales.

The accounts receivable turnover formula includes both income statement and balance sheet figures, so the average accounts receivable balance is used to capture the average receivables over the year.

Figures 6.10 and 6.11 show where to find the figures to calculate Macy's accounts receivable turnover.

FIGURE 6.10

Macy's Inc
Consolidated Statements of Income (Unaudited)
(All amounts in millions)

	52 weeks ended February 1, 2014
Net sales	$ 27,931
Cost of sales	16,725
Gross margin	11,206
Selling, general and administrative expenses	(8,440)
Impairments, store closing, and other costs	(88)
Operating income	2,678
Interest expense	(388)
Premium on early retirement of debt	-
Income before taxes	2,290
Federal, state and local income tax expense	(804)
Net income	$ 1,486

FIGURE 6.11

Macy's Inc
Consolidated Balance Sheets (Unaudited)
(All amounts in millions)

	February 1, 2014	February 3, 2013
ASSETS:		
Current Assets:		
Cash and cash equivalents	$ 2,273	$ 1,836
Receivables	438	371
Merchandise inventories	5,557	5,308
Prepaid expenses and other current assets	420	361
Total Current Assets	8,688	7,876
Property and Equipment – net	7,930	8,196
Goodwill	3,743	3,743
Other Intangible Assets – net	527	561
Other Assets	746	615
Total Assets	$ 21,634	$ 20,991

For Macy's, accounts receivable turnover for fiscal year 2013 was 69x. So, Macy's collects its receivables from customers about 69 times per year.

Net Sales	$ 27,931
Beginning Accounts Receivable Balance	371
Ending Accounts Receivable Balance	438
Average Accounts Receivable Balance	405

$$\text{Accounts Receivable Turnover} = \frac{\text{Net Sales}}{\text{Average Accounts Receivable Balance}} = \frac{27{,}931}{405} = \mathbf{69x}$$

Another ratio closely related to AR turnover is the average collection period. This is also known as days sales outstanding (DSO) or days sales in receivables, and it shows the average number of days it took to collect cash from a customer. The relationship between AR turnover and average collection period is the same as the relationship between inventory turnover and days inventory.

The formula for the average collection period is:

$$\text{Average Collection Period} = \frac{\text{Average Accounts Receivable}}{(\text{Net Credit Sales} / 365)}$$

The average collection period is particularly helpful when compared to the cash collection policy of the firm. If a company requires customers to pay within 30 days, but the average collection period is 45 days, this shows us that the company is having trouble collecting payments from its customers. Perhaps the company should instill more incentives to pay early or enforce stricter penalties for paying late. If the company has to pay its suppliers on time but constantly receives cash late from customers, there could be cash flow issues. Businesses can impact their average collection period with incentives or penalties, but they need to make sure they don't have requirements that are too stringent because customers typically appreciate the ability to pay by credit.

For Macy's, the average collection period for 2013 was 5.3 days. Taking only 5 days to collect cash is fast, but it makes sense in Macy's case because the majority of customers probably pay for their purchases by credit cards, debit cards, or cash. Credit card companies transfer cash to vendors within a few days. A retail store would generally consider purchases made by credit cards as cash purchases because the store does not deal with the hassle of collecting payment; it simply receives the cash from credit card companies and banks within a few days.

When businesses pay other businesses, they usually establish their own **credit terms**, and the collection periods are longer than collection periods for customers.

$$\text{Average Collection Period} = \frac{\text{Average Accounts Receivable}}{(\text{Net Sales} / 365)} = \frac{405}{77} = \mathbf{5.3}$$

An alternative way to calculate the average collection period is:

$$\text{Average Collection Period} = \frac{365}{\text{Accounts Receivable Turnover}}$$

This will give the same number as the previous formula and is simply a different way to think about the average collection period.

For answers to the following questions, please see the end of Chapter 6.

Review 6.4 Question 1

ABC Company has an accounts receivable turnover of 45x. What does ratio imply?

    a.   ABC Company collects receivables from customers every 45 days.

    b.   ABC Company collects receivables from customers 45 times per year.

    c.   ABC Company is slower than its competitors at collecting its receivables.

    d.   ABC Company is faster than its competitors at collecting its receivables.

Review 6.4 Question 2

Suppose a company has net credit sales of $4K, net sales of $10K, and average accounts receivable of $1K. What is the company's average collection period?

    a.   4 days

    b.   10 days

    c.   37 days

    d.   91 days

6.3.4   Accounts Payable Turnover

Another efficiency ratio is accounts payable turnover, or AP turnover, which tells us how quickly a company pays its vendors. Both suppliers of inventory as well as suppliers of services or other non-inventory items are included in the vendor category. This ratio can be thought of as the number of times a year that the average payables balance is paid off.

The formula for accounts payable turnover is:

$$\text{Accounts Payable Turnover} = \frac{\text{Credit Purchases}}{\text{Average Accounts Payable}}$$

Credit purchases are a major input for this ratio, but it can be hard to determine the amount if you're not an insider at the company. For merchandising companies, a good approximation of credit purchases is cost of goods sold. Changes in inventory or other current asset accounts could mean that more or less was sold or used than was actually purchased, so credit purchases and cost of goods sold will not be perfectly aligned, but it is a good estimate. For manufacturing companies, there are additional costs in cost of goods sold, such as labor and overhead, which are not part of actual purchases. It is much harder to figure out the added labor costs, so COGS is not an ideal approximation of credit purchases for manufacturing companies.

Throughout this book, COGS will be used as a proxy for credit purchases. Ratios using this number are particularly helpful when analyzed over time, as this draws out important trends. This approach also assumes that customers purchase all the goods on credit, not with cash. If a business tracks its cash payments, it can adjust this figure to get a more accurate ratio.

When there is no credit purchase data available, the formula for accounts payable turnover is:

$$\text{Accounts Payable Turnover} = \frac{\text{COGS}}{\text{Average Accounts Payable}}$$

When analyzing accounts payable, it's important to take into account the context of the business, looking at how the ratio has changed over time and at the terms with the suppliers. It can be beneficial for a company to have a small AP turnover and take a while to pay its suppliers. It's just important that the company is in line with the suppliers' expectations and the **credit terms**. Establishing generous payment terms with a supplier is advantageous because it basically acts as free short-term financing. But the suppliers probably build in the cost of such financing into the price of the product.

Figures 6.12, 6.13, and 6.14 show where to find the figures to calculate Macy's accounts payable turnover.

FIGURE 6.12

Macy's Inc
Consolidated Statements of Income (Unaudited)
(All amounts in millions)

	52 weeks ended February 1, 2014
Net sales	$ 27,931
Cost of sales	**16,725**
Gross margin	11,206
Selling, general and administrative expenses	(8,440)
Impairments, store closing, and other costs	(88)
Operating income	2,678
Interest expense	(388)
Premium on early retirement of debt	-
Income before taxes	2,290
Federal, state and local income tax expense	(804)
Net income	$ 1,486

FIGURE 6.13

Macy's Inc
Consolidated Balance Sheets (Unaudited)
(All amounts in millions)

	February 1, 2014		February 3, 2013	
ASSETS:				
Current Assets:				
Cash and cash equivalents	$	2,273	$	1,836
Receivables		438		371
Merchandise inventories		5,557		5,308
Prepaid expenses and other current assets		420		361
Total Current Assets		8,688		7,876
Property and Equipment – net		7,930		8,196
Goodwill		3,743		3,743
Other Intangible Assets – net		527		561
Other Assets		746		615
Total Assets	$	21,634	$	20,991
LIABILITIES AND SHAREHOLDERS' EQUITY:				
Current Liabilities:				
Short-term debt	$	463	$	124
Merchandise accounts payable		1,691		1,579
Accounts payable and accrued liabilities		2,810		2,610
Income taxes		362		355
Deferred income taxes		400		407
Total Current Liabilities		5,726		5,075
Long-Term Debt		6,728		6,806
Deferred Income Taxes		1,273		1,238
Other Liabilities		1,658		1,821
Shareholders' Equity		6,249		6,051
Total Liabilities and Shareholders' Equity	$	21,634	$	20,991

FIGURE 6.14

Notes to the Financial Statements
Accounts Payable and Accrued Liabilities

	February 1, 2014	February 2, 2013
Accounts payable	$ 746	$ 625
Gift cards and customer award certificates	840	801
Accrued wages and vacation	190	226
Taxes other than income taxes	157	195
Lease related liabilities	153	145
Current portion of workers' compensation and general liability reserves	131	138
Current portion of post employment and postretirement benefits	110	100
Accrued interest	89	78
Allowance for future sales returns	85	81
Severance and relocation	43	3
Other	266	218
	$ 2,810	$ 2,610

Macy's balance sheet has two line items about accounts payable; one is called merchandise accounts payable, and the other is called accounts payable and **accrued liabilities**. The notes to the financial statements break down the line items, mentioning that accrued liabilities included items such as retirement benefits and severance costs. These shouldn't be included in the ratio. When calculating ratios, it's important to look at the notes to the financial statements to make sure you are capturing the correct items and using the most appropriate figure.

Macy's accounts payable turnover for fiscal year 2013 was 7.2x, so Macy's pays its vendors approximately 7 times per year.

COGS	$ 16,725
Beginning Accounts Payable	625 + 1579
Ending Accounts Payable	746 + 1691
Average Accounts Payable	2,321

$$\textbf{Accounts Payable Turnover} = \frac{\text{COGS}}{\text{Average Accounts Payable}} = \frac{16,725}{2,321} = \textbf{7.21x}$$

It's also possible to convert accounts payable turnover to a measure that shows average days outstanding for payables. This ratio is called days purchases outstanding. If the days purchases outstanding is longer than the terms offered by the vendor, it could imply that the business is having trouble paying its vendors.

The formula for days purchases outstanding is:

$$\text{Days Purchases Outstanding} = \frac{\text{Average Accounts Payable}}{(\text{Annual Credit Purchases} / 365)}$$

or, if the credit purchases figure isn't available,

$$\text{Days Purchases Outstanding} = \frac{\text{Average Accounts Payable}}{(\text{COGS} / 365)}$$

For Macy's, the days purchases outstanding in 2013 was 51 days, which means that Macy's pays back its vendors within about 51 days.

$$\text{Days Purchases Outstanding} = \frac{365}{\text{Accounts Payable Turnover}} = \frac{365}{7.21} = 50.6$$

An alternate way to calculate days purchases outstanding is:

$$\text{Days Purchases Outstanding} = \frac{365}{\text{Accounts Payable Turnover}}$$

This will give the same number as the previous formula and is simply a different way to think about days purchases outstanding.

For answers to the following questions, please see the end of Chapter 6.

Review 6.5 Question 1

Suppose a company has sales of $10K, COGS of $6K, credit purchases of $2K and average accounts payable of $1K. What is the company's accounts payable turnover?

    a.   0.5x

    b.   2x

    c.   4x

    d.   6x

ABC Company has days purchases outstanding of 30. What does this imply?

    a.   ABC Company pays back its vendors about 30 times per year.

    b.   ABC Company pays back its vendors within about 30 days.

    c.   ABC Company must pay back its vendors every 30 days.

6.3.5   Cash Conversion Cycle

Three of the ratios we have just covered, days purchases outstanding, days inventory and the average collection period, can be used together to calculate the cash conversion cycle for a company. This shows the time it takes a company to pay its vendors from the time it receives cash from its customers.

The formula is:

$$\text{Cash Conversion Cycle} = \text{Days Inventory} + \text{Average Collection Period} - \text{Days Purchases Outstanding}$$

For Macy's, the cash conversion cycle would be 73 days. So, from the time Macy's receives cash from its customers, it takes the company about 73 days to pay back its vendors.

Days Inventory	118.5
Plus: Average Collection Period	5.3
Less: Days Purchases Outstanding	(50.6)
Cash Collection Period	73.2

The cash conversion cycle is an important figure because it shows us how long it takes a company to convert its resources into more cash. In general, the lower the number for the cash conversion cycle, the better. A low number implies the company is efficient, and if it has a short cash conversion cycle, it needs less financing.

Sometimes, a business can have a negative cash conversion cycle. This can occur when a company buys goods on credit from a supplier and can sell its inventory and collect cash very quickly, before payment is required by the supplier. Negative cash conversion cycles can be quite useful because a company can rely on credit from its suppliers to provide cash to purchase new inventory. This is especially true for businesses that are growing quickly.

For the answer to the following question, please see the end of Chapter 6.

Review 6.6 Question 1

Suppose a company had days purchases outstanding of 45, days inventory of 100, and an average collection period of 25 days. What would be the company's cash conversion cycle?

    a.   25

    b.   30

    c.   80

    d.   120

Section 4
Leverage

6.4.1   Leverage

The final component of the DuPont framework is financial leverage, also called the equity multiplier or gearing. This figure shows us how a company uses debt to finance its assets. If the company has an equity multiplier of 1, this means the company only uses equity for financing its purchases. As it takes out more debt, the ratio increases from 1, leading to a greater impact on the company's ROE.

If someone invests $1,000 in a firm that does not have any debt, the firm can spend $1,000 to buy assets that will generate earnings. If the firm took out some debt, it could use the extra capital to buy even more assets that will generate more profits for shareholders, if the firm's return on its assets is higher than the cost of its debt.

Taking on more leverage can be a good or bad business decision; it really depends on the circumstances. Leverage has the potential to increase the amount of cash available to spend, thus allowing a company to buy resources that will generate even more earnings. However, leverage is also risky because it magnifies losses. Equity holders for highly leveraged companies feel more of an impact when a loss occurs than equity holders for a company with little to no leverage. Even more, equity holders can face a total loss if the company goes bankrupt because debt holders are always repaid first.

The formula for leverage is:

$$\textbf{Leverage} \quad = \quad \frac{\text{Average Total Assets}}{\text{Average Total Equity}}$$

Figure 6.15 shows where to find the figures to calculate Macy's leverage.

FIGURE 6.15

Macy's Inc
Consolidated Balance Sheets (Unaudited)
(All amounts in millions)

	February 1, 2014		February 3, 2013	
ASSETS:				
Current Assets:				
Cash and cash equivalents	$	2,273	$	1,836
Receivables		438		371
Merchandise inventories		5,557		5,308
Prepaid expenses and other current assets		420		361
Total Current Assets		8,688		7,876
Property and Equipment – net		7,930		8,196
Goodwill		3,743		3,743
Other Intangible Assets – net		527		561
Other Assets		746		615
Total Assets	$	21,634	$	20,991
LIABILITIES AND SHAREHOLDERS' EQUITY:				
Current Liabilities:				
Short-term debt	$	463	$	124
Merchandise accounts payable		1,691		1,579
Accounts payable and accrued liabilities		2,810		2,610
Income taxes		362		355
Deferred income taxes		400		407
Total Current Liabilities		5,726		5,075
Long-Term Debt		6,728		6,806
Deferred Income Taxes		1,273		1,238
Other Liabilities		1,658		1,821
Shareholders' Equity		6,249		6,051
Total Liabilities and Shareholders' Equity	$	21,634	$	20,991

Macy's leverage for 2013 was 3.47x, which means that for every dollar of equity outstanding, Macy's had $3.47 dollars of assets. This implies the company is more heavily financed by debt than by equity.

$$\textbf{Leverage} = \frac{\text{Average Total Assets}}{\text{Average Total Equity}} = \frac{21,313}{6,150} = \textbf{3.47x}$$

6.4.2 Debt to Equity

Another useful for ratio for analyzing a company's leverage is the debt to equity ratio.

The formula for debt to equity is:

$$\textbf{Debt to Equity} = \frac{\text{Average Total Liabilities}}{\text{Average Total Equity}}$$

While the equity multiplier uses total assets in the numerator, the debt to equity ratio excludes equity from the numerator and only uses liabilities.

A debt to equity ratio of 1 implies that half of the company's assets are financed by equity and half are financed by debt. A debt to equity ratio greater than 1 means that more of the company's assets are financed by debt than by equity.

Lenders typically prefer a lower debt to equity ratio because it indicates less risk for the lender and suggests that the borrower will be able to pay the lenders back.

Figure 6.16 shows where to find the figures to calculate Macy's debt to equity.

FIGURE 6.16

Macy's Inc
Consolidated Balance Sheets (Unaudited)
(All amounts in millions)

		February 1, 2014		February 3, 2013
ASSETS:				
Current Assets:				
Cash and cash equivalents	$	2,273	$	1,836
Receivables		438		371
Merchandise inventories		5,557		5,308
Prepaid expenses and other current assets		420		361
Total Current Assets		8,688		7,876
Property and Equipment – net		7,930		8,196
Goodwill		3,743		3,743
Other Intangible Assets – net		527		561
Other Assets		746		615
Total Assets	$	21,634	$	20,991
LIABILITIES AND SHAREHOLDERS' EQUITY:				
Current Liabilities:				
Short-term debt	$	463	$	124
Merchandise accounts payable		1,691		1,579
Accounts payable and accrued liabilities		2,810		2,610
Income taxes		362		355
Deferred income taxes		400		407
Total Current Liabilities		5,726		5,075
Long-Term Debt		6,728		6,806
Deferred Income Taxes		1,273		1,238
Other Liabilities		1,658		1,821
Shareholders' Equity		6,249		6,051
Total Liabilities and Shareholders' Equity	$	21,634	$	20,991

For Macy's, debt to equity was 2.47x for fiscal year 2013. This means that, for each dollar of assets provided by shareholders, creditors provide $2.47 of assets.

Beginning Liabilities	$14,940
Ending Liabililities	15,385
Average Liabilities	15,163
Beginning Equity	6,051
Ending Equity	6,249
Average Equity	6,150

$$\textbf{Debt to Equity} \ = \ \frac{\text{Average Total Liabilities}}{\text{Average Total Equity}} \ = \ \frac{15{,}163}{6{,}150} \ = \ \textbf{2.47x}$$

Given the following figure, let's analyze the leverage for ABC Company.

	2012	2013
Total assets	$ 7,000	$ 9,000
Current liabilities	1,400	1,000
Long-term liabilities	1,600	2,000
Shareholder's equity	4,000	6,000
Total liabilites and shareholder's equity	$ 7,000	$ 9,000

For answers to the following questions, please see the end of Chapter 6.

Review 6.7 Question 1

The leverage ratio for ABC Company in 2013 is:

- a. 1.17x
- b. 1.50x
- c. 1.60x
- d. 1.75x

Review 6.7 Question 2

The debt to equity ratio for ABC Company in 2013 is:

- a. 0.33x
- b. 0.50x
- c. 0.60x
- d. 0.75x

Section 5
Other Ratios

Concepts

1. Current Ratio

2. Quick Ratio

3. Interest Coverage Ratio

6.5.1   Current Ratio

There are plenty of other ratios that are helpful to look at when analyzing a company's performance over time. These don't directly relate to the DuPont framework, but they still provide useful insights.

One common liquidity ratio is the current ratio, which shows a company's ability to pay its short-term obligations. The formula for the current ratio is:

$$\textbf{Current Ratio} = \frac{\text{Current Assets}}{\text{Current Liabilities}}$$

This ratio looks at a firm's ability to use its current assets to pay its current liabilities, those that are due within a year. Current assets are short-term assets such as cash, inventory and accounts receivables, and current liabilities include items such as accounts payable and wages payable. If a company has more current liabilities than current assets, leading to a current ratio of less than 1x, it could face difficulties in paying its short-term obligations. Typically, a high current ratio implies a business is in a good position to meet its near-term obligations. However, a current ratio that is too high can be negative because it could mean the business doesn't effectively manage its working capital, which is the cash available for a company's day to day operations.

Figure 6.17 shows where to find the figures to calculate Macy's current ratio.

FIGURE 6.17

Macy's Inc
Consolidated Balance Sheets (Unaudited)
(All amounts in millions)

		February 1, 2014
ASSETS:		
Current Assets:		
Cash and cash equivalents	$	2,273
Receivables		438
Merchandise inventories		5,557
Prepaid expenses and other current assets		420
Total Current Assets		**8,688**
Property and Equipment – net		7,930
Goodwill		3,743
Other Intangible Assets – net		527
Other Assets		746
Total Assets	$	21,634
LIABILITIES AND SHAREHOLDERS' EQUITY:		
Current Liabilities:		
Short-term debt	$	463
Merchandise accounts payable		1,691
Accounts payable and accrued liabilities		2,810
Income taxes		362
Deferred income taxes		400
Total Current Liabilities		**5,726**
Long-Term Debt		6,728
Deferred Income Taxes		1,273
Other Liabilities		1,658
Shareholders' Equity		6,249
Total Liabilities and Shareholders' Equity	$	21,634

Macy's had current assets of $8.7 billion and current liabilities of $5.7 billion as of February 1, 2014. Dividing current assets by current liabilities gives us a current ratio of 1.52x, which means that for every dollar in current liabilities, Macy's has 1.52 dollars in short-term assets to pay those short-term obligations.

$$\textbf{Current Ratio} \ = \ \frac{\text{Current Assets}}{\text{Current Liabilities}} \ = \ \frac{8,688}{5,726} \ = \ \textbf{1.52x}$$

FIGURE 6.18

Balance Sheet as of December 31, 2013

Assets

Cash	$ 345,000
Accounts receivable	91,000
Inventory	75,800
Prepaid rent	4,500
Equipment	5,500
Total Assets	$ 521,800

Liabilities

Accounts payable	22,000
Wages payable	13,000
Accrued utilities liability	2,200
Accrued interest liability	4,600
Bank loan	150,000
Total Liabilities	$ 191,800

Stockholders' Equity

Preferred stock	20,000
Common stock	90,000
Retained earnings	220,000
Total Stockholders' Equity	$ 330,000
Total Liabilities and Stockholders' Equity	$ 521,800

For answers to the following questions, please see the end of Chapter 6.

Review 6.8 Question 1

Calculate the current ratio from the balance sheet information in Figure 6.18.

- a. 2.69x
- b. 2.72x
- c. 12.35x
- d. 12.48x

If a company has a current ratio of less than 1x, it means

    a.   The company may have difficulties meeting its current obligations

    b.   The company is in a good position to meet its current obligations

    c.   Nothing – it's important to compare this ratio to other companies within the industry

6.5.2   Quick Ratio

Another liquidity ratio that measures a company's ability to pay its short term obligations is called the quick ratio. It is similar to the current ratio, but it only includes highly liquid current assets, so it excludes inventory. Some companies cannot immediately turn inventory into cash, so the quick ratio is a more conservative way to determine a company's ability to pay for its current liabilities because the ratio only uses current assets that can quickly be turned into cash. Items such as cash, short-term investments, and accounts receivable should be included as highly liquid current assets. The quick ratio is also known as an acid test ratio.

Figure 6.19 shows where to find the figures to calculate Macy's quick ratio.

FIGURE 6.19

Macy's Inc
Consolidated Balance Sheets (Unaudited)
(All amounts in millions)

	February 1, 2014
ASSETS:	
Current Assets:	
Cash and cash equivalents	$ 2,273
Receivables	438
Merchandise inventories	5,557
Prepaid expenses and other current assets	420
Total Current Assets	8,688
Property and Equipment – net	7,930
Goodwill	3,743
Other Intangible Assets – net	527
Other Assets	746
Total Assets	$ 21,634
LIABILITIES AND SHAREHOLDERS' EQUITY:	
Current Liabilities:	
Short-term debt	$ 463
Merchandise accounts payable	1,691
Accounts payable and accrued liabilities	2,810
Income taxes	362
Deferred income taxes	400
Total Current Liabilities	5,726
Long-Term Debt	6,728
Deferred Income Taxes	1,273
Other Liabilities	1,658
Shareholders' Equity	6,249
Total Liabilities and Shareholders' Equity	$ 21,634

Macy's quick ratio for 2013 was 0.55x, which is much lower than its current ratio of 1.52x. Macy's had a lot of inventory, so excluding this number decreases the ratio significantly. A quick ratio of 0.55x implies that Macy's would be able to settle about half of its current liabilities immediately with its highly liquid current assets.

Cash and cash equivalents	$ 2,273
Receivables	438
Prepaid expenses and other current assets	420
Highly Liquid Current Assets	3,131

$$\text{Quick Ratio} = \frac{\text{Highly Liquid Current Assets}}{\text{Current Liabilities}} = \frac{3,131}{5,726} = \textbf{0.55x}$$

6.5.3   Interest Coverage Ratio

It's important for a business to make timely interest payments on debt in order to maintain good relationships with creditors and not default on loans. The interest coverage ratio can be used to determine a company's ability to make interest payments on its debt. An interest coverage ratio below 1 implies the company is unable to make its interest payments. The formula is:

$$\text{Interest Coverage} = \frac{\text{EBIT}}{\text{Interest Expense}}$$

EBIT (Earnings Before Interest and Taxes) is calculated by adding back interest expense and tax expense to net income.

Figure 6.20 shows where to find the figures to calculate Macy's interest coverage ratio.

FIGURE 6.20

Macy's Inc
Consolidated Statements of Income (Unaudited)
(All amounts in millions)

	52 weeks ended February 1, 2014
Net sales	$ 27,931
Cost of sales	16,725
Gross margin	11,206
Selling, general and administrative expenses	(8,440)
Impairments, store closing, and other costs	(88)
Operating income	2,678
Interest expense	(388)
Premium on early retirement of debt	-
Income before taxes	2,290
Federal, state and local income tax expense	(804)
Net income	$ 1,486

Since Macy's did not have a lot of interest expense for the period, its interest coverage ratio was 6.9x. This implies that Macy's would be able to cover its interest payments nearly 7 times over.

The calculation of Macy's interest coverage ratio is shown below.

Net Income	$ 1,486
Plus: Interest Expense	388
Plus: Tax Expense	804
EBIT	$ 2,678

$$\text{Interest Coverage} = \frac{\text{EBIT}}{\text{Interest Expense}} = \frac{2{,}678}{388} = \textbf{6.90x}$$

Section 6
The Impact of Policy Differences

Concepts

1. Introduction

2. Revenue Recognition

3. Capitalizing Expenditures

4. Depreciation

5. Seasonality

6.6.1   Introduction

Ratios are an excellent way to compare performance between companies because they show performance within the context of the business. For the most part, ratios can eliminate the impact of size differences and standardize comparisons.

For example, just looking at the accounts receivable balance for one company and comparing it to another company's AR balance is not very useful because you're not factoring in the overall sales of the companies. The AR turnover ratio takes the overall sales into account, and is a much better way to see how efficient a business is at collecting its receivables.

However, it is important to be aware of the different ways companies can calculate figures that are used in ratio analysis because there is some flexibility in the way managers can record transactions. When using ratios, we want to make sure the figures are calculated similarly so we are comparing apples to apples. Accounting standards try to minimize the differences between companies, but there are occasions when two companies will choose different ways to record items that seem similar, and both ways are accepted under GAAP.

Sometimes, you need to alter the financial statements to adjust for the differences before using them for comparisons. The next few sections will examine some of these common situations.

6.6.2   Revenue Recognition

Standards for revenue recognition state that revenue should be recognized when it is earned, but complicated business models and unique situations can make this policy challenging to follow. Not every situation is accounted for in the accounting standards, so the new questions that arise can leave room for managers to decide when to recognize revenue.

For example, some retail stores have lax return policies where a customer can return an item at any time for a full refund. In the airline industry, some airlines sell tickets where part of the ticket has a life of a year or more, and there are questions about when to recognize unredeemed tickets. Some airlines sell non-refundable tickets.

The way a business chooses to handle these situations can influence the amount of revenue recognized for the period. If we're comparing two businesses that handled the situation differently, the analysis could make one appear better than the other, even if they are fundamentally the same.

6.6.3   Capitalizing Expenditures

Capitalizing expenditures is another big issue in the accounting world. Capitalization is the practice of recording a purchased item as an asset instead of an expense. Accounting standards have many rules to guide companies about whether purchased assets should be expensed or capitalized, but there is still room for judgment. How should it be handled if a business upgrades equipment that extends the useful life of the assets they already owned? Perhaps there are two firms in the same industry, and one company chooses to purchase and capitalize its assets while another leases the assets and recognizes expenses each period. The financial statements for these companies would look very different, even though they are quite similar operationally.

6.6.4   Depreciation

There are many assumptions that are made when determining how to depreciate a long-lived asset., and it's not always reasonable to assume the assumptions will remain the same throughout the lifetime of the asset. For example, there can be improvements to an asset, changes in the useful life of the asset, or changes in market conditions, all of which can affect assumptions and impact the financials and ratio analysis.

As we've seen previously, a company can also choose which depreciation method it wants to use, and this choice affects the company's ratios. Suppose a company is using the accelerated depreciation method. This method would increase depreciation expense, thereby lowering a company's profit in the early years of the asset's life. So, this would result in a lower profit margin than using the straight-line method. ROA, debt to assets, and debt to equity are some other ratios that could also be affected by differences in depreciation calculations.

6.6.5   Seasonality

The financial statements of some businesses can vary a lot due to seasonality. The fluctuations repeat themselves, often over the course of a year. Most of the ratios we have looked at have analyzed performance over a year, but if we look at financial statements over smaller time frames, such as quarters or months, we could see the variations.

It's important to consider these cycles because a business needs to be able to survive both the highs and the lows. The ratios of a business could look very different depending on where they are in their cycle. For example, retailers often sell a lot of their inventory in the fourth quarter, during the holidays. At the end of this time period, it's likely they would have a lot of cash and very little inventory. On the other hand, at the end of the third quarter, they likely used a lot of their cash to purchase inventory. Some other examples of seasonal businesses include ski shops, summer camps, and lawn care companies. It's easy to see how seasonality could change the ratios. Management needs to take into account the seasonality of a business when planning for its future.

Section 7

DuPont Ratios and Common Size Statements

Concepts

1. Summary of DuPont Ratios

2. Common Size Statements

6.7.1   Summary of DuPont Ratios

The DuPont framework consists of three areas, profitability, efficiency, and leverage, that combine together to give us the ROE for the firm.

$$\textbf{ROE} = \text{Profit Margin} * \text{Asset Turnover} * \text{Leverage}$$

$$\textbf{ROE} = \frac{\text{Net Income}}{\text{Sales}} * \frac{\text{Sales}}{\text{Average Assets}} * \frac{\text{Average Assets}}{\text{Average Equity}}$$

For Macy's, the profit margin was 5%, the asset turnover was 1.31x, and leverage was 3.47x, which gives us 0.24, or 24%, for the ROE for 2013.

$$\textbf{ROE} = 0.05 * 1.31 * 3.47 = \textbf{0.24}$$

When we divide net income by equity, we get the same number. The DuPont framework just breaks out more details, making it easier to see the key drivers of the ROE.

$$\textbf{ROE} = \frac{\text{Net Income}}{\text{Average Equity}} = \frac{1,486}{6,150} = \textbf{0.24}$$

The insights gained from analyzing the DuPont ratios can help managers identify the areas to focus on to improve the business. If a profitable company increases any one of the areas, it can increase its ROE and generate more returns for investors. But if the company chooses to increase leverage, it also makes the business a riskier investment. If the business makes a loss, the higher leverage magnifies the negative ROE.

When analyzing one company, a higher ROE is typically better than a lower ROE, but when analyzing companies in different industries, a higher ROE does not automatically imply that one business is better than another. It's essential to take into consideration other aspects of the business, operations, and industry.

The individual components of ROE can vary greatly between companies depending on the type of business. For example, an online retailer might have a very low profit margin because it fights stiff competition and doesn't add a lot of value to the product that it is purchasing from the vendor. However, a manufacturer or technology company that uses proprietary techniques can likely demand a much higher premium for their product, which results in a higher profit margin.

This chapter covered the formulas and interpretations of many ratios that are commonly used in financial analysis. Figure 6.21 summarizes the direction that indicates better or improving financial performance for each ratio. However, you should always keep in mind that ratios are best analyzed within the context of an industry or a company over time.

FIGURE 6.21

Ratio	Metric	Which direction reflects better / improving financial performance?
Profitability Ratios		
Profit Margin	%	Higher
Gross Profit Margin	%	Higher
Efficiency Ratios		
Asset Turnover	x	Higher
Inventory Turnover	x	Higher
Days Inventory Outstanding	days	Lower
Accounts Receivable Turnover	x	Higher
Average Collection Period	days	Lower
Accounts Payable Turnover	x	Lower
Days Purchases Outstanding	days	Higher
Cash Conversion Cycle	days	Lower
Leverage Ratios		
Leverage	x	Depends*
Debt to Equity	x	Depends*
Current Ratio	x	Depends*
Quick Ratio	x	Depends*
Interest Coverage Ratio	x	Higher

*A higher ratio is more risky, but it can also bring more rewards. It often indicates more liquidity, but if the number is too high, it could imply inefficient deployment of capital.

6.7.2   Common Size Statements

One common problem when comparing financial statements from different companies is that different sizes and scales of businesses can make it difficult to compare them. To make it easier to compare financials across companies, an analyst can prepare common-size financial statements.

Common size financial statements divide each number on the balance sheet by total assets and each number on the income statement by sales. This converts the financial statement items into ratios that help us see trends and can easily be compared from one company to another.

Figures 6.22 and 6.23 show the common size statements for Macy's.

FIGURE 6.22

Macy's Inc
Common Size Income Statement

	52 weeks ended February 1, 2014	52 weeks ended February 2, 2013
Net sales	100%	100%
Cost of sales	60%	60%
Gross margin	40%	40%
Selling, general and administrative expenses	(30%)	(31%)
Impairments, store closing, and other costs	-	-
Operating income	10%	10%
Interest expense	(1%)	(2%)
Premium on early retirement of debt	-	-
Income before taxes	8%	8%
Federal, state and local income tax expense	(3%)	(3%)
Net income	5%	5%

FIGURE 6.23

Macy's Inc
Common Size Balance Sheet

	February 1, 2014	February 3, 2013
ASSETS:		
Current Assets:		
Cash and cash equivalents	11%	9%
Receivables	2%	2%
Merchandise inventories	26%	25%
Prepaid expenses and other current assets	2%	2%
Total Current Assets	40%	38%
Property and Equipment – net	37%	39%
Goodwill	17%	18%
Other Intangible Assets – net	2%	3%
Other Assets	3%	3%
Total Assets	100%	100%
LIABILITIES AND SHAREHOLDERS' EQUITY:		
Current Liabilities:		
Short-term debt	2%	1%
Merchandise accounts payable	8%	8%
Accounts payable and accrued liabilities	13%	12%
Income taxes	2%	2%
Deferred income taxes	2%	2%
Total Current Liabilities	26%	24%
Long-Term Debt	31%	32%
Deferred Income Taxes	6%	6%
Other Liabilities	8%	9%
Shareholders' Equity	29%	29%
Total Liabilities and Shareholders' Equity	100%	100%

Section 8

Review

Ratio analysis is a useful tool of financial statement analysis that allows us to understand how a business is performing and discover relationships between financial statement items. Ratios are used for comparisons, so it's really important to understand the company and its industry to draw meaningful conclusions.

ROE, or **return on equity**, is a good indicator of how well a business' management creates value for its owners. It shows the return generated by a business on the equity invested by the business owners.

$$\textbf{ROE} = \frac{\text{Net Income}}{\text{Average Total Owners' Equity}}$$

To understand what drives ROE, we use the **DuPont framework**, which includes components related to profitability, operating efficiency, and financial leverage.

$$\textbf{ROE} = \text{Profit Margin * Asset Turnover * Leverage}$$

$$\frac{\text{Net Income}}{\text{Avg Equity}} = \frac{\text{Net Income}}{\text{Sales}} * \frac{\text{Sales}}{\text{Avg Total Assets}} * \frac{\text{Avg Total Assets}}{\text{Avg Equity}}$$

Although profit margin, asset turnover, and the leverage ratio are the key ratios used in the DuPont framework, there are many other ratios that are helpful for measuring the profitability, efficiency, and leverage of a business.

Profitability

Profit margin tells us how much a company keeps in earnings for every dollar of sales after all the expenses have been subtracted. It's particularly useful for comparing companies in similar industries.

$$\textbf{Profit Margin} = \frac{\text{Net Income}}{\text{Total Sales}}$$

Gross profit margin is the percentage of revenue available to pay for a company's expenses after the cost of goods sold is subtracted.

$$\textbf{Gross Profit Margin} = \frac{\text{Gross Profit}}{\text{Sales}}$$

Earnings before interest after taxes, or **EBIAT**, shows the earnings a company has generated without the effects of the company's capital structure. EBIAT is sometimes referred to as Net Operating Profit After Taxes (NOPAT).

$$\text{EBIAT} = (\text{Income Before Taxes} + \text{Interest}) * \left(1 - \frac{\text{Tax expense}}{\text{Income before taxes}}\right)$$

$$\text{EBIAT} = \text{EBIT} * (1 - \text{Corporate tax rate})$$

Efficiency

Asset turnover measures the efficiency with which a company uses its assets to generate revenues. The company that uses fewer assets to produce more sales operates better from an efficiency perspective.

For ratios that use both income statement and balance sheet items, we generally use the average of the beginning and ending balance sheet items.

$$\textbf{Asset Turnover} = \frac{\text{Revenues}}{\text{Average Total Assets}}$$

Inventory turnover is the number of times a company sells through and replaces its inventory during a year. A higher inventory turnover ratio indicates more efficient inventory management. It's important to remember to use average inventory in the denominator because inventory levels can vary significantly over the course of an accounting period.

$$\textbf{Inventory Turnover} = \frac{\text{COGS}}{\text{Average Inventory}}$$

Days inventory is the average number of days that items sit in inventory before being sold.

$$\textbf{Days Inventory} = \frac{\text{Average Inventory}}{(\text{COGS} / 365)}$$

$$\textbf{Days Inventory} = \frac{365}{\text{Inventory Turnover}}$$

Accounts receivable turnover, or **AR turnover**, shows how quickly a company collects payment from its customers. It's defined as the number of times per year that a company collects its receivables. A higher AR turnover indicates more efficient cash collections.

$$\textbf{Accounts Receivable Turnover} = \frac{\text{Net Credit Sales}}{\text{Average Accounts Receivable Balance}}$$

Average collection period, also called **days sales outstanding (DSO)** or **days sales in receivables**, shows the average number of days it took to collect cash from a customer. This ratio can be compared to the company's collection policy to see whether it is efficient at collecting from customers.

$$\textbf{Average Collection Period } = \frac{\text{Average Accounts Receivable}}{(\text{Net Credit Sales} / 365)}$$

$$\textbf{Average Collection Period } = \frac{365}{\text{Accounts Receivable Turnover}}$$

Accounts payable turnover, or **AP turnover**, is defined as the number of times per year a company pays its vendors. It's ideal to use credit purchases for the numerator of this ratio, but when the figure isn't available, COGS is a reasonable estimate.

$$\textbf{Accounts Payable Turnover } = \frac{\text{Credit Purchases}}{\text{Average Accounts Payable}}$$

When there is no credit purchase data available, the formula for accounts payable turnover is:

$$\textbf{Accounts Payable Turnover } = \frac{\text{COGS}}{\text{Average Accounts Payable}}$$

Days purchases outstanding shows the average days outstanding for payables.

$$\textbf{Days Purchases Outstanding } = \frac{\text{Average Accounts Payable}}{(\text{Annual Credit Purchases} / 365)}$$

Or, if the credit purchases figure isn't available,

$$\textbf{Days Purchases Outstanding } = \frac{\text{Average Accounts Payable}}{(\text{COGS} / 365)}$$

$$\textbf{Days Purchases Outstanding } = \frac{365}{\text{Accounts Payable Turnover}}$$

The **cash conversion cycle** shows the time it takes a company to pay its vendors from the time it receives cash from its customers.

$$\text{Cash Conversion Cycle} = \text{Days Inventory} + \text{Average Collection Period} - \text{Days Purchases Outstanding}$$

The cash conversion cycle is an important figure because it shows us how long it takes a company to convert its resources into more cash. In general, the lower the number for the cash conversion cycle, the better. A low number implies the company is efficient, and if it has a short cash conversion cycle, it needs less financing.

Leverage

Financial leverage, also called the **equity multiplier**, shows us how a company uses debt to finance its assets. A company that is completely financed by equity has an equity multiplier of 1. As debt increases, the equity multiplier increases.

Leverage has the potential to increase the amount of cash available to spend, thus allowing a company to buy resources that will generate even more earnings. However, leverage is also risky because it magnifies losses.

$$\textbf{Leverage} = \frac{\text{Average Total Assets}}{\text{Average Total Equity}}$$

A **debt to equity** ratio of 1 implies that half of the company's assets are financed by equity and half are financed by debt. A debt to equity ratio greater than 1 means that more of the company's assets are financed by debt than by equity.

$$\textbf{Debt to Equity} = \frac{\text{Average Total Liabilities}}{\text{Average Total Equity}}$$

Other Ratios

Current ratio shows a company's ability to pay its short-term obligations.

$$\textbf{Current Ratio} = \frac{\text{Current Assets}}{\text{Current Liabilities}}$$

Another liquidity ratio that measures a company's ability to pay its short-term obligations is called the **quick ratio**, or the **acid test ratio**. It is similar to the current ratio, but it only includes highly liquid current assets, so it excludes inventory.

$$\textbf{Quick Ratio} \quad = \quad \frac{\text{Highly Liquid Current Assets}}{\text{Current Liabilities}}$$

The **interest coverage ratio**, also called **times interest earned**, can be used to determine a company's ability to make interest payments on its debt. An interest coverage ratio below 1 implies the company is unable to make its interest payments. The number used in the numerator, EBIT, or Earnings Before Interest and Taxes, is calculated by adding back interest expense and tax expense to net income.

$$\textbf{Interest Coverage} \quad = \quad \frac{\text{EBIT}}{\text{Interest Expense}}$$

Impact of Timing Differences

For the most part, ratios can eliminate the impact of size differences and standardize comparisons between companies. However, it's important to be aware of timing differences and the flexibility in calculating ratios in some industries. Some common situations involve revenue recognition, the capitalization of expenditures, the depreciation of assets, and the seasonality of a business.

Revenue should be recognized when it is earned, but unique situations, such as refund or return policies, can make this revenue recognition policy challenging to follow.

Capitalization is the practice of recording a purchased item as an asset instead of an expense, and although there are accounting standards regarding capitalization, there is still some room for judgment.

Different depreciation methods or changes in the assumptions made when recognizing depreciation can impact ratio analysis.

The seasonality of some businesses significantly affects their ratios, which can look very different depending on where they are in their cycle.

Common Size Financial Statements

Different sizes and scales of businesses can make it difficult to compare their financials, so analysts often prepare common-size financial statements to make it easier to compare them. Common size financial statements divide each number on the balance sheet by total assets and each number on the income statement by sales.

Section 9
Review Questions

For answers to the following questions, please see the end of Chapter 6.

Review 6.9 Question 1

Profitability, operating efficiency, and leverage are the major components of

- a.   the DuPont Framework
- b.   the Cash Conversion Cycle
- c.   EBIAT

Review 6.9 Question 2

The DuPont framework uses the following ratios...
Please select all that apply.

- a.   Profit margin
- b.   Gross profit margin
- c.   Inventory turnover
- d.   Debt to equity
- e.   Asset turnover
- f.   Equity multiplier

Review 6.9 Question 3

Select which items are used to calculate the ratio.

Profit Margin

- a.   Net income
- b.   Total sales
- c.   Cost of sales
- d.   Operating income

Review 6.9 Question 4

Select which items are used to calculate the ratio.

Gross Profit Margin

    a.   Sales

    b.   COGS

    c.   Gross profit

    d.   EBIAT

Review 6.9 Question 5

Select which items are used to calculate the ratio.

Asset Turnover

    a.   Sales

    b.   Ending Assets

    c.   Average Assets

    d.   Net Income

Review 6.9 Question 6

Select which items are used to calculate the ratio.

Days Inventory

    a.   Net Credit Sales

    b.   Average Inventory

    c.   Inventory Turnover

    d.   365

Review 6.9 Question 7

Select which items are used to calculate the ratio.

AR Turnover

a.   Net Credit Sales

b.   Beginning Inventory Balance

c.   Ending Inventory Balance

d.   Average AR balance

e.   365

Review 6.9 Question 8

Asset turnover and AR turnover are measures of

a.   profitability

b.   efficiency

c.   leverage

Review 6.9 Question 9

Inventory turnover uses figures from

a.   the balance sheet

b.   the income statement

c.   both the balance sheet and the income statement

Review 6.9 Question 10

For the AP Turnover ratio, COGS can be used to replace credit purchases for

a.   Merchandising companies

b.   Manufacturing companies

c.   All companies

Review 6.9 Question 11

The profit margin for The Flower Shop (TFS) for the year 2013 was 4.62%. Select the correct interpretation.

    a.   TFS generated $4.62 of revenues for each dollar of assets.
    b.   TFS earned $4.62 for every $100 of sales.
    c.   TFS earned $1.00 of revenue for $4.62 of assets.
    d.   TFS earned $1.00 for every $4.62 of sales.

Review 6.9 Question 12

If inventory turnover is 4x, it means the company sells through its inventory

    a.   every 4 months
    b.   every 3 months
    c.   4 times per month

Review 6.9 Question 13

A low inventory turnover could suggest...
Please select all that apply.

    a.   good inventory management
    b.   good receivable collection methods
    c.   excess production
    d.   poor inventory management

Review 6.9 Question 14

Suppose you are looking at the asset turnover ratios of a financial advisory firm and a manufacturing company. Which one would likely have a higher asset turnover ratio?

    a.   the financial advisory firm
    b.   the manufacturing company

Review 6.9 Question 15

A low-margin industry would likely have a

a. higher inventory turnover than a high-margin industry
b. lower inventory turnover than a high-margin industry
c. similar inventory turnover to a high-margin industry

Review 6.9 Question 16

Suppose a company in the retail industry has a low inventory turnover. This could imply...
Please select all that apply.

a. poor sales
b. good sales
c. excess inventory levels
d. inadequate inventory levels

Review 6.9 Question 17

Suppose average accounts payable is $3,000 and COGS is $15,000. Approximately what is days purchases outstanding?

a. 5
b. 6
c. 60
d. 73

Review 6.9 Question 18

Suppose the average collection period is 6.0x. Net credit sales is $18,250 and the ending accounts receivable was $350. What was beginning accounts receivable?

a. 250
b. 300
c. 350
d. 400

Review 6.9 Question 19

The average collection period...
Please select all that apply.

    a.   is also known as days purchases outstanding
    b.   is also known as days sales outstanding
    c.   is also known as days sales in receivables
    d.   shows the average days outstanding for payables

Review 6.9 Question 20

Common size financial statements divide each number on the balance sheet by

    a.   total assets
    b.   current assets
    c.   total sales
    d.   COGS

Review 6.9 Question 21

Suppose there are two companies in the same industry. Company A's leverage is 4.0x and Company B's leverage is 0.5x. Based on leverage, other things being equal, which one is less risky for equity holders?

    a.   Company A
    b.   Company B

Review 6.9 Question 22

For fiscal year 2013, Company A has an ROE of 25%, profit margin of 10%, sales of $20,000 and assets of $40,000. What was Company A's average total equity for fiscal year 2013?

    a. $4,000
    b. $6,000
    c. $8,000
    d. $10,000

Review 6.9 Question 23

Suppose two companies in the same industry have an ROE of 0.20. Company A has a profit margin of 10% and an asset turnover of 2x. Company B has an asset turnover of 1.3x and leverage of 3.0x.

Which one has greater profit margin?

    a.   Company A
    b.   Company B

Review 6.9 Question 24

Suppose two companies in the same industry have an ROE of 0.20. Company A has a profit margin of 10% and an asset turnover of 2x. Company B has an asset turnover of 1.3x and leverage of 3.0x.

Which one uses its assets more efficiently?

    a.   Company A
    b.   Company B

Review 6.9 Question 25

Suppose two companies in the same industry have an ROE of 0.20. Company A has a profit margin of 10% and an asset turnover of 2x. Company B has an asset turnover of 1.3x and leverage of 3.0x.

Which one is more highly levered?

    a.   Company A
    b.   Company B

Section 10

Answer Key

Review 6.1 Explanations

Question 1

Answer: B

Profit margin = net income / total sales = $4,000 / $50,000 = 0.08 = 8%.

Question 2

Answer: C

Gross profit margin = gross profit / sales = $20,000 / $50,000 = 0.4 = 40%.

Review 6.2 Explanations

Question 1

Answer: D

Asset turnover = revenues / average total assets. Average total assets = ($3,000 + $5,000)/2 = $4,000. So, asset turnover = $5,000 / $4,000 = 1.25x.

Review 6.3 Explanations

Question 1

Answer: D

Inventory turnover = COGS / average inventory = $3,000 / $1,000 = 3x.

Question 2

Answer: B

Days inventory outstanding = 365/ inventory turnover = average inventory / (COGS / 365) = $1,000 / ($3,000/365) = 122 days.

Review 6.4 Explanations

Question 1

Answer: B

Accounts receivable turnover = net sales / average accounts receivable, and it shows how quickly a company collects payment from its customers. An accounts receivable turnover of 45x implies that ACB Company collects receivables from customers 45 times per year. The average collection period tells us how many days it takes to collect receivables from customers. In order to know how efficient ABC Company is at collecting receivables compared to its competitors, we would also need to know the competitors' accounts receivable turnover ratios.

Question 2

Answer: D

Average collection period = 365 / accounts receivable turnover = average accounts receivable / (net credit sales / 365) = $1,000 / ($4,000 / 365) = 91 days.

Review 6.5 Explanations

Question 1

Answer: B

Accounts payable turnover = credit purchases / average accounts payable = $2,000 / $1,000 = 2x.

Question 2

Answer: B

Days purchases outstanding shows the average number of days outstanding for payables. If ABC Company has days purchases outstanding of 30, it implies that ABC Company pays back its vendors within about 30 days. Accounts payable turnover tells us the number of times a company pays its vendors per year. Credit terms define the number of days a vendor gives a company to pay its bills.

Review 6.6 Explanations

Question 1

Answer: C

Cash conversion cycle = days inventory outstanding + average collection period – days purchases outstanding = 100 + 25 – 45 = 80.

Review 6.7 Explanations

Question 1

Answer: C

Leverage = average total assets / average total equity. Average total assets = ($7,000+$9,000)/2 = $8,000 and average total equity = ($4,000 + $6,000)/2 = $5,000. So, the leverage ratio for ABC Company = $8,000 / $5,000 = 1.60x.

Question 2

Answer: C

Debt to equity = average total liabilities / average total equity. Average total liabilities = ($1,400+$1,600+$1,000+$2,000)/2 = $3,000 and average total equity = ($4,000 + $6,000)/2 = $5,000. So, the debt to equity ratio for ABC Company = $3,000 / $5,000 = 0.60x.

Review 6.8 Explanations

Question 1

Answer: C

Current ratio = current assets / current liabilities. Current assets = cash + accounts receivable + inventory + prepaid rent = $345,000 + $91,000 + $75,800 +$4,500= $516,300. Equipment is not a current asset because it will provide a benefit to the company for over one year. Current liabilities = accounts payable + wages payable + accrued utilities liability +accrued interest liability = $22,000 + $13,000 + $2,200 +$4,600 = $41,800. So, the current ratio = $516,300 / $41,800 = 12.35x. The bank loan of $150,000, appearing at the bottom of the list of liabilities is a long-term obligation and should not be included in the calculation of current liabilities for the current ratio.

Question 2

Answer: A

A company with a current ratio of less than 1, has more current liabilities coming due, than assets being turned into ready cash in the near term. Companies in this position may have difficulty meeting payments of their short-term obligations.

Chapter Review 6.9 Explanations

Question 1

Answer: A

The DuPont Framework breaks down ROE into three components that measure profitability, operating efficiency and leverage. The DuPont Framework formula is

ROE = profit margin * asset turnover * leverage. The cash conversion cycle shows the amount of time it takes a company to pay its vendors from the time it receives cash from its customers. EBIAT stands for Earnings Before Interest After Taxes and is measure of profitability.

Question 2

Answers: A, E, F

The DuPont Framework formula is ROE = profit margin * asset turnover * equity multiplier.

Question 3

Answers: A, B

Profit margin = net income / total sales

Question 4

Answers: A, C

Gross profit margin = gross profit / sales

Question 5

Answers: A, C

Asset turnover = average assets / sales

Question 6

Answers: C, D

Days inventory outstanding =365 / inventory turnover

Question 7

Answers: A, D

AR turnover = net credit sales / average AR balance

Question 8

Answer: B

Asset turnover and AR turnover are measures of efficiency. Asset turnover shows the efficiency with which a company uses its assets to generate revenues. AR turnover shows how quickly a company collects payment from its customers.

Question 9

Answer: C

Inventory turnover uses figures from both the balance sheet and the income statement. Inventory turnover = COGS / average inventory, and COGS is found on the income statement while average inventory is found on the balance sheet.

Question 10

Answer: A

For the AP turnover ratio, COGS can be used to replace credit purchases for merchandising companies since COGS is a relatively good estimate of credit purchases. For manufacturing companies, COGS includes many other costs, such as labor and overhead, so it is not a good approximation of credit purchases.

Question 11

Answer: B

The profit margin for TFS was 4.62%, which means that TFS earned $4.62 dollars for every $100 of sales. Profit margin = net income / total sales.

Question 12

Answer: B

If inventory turnover is 4x, it means the company sells through its inventory 4 times per year, or every three months (12 months / 4 times = 3 months).

Question 13

Answers: C, D

A low inventory turnover could suggest excess production and / or poor inventory management. Inventory turnover = COGS / average inventory and measures how fast a company sells through its inventory. A low inventory turnover ratio implies the company does not sell through its inventory quickly. This could be because it has too much inventory that simply sits at the company instead of being sold. Receivables are not related to the inventory turnover ratio.

Question 14

Answer: A

The asset turnover ratio of a financial advisory firm would likely be higher than the asset turnover ratio of a manufacturing company. Asset turnover = revenues / average total assets. A manufacturing company likely has a lot more assets to manufacture its products, and higher denominator would create a lower asset turnover ratio.

Question 15

Answer: A

A low margin industry would likely have higher inventory turnover than a high-margin industry. A low margin industry is one where a company does not earn a large profit on each item it sells. So, the company would need to sell a lot more inventory in order to earn profit. This would cause inventory turnover to be higher for a low margin industry than a high margin industry.

Question 16

Answers: A, C

If a company in the retail industry has a low inventory turnover, it could imply poor sales and / or excess inventory. Inventory turnover = COGS / average inventory. Either having low COGS (poor sales), or having high average inventory (excess inventory) could cause the inventory turnover ratio to be low. If the company had inadequate inventory, the denominator would be very low, and the inventory turnover would be high.

Question 17

Answer: D

Days purchases outstanding = 365 / accounts payable turnover = average accounts payable / (COGS / 365) = $3,000 / ($15,000 / 365) = 73 days.

Question 18

Answer: A

Average collection period = average accounts receivable / (net credit sales / 365) = ((beginning AR + ending AR)/2) / (net credit sales / 365). So, ((Beginning AR + 350) / 2) / (18,250 / 365) = 6.0x. This equation gives us (Beginning AR + 350) / 2 = 300, and when we solve for beginning AR, we get $250.

Question 19

Answers: B, C

The average collection period is also known as days sales outstanding and as days sales in receivables. The formula is average collection period = average accounts receivable / (net credit sales / 365).

Question 20

Answer: A

Common size financial statements divide each number on the balance sheet by total assets and divide each number on the income statement by total sales.

Question 21

Answer: B

Leverage = average total assets / average total equity. Leverage shows us how a company uses debt to finance its assets, and a leverage ratio of 1.0x means the company only uses equity to finance its purchases. The leverage ratio increases as a company uses more debt to finance its assets. Company A's leverage ratio is 4.0x and Company B's leverage is 0.5x, so Company A has more leverage and is more risky for equity holders and Company B is less risky for equity holders.

Question 22

Answer: C

ROE = net income / average total equity

Profit margin – net income / sales

We know that ROE = net income / average total equity and profit margin = net income / sales. We can calculate net income by using the profit margin formula and the information in the question: 10% = net income / $20,000, so net income = $2,000. Then we can calculate average total equity by using the ROE formula, the information in the question, and the net income we calculated. 25% = $2,000 / average total equity, so average total equity = $8,000. We didn't need to know the assets in order to determine average total equity.

Question 23

Answer: A

We need to calculate the profit margin for Company B in order to see which company appears more profitable. ROE = profit margin * asset turnover * leverage. For Company B, 0.20 = profit margin * 1.3 * 3.0, so profit margin = 5%. Since Company A has a higher profit margin than Company B (10% vs. 5%), Company A appears more profitable.

Question 24

Answer: A

Asset turnover = revenues / average total assets. Company A has an asset turnover of 2x and Company B has an asset turnover of 1.3x, so Company A uses its assets more efficiently. Company A generated $2 of revenues for each dollar of assets whereas Company B generated $1.30 of revenues for each dollar of assets.

Question 25

Answer: B

We need to calculate the leverage for Company A in order to see which company is more highly levered. ROE = profit margin * asset turnover* leverage. For Company A, 0.20 = 10% * 2.0 * leverage, so leverage = 1.0x. A higher leverage ratio means a company has more debt and is more highly levered, so Company B is more highly levered than Company A (3.0x vs. 1.0x).

7

Forecasting and Valuation

Sections

Section 1

Introduction

Concepts

1. Introduction to Forecasting

7.1.1   Introduction to Forecasting

It's extremely important to know how to analyze historical statements so we can understand how a business is performing and identify the key drivers behind that performance. The past few chapters have covered these topics in-depth.

However, it's also essential to anticipate how a business might perform in the future so that investors can make smart decisions and management can prepare for upcoming challenges. Obviously, it's impossible to know exactly how a business will perform, but many businesses create projected financial statements based on certain assumptions that show what management expects to happen. These statements are called forecasts, financial projections, pro-formas, plans, or budgets.

Budgets are very useful to companies because they allow them to plan in advance for future needs. For example, if a company believes sales will increase significantly in the coming years, it may need to purchase additional inventory or hire more factory workers. Budgets can also be helpful in terms of financing; in order to fund those purchases or new hires, a company might need to obtain additional loans. If a company doesn't have a budget, it could be taken by surprise and learn too late that it needs more financing. Management needs to plan ahead and anticipate the future needs of a business.

A business also uses forecasts when evaluating the different directions it can take or which strategy it should pursue. Sometimes, a business creates multiple forecast scenarios to determine the impact of various events on the business. This can help a business decide which market to focus on or what product to manufacture.

Projections are also used by investors and lenders when they are deciding whether to invest or extend credit to a business.

A business' financial projections are never guaranteed and involve a lot of uncertainty because it is challenging to predict the future. Despite the potential that the forecasts won't be accurate, it is helpful for businesses to make predictions based on the most accurate information available.

This chapter will focus on how to create financial forecasts, how to convert them into cash flows, and how to value cash flow forecasts.

Section 2
Pro-Forma Financial Statements

Concepts

1. Percent of Sales Forecasting

2. Property, Plant, and Equipment

3. Current Portion of Long-Term Debt

4. Interest Expense

5. Income Tax Expense

6. Retained Earnings

7. Borrowings

8. Review

7.2.1   Percent of Sales Forecasting

Many businesses use pro-forma financial statements to create forecasts. Pro-formas show what management expects the business' financials to look like over a certain period of time, if the assumptions that management made hold true. The first step in creating pro-formas is to consider the strategic goals of the company, which will then guide the projections for the company's resources and operations. In this chapter, we will create a pro-forma income statement and balance sheet for Java Joe.

One common method of forecasting is called the percent of sales method. It's based on the assumption that many balance sheet and income statement accounts vary with sales.

To create the pro-formas, the company uses the strategic goals, in addition to the expected market conditions, to predict the top line of the income statement for the forecast period. It's important that the company has an accurate estimate for the sales figures because many other items in the statements are based off of expected sales. For 2014, Java Joe was expecting sales growth of approximately 20%, so this assumption will be used in the forecasts.

After estimating the expected sales, management needs to analyze recent financial statements to identify patterns among different items of the statements. For example, there is often a relationship between a given account and the level of sales, so the percent of sales forecasting method is typically used for these accounts. This method includes accounts such as current asset accounts, current liability accounts, and variable costs. These accounts increase proportionately as sales increase.

Variable costs are expenses that change proportionately with a company's production levels. For Java Joe, coffee beans would be a variable cost. As Java Joe sells more coffee, it must buy more coffee beans. It's also logical that inventory and accounts receivable would increase as sales increase. Similarly, current liabilities, such as accounts payable, would increase because the company would be purchasing more products from suppliers to keep up with sales.

For Java Joe, we will assume many costs are variable, but there are some situations where costs are not directly tied to revenue, and those require very detailed cost forecasts in order to create useful pro-formas. For example, a pharmaceutical company can spend a significant amount of money on research and development (R&D) that isn't necessarily tied to revenue in the current period but can be tied to revenue in future periods. The level of detail required for costs depends on the type of company and the purpose of the pro-formas.

The balance sheet and income statement for Java Joe are shown below in Figures 7.1 and 7.2. Which accounts can be forecasted using the percent of sales method?

FIGURE 7.1

Java Joe Income Statement
For the Year Ended December 31, 2013
$ in thousands

Sales	$ 420,000
Cost of goods sold	185,305
Gross profit	234,695
Operating expenses	112,522
Selling, general and administrative	25,789
Depreciation and amortization	15,400
Total operating expenses	153,711
Income from operations	80,984
Interest income (expense)	(325)
Income before income taxes	80,659
Income tax provision	28,231
Net income	$ 52,428

FIGURE 7.2

Java Joe Balance Sheet
As of December 31, 2013
$ in thousands

Assets

Cash	$ 30,705
Accounts receivable	20,603
Inventory	53,250
Prepaid expenses and other	9,238
Total current assets	113,796
Property, plant & equipment	104,616
Accumulated depreciation	(22,500)
Net property, plant & equipment	82,116
Total Assets	$ 195,912

Liabilities and Shareholders' Equity

Current liabilities

Accounts payable	$ 11,563
Accrued compensation and benefits	10,115
Deferred revenue	6,022
Current portion of long-term debt	1,200
Accrued expenses	1,032
Total current liabilities	32,072

Long-term liabilities

Long-term debt	2,050
Total Liabilities	34,122

Shareholders' equity

Common stock and paid-in capital	69,500
Retained earnings	92,290
Total shareholders' equity	161,790
Total liabilities and equity	$ 195,912

The next step is to determine the relationship between certain accounts on the income statement and sales. Projected depreciation and amortization expense is not calculated as a percentage of sales, so it is listed as N/A in Figure 7.3.

FIGURE 7.3

	2013	% of sales
Sales	$ 420,000	100.00%
Cost of goods sold	185,305	44.12%
Gross profit	234,695	55.88%
Operating expenses	112,522	26.79%
Selling, general and administrative	25,789	6.14%
Depreciation and amortization	15,400	N/A
Total operating expenses	153,711	36.60%

We already know that Java Joe expects sales for fiscal year 2014 to grow by 20%. In order to calculate projected sales, we need to multiply the 2013 sales figure by 1+ growth rate. So, sales for fiscal year 2014 is expected to be $420,000 * (1 + 0.20) = $504,000. Using this figure, and the relationship between sales and other income statement accounts, we can determine the figures for several other 2014 accounts.

FIGURE 7.4

	FY 2013	% of sales	Calculation	PF 2014
Sales	$ 420,000	100.00%	420,000 * 120%	$ 504,000
Cost of goods sold	185,305	44.12%	504,000 * 44.12%	222,365
Gross profit	234,695	55.88%		281,635
Operating expenses	112,522	26.79%	504,000 * 26.79%	$ 135,022
Selling, general and administrative	25,789	6.14%	504,000 * 6.14%	$ 30,946

We follow a similar process for current asset and current liability accounts on the balance sheet. The property, plant and equipment account does not necessarily vary with sales; this account will be covered in the next subsection of this chapter. Determining the figure for the current portion of long-term debt will also be covered in a later subsection of this chapter.

FIGURE 7.5

Assets	12/31/13	% of sales
Cash	$ 30,705	7.31%
Accounts receivable	20,603	4.91%
Inventory	53,250	12.68%
Prepaid expenses and other	9,238	2.20%
Total current assets	113,796	27.09%

	12/31/13	Addit PP&E
Property, plant & equipment	104,616	15,000
Accumulated depreciation	(22,500)	
Net property, plant & equipment	82,116	

Total Assets	$ 195,912	

Liabilities and Shareholders' Equity

Current liabilities	12/31/13	% of sales
Accounts payable	$ 11,563	2.75%
Accrued compensation and benefits	10,115	2.41%
Deferred revenue	6,022	1.43%
Current portion of long-term debt	1,200	N/A
Accrued expenses	1,032	0.25%
Total current liabilities	32,072	7.64%

FIGURE 7.6

	2014 Projected Sales:		$504,000	
Assets	**12/31/13**	**% of sales**	**Calculation**	**PF 2014**
Cash	$ 30,705	7.31%	504,000 * 7.31%	$ 36,842
Accounts receivable	20,603	4.91%	504,000 * 4.91%	24,746
Inventory	53,250	12.68%	504,000 * 12.68%	63,907
Prepaid expenses and other	9,238	2.20%	504,000 * 2.20%	11,088
Total current assets	113,796	27.09%		$ 136,584
	12/31/13	**Addit PP&E**	**Calculation**	**PF 2014**
Property, plant & equipment	104,616	15,000	104,616 + 15,000	119,616
Accumulated depreciation	(22,500)		(22,500) + (13,423)	(35,923)
Net property, plant & equipment	82,116			83,693
Total Assets	$ 195,912			
Liabilities and Shareholders' Equity				
Current liabilities	**12/31/13**	**% of sales**	**Calculation**	**PF 2014**
Accounts payable	$ 11,563	2.75%	504,000 * 2.75%	$ 13,860
Accrued compensation and benefits	10,115	2.41%	504,000 * 2.41%	12,146
Deferred revenue	6,022	1.43%	504,000 * 1.43%	7,207
Current portion of long-term debt	1,200	N/A		??
Accrued expenses	1,032	0.25%	504,000 * 0.25%	1,260
Total current liabilities	32,072	7.64%		$ 34,474

7.2.2 Property, Plant, and Equipment

The next step for creating pro-formas is looking at some other accounts on the balance sheet that might not vary proportionately with sales. Capital investments, the investments that a business makes in property and equipment, do tend to grow proportionately with sales in the long-run, but in the short-term, growth generally follows a more stepped pattern.

Investments in Property, Plant and Equipment (PP&E) can be quite large and typically require a big time commitment. So, businesses usually take that fact into account and plan ahead, purchasing additional capacity to allow for future growth. This causes capital investments to vary considerably, growing a lot faster than sales in certain years, and a lot slower in others.

The majority of businesses plan their capital expenditures far in advance, which allows them to better forecast costs in the pro-forma statements. Many public companies include information about expected capital expenditures in the notes to the financial statements.

These expected expenditures are also used to project depreciation. Management can look at the relationship between past capital expenditures and historical depreciation and use it to forecast expected depreciation for the future.

Java Joe is not planning to expand and open any new stores in 2014, but it is expecting to complete some store renovations and increase its manufacturing capacity. Java Joe expects to increase its PP&E expenditures by $15 million for the year 2014.

FIGURE 7.7

	12/31/13	Addit PP&E	Calculation	PF 2014
Property, plant & equipment	104,616	15,000	104,616 + 15,000	119,616

Depreciation is calculated off of property, plant and equipment. It can be a tricky number to forecast because depreciation varies depending on the item being depreciated. Land is never depreciated, so it needs to be removed from PP&E for the depreciation calculation. For Java Joe in 2013, PP&E includes $20,000 of land. The other items included in PP&E are buildings and equipment. For 2013, PP&E included $30,000 of buildings and $54,616 of equipment. Since Java Joe did not buy new land or open new stores, building and land would remain the same in 2014, and equipment would now be $69,616 ($119,616 - $30,000 - $20,000).

Java Joe uses the straight line depreciation method and depreciates its buildings over 30 years and its equipment over 5 years. Java Joe has no salvage value for its equipment.

To calculate depreciation, we take the average gross book value of the equipment and divide it by the useful life of the equipment. For Java Joe, depreciation expense in 2014 would be ((($54,616 + $69,616) / 2) / 5 years)+ $30,000 / 30 years = $13,423.

FIGURE 7.8

	12/31/2013	Calculation	PF 2014
Depreciation and amortization	15,400	((54,616 + 69,616)/2)/5 + 30,000/30	$ 13,423

Accumulated depreciation is calculated by adding the depreciation expense for the forecasted year to the accumulated depreciation from the previous year. For Java Joe, accumulated depreciation was ($22,500) for 2013, and the depreciation expense we forecasted for 2014 was ($13,423). So, accumulated depreciation for 2014 would be projected to be ($22,500) + ($13,423) = ($35,923).

FIGURE 7.9

	12/31/2013	Addit PP&E	Calculation	PF 2014
Property, plant & equipment	104,616	15,000	104,616 + 15,000	119,616
Accumulated depreciation	(22,500)		(22,500) + (13,423)	(35,923)
Net property, plant & equipment	82,116			83,693

7.2.3   Current Portion of Long-term Debt

In order to determine the current portion of long-term debt, management needs to look at the contracts for existing loans. The portion of the principal of long-term debt that will be repaid within a year should be moved to current liabilities.

The notes to the financial statements often provide a breakdown of debt obligations, but it may be necessary to look at contracts to find the exact portion due in under a year.

The notes to the 2013 financial statements for Java Joe show the following breakdown of debt obligations.

FIGURE 7.10

$ in thousands		Payments due by period		
	Total	Less than 1 year	1- 3 years	3-5 years
Debt obligations	$ 3,250	1,200	1,800	250

The loan contracts state that, of the $1,800,000 due in 1-3 years, the portion due in 2014 will be $600,000.

The pro forma balance sheet for Java Joe now looks like the following figure.

FIGURE 7.11

Assets	12/31/13	% of sales	Calculation	PF 2014
Cash	$ 30,705	7.31%	504,000 * 7.31%	$ 36,842
Accounts receivable	20,603	4.91%	504,000 * 4.91%	24,746
Inventory	53,250	12.68%	504,000 * 12.68%	63,907
Prepaid expenses and other	9,238	2.20%	504,000 * 2.20%	11,088
Total current assets	113,796	27.09%		$ 136,584

	12/31/13	Addit PP&E	Calculation	PF 2014
Property, plant & equipment	104,616	15,000	104,616 + 15,000	119,616
Accumulated depreciation	(22,500)		(22,500) + (13,423)	(35,923)
Net property, plant & equipment	82,116			83,693

Total Assets	$ 195,912

Liabilities and Shareholders' Equity

Current liabilities	12/31/13	% of sales	Calculation	PF 2014
Accounts payable	$ 11,563	2.75%	504,000 * 2.75%	$ 13,860
Accrued compensation and benefits	10,115	2.41%	504,000 * 2.41%	12,146
Deferred revenue	6,022	1.43%	504,000 * 1.43%	7,207
Current portion of long-term debt	1,200	N/A	See contracts.	600
Accrued expenses	1,032	0.25%	504,000 * 0.25%	1,260
Total current liabilities	32,072	7.64%		$ 35,074

7.2.4   Interest Expense

Interest expense is one of the more challenging line items to forecast because a business often uses this figure to decide how much money it needs to borrow to pay off its expenses. But the amount of money the business borrows affects the interest expense. If a business decides it needs more funding, it will increase its projected borrowings, which then increase interest expense. The increase in interest expense decreases profits and creates a need for more funding. How can we forecast the correct amount when there is a circular relationship?

One option is to use computer programs that can solve for the variables simultaneously. Another option that would give us a reasonably close estimate is to use beginning borrowings to forecast interest expense. There is a lot of uncertainty about other aspects of the forecast, so, in general, it's not necessary to be extremely precise when estimating interest expense.

In order to demonstrate the effects of circularity, we will show the more complex approach that uses the average of beginning and ending borrowings to determine interest expense. The calculation of ending borrowings also includes interest expense. When calculated in Excel, you get the following error:

FIGURE 7.12

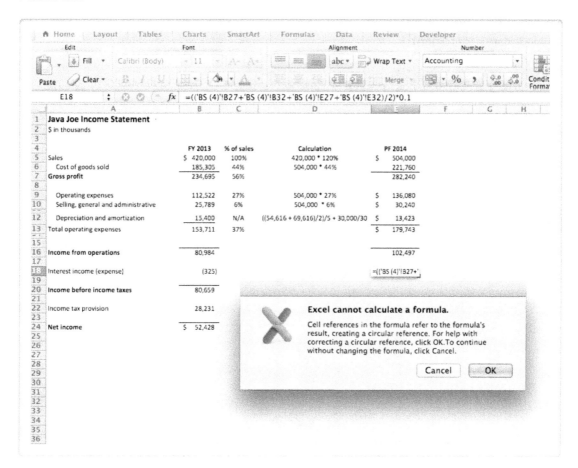

So, in this case, we modified the interest expense calculation to be based off of borrowings at the beginning of 2014. We multiplied the 10% interest rate with the total interest-bearing debt of $3.25 million. This calculation resulted in interest expense of $325,000.

FIGURE 7.13

Java Joe Income Statement

$ in thousands

	FY 2013	% of sales	Calculation	PF 2014
Sales	$ 420,000	100.00%	420,000 * 120%	$ 504,000
Cost of goods sold	185,305	44.12%	504,000 * 44.12%	222,365
Gross profit	234,695	55.88%		281,635
Operating expenses	112,522	26.79%	504,000 * 26.79%	$ 135,022
Selling, general and administrative	25,789	6.14%	504,000 * 6.14%	$ 30,946
Depreciation and amortization	15,400	N/A	((54,616 + 69,616)/2)/5 + 30,000/30	$ 13,423
Total operating expenses	153,711	36.60%		$ 179,390
Income from operations	80,984			102,245
			Calculate off of beginning debt	
Interest income (expense)	(325)		balance or use a computer program	**(325)**
Income before income taxes	80,659			101,920

7.2.5   Income Tax Expense

Income tax expense is another example of an account that is not projected based off of its relationship with sales. Just as depreciation varies with the amount of capital expenditures, there are other pairings of accounts that have relationships with each other. Income tax expense is generally a certain percentage of income before taxes. This relationship is usually quite consistent if the operations of a business are stable. Analysts in the US often use a typical corporate tax rate of 35% when calculating taxes.

Based on the forecasts we already created, income before taxes is expected to be $101,920 for Java Joe in 2014. Let's determine taxes using a 35% tax rate.

$101,920 * 35% = $35,672

FIGURE 7.14

Java Joe Income Statement
$ in thousands

	FY 2013	PF 2014
Sales	$ 420,000	$ 504,000
Cost of goods sold	185,305	222,365
Gross profit	234,695	281,635
Operating expenses	112,522	135,022
Selling, general and administrative	25,789	30,946
Depreciation and amortization	15,400	$ 13,423
Total operating expenses	153,711	179,390
Income from operations	80,984	102,245
Interest income (expense)	(325)	(325)
Income before income taxes	80,659	101,920
Corporate tax rate	35%	35%
Income tax provision	28,231	35,672
Net income	$ 52,428	$ 66,248

7.2.6　Retained Earnings

In order to forecast the retained earnings for the end of the year, we take the retained earnings balance from the previous year, add the projected net income and subtract the dividends expected to be declared. So, retained earnings is essentially the remainder of net income that isn't paid out as dividends. If Java Joe expects to pay $50 million in dividends, the estimated retained earnings for 2014 would be $109 million.

FIGURE 7.15

2013 Retained earnings	$ 92,290
Add: 2014 Projected net income	66,248
Less: 2014 Projected dividends	50,000
2014 Projected retained earnings	$ 108,538

Common stock is the other account in the equity section of the balance sheet. In general, common stock is projected to stay the same, unless a company has big plans for issuing or buying back stock. Java Joe does not expect to issue any stock, so it will remain the same for 2014.

The pro-forma 2014 equity section of the balance sheet for Java Joe is shown below.

FIGURE 7.16

Shareholders' equity	
Common stock and paid-in capital	$ 69,500
Retained earnings	108,538
Total shareholders' equity	$ 178,038

7.2.7   Borrowings

The final figure to determine for pro-forma statements is borrowings. This number is a plug in based off of the projections we have already established. What is a plug in or a plug number? As we know, the balance sheet equation must balance and assets must equal the sum of liabilities and owner's equity. So, borrowings should be the "plug in or plug" number that causes the equation to balance.

However, there is the circularity problem once again. Other numbers, such as interest expense, depend on the amount of borrowings, and borrowings depend on interest expense and retained earnings, so it might take a few iterations in order to get the number that makes the equation balance.

Using only the beginning borrowing balance for the interest expense calculation eliminates the circularity problem for borrowings (although it also slightly reduces accuracy).

FIGURE 7.17

Java Joe Balance Sheet

$ in thousands

	2014 Projected Sales:		$504,000	
Assets	**12/31/13**	**% of sales**	**Calculation**	**PF 2014**
Cash	$ 30,705	7.31%	504,000 * 7.31%	$ 36,842
Accounts receivable	20,603	4.91%	504,000 * 4.91%	24,746
Inventory	53,250	12.68%	504,000 * 12.68%	63,907
Prepaid expenses and other	9,238	2.20%	504,000 * 2.20%	11,088
Total current assets	113,796	27.09%		$ 136,584
	12/31/13	**Addit PP&E**	**Calculation**	**PF 2014**
Property, plant & equipment	104,616	15,000	104,616 + 15,000	119,616
Accumulated depreciation	(22,500)		(22,500) + (13,423)	(35,923)
Net property, plant & equipment	82,116			83,693
Total Assets	$ 195,912			$ 220,277

Liabilities and Shareholders' Equity

Current liabilities	**12/31/13**	**% of sales**	**Calculation**	**PF 2014**
Accounts payable	$ 11,563	2.75%	504,000 * 2.75%	$ 13,860
Accrued compensation and benefits	10,115	2.41%	504,000 * 2.41%	12,146
Deferred revenue	6,022	1.43%	504,000 * 1.43%	7,207
Current portion of long-term debt	1,200	N/A	See contracts.	600
Accrued expenses	1,032	0.25%	504,000 * 0.25%	1,260
Total current liabilities	32,072	7.64%		$ 35,074

Long-term liabilities				
Long-term debt	2,050		**Plug in.**	**7,165**
Total Liabilities	34,122			42,239

Shareholders' equity				
Common stock and paid-in capital	69,500			69,500
Retained earnings	92,290			108,538
Total shareholders' equity	161,790			178,038
Total liabilities and equity	$ 195,912			$ 220,277

Java Joe's complete pro-forma balance sheet is shown below.

FIGURE 7.18

Java Joe Pro Forma Balance Sheet
$ in thousands

Assets	2014
Cash	$ 36,842
Accounts receivable	24,746
Inventory	63,907
Prepaid expenses and other	11,088
Total current assets	136,584
Property, plant & equipment	119,616
Accumulated depreciation	(35,923)
Net property, plant & equipment	83,693
Total Assets	$ 220,277

Liabilities and Shareholders' Equity

Current liabilities	
Accounts payable	$ 13,860
Accrued compensation and benefits	12,146
Deferred revenue	7,207
Current portion of long-term debt	600
Accrued expenses	1,260
Total current liabilities	35,074
Long-term liabilities	
Long-term debt	7,165
Total Liabilities	42,239
Shareholders' equity	
Common stock and paid-in capital	69,500
Retained earnings	108,538
Total shareholders' equity	178,038
Total liabilities and equity	$ 220,277

7.2.8   Review

It's very important for companies to plan and budget so that they can anticipate future challenges and be well-prepared. Oftentimes people perform sensitivity analysis on forecasts to see what happens to the forecasts when key assumptions are changed. You can see the effects on future financials of many different scenarios, such as what happens if the company earns more revenue than expected or if operating costs are higher or lower as a percentage of revenue. Using formulas when creating pro-formas, instead of using a calculator and hardcoding numbers, makes it much easier to perform sensitivity analysis.

Use the following assumptions and Figures 7.19 and 7.20 to create forecasted financials for Calvin Technology (CT) for the next three years.

Assumptions for the income statement:

- CT expects a 10% sales growth rate for the next 3 years.

- CT does not own any land or buildings and depreciates its equipment using the straight line method over a period of ten years and assuming no salvage value.

- Calculate interest expense based off of beginning borrowings. CT expects to pay 5% interest on its interest-bearing debt.

- CT expects its corporate tax rate to be 35%.

FIGURE 7.19

Calvin Technology Income Statement
For the year ended December 31, 2013
$ in thousands

Sales	$ 162,864
Cost of Sales	133,273
Gross Profit	29,591
Selling, General & Administrative Expenses	12,131
Research & Development	1,538
EBITDA	15,922
Depreciation	6,237
EBIT	9,685
Interest Income (Expense)	(1,920)
Pretax Income	7,765
Income Tax	2,718
Net Income	$ 5,047

Assumptions for the balance sheet:

- CT expects to increase its PP&E by 25% in 2014 and by 10% each year after.

- CT does not own any land or buildings and depreciates its equipment using the straight line method over a period of ten years and assuming no salvage value.

- CT expects short-term debt and the current portion of LTD to remain relatively constant at $9.542 million over the next few years.

- CT is not planning to issue new stock.

- CT expects to pay approximately $2 million in dividends each year from 2014 - 2016.

FIGURE 7.20

Calvin Technology Balance Sheet
As of December 31, 2013
$ in thousands

Assets
Current:

Cash and Marketable Securities	$ 2,391
Accounts Receivable	12,683
Inventories	17,610
Total Current Assets	32,684
Property, Plant & Equipment	62,366
Less: Depreciation	26,077
Net Property, Plant & Equipment	36,289
Other Noncurrent Assets	6,546
Total Assets	75,519

Liabilities
Current:

Short-term debt and current portion of LTD	9,542
Accounts payable	12,361
Accrued expenses	1,638
Total current liabilities	23,541
Long-term debt	28,655
Total liabilities	52,196
Common stock	12,000
Retained earnings	11,323
Total shareholders' equity	23,323
Total liabilities and shareholders' equity	$ 75,519

Use the following templates to forecast the financials for Calvin Technology.

Calvin Technology Income Statement

$ in thousands

	Historical	Projected		
	2013	2014	2015	2016
Sales	$ 162,864			
Cost of Sales	133,273			
Gross Profit	29,591			
Selling, General & Administrative Expenses	12,131			
Research & Development	1,538			
EBITDA	15,922			
Depreciation	6,237			
EBIT	9,685			
Interest Income (Expense)	(1,920)			
Pretax Income	7,765			
Income Tax	2,718			
Net Income	$ 5,047			

Calvin Technology Balance Sheet

$ in thousands

	Historical	Projected		
	2013	2014	2015	2016
Assets				
Current:				
Cash and Marketable Securities	$ 2,391			
Accounts Receivable	12,683			
Inventories	17,610			
Total Current Assets	32,684			
Property, Plant & Equipment	62,366			
Less: Depreciation	26,077			
Net Property, Plant & Equipment	36,289			
Other Noncurrent Assets	6,546			
Total Assets	75,519			
Liabilities				
Current:				
Short-term debt and current portion of LTD	9,542			
Accounts payable	12,361			
Accrued expenses	1,638			
Total current liabilities	23,541			
Long-term debt	28,655			
Total liabilities	52,196			
Common stock	12,000			
Retained earnings	11,323			
Total shareholders' equity	23,323			
Total liabilities and shareholders' equity	$ 75,519			

Answer the following questions based on your forecasted financials. Note that percentages were not rounded to calculate the forecasted financials. If you used rounded figures, select the closest answer.

To check your answers to the questions, please see the end of Chapter 7.

Review 7.1 Question 1

What is projected sales for CT for 2016?

    a. $179,150
    b. $197,065
    c. $209,330
    d. $216,772

Review 7.1 Question 2

What is projected cost of sales for CT for 2016?

    a. $138,300
    b. $146,600
    c. $161,260
    d. $177,386

Review 7.1 Question 3

What is projected gross profit for CT for 2014?

    a. $31,450
    b. $32,550
    c. $33,605
    d. $35,805

Review 7.1 Question 4

What is projected SG&A for CT for 2016?

    a. $14,679
    b. $15,990
    c. $16,146
    d. $17,320

Review 7.1 Question 5

What is projected depreciation expense for CT for 2014?

    a. $7,016
    b. $8,556
    c. $26,077
    d. $33,093

Review 7.1 Question 6

What is projected interest income (expense) for CT for 2015?

    a. $(1,910)
    b. $(1,920)
    c. $(2,219)
    d. $(2,286)

Review 7.1 Question 7

What is projected net income for CT for 2016?

    a. $4,655
    b. $5,446
    c. $6,480
    d. $9,969

Review 7.1 Question 8

What is projected accounts receivable for CT for 2014?

    a. $13,245
    b. $13,951
    c. $14,346
    d. $14,881

Review 7.1 Question 9

What is projected PP&E for CT for 2015?

    a. $77,958
    b. $85,753
    c. $94,329
    d. $103,561

Review 7.1 Question 10

What is projected total assets for CT for 2016?

    a. $75,519
    b. $87,548
    c. $96,261
    d. $107,102

Review 7.1 Question 11

What is projected short-term debt and current portion of long-term debt for CT for 2015?

    a. $9,542
    b. $10,450
    c. $11,452
    d. $12,500

Review 7.1 Question 12

What is projected retained earnings for CT for 2015?

    a. $11,323
    b. $12,965
    c. $15,133
    d. $18,622

Review 7.1 Question 13

What is projected long-term debt for CT for 2014?

    a. $26,905
    b. $36,171
    c. $38,651
    d. $42,089

Review 7.1 Question 14

What is projected sum of total liabilities and shareholders' equity for CT for 2015?

    a. $75,519
    b. $61,321
    c. $91,943
    d. $97,366

Review 7.1 Question 15

What is the projected profit margin for CT for 2014?

    a.   2.17%
    b.   3.12%
    c.   4.79%
    d.   18.17%

The projected income statement and balance should look like Figures 7.21 and 7.22

FIGURE 7.21

Calvin Technology Income Statement

$ in thousands

	Historical	Projected		
	2013	2014	2015	2016
Sales	$ 162,864	$ 179,150	$ 197,065	$ 216,772
Cost of Sales	133,273	146,600	161,260	177,386
Gross Profit	29,591	32,550	35,805	39,386
Selling, General & Administrative Expenses	12,131	13,344	14,679	16,146
Research & Development	1,538	1,692	1,861	2,047
EBITDA	15,922	17,514	19,266	21,192
Depreciation	6,237	7,016	8,186	9,004
EBIT	9,685	10,498	11,080	12,188
Interest Income (Expense)	(1,920)	(1,910)	(2,286)	(2,219)
Pretax Income	7,765	8,588	8,794	9,969
Income Tax	2,718	3,006	3,078	3,489
Net Income	$ 5,047	$ 5,582	$ 5,716	$ 6,480

FIGURE 7.22

Calvin Technology Balance Sheet

$ in thousands

	Historical	Projected		
	2013	2014	2015	2016
Assets				
Current:				
Cash and Marketable Securities	$ 2,391	$ 2,630	$ 2,893	$ 3,182
Accounts Receivable	12,683	13,951	15,346	16,881
Inventories	17,610	19,371	21,308	23,439
Total Current Assets	32,684	35,952	39,548	43,502
Property, Plant & Equipment	62,366	77,958	85,753	94,329
Less: Depreciation	26,077	33,093	41,279	50,283
Net Property, Plant & Equipment	36,289	44,864	44,475	44,046
Other Noncurrent Assets	6,546	7,201	7,921	8,713
Total Assets	75,519	88,017	91,943	96,261
Liabilities				
Current:				
Short-term debt and current portion of LTD	9,542	9,542	9,542	9,542
Accounts payable	12,361	13,597	14,957	16,452
Accrued expenses	1,638	1,802	1,982	2,180
Total current liabilities	23,541	24,941	26,481	28,175
Long-term debt	28,655	36,171	34,840	32,985
Total liabilities	52,196	61,112	61,321	61,159
Common stock	12,000	12,000	12,000	12,000
Retained earnings	11,323	14,905	18,622	23,102
Total shareholders' equity	23,323	26,905	30,622	35,102
Total liabilities and shareholders' equity	$ 75,519	$ 88,017	$ 91,943	$ 96,261

Section 3
Projecting Free Cash Flows

Concepts

1. Introduction

2. EBIT and EBIAT

3. Depreciation

4. Capital Expenditures

5. Net Working Capital

7.3.1　Introduction

The pro-forma financial statements are very useful for understanding how a business is likely to perform in the future, but it's also important to know what the cash flows of a business will look like. As we have discussed in previous chapters, cash flows are very meaningful and need to be analyzed along with the other financial statements to truly have an accurate picture of a company's position.

Net income shows a company's profit over a period of time, not the cash it generated during that time. When a business sells a good to a customer, it recognizes revenue once it delivers the product, not when it actually receives the cash from the customer.

In contrast, cash flow shows how much cash is generated and available to be used for various purposes, such as paying down debt or purchasing new equipment.

Cash flow plays a large role in many management decisions – a company needs to have enough cash on hand to invest in new equipment or fund an acquisition. Looking at the cash flows instead of the pro-forma financials is helpful because they highlight when cash will be received or need to be paid.

It's relatively simple to convert the accrual basis financial statements to cash flows. By making a few adjustments, we can determine the free cash flows of the business. Free cash flows are cash flows that are free, or available, to distribute to investors or to reinvest in the business after the business has covered all its expenses.

The formula to calculate free cash flow is:

$$FCF = (1 - t) * EBIT + Dep - CapEx - \Delta NWC$$

where

    FCF = free cash flows

    t = tax rate

    EBIT = Earnings Before Interest and Taxes

    Dep = depreciation and amortization

    CapEx = capital expenditures

    Change in NWC = change in net working capital

The next few sections will walk through the components of free cash flow in detail.

7.3.2   EBIT and EBIAT

In order to calculate free cash flows, we first need to calculate EBIT, or Earnings Before Interest and Taxes. To get this figure, we just need to add back interest expense and tax expense to the bottom line of the income statement, net income.

EBIT = Net income + Interest Expense + Tax Expense

To calculate EBIAT, Earnings Before Interest After Taxes, we subtract taxes on EBIT from EBIT. Taxes are generally assumed to be a certain percentage of EBIT. Many people use 35 – 40% as the typical corporate tax rate. The calculation for Calvin Technology is shown below.

FIGURE 7.23

Calvin Technology Free Cash Flow Calculation

	Projected		
	2014	2015	2016
Net income	$ 5,582	$ 5,716	$ 6,480
Add: Interest expense	1,910	2,286	2,219
Add: Tax expense	3,006	3,078	3,489
EBIT	$ 10,498	$ 11,080	$ 12,188
Less: Tax expense	3,674	3,878	4,266
EBIAT	$ 6,824	$ 7,202	$ 7,922

Notice that the taxes added back to Net Income to calculate EBIT are the company's actual tax expenses. To calculate EBIAT, we calculate a notional tax expense on EBIT at the tax rate. One way to think about EBIAT is that EBIAT is the after-tax income of a hypothetical company with the same operations and cash flows as the company we are studying, except that the hypothetical company is financed entirely by equity capital and has zero borrowings.

7.3.3 Depreciation

The next step is to add back depreciation, a non-cash expense. It might seem strange that we subtracted depreciation to obtain EBIAT and now need to add it back. But, we needed to initially subtract depreciation and use EBIT to calculate taxes because depreciation has an effect on taxes. After we have already calculated the taxes and have EBIAT, we can add depreciation back to get free cash flows.

It's also necessary to add back amortization from intangible assets at this step.

FIGURE 7.24

Calvin Technology Free Cash Flow Calculation

	Projected		
	2014	2015	2016
Net income	$ 5,582	$ 5,716	$ 6,480
Add: Interest expense	1,910	2,286	2,219
Add: Tax expense	3,006	3,078	3,489
EBIT	$ 10,498	$ 11,080	$ 12,188
Less: Tax expense	3,674	3,878	4,266
EBIAT	$ 6,824	$ 7,202	$ 7,922
Add: Depreciation & amortization	7,016	8,186	9,004
EBIAT + D&A	$ 13,840	$ 15,388	$ 16,926

7.3.4   Capital Expenditures

The next step is considering the cash inflows and outflows of the capital expenditures. This refers to the cash actually paid for the property and equipment, not the depreciation recognized on it.

If a company sells an asset, the money earned from the sale will be included in the calculation. There's also the possibility that there will be a gain or a loss on the sale of the asset.

Gains and losses are important to take into account because they impact taxes. Gains and losses are not cash transactions, but they affect net income and taxes, which affect cash flow.

Multiplying the gain or loss by the tax rate gives us the tax impact of the gain or loss. If a business realizes a loss on the sale of an asset, there is a tax shelter that will increase its cash flows. A gain on the sale of an asset causes the business to pay additional taxes, which decreases its cash flows.

The cash for the capital expenditures can be found on the pro forma cash flow statement.

For Calvin Technology, the projected capital expenditures were:

FIGURE 7.25

	Projected		
	2014	2015	2016
Capital expenditures	4,400	2,800	2,800

FIGURE 7.26

Calvin Technology Free Cash Flow Calculation

	Projected		
	2014	2015	2016
Net income	$ 5,582	$ 5,716	$ 6,480
Add: Interest expense	1,910	2,286	2,219
Add: Tax expense	3,006	3,078	3,489
EBIT	$ 10,498	$ 11,080	$ 12,188
Less: Tax expense	3,674	3,878	4,266
EBIAT	$ 6,824	$ 7,202	$ 7,922
Add: Depreciation & amortization	7,016	8,186	9,004
EBIAT + D&A	$ 13,840	$ 15,388	$ 16,926
Less: Capital expenditures	**4,400**	**2,800**	**2,800**
EBIAT + D&A - CapEx	**$ 9,440**	**$ 12,588**	**$ 14,126**

7.3.5   Net Working Capital

Net working capital is the difference between a firm's current assets and current liabilities. However, when finding the change in net working capital for the purpose of calculating free cash flows, we exclude cash and cash equivalents, notes payable, and short-term debt. Net working capital is money that can be used to fund day to day operations and isn't available for other purposes.

To determine the change in net working capital for Calvin Technology, we should only include accounts receivable, inventory, accounts payable, and accrued expenses, such as wages payable.

To determine the change in net working capital, which will be used in the calculation of free cash flows, we take the projected net working capital and subtract the net working capital from the previous year.

FIGURE 7.27

	Historical	Projected		
	2013	2014	2015	2016
Accounts receivable	$ 12,683	$ 13,951	$ 15,346	$ 16,881
Inventory	17,610	19,371	21,308	23,439
Total current assets	30,293	33,322	36,655	40,320
Less: Accounts payable	12,361	13,597	14,957	16,452
Less: Accrued expenses	1,638	1,802	1,982	2,180
Total current liabilities	13,999	15,399	16,939	18,633
Working capital	$ 16,294	$ 17,923	$ 19,716	$ 21,687
Change in net working capital		$ 1,629	$ 1,793	$ 1,971

All of these adjustments combined together give us the free cash flows for the period. Free cash flows can be determined for a specific project or for a company over a period of time. The free cash flow for Calvin Technology is shown below.

FIGURE 7.28

Calvin Technology Free Cash Flow Calculation

	Projected		
	2014	2015	2016
Net income	$ 5,582	$ 5,716	$ 6,480
Add: Interest expense	1,910	2,286	2,219
Add: Tax expense	3,006	3,078	3,489
EBIT	$ 10,498	$ 11,080	$ 12,188
Less: Tax expense	3,674	3,878	4,266
EBIAT	$ 6,824	$ 7,202	$ 7,922
Add: Depreciation & amortization	7,016	8,186	9,004
EBIAT + D&A	$ 13,840	$ 15,388	$ 16,926
Less: Capital expenditures	4,400	2,800	2,800
EBIAT + D&A - CapEx	$ 9,440	$ 12,588	$ 14,126
Less : Change in net working capital	1,629	1,793	1,971
Free Cash Flow	$ 7,810	$ 10,795	$ 12,155

Section 4

Valuation

Concepts

1. The Time Value of Money

2. Terminal Value

3. Net Present Value

4. Other Measures

5. Sensitivity

6. Determining Relevant Cash Flows

7.4.1   The Time Value of Money

As discussed in the last section, free cash flows are extremely important to project because they show the cash available to be used for various purposes, such as distributing dividends or reinvesting in the business. Free cash flows are also an essential component of a common valuation methodology, the discounted cash flow analysis. A discounted cash flow (DCF) calculates the value of a company by taking a company's free cash flows over many years, discounting them back to the present and then adding them up.

We must discount the cash flows back to the present because of the concept of the time value of money. This concept is central to finance and is one of the reasons why we project the free cash flows of a company in the first place. The basic idea is that a dollar received today is worth more than a dollar received a year from now.

There are many reasons why this statement is true. First, we must consider the opportunity cost. If you have a dollar now, you can invest it in projects that can earn money. If you only receive a dollar a year from now, you have lost the opportunity to invest the dollar and make a return on your investment.

The second factor is inflation. Most economies experience inflation, and the purchasing power of a currency decreases over time, which increases prices. It's easy to think about this in terms of a real-world situation; in 1950, you could buy

20 candy bars for a dollar, whereas now you can barely buy 1 candy bar for a dollar. A dollar today can buy a lot less than a dollar 50 years ago could.

Lastly, the uncertainty factor contributes to a dollar being worth less in the future. The extra time that passes between now and when the dollar is supposed to be received is extra time for something to go wrong and cause the dollar not to be transferred. For example, the person owing the dollar could go bankrupt during that time. Uncertainty causes there to be more value associated with the dollar that is received sooner.

Let's discuss an example to better understand the concept of the time value of money. Suppose someone owed you $5,000 and paid you immediately. Then you chose to invest it at a bank that paid 5% annual interest. At the end of the year, you would have $5,250. However, if the person didn't pay you immediately and instead promised to pay you a year later, you would not have been able to earn the extra $250. Furthermore, there's the possibility that something happened and he wouldn't even be able to pay you.

When analyzing the value of a project to a business, it's important to factor in the time value of money to the projected free cash flows. Spreadsheets are helpful tools for performing the time value of money calculations.

The formula for the present value of a series of future cash flows is:

$$\text{Present Value} = \sum_{t=0}^{n} \frac{(\text{Future Value})_t}{(1+r)^t}$$

where

r = the discount rate or the interest rate for the period

t = the period

n = the total number of periods.

Suppose you are promised $500 a year from now and another $500 two years from now. If your discount rate is 10%, how much would you be willing to pay to receive the money now?

The answer is $868, which can be calculated by the following formula:

$$\frac{500}{(1+0.1)} + \frac{500}{(1+0.1)^2} = 868$$

The first year's $500 payment is discounted at 10%, but the second year's payment is discounted by 1.21, which is 1.1 *1.1. This reflects the greater uncertainty and the opportunity cost of the second year's payment.

It's also important to note that we can add the cash flows from multiple years, but only after converting the future cash flows into the present value of the cash flows. Cash flows from different years are analogous to cash flows from different currencies. It's possible to add or subtract them, but first you need to make sure they are all from the same time period or in the same currency. Oftentimes, the present time period is used to perform these calculations, which is why we use the term present value.

Sometimes, the cash flows received are the same over many periods. This is called an annuity. While the present value formula previously shown can calculate the present value of an annuity, there is a quicker formula that saves us the step of calculating the present value for each year and then adding them up.

The formula for the present value of an annuity is:

$$\text{PV of ordinary annuity} = C * \frac{(1 - (1 + r)^{-n})}{r}$$

where

C = the cash flow per period

r = the discount rate or the interest rate for the period

n = the total number of periods.

Let's look at an example to verify that both present value formulas give us the same result. Suppose you are promised $300 for the next 3 years, and your discount rate is 5%.

The table below shows the present value of the payments if each year is calculated individually.

Year	Cash Flows	Present Value		
1	$ 300	$300 / (1 +.05)^1$	=	$ 285.71
2	300	$300 / (1 +.05)^2$	=	272.11
3	300	$300 / (1 +.05)^3$	=	259.15
		Total	=	$ 816.97

If we use the formula for the present value of an ordinary annuity, we get the same result:

$$\text{PV of ordinary annuity} = 300 * \frac{(1 - (1 + .05)^{-3})}{0.05} = \$\ 816.97$$

For answers to the following questions, please see the end of Chapter 7.

Review 7.2 Question 1

Suppose you are promised $200 one year from now and $400 two years from now. If the interest rate is 5%, how much would you be willing to pay to receive the money now?

    a. $600
    b. $571
    c. $562
    d. $553

Review 7.2 Question 2

The time value of money concept states that

    a.   A dollar today is worth more than a dollar in the future
    b.   A dollar in the future is worth more than a dollar today
    c.   The value of a dollar remains relatively constant over time

---

Review 7.2 Question 3

Which option has the greater present value? Receiving $250 for 3 years at a 5% interest rate or receiving $400 for 2 years at a 10% interest rate?

    a. $250 for 3 years, 5% rate
    b. $400 for 2 years, 10% rate

7.4.2   Terminal Value

Sometimes, it's necessary to estimate cash flows far into the future because projects can last many years, and some even go on indefinitely. It's not practical to determine the cash flow for every year. In these cases, we need to estimate a terminal value, which will give us an approximate sum of the cash flows for the final years. There are several different ways to determine this value.

One method is the Gordon Growth Model, which is given by the following formula:

$$\text{Terminal Value} = \frac{CF}{r - g}$$

where

CF = cash flows in the final year of the projection

r = discount rate

g = growth rate.

This model makes several assumptions:

1. the growth rate will remain constant indefinitely

2. margins will remain the same

3. turnovers will remain the same

4. the capital structure will remain the same.

The model should only be used when a business believes the cash flows will be stable. If cash flows are still fluctuating, it's best to forecast on a yearly basis until they are stable.

It's important to note that this formula gives us the value of all future cash flows as of the end of the forecast period, so we still need to discount the cash flows using the previous formula to get the present value as of the beginning of the forecast period.

Let's look at an example to see how to calculate the terminal value. Suppose a company is investing in a new project that will pay the cash flows listed below for the years 2015 to 2017. After 2017, the company expects the cash flows to stabilize at a 3% growth rate. The discount rate is 7%.

Year	Cash flows
2014	$ 2,000
2015	2,400
2016	2,800
2017	3,200

What would be the terminal value of the project on 1/1/2018?

In order to calculate the terminal value, we first need to calculate the cash flow of 2018, the first stabilized period. Since the cash flow is expected to have constant growth of 3%, the cash flow of 2018 would be $3,200 * 1.03 = $3,296.

Next, we would use the Gordon Growth Model to calculate the terminal value.

Terminal Value = CF / (r - g) = $3,296 / (7% - 3%) = $82,400.

On 1/1/2018, the terminal value of the project would be $82,400.

7.4.3   Net Present Value

The next step is to use the present value calculations to value a project's cash flows. A widely used method is the net present value, or NPV, calculation. This method combines all of the present values of a project's cash inflows and outflows to get the net value, a figure that indicates what value the project would add to the business. This calculation doesn't have to be solely related to a project; it can also be used to value an entire business.

Most companies use the weighted average cost of capital, or the WACC, to discount the cash flows for the NPV method. Some companies choose to use a discount rate specific to a project that captures the project's riskiness, but it can be challenging to estimate a rate for every project, so typically the more general WACC discount rate is used.

The WACC is essentially a business' cost of raising funds. It takes into account a company's debt and equity profile as well as the costs associated with debt and equity. The WACC can be used when valuing an entire company, but when you only value a component, such as the equity of a company, you should use a different discount rate, namely the cost of equity.

A company's return on an investment needs to be greater than the WACC in order for the investment to be worth it and the company to make money. Sometimes the WACC is also adjusted for operational or strategic considerations. While the actual calculation of the WACC is beyond the scope of this book, it's important to understand what the WACC represents and how it plays a role in valuation.

The net present value calculation reiterates the key concept about the time value of money; cash flows received sooner are worth more than those received later. Also, the longer cash outflows are delayed, the better.

The general formula for the NPV calculation is:

$$\sum_{t=1}^{T} \frac{C_t}{(1+r)^t} - C_o$$

where

C_t = net cash inflow during the period

C_o = initial investment

r = discount rate

t = number of periods

Suppose we are considering a project with the cash flows shown below and a discount rate of 5%

Year	Cash flows
0	$ (600)
1	120
2	240
3	350

What would be the NPV?

We should plug the cash flows and the discount rate into the NPV formula to calculate the NPV of $34.

$$NPV = -600 + \frac{120}{(1+.05)^1} + \frac{240}{(1+.05)^2} + \frac{350}{(1+.05)^3} = 34$$

7.4.4   Other Measures

There are other popular methods that companies use to evaluate a business or an investment, namely the internal rate of return, or the IRR, and the payback period.

The IRR is the discount rate that causes the NPV of all cash flows to be equal to zero. It's the rate at which an investment breaks even and the net present value of the costs equals the net present value of the benefits. This method factors in the time value of money, just like the NPV calculation does. Oftentimes, the IRR is used when a company is not sure what discount rate to input for the NPV calculation.

The other common metric to determine the attractiveness of an investment is the payback period. This number tells us how long it would take for investors to recoup their money. It is a relatively straightforward metric that is simple to calculate, but it doesn't reveal as much information as the other measures. The payback period is helpful for those focused on limiting downsides, but it doesn't incorporate the time value of money or cash flows post-payback period and doesn't truly evaluate the project as a whole.

The formula for the payback period is:

$$Payback\ Period = \frac{Cost\ of\ Project}{Annual\ Cash\ Inflows}$$

If the inflows are not even, then we must calculate the cumulative cash flows for each year, find the last year with negative cumulative cash flows, and determine the point during the following year where the cumulative cash flows turn positive.

Although these methods have limitations compared to the NPV calculation, they are often used because they are intuitive and straightforward.

Let's look at how the IRR is calculated. Suppose a project has the following expected cash flows.

Year	Cash flows
0	$ (5,000)
1	2,000
2	2,500
3	3,000

What would be the discount rate that causes the NPV of the cash flows to be equal to zero?

$$NPV = -5000 + \frac{2000}{(1+r)^1} + \frac{2500}{(1+r)^2} + \frac{3000}{(1+r)^3} = 0$$

We can plug in values for r to get the interest rate that satisfies the equation, but a simpler way to determine r is to use Excel's IRR function. For this project, the IRR is 22%.

Now let's determine what the payback period would be for this project. The cumulative cash flows for the project are shown below.

Year	Cash flows	Cumulative cash flows
0	$ (5,000)	$ (5,000)
1	2,000	(3,000)
2	2,500	(500)
3	3,000	2,500

If the initial investment in the project is $5,000, the company will recoup most of its money ($4,500 = $2,000 + $2,500) after 2 years. Then it will take 0.16 = (500 / 3,000) of year 3 to earn back all of its money. Thus the payback period is 2.16 years.

7.4.5 Sensitivity

The net present value calculation is very sensitive to changes in assumptions and discount rates. It's important to consider how small changes can affect the attractiveness of an investment.

There are a lot of estimates and a lot of uncertainty involved in the NPV calculation. Suppose a company has three different potential projects to undertake and asks its management team to determine which one is the best. It's very possible for each project to receive an equal number of votes; the different assumptions made by managers can lead to different conclusions.

It's also easy for personal biases to influence assumptions and the valuation of a project. One might think that valuation is objective because it is based on hard numbers and quantitative analysis, but decisions are subjective. It's important to be aware of these biases, check and re-check assumptions, and ask others to challenge assumptions in order to make the forecasting process more rigorous.

7.4.6   Determining Relevant Cash Flows

When evaluating a project, it's important to include only the relevant cash flows in the calculation. These are the costs that will be incurred or money that will be generated specifically if the project is undertaken.

A company might incur other costs, regardless of whether the project is undertaken or not, which should not be included because they're not directly relevant to the project. A company might also use already existing equipment to complete a project. The costs related to this equipment would not be included because the company did not directly purchase it for the purpose of the project. These are sunk costs that the company has already paid for.

Determining which cash flows are relevant can be very challenging, but as you gain experience valuing projects, you will get a better sense of which cash flows are relevant and which aren't.

For answers to the following questions, please see the end of Chapter 7.

Review 7.3 Question 1

A shoe company spent $2 million to advertise its new muscle-toning sneakers. It then spent $100,000 on a marketing study to determine if its new product would be successful. The study determined the product would not be profitable. The company is now deciding whether to continue manufacturing its new product. Which of the following is a relevant cash flow? Please select all that apply.

    a. $2 million for advertising
    b. $100,000 for the marketing study
    c.   Neither

Review 7.3 Question 2

A domestic-only airline company is considering expanding internationally. Half of its current fleet of planes needs to be replaced. In addition, if it expands, the company would need to purchase bigger planes that are able to fly longer distances. Which of the following is considered a relevant cash flow when deciding whether to expand internationally? Please select all that apply.

    a.   Replacing half of the company's current fleet of planes
    b.   Purchasing bigger planes
    c.   Neither

Section 5

Review

Businesses often create **forecasts**, also called **financial projections** or **pro formas**, to estimate how they will perform in the future based on a set of assumptions. Anticipating how a business will perform in the future is important so that investors can make good decisions and management can prepare for challenges.

The **percent of sales method** is based on the assumption that many balance sheet and income statement accounts vary with sales.

- The company first projects its sales based on its goals and expected market conditions.

- Next, the company determines the relationship between sales and several accounts that typically vary with sales, such as current asset accounts, current liability accounts, and variable costs. The company assumes that the relationship between these accounts and sales will be the same in future years, so the company uses the forecasted sales figures to calculate the forecasted figures of these accounts.

- The next step is to determine the projections for accounts that do not vary proportionately with sales.

  - Many companies predict their capital expenditures far into the future and disclose the information in their financial statements. This information is used to project property, plant and equipment. Then, the new property, plant and equipment figure can be used to calculate future depreciation using the same method the company has historically used.

  - The projections for the current portion of long-term debt are based on contracts for existing loans.

  - Interest expense is challenging to forecast because a business often uses this figure to decide how much money it needs to borrow to pay off its expenses, but the amount of money the business borrows affects the interest expense. This creates a circularity problem. To avoid the circularity problem, we often forecast interest expense using computer program or estimating the expense based on beginning borrowings.

  - Income tax expense is generally a certain percentage of income before taxes, so projections for this figure are calculated off of income before taxes.

  - In order to forecast the retained earnings for the end of the year, we take the retained earnings balance from the previous year, add the projected net income and subtract the dividends expected to be declared.

  - Common stock is typically projected to stay the same, unless a company has big plans for issuing or buying back stock.

  - Borrowings is typically a plug in based off the projections already established.

Projecting Free Cash Flows

Cash flow plays a large role in many management decisions – a company needs to have enough cash on hand to invest in new equipment or fund an acquisition. Looking at the cash flows instead of the pro-forma financials is helpful because they highlight when cash will be received or need to be paid.

Free cash flows are cash flows that are free, or available, to distribute to investors or to reinvest in the business after the business has covered all its expenses.

The formula to calculate free cash flows is:

$$FCF = (1 - t) * EBIT + Dep - CapEx - \Delta NWC$$

where

FCF = free cash flows

t = tax rate

EBIT = Earnings Before Interest and Taxes

Dep = depreciation and amortization

CapEx = capital expenditures

Change in NWC = change in net working capital

Time Value of Money

The time value of money is the concept that a dollar received today is worth more than a dollar received a year from now, due to factors such as opportunity costs, inflation, and the certainty of payments.

To fairly compare projects, we look at the present value of the cash flows, which is what the cash flows would be worth today. To determine the present value of the cash flows, we discount them by the discount rate, which reflects the riskiness of the estimated cash flows.

Sometimes, projects can extend far into the future and it's necessary to estimate a **terminal value**, which will give us an approximate sum of the cash flows for the final years. The **Gordon Growth Model** is a common method to estimate the terminal value of a project.

The formula is:

$$\text{Terminal Value} = \frac{\text{Cash flows in the final year of the projection}}{\text{Discount rate - Growth rate}}$$

The **net present value**, or **NPV**, calculation combines all of the present values of a project's cash inflows and outflows to get the net value, a figure that indicates what value the project would add to the business. It can also be used to value an entire business.

Most companies use the **weighted average cost of capital**, or the **WACC**, as the discount rate for the NPV calculation. The WACC is essentially a business' cost of raising funds, and it takes into account a company's debt and equity profile as well as the costs associated with debt and equity.

The **IRR** is the discount rate that causes the NPV of all cash flows to be equal to zero. It's the rate at which an investment breaks even and the net present value of the costs equals the net present value of the benefits.

The **payback period** tells us how long it would take for investors to recoup their money.

Since the net present value calculation is very sensitive to changes in assumptions and discount rates, it's important to be very rigorous when making assumptions and consider how small changes can affect the attractiveness of an investment. It's also important to include only the relevant cash flows related to a project when making calculations. These are the costs that will be incurred or money that will be generated specifically if the project is undertaken.

Section 6
Review Questions

For answers to the following questions, please see the end of Chapter 7.

Review 7.4 Question 1

Forecasts

a. help a business plan ahead for future needs
b. help a business evaluate the strategy and direction of the business
c. help investors decide whether to invest
d. help lenders decide whether to extend credit
e. all of the above

Review 7.4 Question 2

Which accounts can be forecasted using the percent of sales method?
Please select all that apply.

a. COGS
b. PP&E
c. Accounts payable
d. Long-term debt
e. Retained Earnings

Review 7.4 Question 3

Suppose ABC Company had $6,000 in sales and $3,500 in COGS for fiscal year 2013. ABC Company expects sales to grow by 10% for 2014. Under the percent of sales method, what would be the projected COGS for 2014?

a. $3,300
b. $3,500
c. $3,850
d. $4,000

Review 7.4 Question 4

Accounts that generally are NOT forecasted using the percent of sales method include...
Please select all that apply.

a. Current portion of long-term debt
b. Interest expense
c. Accounts receivable
d. Accrued compensation

Review 7.4 Question 5

EBIT is calculated by

a. subtracting interest and taxes from net income
b. adding interest and taxes to net income
c. subtracting interest and taxes from gross profit
d. adding interest and taxes to gross profit

Review 7.4 Question 6

Which calculations take into account the concept of the time value of money?
Please select all that apply.

a. DCF
b. NWC
c. EBIAT
d. IRR

Review 7.4 Question 7

The formula for free cash flow is

a. Net income + interest expense - D&A - CapEx - change in working capital
b. Net income + tax expense - D&A - CapEx - change in working capital
c. EBIAT + D&A - CapEx - change in working capital
d. EBIT + tax expense + D&A + CapEx - change in working capital

Review 7.4 Question 8

Suppose you are promised $100 a year from now and $200 two years from now. If your discount rate is 10%, how much would you be willing to pay to receive the money now?

    a. $248
    b. $256
    c. $272
    d. $352

Review 7.4 Question 9

Suppose you have the cash flows listed below. What is the IRR?

Year	Cash flow
0	-800
1	400
2	550

    a.   8%
    b.   10%
    c.   12%
    d.   14%

Review 7.4 Question 10

Suppose a company invests $30,000 in a project and it generates cash as follows: $6,000 in year 1, $12,000 in year 2 and $18,000 in year 3. What is the payback period?

    a.   2 years
    b.   2 years 6 months
    c.   2 years 8 months
    d.   3 years
    e.   not enough information

Section 7

Answer Key

Review 7.1 Explanations

For the calculations for questions 1-15, see the figures on the following pages. Percentages were **not** rounded for the calculations.

Calvin Technology Income Statement

$ in thousands

	Historical	Projected					
	2013	2014		2015		2016	
Sales	$ 162,864	162,864 * (1 + 0.1) =	$179,150	179,150 * (1 + 0.1) =	$197,065	197,065 * (1 + 0.1) =	$216,772
Cost of Sales	133,273	179,150 * 82% =	146,600	197,065 * 82% =	161,260	216,772 * 82% =	177,386
Gross Profit	29,591		32,550		35,805		39,386
SG&A	12,131	179,150 * 7% =	13,344	197,065 * 7% =	14,679	216,772 * 7% =	16,146
R&D	1,538	179,150 * 1% =	1,692	197,065 * 1% =	1,861	216,772 * 1% =	2,047
EBITDA	15,922		17,514		19,266		21,192
Depreciation	6,237	((62,366 + 77,958) / 2) / 10 =	7,016	((77,958+85,753) / 2) / 10 =	8,186	((85,753 + 94,329) / 2) / 10 =	9,004
EBIT	9,685		10,498		11,080		12,188
Interest Income (Expense)	(1,920)	(9,542 + 28,655) * 5% =	(1,910)	(9,500 + 36,213) * 5% =	(2,286)	(9,500 + 34,882) * 5% =	(2,219)
Pretax Income	7,765		8,588		8,794		9,969
Income Tax	2,718	8,588 * 35% =	3,006	8,794 * 35% =	3,078	9,969 * 35% =	3,489
Net Income	$ 5,047		$ 5,582		$ 5,716		$ 6,480

Calvin Technology Balance Sheet

$ in thousands

	Historical 2013	Projected 2014		2015		2016		% of sales
Assets								
Current:								
Cash and Marketable Securities	$ 2,391	179,150 * 1%=	$ 2,630	197,065 * 1%=	$ 2,893	216,772 * 1%=	$ 3,182	1%
Accounts Receivable	12,683	179,150 * 8%=	13,951	197,065 * 8%=	15,346	216,772 * 8%=	16,881	8%
Inventories	17,610	179,150 * 11%=	19,371	197,06 * 11%=	21,308	216,772 * 11%=	23,439	11%
Total Current Assets	32,684		35,952		39,548		43,502	
Property, Plant & Equipment	62,366	62,366 * (1 + 0.25)=	77,958	77,958 * (1 + 0.1)=	85,753	85,753 * (1 + 0.1)=	94,329	
Less: Depreciation	26,077	26,077 + 7,016=	33,093	33,093 + 8,186=	41,279	41,279 + 9,004=	50,283	
Net Property, Plant & Equipment	36,289		44,864		44,475		44,046	
Other Noncurrent Assets	6,546	179,150 * 4%=	7,201	197,065 * 4%=	7,921	216,772 * 4%=	8,713	4%
Total Assets	75,519		88,017		91,943		96,261	
Liabilities								
Current:								
Short-term debt and current portion of LTD	9,542	Plug in from assumptions	9,542	Plug in from assumptions	9,542	Plug in from assumptions	9,542	
Accounts payable	12,361	179,150 * 8%=	13,597	197,065 * 8%=	14,957	216,772 * 8%=	16,452	8%
Accrued expenses	1,638	179,150 * 1%=	1,802	197,065 * 1%=	1,982	216,772 * 1%=	2,180	1%
Total current liabilities	23,541		24,941		26,481		28,175	
Long-term debt	28,655	88,017 - 24,941 - 26,905=	36,171	91,943 - 26,481 - 30,622=	34,840	96,261 - 28,175 - 35,102 =	32,985	
Total liabilities	52,196		61,112		61,321		61,159	
Common stock	12,000	Plug in from assumptions	12,000	Plug in from assumptions	12,000	Plug in from assumptions	12,000	
Retained earnings	11,323	11,323 + 5,582 - 2,000=	14,905	14,905 + 5,716 - 2,000=	18,622	18,622 + 6,480 - 2,000=	23,102	
Total shareholders' equity	23,323		26,905		30,622		35,102	
Total liabilities and shareholders' equity	$ 75,519		$ 88,017		$ 91,943		$ 96,261	

Question 1

Answer: D

According to the assumptions, Calvin Technology expects a 10% sales growth rate for the next three years. Historical sales for the fiscal year ended 2013 were $162,864. To calculate projected sales for a year, we multiply sales from the previous year by (1+ growth rate). So, in 2014, projected sales are $162,864 * (1 + 0.1) = $179,150. In 2015, projected sales = $179,150 * (1 + 0.1) = $197, 065. In 2016, projected sales = $197, 065 * (1 + 0.1) = $216,772, so D is the correct answer.

Question 2

Answer: D

In order to determine projected cost of sales, we need to determine the historical relationship between sales and cost of sales by dividing the cost of sales in 2013 by sales in 2013. Then we multiply this figure by 2016 projected sales. So, 2013 cost of sales / 2013 sales = $133,273 / $162,864 = 82%. We calculated 2016 sales in the previous question and determined it was $216,772. So, projected cost of sales for 2016 = $216,772 * 82% = $177,386, so D is the correct answer.

Question 3

Answer: B

Gross profit = sales – cost of sales. For 2014, projected sales – projected cost of sales = $179,150 - $146,600 = $32,550.

Question 4

Answer: C

In order to determine projected SG&A, we need to determine the historical relationship between sales and SG&A by dividing SG&A in 2013 by sales in 2013. Then we multiply this figure by 2016 projected sales. So, 2013 SG&A / 2013 sales = $12,131 / $162,864 = 7%. . So, projected SSG&A for 2016 = $216,772 * 7% = $16,146, so C is the correct answer.

Question 5

Answer: A

According to the assumptions, CT does not own any land or buildings and depreciates its equipment using the straight-line method over a period of 10 years and assuming no salvage value. We need to know beginning and ending PP&E in order to calculate depreciation expense. So, the first step is to project PP&E for 2014 – 2016. The assumptions stated PP&E is expected to grow by 25% in 2014 and 10% each year after. So, PP&E in 2014 = PP&E in 2013 * 1.25 = $62,366*1.25 = $77,958. Then, depreciation expense for 2014 = average PP&E / useful life = ((PP&E in 2013 + PP&E in 2014) / 2) / 10 years = (($62,366 + $77,958) / 2) / 10 = $7,016.

Question 6

Answer: D

According to the assumptions, interest expense should be calculated off of beginning borrowings, and CT expects to pay 5% interest on its debt. Beginning borrowings for 2015 is the same as ending borrowings for 2014. For 2014, interest-bearing debt = short-term debt and current portion of long-term debt + long-term debt = $9,542 + $36,171 = $45,713. So, interest expense = interest-bearing debt * interest rate = $45,713 * 5% = $2,286. The long-term debt figure for 2014 was a plug-in. Since assets = liabilities + shareholders' equity, the long-term debt = total assets – total current liabilities – total shareholders' equity= $88,017 - $24,941 - $26,905 = $36,171.

Question 7

Answer: C

In order to determine 2016 projected net income, we need to know CT's income taxes for 2016. According to the assumptions, CT expects its corporate tax rate to be 35%. So, taxes = pretax income * tax rate = $9,969 * 35% = $3,489. With this figure, we can determine that projected net income for 2016 = pretax income – income taxes = $9,969 - $3,489 = $6,480, so the correct answer is C.

Question 8

Answer: B

In order to determine projected accounts receivable, we need to determine the historical relationship between sales and accounts receivable by dividing accounts receivable in 2013 by sales in 2013. Then we multiply this figure by 2014 projected sales. So, 2013 accounts receivable / 2013 sales = $12,683 / $162,864 = 8%. We calculated 2014 sales previously and determined it was $179,150. So, projected accounts receivable for 2014 = $179,150 * 8% = $13,951, so B is the correct answer.

Question 9

Answer: B

According to the assumptions, CT expects to increase its PP&E expenditures by 25% in 2014 and by 10% each year after. So, in order to determine projected PP&E in 2015, we need to know projected PP&E in 2014. Projected PP&E in 2014 = PP&E in 2013 * (1 + 0.25) = $62,366 * (1.25) = $77,958. Projected PP&E in 2015 = PP&E in 2013 * (1+0.1) = $77,958 * (1.1) = $85,753, so the correct answer is B.

Question 10

Answer: C

Projected total assets = sum of all assets in 2016. The current asset accounts (cash and marketable securities, accounts receivable and inventories) and other noncurrent assets are all calculated using the percent of sales method. PP&E is calculated based on the assumptions (see the explanation for question 9), and accumulated depreciation is calculated by adding the previous year's depreciation and the current year's projected depreciation expense. The sum of all those asset accounts is equal to total assets, which is $96,261 in 2016.

Question 11

Answer: A

Projected short-term debt and current portion of long-term debt comes directly from the assumptions. The assumptions state that projected short-term debt and current portion of long-term debt is expected to remain relatively constant at $9.542 million over the next few years, so the correct answer is A.

Question 12

Answer: D

Retained earnings in 2015 = retained earnings in 2014 + projected net income in 2015 – projected dividends in 2015. The assumptions state that CT expects to pay approximately $2 million in dividends each year from 2014 to 2016. In 2015, projected retained earnings are $18,622.

Question 13

Answer: B

Long-term debt is a plug in that is calculated after all the other balance sheet figures have been determined. Since assets = liabilities + shareholders' equity, and long-term debt is CT's only non-current liability, we know that long-term debt = total assets – total current liabilities – total shareholders' equity= $88,017 - $24,941 - $26,905 = $36,171.

Question 14

Answer: C

The sum of total liabilities and shareholders' equity is found by adding up the current liabilities, the long-term liabilities, and shareholders' equity. For 2015, total liabilities and shareholders' equity = $26,439 + $34,882 +$30,622 = $91,043. This also equals projected total assets for 2015.

Question 15

Answer: B

Profit margin = net income / sales. Profit margin in 2014 = $5,582 / $179,150 = 3.12%.

Review 7.2 Explanations

Question 1

Answer: D

In order to determine how much you would be willing to pay, you need to figure out the present value of the future cash flows. The formula is Present value = CF1 / (1+r)^1 + CF2 / (1+r)^2 = 200 / 1.05^1 + 400 / 1.05^2 = $553.29.

Question 2

Answer: A

The time value of money concept states that a dollar today is worth more than a dollar in the future. There are many reasons why this statement holds true, such as the opportunity cost of investing a dollar, inflation, and uncertainty.

Question 3

Answer: B

In order to see which option has the greater present value, we need to use the formula for calculating the present value of future cash flows. For the first option, we have Present value = CF1 / (1+r)^1 + CF2 / (1+r)^2 + CF3 / (1+r)^3 = 250 / 1.05 + 250 / 1.05^2 + 250 / 1.05^3 = \$680.81. For the second option, we have Present value = CF1 / (1+r)^1 + CF2 / (1+r)^2 = 400 / 1.1 + 400 / 1.1^2 = \$694.21. So, the second option, receiving \$400 for two years at a 10% interest rate has the greater present value.

Review 7.3 Explanations

Question 1

Answer: C

Relevant cash flows are costs that will be incurred or cash that will be generated if the project is undertaken. The money spent on advertising and the money spent on the marketing study are both sunk costs that the company has already paid for. The shoe company is trying to decide whether it should continue manufacturing its new product in the future, and in order to decide, it should look at costs that will be incurred or money that will be generated if it manufactures the product in the future.

Question 2

Answer: B

The cash required to purchase bigger planes that can fly internationally would be considered a relevant cash flow because it is a cost that will be incurred if the company decides to expand. However, the cash required to replace half of the company's current fleet of planes is a cost that will be incurred regardless of whether the company expands internationally. Thus, it is not a relevant cash flow.

Chapter Review 7.4 Explanations

Question 1

Answer: E

Forecasts are used by many different parties for different reasons. Forecasts help businesses plan ahead and evaluate their strategies, they help investors understand the direction of the business and whether they should invest, and they also help lenders learn about the liquidity and solvency of the business, allowing them to make a decision about extending credit.

Question 2

Answer: A, C

COGS and accounts payable can be forecasted using the percent of sales method. These two accounts have a strong relationship with sales, so they can be reasonably forecasted using the percent of sales method. PP&E tends to grow in a step-like pattern and does not grow proportionately with sales in the short-term. It's best to forecast PP&E by looking at the company's discussion about future capital expenditures, often found in the notes to the financial statements. Long-term debt is usually a plug-in that is calculated after the other accounts have been forecasted. Retained earnings is forecasted by taking the previous year's retained earnings, adding projected net income, and subtracting projected dividends.

Question 3

Answer: C

To forecast COGS for 2014, we need to determine the relationship between sales and COGS in 2013. In 2013, COGS / Sales = $3,500 / $6,000 = 58.3%. In 2014, ABC Company expects sales to grow by 10%, so sales will grow by $6,000*10% = $600, and projected sales for 2014 = $6,000 + $600 = $6,600. So, COGS for 2014 should be $6,600* 58.3% = $3,850.

Question 4

Answer: A, B

The current portion of long-term debt and interest expense are not forecasted using the percent of sales method. The current portion of long-term debt should be forecasted by looking at contracts for existing loans and determining the portion of the principal that will be repaid within one year. Interest expense can be projected using computer programs or based off of average borrowings. Current assets and current liabilities, such as accounts receivable and accrued compensation, are forecasted using the percent of sales method.

Question 5

Answer: B

EBIT stands for Earnings Before Interest and Taxes, and it can be calculated by adding interest and taxes back to net income. Net income is the amount of revenue remaining after all a business' expenses, including interest and taxes, have been subtracted, so interest and taxes must be added back, not subtracted, in order to get to EBIT.

Question 6

Answer: A, D

DCF stands for discounted cash flow, and it calculates the value of a company by taking a company's free cash flows over many years, discounting them back to the present (reflecting the time value of money) and then adding them up. IRR stands for the internal rate of return, and it is the discount rate that causes the net present value of all cash flows to be equal to zero. The IRR factors in the time value of money, reflecting that cash flows received sooner are worth more than those received later. NWC stands for net working capital, which is essentially current assets – current liabilities. This is a figure for a particular point in time and does not take into account the time value of money. EBIAT stands for Earnings Before Interest After Taxes and is a figure that reflects earnings over a period of time, but it does not take into account the time value of money.

Question 7

Answer: C

The formula for free cash flow is EBIAT + D&A - CapEx - change in working capital. Answer A is incorrect because it net income + interest expense does not equal EBIAT and Answer A subtracts, instead of adding, D&A. Answer B is incorrect because net income + tax expense does not equal EBIAT, and Answer B subtracts, instead of adding, D&A. Answer D is incorrect because tax expense should be subtracted from EBIT in order to get to EBIAT, and CapEx should be subtracted, not added to get to free cash flows.

Question 8

Answer: B

In order to determine how much you would be willing to pay, you need to figure out the present value of the future cash flows. The formula is Present value = CF1 / (1+r)^1 + CF2 / (1+r)^2 = 100 / 1.10^1 + 200 / 1.10^2 = $256.20.

Question 9

Answer: C

The IRR is the discount rate that causes the NPV of the cash flows to equal zero. So, the IRR is the rate that makes this equation hold true: NPV = 0 = CF0 + CF1/ (1+r)^1 + CF2 / (1+r)^2 = -$800 + $400 / (1+r)^1 + $550 / (1+r)^2. You can solve for r or use Excel's IRR function to determine the rate. When you solve for r, you find that IRR = 11.6%.

Question 10

Answer: C

The payback period is the amount of time it will take for a company to recoup its initial investment. The company initially invested $30,000, and it will recoup most of its money after two years ($6,000 in year 1 + $12,000 in year 2 = $18,000). Then it has to make $30,000 - $18,000 = $12,000 in year 3, and it will take $12,000 / $18,000, or 2/3 of a year to do so. So, the payback period is 2 years and 8 months.

8

Practice Tests

Sections

Section 1

Practice Test 1

For answers to the following questions, please see the end of Chapter 8.

Review 8.1 Question 1

A small coffee shop, Central Perk, with annual income of $200,000, just settled a lawsuit for selling coffee that was too hot, and it owes $2 million to the plaintiff. The company isn't expecting any lawsuits next year, so it won't be a recurring cost. Should it be disclosed as a separate line item in its financial statements?

    a.   Yes, it is a significant cost.

    b.   No, it won't be a recurring cost.

    c.   No, as it will reduce the market value of Central Perk.

    d.   It's the auditor's decision.

Review 8.1 Question 2

Suppose two companies in the same industry have an ROE of 10%. Company A has a profit margin of 2% and an asset turnover of 1.5x. Company B has an asset turnover of 0.5x and leverage of 2.0x. Which one is more highly levered?

    a.   Company A

    b.   Company B

Review 8.1 Question 3

Given the following figures, calculate free cash flow.

EBIT	$800
EBIAT	$550
D&A	$130
CapEx	$320
Increase in working capital	$35

    a. $65

    b. $325

    c. $360

    d. $575

Review 8.1 Question 4

Which account can be forecasted using the percent of sales method?
Please select all that apply.

a. Interest expense
b. PP&E
c. Accounts receivable
d. Current portion of long-term debt

Review 8.1 Question 5

Which of the following is an example of operating revenue for a pizza shop? Please select all that apply.

a. Cash from pizza sales
b. Income earned from renting out buildings
c. Dividends from investments

Review 8.1 Question 6

Which of the following is a liquidity ratio?

a. inventory turnover
b. debt to equity
c. current ratio
d. profit margin

Review 8.1 Question 7

Suppose Max bought a new suit from Simon and Sons for $700 and paid in cash on 6/1/14. It cost Simon and Sons $400 to make the suit. What would be the correct accounts to debit and credit in this journal entry for Simon and Sons to recognize the expense of the goods?

Date	Account Name	Debit	Credit
June 1, 2014	1) ??	$400.00	
	2) ??		$400.00

    a.   1) Inventory
    b.   1) COGS
    c.   2) Inventory
    d.   2) COGS

Review 8.1 Question 8

Which of the following would be classified under the Cash Flow from Operations section under both IFRS and US GAAP?

    a.   Wages paid
    b.   Depreciation
    c.   Inventory purchased
    d.   Dividends paid

Review 8.1 Question 9

State whether you would debit or credit the account to achieve the following result.

Increase accounts payable

    a.   Debit
    b.   Credit

Review 8.1 Question 10

A deferred tax asset occurs when taxable income is smaller than financial net income.

    a.   True
    b.   False

Review 8.1 Question 11

Suppose Max bought a new suit from Simon and Sons for $700 and paid in cash on 6/1/14. It cost Simon and Sons $400 to make the suit. What would be the correct account to debit in this journal entry for Simon and Sons?

Date	Account Name	Debit	Credit
June 1, 2014	??	$700.00	
	XX		$700.00

   a.   Revenue
   b.   Inventory
   c.   COGS
   d.   Cash

Review 8.1 Question 12

Depreciation expense is recorded on the

   a.   balance sheet
   b.   income statement

Review 8.1 Question 13

Calculate operating income based on the following information.

Revenues	$350
COGS	$100
Operating expenses	$60
Interest expense	$30

   a. $290
   b. $250
   c. $190
   d. $160

Review 8.1 Question 14

Under IFRS, balance sheet accounts

    a.   are ordered from the most liquid to the least liquid

    b.   are ordered from the least liquid to the most liquid

    c.   can be ordered however the company chooses, as long as it is consistent in its choice

Review 8.1 Question 15

When a company pays cash for an item that it will recognize as an expense in a later period, it is:

    a.   a deferred expense

    b.   an accrued expense

    c.   a deferred revenue

    d.   an accrued revenue

Review 8.1 Question 16

The income statement

    a.   shows a snapshot of a company's assets, liabilities and equity at a certain point in time

    b.   shows revenues, gains, expenses, and losses over a period of time

    c.   shows the cash flows of a company over a period of time

    d.   shows all the profits retained by a business over its lifetime

Review 8.1 Question 17

Suppose The Dog Academy sold 5 training sessions to Felix. Felix prepaid $100 in cash on 1/1/14 and had 3 months to use the training sessions before they expire. What would be the correct accounts to debit and credit in this journal entry for The Dog Academy?

Date	Account Name	Debit	Credit
January 1, 2014	1) ??	$100.00	
	2) ??		$100.00

    a.   1) Accounts Receivable

    b.   1) Cash

    c.   2) Revenue

    d.   2) Unearned Revenue

Review 8.1 Question 18

Which of the following is an example of an asset? Please select all that apply.

a. Cash
b. Accounts payable
c. Property, plant, & equipment
d. Notes Payable

Review 8.1 Question 19

Suppose that Ben & Jerry's issued a 5 year bond on 9/1/2014. When preparing the balance sheet as of 12/31/2014, where should Ben & Jerry's place the bond?

a. Current assets
b. Non-current assets
c. Current liabilities
d. Non-current liabilities

Review 8.1 Question 20

Which depreciation method results in higher net income in the earlier years?

a. Straight line method
b. Double declining balance method
c. Cannot be determined

Review 8.1 Question 21

State whether the following transaction is implicit or explicit.

Expiration of prepaid insurance

a. Implicit
b. Explicit

Review 8.1 Question 22

Suppose a company has sales of $15,000, COGS of $9,000, credit purchases of $3,000K and average accounts payable of $2,000. What is the company's accounts payable turnover?

a. 0.2x
b. 1.5x
c. 3.0x
d. 4.5x

Review 8.1 Question 23

Suppose Max bought a new suit from Simon and Sons for $700 and paid in cash on 6/1/14. It cost Simon and Sons $400 to make the suit. What would be the correct account to credit in this journal entry for Simon and Sons?

Date	Account Name	Debit	Credit
June 1, 2014	Cash	$700.00	
	??		$700.00

a. Revenue
b. Inventory
c. COGS
d. Accounts Payable

Review 8.1 Question 24

Suppose Central Perk sold a 10-coffee punch card to Ellen that expires 3 months after drinking the first coffee. Suppose Ellen bought the $50 card in January and drank 4 coffees that month. In February, she started a diet and decided to stop drinking coffee. When should Central Perk recognize the revenue?

a. Recognize $16.66 ($50 / 3) of revenue at the end of each month from January until March.
b. Recognize $20 of revenue at the end of January and $30 of revenue at the end of March.
c. Recognize $50 of revenue at the end of January.
d. Recognize $50 of revenue at the end of March.

Review 8.1 Question 25

Which method can help a business decide whether or not it should invest in a project? Please select all that apply.

    a.   Net Present Value

    b.   Internal Rate of Return

    c.   Discounted Cash Flow Analysis

    d.   All of the above

Review 8.1 Question 26

If a company has positive cash flows, it must have positive net income.

    a.   True

    b.   False

Review 8.1 Question 27

Suppose a company had $400 of inventory on hand on July 1, 2014. It bought $350 of inventory during the accounting period July 1, 2014 to September 30, 2014 and had $250 on hand on September 30, 2014. What entries would the company make to its books?

    a.   Debit cost of goods sold by $350

    b.   Credit cost of goods sold by $350

    c.   Debit cost of goods sold by $500

    d.   Credit cost of goods sold by $500

    e.   Debit inventory $350

    f.   Credit inventory $500

Review 8.1 Question 28

The cash flow statement shows information about a company's…
Please select all that apply.

    a.   asset utilization efficiency

    b.   financial position at a point in time

    c.   revenues and expenses

    d.   cash inflows and outflows

Review 8.1 Question 29

Using the indirect method to build the Cash Flow from Operations section, increases in operating current assets should be

    a.   subtracted from net income in order to get to operating cash flow
    b.   added to net income in order to get to operating cash flow

---

Review 8.1 Question 30

Suppose you have the following information:

2013 revenues	$50,000
2013 COGS	$30,000
2014 projected revenues	$57,500

What would be the projected COGS for FY 2014?

    a. $30,000
    b. $34,500
    c. $37,500
    d. $40,000

Review 8.1 Question 31

Calculate gross profit based on the following information.

Revenues	$350
COGS	$100
Operating expenses	$60
Interest expense	$30

    a. $290
    b. $250
    c. $190
    d. $160

Review 8.1 Question 32

Peter's Pet Shop purchased a litter of puppies for $3,000, and it paid cash to complete the transaction. How will this transaction impact the accounting equation? Please select all that apply.

a. Increase inventory by $3,000
b. Increase owners' equity by $3,000
c. Decrease cash by $3,000
d. Decrease accounts payable by $3,000

Review 8.1 Question 33

An annuity is

a. a series of equal payments made over a specified period of time
b. a series of varying payments made over a specified period of time

Review 8.1 Question 34

Suppose there are two companies in the same industry, and Company A has an asset turnover of 2.0x whereas Company B has an asset turnover of 4.0x. Which one uses its assets more efficiently?

a. Company A
b. Company B

Review 8.1 Question 35

Suppose you are promised $300 one year from now and $500 two years from now. If the interest rate is 5%, how much would you be willing to pay to receive the money now?

a. $726
b. $739
c. $762
d. $800

Review 8.1 Question 36

Permanent accounts are found on the

    a.   balance sheet
    b.   income statement

Review 8.1 Question 37

Suppose a company has net credit sales of $6K, net sales of $10K, and average accounts receivable of $2K. What is the company's average collection period?

    a.   46 days
    b.   73 days
    c.   122 days
    d.   219 days

Review 8.1 Question 38

Which type of company often has negative or very low cash flow from operations? Please select all that apply.

    a.   Startup
    b.   Growing
    c.   Mature
    d.   In decline

Review 8.1 Question 39

Accounts receivable turnover and accounts payable turnover are measures of

    a.   profitability
    b.   efficiency
    c.   leverage

Review 8.1 Question 40

Calculate net income based on the following information.

Revenues	$650
COGS	$220
Income before taxes	$100
Interest	$35
Taxes	$30

    a. $430

    b. $330

    c. $70

    d. $35

Review 8.1 Question 41

State whether you would debit or credit the account to achieve the following result.

Decrease equity

    a.   Debit

    b.   Credit

Review 8.1 Question 42

It's possible to build the cash flow statement by using just a company's income statement.

    a.   True

    b.   False

Section 2
Practice Test 2

For answers to the following questions, please see the end of Chapter 8.

Review 8.2 Question 1

Which of the following is an example of a liability? Please select all that apply.

   a.   Equipment
   b.   Accounts payable
   c.   Inventory
   d.   Accounts receivable

Review 8.2 Question 2

State whether you would debit or credit the account to achieve the following result.

Increase cash

   a.   Debit
   b.   Credit

Review 8.2 Question 3

Revenue is a

   a.   permanent account
   b.   temporary account

Review 8.2 Question 4

State whether the following transaction is implicit or explicit.

Purchasing a factory

   a.   Implicit
   b.   Explicit

Review 8.2 Question 5

How would the following transaction impact the cash flow of a business?

Purchasing land

a.   Increase cash flow
b.   Decrease cash flow
c.   No impact

Review 8.2 Question 6

Suppose a company had sales of $80K, cost of goods sold of $30K, gross profit of $50K, and net income of $8K. What is the company's gross profit margin?

a.   10%
b.   25%
c.   37.5%
d.   62.5%

Review 8.2 Question 7

Suppose you are promised $100 one year from now, $250 two years from now and $500 three years from now. If the interest rate is 7%, how much would you be willing to pay to receive the money now?

a. $720
b. $742
c. $794
d. $850

Review 8.2 Question 8

Under US GAAP, which account is listed first under the current asset section of the balance sheet?

a.   Short-term investments
b.   Accounts receivable
c.   Cash
d.   Inventory

Review 8.2 Question 9

Which of the following is considered a financing activity under US GAAP?

    a.   Interest received

    b.   Dividends received

    c.   Interest paid

    d.   Dividends paid

Review 8.2 Question 10

Suppose The Shoe Shop had $200,000 in sales and $80,000 in COGS for fiscal year 2013. The Shoe Shop expects sales to grow by 10% for 2014. Under the percent of sales method, what would be the projected COGS for 2014?

    a. $80,000

    b. $88,000

    c. $100,000

    d. $120,000

Review 8.2 Question 11

Suppose The Construction Company needed more tools to complete its newest construction project. The Construction Company purchased $5,000 of tools and paid in cash. How would this impact the accounting equation? Please select all that apply.

    a.   Increase cash by $5,000

    b.   Increase Property, Plant & Equipment (PP&E) by $5,000

    c.   Decrease cash by $5,000

    d.   Increase owner's equity by $5,000

Review 8.2 Question 12

State whether you would debit or credit the account to achieve the following result.

Decrease expenses

    a.   Debit

    b.   Credit

Review 8.2 Question 13

Which accounts should be depreciated over time?

    a.   Equipment
    b.   Inventory
    c.   Land
    d.   Patents

Review 8.2 Question 14

Company A had a current ratio of 2.0x and a quick ratio of 0.5x. Which of the following statements is true?

    a.   Company A would be able to settle about half its current liabilities immediately with its highly liquid current assets.
    b.   For every dollar in current liabilities, Company A has $0.5 dollars in short-term assets to pay those short-term obligations.
    c.   Company A will likely face difficulties paying its short-term obligations.

Review 8.2 Question 15

Suppose a coffee shop bought coffee beans for $15K from a local farmer on 1/1/14. The coffee shop had 30 days to pay the farmer. How would this transaction affect the coffee shop's accounting equation on 1/1/14?

    a.   Accounts receivable increases by $15K
    b.   Accounts payable increases by $15K
    c.   Owners' equity decreases by $15K
    d.   Inventory increases by $15K
    e.   Inventory decreases by $15K

Review 8.2 Question 16

On 7/1/14, Emily signed up for a 6-month membership to Family Farm Share (FFS) where she would receive fresh farm products at the beginning of a month and pay at the end of the month. The membership cost $50 per month. What would the journal entry in the books of FFS look like to record this transaction on 7/1/14?

Date	Account Name	Debit	Credit
July 1, 2014	1) ??	$50.00	
	2) ??		$50.00

    a.   1) Revenue
    b.   1) Unearned Revenue
    c.   1) Accounts Receivable
    d.   2) Revenue
    e.   2) Unearned Revenue
    f.   2) Accounts Receivable

Review 8.2 Question 17

Which of the following is an example of a current asset?

    a.   Unearned revenue
    b.   Land
    c.   Accounts receivable
    d.   Current portion of long-term debt

Review 8.2 Question 18

Suppose a company had a machine with a net book value of $600, historical cost of $750, and accumulated depreciation of $150. The machine was damaged by a flood, and the company determined the market value decreased to $350. What journal entries should the company make to record this transaction? Please select all that apply.

    a.   Debit loss on impairment for $250
    b.   Debit accumulated depreciation for $350
    c.   Credit loss on impairment for $250
    d.   Credit machine for $350
    e.   Credit accumulated depreciation for $250

Review 8.2 Question 19

Select whether the following transaction should be an operating, investing or financing activity under US GAAP. ABC Company paid $5,000 to replace its old equipment.

    a.   Operating

    b.   Investing

    c.   Financing

Review 8.2 Question 20

Which ratio uses both income statement and balance sheet figures?

    a.   leverage

    b.   profit margin

    c.   asset turnover

Review 8.2 Question 21

When using the percent of sales forecasting method, which accounts are plug ins?

    a.   Accounts payable

    b.   Interest expense

    c.   Income tax expense

    d.   Bank borrowings

Review 8.2 Question 22

Calculate EBT based on the following information.

Revenues	$400
COGS	$120
EBIT	$230
Interest expense	$50
Other Income / Expense	$25
Taxes	$40

    a. $280

    b. $180

    c. $155

    d. $115

Review 8.2 Question 23

Using the indirect method to build the Cash Flow from Operations section, decreases in operating current liabilities should be

    a.   subtracted from net income in order to get to operating cash flow

    b.   added to net income in order to get to operating cash flow

---

Review 8.2 Question 24

Suppose you have the following information for a company:

2013 retained earnings $18,000
2014 retained earnings $22,000
2015 projected net income $5,500
2015 projected dividends $2,100

What is projected retained earnings for 2015?

    a. $21,400

    b. $22,000

    c. $23,400

    d. $25,400

Review 8.2 Question 25

Suppose Acorns sells a muffin to a customer for $2.50, and the customer paid cash. How would the cash inflow and revenue from this sale impact the accounting equation? Please select all that apply.

    a.   Cash increases by $2.50

    b.   Owners' equity increases by $2.50

    c.   Accounts payable increases by $2.50

    d.   Cash decreases by $2.50

Review 8.2 Question 26

On 7/1/14, Emily signed up for a 6-month membership to Family Farm Share (FFS) where she would receive fresh farm products at the beginning of a month and pay at the end of the month. The membership cost $50 per month. What would the journal entry in the books of FFS look like to record this transaction on 7/31/14?

Date	Account Name	Debit	Credit
July 31, 2014	1) ??	$50.00	
	2) ??		$50.00

- a. 1) Unearned Revenue
- b. 1) Accounts Receivable
- c. 1) Cash
- d. 2) Unearned Revenue
- e. 2) Accounts Receivable
- f. 2) Cash

Review 8.2 Question 27

Pierre owns a paint shop. On July 1, he buys 200 cans of paint for $20 each. On July 15, he buys 300 cans of paint for $22 each. On July 25, he sells 10 cans of paint for $25 each. Select the correct value(s) for the COGS.

- a. COGS under LIFO is $200.
- b. COGS under LIFO is $220.
- c. COGS under LIFO is $250.
- d. COGS under FIFO is $200.
- e. COGS under FIFO is $220.
- f. COGS under FIFO is $250.

Review 8.2 Question 28

The equity multiplier and debt to equity are measures of

- a. profitability
- b. efficiency
- c. leverage

Review 8.2 Question 29

Suppose the owner of Pizza Pizza asked his family to lend the company $50,000 to get the business started. How would the loan impact the accounting equation of Pizza Pizza? Please select all that apply.

    a.   Increase cash by $50,000
    b.   Increase accounts receivable by $50,000
    c.   Increase loans payable by $50,000
    d.   Increase owners' equity by $50,000

Review 8.2 Question 30

On 7/1/14, Emily signed up for a 6-month membership to Family Farm Share (FFS) where she would receive fresh farm products at the beginning of a month and pay at the end of the month. The membership cost $50 per month. How would the transaction be posted to the t-accounts in the books of FFS on 7/1/14?

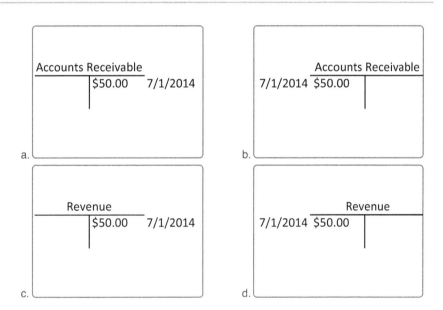

427

Review 8.2 Question 31

Calculate gross profit based on the following information.

Revenues	$400
COGS	$120
Operating expenses	$60
Interest expense	$30

a. $310
b. $280
c. $220
d. $190

Review 8.2 Question 32

If a company owes interest for November 2013 but doesn't pay it until December 2013, it has to make a provision for _____ while preparing financial statements for November 2013.

a. Accrued revenue
b. Deferred revenue
c. Accrued expense
d. Deferred expense

Review 8.2 Question 33

Using the indirect method to build the Cash Flow from Operations section, depreciation should be

a. subtracted from net income in order to get to operating cash flow
b. added back to net income in order to get to operating cash flow

Review 8.2 Question 34

Suppose that Company A has an inventory turnover of 10.0x, and the industry average inventory turnover is 6.0x. How is Company A's operating efficiency compared to others in its industry?

a. Company A sells through its inventory faster than others in the industry.
b. Company A sells through its inventory slower than others in the industry.
c. Company A maintains a higher average inventory than others in the industry.

Review 8.2 Question 35

The Gordon Growth Model

    a.   estimates the terminal value of a project

    b.   assumes the growth rate will increase slightly over time

    c.   assumes margins are declining

Review 8.2 Question 36

Calculate net income based on the following information.

EBT	$650
Interest expense	$220
Other income / expenses	$50
Taxes	$200

    a. $430

    b. $450

    c. $400

    d. $180

Review 8.2 Question 37

Which type of company would be most likely to have positive cash flow from investing?

    a.   Startup

    b.   Growing

    c.   Mature

    d.   In decline

Review 8.2 Question 38

Suppose you have the following information:

12/31/13 revenues	$20,000
12/31/13 COGS	$12,000
12/31/13 accounts receivable	$3,000

10% projected sales growth rate for 2014 – 2016

What is projected accounts receivable on 12/31/15?

a. $3,000
b. $3,300
c. $3,630
d. $4,000

Review 8.2 Question 39

Which of the following hypothetical examples demonstrate the principle of conservatism? Please select all that apply.

a. One of Pizza Pizza's customers is going bankrupt. The customer owes Pizza Pizza $4,000 for purchases it made last month, but Pizza Pizza doesn't think it will receive the money, so it writes off the $4,000 in its accounts receivable account.

b. Pizza Pizza signed a new contract with Boston Public Schools and thinks it will earn $8,000 in revenues next month. Pizza Pizza wants to record $8,000 in accounts receivable for this month.

Review 8.2 Question 40

On 7/1/14, Emily signed up for a 6-month membership to Family Farm Share (FFS) where she would receive fresh farm products at the beginning of a month and pay at the end of the month. The membership cost $50 per month. How would the transaction be posted to the t-accounts in the books of FFS on 7/31/14?

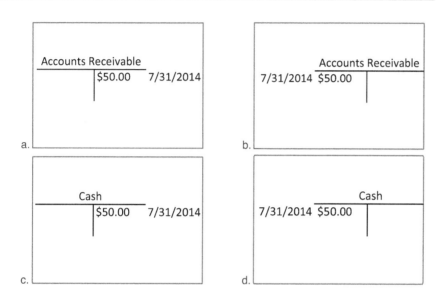

a.
Accounts Receivable
$50.00   7/31/2014

b.
Accounts Receivable
7/31/2014 $50.00

c.
Cash
$50.00   7/31/2014

d.
Cash
7/31/2014 $50.00

Review 8.2 Question 41

A company bought a building for $5 million 1/1/2014 and expects to sell it for $3 million on 12/31/2023. Based on the straight line depreciation method, what would the depreciation listed on the income statement be for the year ended 12/31/2018?

    a. $100,000
    b. $200,000
    c. $1,000,000
    d. $2,000,000

Review 8.2 Question 42

Suppose two companies in the same industry have an ROE of 10%. Company A has a profit margin of 2% and an asset turnover of 1.5x. Company B has an asset turnover of 0.5x and leverage of 2.0x. Which one has higher margin on sales?

    a.   Company A

    b.   Company B

Section 3

Answer Key

Review 8.1 Explanations

Question 1

Answer: A

The materiality concept states that it is necessary to do detailed record keeping and reporting for material items. The $2 million settlement payment is a significant cost, so it should be disclosed as a separate line item in the financial statements. The fact that it may reduce the market value of Central Perk should not affect the decision to disclose the settlement payment, and the auditor does not get to make the decision about whether or not to disclose the settlement.

Question 2

Answer: A

We need to calculate the leverage for Company A in order to see which company is more highly levered. ROE = profit margin * asset turnover* leverage. For Company A, 10% = 2% * 1.5x * leverage, so leverage = 3.33x. A higher leverage ratio means a company has more debt and is more highly levered, so Company A is more highly levered than Company B (3.33x vs. 2.0x). Note that leverage for Company B was given while it had to be calculated for Company A.

Question 3

Answer: B

We need to use the formula free cash flow = EBIAT + D&A - CapEx - increase in working capital = $550 + $130 - $320 - $35 = $325, so Answer B is correct. Answer A was calculated by subtracting D&A instead of adding it ($550 - $130 - $320 - $35). Answer C was calculated by not subtracting the change in working capital ($550 + $130 - $320). Answer D was calculated by incorrectly using EBIT instead of EBIAT ($800 + $130 - $320 - $35).

Question 4

Answer: C

Accounts receivable can be forecasted using the percent of sales method because it has a strong relationship with sales. Interest expense should not be forecasted using the percent of sales method; it can be projected using computer programs or based off of average borrowings. PP&E tends to grow in a step-like pattern and does not grow proportionately with sales in the short-term. It's best to forecast PP&E by looking at the company's discussion about future capital expenditures, often found in the notes to the financial statements. The current portion of long-term debt should be forecasted by looking at contracts for existing loans and determining the portion of the principal that will be repaid within one year.

Question 5

Answer: A

Operating revenue is revenue earned from the main activities of a business. The main activity of a pizza shop is selling pizza, so cash from pizza sales is an example of operating revenue. Renting out buildings and investing in securities are not the main activities of the pizza shop, so any income earned from those activities would be examples of non-operating revenues.

Question 6

Answer: C

The current ratio measures liquidity and shows a company's ability to pay its short-term obligations. The formula is: current ratio = current assets / current liabilities. Inventory turnover measures efficiency, profit margin measures profitability, and debt to equity measures leverage.

Question 7

Answers: B, C

Simon and Sons needs to recognize an expense for selling the suit. It needs to decrease inventory by $400 and increase COGS by $400. In order to increase COGS, Simon and Sons needs to debit the account. In order to decrease the asset inventory, Simon and Sons needs to credit the account.

Question 8

Answers: A, C

Wages paid and inventory purchased would be classified as operating activities under both IFRS and US GAAP. Depreciation is a non-cash expense that does not affect CFO. Dividends paid is considered a financing activity under US GAAP but can be an operating or a financing activity under IFRS.

Question 9

Answer: B

Credits increase liabilities, so, in order to increase accounts payable, we would credit the account.

Question 10

Answer: B

A deferred tax asset arises when a company has higher taxable income reported on its tax returns than it has income before taxes reported on the income statement due to temporary timing differences. A deferred tax liability occurs when taxable income on the tax returns is smaller than income before taxes on the income statement due to temporary timing differences.

Question 11

Answer: D

Simon and Sons should increase its cash account. In order to increase the asset cash, Simon and Sons should debit cash. Simon and Sons also needs to recognize revenue, but it should be credited, not debited. COGS and inventory will also be affected by this transaction, but they are affected by $400, the amount that it cost Simon and Sons to produce the suit.

Question 12

Answer: B

Depreciation expense is a temporary account that is recorded on the income statement. It only shows the expense for the income statement period. Accumulated depreciation, the sum of all the depreciation expense recognized against an asset, is shown on the balance sheet.

Question 13

Answer: C

Operating Income = Gross Profit – Operating Expenses = Revenue – COGS – Operating Expenses =$350 - $100 - $60 = $190. Interest expense is not considered an operating expense.

Question 14

Answer: B

Under IFRS, the least liquid items are listed first, and the other items follow in order of increasing liquidity. This is the opposite of how the balance sheet is ordered under US GAAP, where the accounts are listed in order of how quickly they can be converted to cash.

Question 15

Answer: A

When a company pays cash for an item that it will recognize as an expense in a later period, it is a deferred expense. Deferrals happen when a company delays recognizing revenues or expenses until a later period. Accruals occur when a company recognizes revenues or expenses immediately, before the transfer of cash occurs.

Question 16

Answer: B

The income statement shows revenues and expenses over a period of time. The balance sheet, not the income statement, is a snapshot of a company's resources (assets) and how the resources were financed (liabilities and owners' equity) at a point in time. The cash flow statement, not the income statement, shows the cash flows of a company over a period of time. The Retained Earnings balance in the balance sheet shows the cumulative profits retained by a business over its lifetime. The Income Statement, on the other hand, shows the income or the loss for the current accounting period.

Question 17

Answer: B, D

On 1/1/14, The Dog Academy needs to increase its cash account and increase its unearned revenue account. In order to increase the asset cash, The Dog Academy would debit the account for $100. The account unearned revenue is a liability, so in order to increase the liability, we would credit it for $100. The Dog Academy will recognize revenue and decrease unearned revenue over time as the training classes are used up.

Question 18

Answers: A, C

Cash and Property, Plant and Equipment (PP&E) are assets because they are resources that provide economic benefits to the company. Accounts payable and notes payable refer to payments the company will have to make in the future, so they are liabilities, not assets.

Question 19

Answer: D

Ben & Jerry's should place the bond under non-current liabilities. The bond is a liability because it reflects that Ben & Jerry's has an obligation to pay back the issuer for the funds it borrowed. It is non-current because it will be due in over one year.

Question 20

Answer: A

The double declining balance method is an accelerated depreciation method, meaning a business recognizes more depreciation expense in the earlier years than the straight line method. So, since the straight line method recognizes less depreciation expense, the business would have higher net income than if it had used the double declining balance method.

Question 21

Answer: A

The expiration of prepaid insurance is an implicit transaction. There is no clear event that triggers a journal entry, and the timing and amount are not clearly defined.

Question 22

Answer: B

Accounts payable turnover = credit purchases / average accounts payable = $3,000 / $2,000 = 1.5x.

Question 23

Answer: A

Simon and Sons should increase its revenue account. In order to increase revenue, Simon and Sons should credit revenue for $700. COGS and inventory will also be affected by this transaction, but they are affected by $400, the amount that it cost Simon and Sons to produce the suit. Accounts payable is not affected because Simon and Sons does not owe anyone for selling the suit to Max.

Question 24

Answer: B

Central Perk should recognize revenue when it is earned, which is when Ellen receives the coffee, not evenly over time. Central Perk should recognize $20 (4 * $5) of revenue at the end of January because Ellen received 4 coffees in January. Central Perk should wait until the expiration of the coffee punch card in March to recognize the remaining revenue for the drinks Ellen won't receive.

Question 25

Answer: D

All of the methods can help a business decide whether or not it should invest in a project. NPV stands for net present value, and it combines the present values of a project's cash inflows and outflows to get the net value, which indicates what value the project would add to the business. IRR stands for the internal rate of return, and it is the discount rate that causes the NPV of all cash flows to be equal to zero. It's the rate at which an investment breaks even. DCF stands for discounted cash flow analysis, and it determines the value of a project by adding up the present values of a project's future free cash flows.

Question 26

Answer: B

If a company has positive cash flows, it doesn't mean that the company has positive net income. There are many expenses that appear on the income statement that are non-cash expenses, such as depreciation or prepaid rent. It's possible for a company to have few cash expenses, leading to positive cash flows, but also have a significant amount of non-cash expenses, such as depreciation, leading to negative net income.

Question 27

Answers: C,F

The company had $400 on hand on July 1, 2014, bought $350 of inventory during the accounting period and had $250 on hand on September 30, 2014. We know that beginning inventory + purchased inventory − ending inventory = COGS. So, COGS = $400 + $350 − $250 = $500. The company should debit (increase) COGS by $500 and credit (decrease) inventory by $500 to reflect the inventory sold by the company.

Question 28

Answers: D

The cash flow statement shows information about a company's cash inflows and outflows. The balance sheet tells us about a company's financial position at a point in time, and the income statement shows a company's revenues and expenses over time. Asset utilization efficiency is determined by calculating ratios based on figures from the balance sheet and income statement.

Question 29

Answer: A

All increases in operating current assets should be deducted from net income in order to get to operating cash flow.

Question 30

Answer: B

In order to determine projected COGS, we need to determine the historical relationship between revenues and COGS by dividing COGS in 2013 by revenues in 2013. Then we multiply this figure by 2014 projected revenues. So, 2013 COGS / 2013 revenues = $30,000 / $50,000 = 60%. So, projected COGS for 2014 = $57,500 * 60% = $34,500, so B is the correct answer.

Question 31

Answer: B

Gross Profit = Revenue – COGS = $350 - $100 = $250. Operating expenses and interest expense are not needed to calculate gross profit.

Question 32

Answers: A,C

This transaction will increase inventory by $3,000 to reflect the additional puppies that Peter's Pet Shop owns and can sell in the future. It will also decrease cash by $3,000 because Peter's Pet Shop used cash to purchase the puppies. This transaction will not affect owners' equity because no one is making a contribution to the business. This transaction will not decrease accounts payable because the question stated that Peter's Pet Shop used cash to purchase the puppies.

Question 33

Answer: A

An annuity is a series of equal, fixed payments made over a specified period of time. Payments that differ over time are not annuities.

Question 34

Answer: B

Asset turnover = revenues / average total assets. Company A has an asset turnover of 2.0x and Company B has an asset turnover of 4.0x, so Company B uses its assets more efficiently. Company B generated $4 of revenues for each dollar of assets whereas Company A generated $2.00 of revenues for each dollar of assets.

Question 35

Answer: B

In order to determine how much you would be willing to pay, you need to figure out the present value of the future cash flows. The formula is Present value = $CF1 / (1+r)^1 + CF2 / (1+r)^2$ = $300 / 1.05^1 + 500 / 1.05^2$ = $739.23.

Question 36

Answer: A

Permanent accounts are found on the balance sheet. They are continuous accounts that have a cumulative balance over time.

Question 37

Answer: C

Average collection period = 365 / accounts receivable turnover = average accounts receivable / (net credit sales / 365) = $2,000 / ($6,000 / 365) = 122 days.

Question 38

Answers: A, D

Startups often have low or negative CFO because they are spending a lot of money to get their operations running. Companies in decline often have negative CFO because they are not performing well and earning money. Companies that are growing or in a mature / steady state often enjoy positive CFO because they are earning enough revenue to cover operating expenses.

Question 39

Answer: B

Accounts receivable turnover and accounts payable turnover are measures of efficiency. Accounts receivable turnover shows how quickly a company collects payment from its customers. Accounts payable turnover tells us how quickly a company pays its vendors.

Question 40

Answer: C

Net Income = Income before Taxes − Taxes = $100 - $30 = $70. Income before taxes already factored in interest expense, so it does not need to be subtracted again to calculate net income.

Question 41

Answer: A

Debits decrease equity, so we would debit the account.

Question 42

Answer: B

In order to build a company's cash flow statement for an accounting period, you need the balance sheet from the beginning and end of the accounting period and the income statement. It is not possible to build the statement of cash flows just from an income statement.

Review 8.2 Explanations

Question 1

Answer: B

Accounts payable is a liability. Accounts payable represents a company's obligation to pay others in the future for services or goods previously received. Accounts receivable, equipment, and inventory are not liabilities; they are assets because they will all provide economic benefits to the company. Accounts receivable represents a company's right to receive cash in the future.

Question 2

Answer: A

Debits increase assets, so, in order to increase cash, we would debit the cash account.

Question 3

Answer: B

Revenue is found on the income statement, and it is a temporary account. Temporary accounts show activity over a period of time and reset to zero at the start of a new accounting period.

Question 4

Answer: B

Purchasing a factory is an explicit transaction. There is a clear event that triggers the transaction, and the amount and timing of the transaction can be identified.

Question 5

Answer: B

Purchasing land would decrease cash flow from investing activities.

Question 6

Answer: D

Gross profit margin = gross profit / sales = $50,000 / $80,000 = 0.625 = 62.5%

Question 7

Answer: A

In order to determine how much you would be willing to pay, you need to figure out the present value of the future cash flows. The formula is Present value = CF1 / (1+r)^1 + CF2 / (1+r)^2 = 100 / 1.07^1 + 250 / 1.07^2 + 500 / 1.07^3= $719.97.

Question 8

Answer: C

Under US GAAP, accounts are ordered according to their liquidity. Cash would be listed first because it is the most liquid. After cash, there would be short-term investments, then there would be accounts receivable, and finally inventory.

Question 9

Answer: D

Dividends paid is considered a financing activity under US GAAP. Interest received, dividends received, and interest paid are all considered operating activities under US GAAP.

Question 10

Answer: B

To forecast COGS for 2014, we need to determine the relationship between sales and COGS in 2013. In 2013, COGS / Sales = $80,000 / $200,000 = 40%. In 2014, The Shoe Shop expects sales to grow by 10%, so sales will grow by $200,000*10% = $20,000, and projected sales for 2014 = $200,000 + $20,000 = $220,000. So, COGS for 2014 should be $220,000* 40% = $88,000.

Question 11

Answers: B,C

This purchase would increase PP&E by $5,000 because The Construction Company now owns additional equipment. It would also decrease cash by $5,000 because The Construction Company spent cash to buy the equipment. This purchase would not decrease accounts receivable because the purchase does not affect the cash the company will receive from others. This transaction would not affect owners' equity because no one made a contribution to the business, and the company did not earn revenues or recognize an expense as a result of the transaction.

Question 12

Answer: B

Credits decrease expenses, so we would credit the account.

Question 13

Answer: A

Equipment should be depreciated over time because a business needs to recognize an expense over time for long-lived physical assets. Land should never be depreciated because it is not "used up." Patents should be amortized because patents are non-physical assets. Inventory should not be depreciated because it is not an asset that is held for use by a business; it is sold to others and expensed as COGS.

Question 14

Answer: A

A quick ratio of 0.5x implies that Company A would be able to settle about half its current liabilities immediately with its highly liquid current assets. A current ratio of 2.0x implies that, for every dollar in current liabilities, Company A has

$2.0 dollars in short-term assets to pay its short-term obligations. Generally, a current ratio of less than 1.0x suggests a company could face difficulties in paying its short-term obligations. Since Company A's current ratio is 2.0x, it does not seem like it will have a lot of difficulty paying its short-term obligations.

Question 15

Answers: B, D

Accounts payable would increase by $15K. When the coffee shop bought the beans from the farmer, the coffee shop agreed to pay for them later. Inventory increases by $15K to reflect the $15K of beans the coffee shop added to inventory. Owners' equity would not decrease by $15K because the coffee shop has not yet recognized an expense for the purchase. Inventory would not decrease by $15K because the coffee shop did not sell its inventory. Accounts receivable would not increase by $15K. The coffee shop owes the farmer money and would not expect to receive cash in the future from the farmer.

Question 16

Answers: C, D

Accounts receivable would increase by $50 to reflect that FFS will collect $50 from Emily at the end of the month. In order to increase the asset accounts receivable, we would debit the account. FFS also needs to recognize revenue it earned for delivering the products to Emily. In order to increase revenue, FFS would credit the account. If Emily had prepaid for the whole membership, the account unearned revenue would have been affected. But, in this situation, Emily agreed to pay at the end of the month for each month she participated in the farm share.

Question 17

Answer: C

Accounts receivable is an example of a current asset because it will be turned into cash in under one year. Unearned revenue is an account that is created when a company receives cash before providing the goods or service, and it is a current liability. Land is a long-term asset because it will provide a benefit to a company for over one year. The current portion of long-term debt is a current liability.

Question 18

Answers: A, E

To record the impairment, we would debit loss on impairment for $250 and credit accumulated depreciation for $250 to increase the contra-asset account and reduce the machine to its current market value of $350. Crediting loss on impairment would decrease the account, rather than increase it, and crediting the machine for $350 would decrease the machine to a market value of $250, which is incorrect.

Question 19

Answer: B

Replacing old equipment is an investing activity because the new equipment is an asset that will provide benefits to the company for many years.

Question 20

Answer: C

Asset turnover = revenues / average total assets, so it uses figures from the income statement (revenues) and the balance sheet (average total assets). Profit = net income / sales, so it only uses figures from the income statement. Leverage = average total assets / average total equity, so it only uses balance sheet figures.

Question 21

Answer: D

Bank borrowings is a plug in that is calculated after all the other accounts have been forecasted. Accounts payable is forecasted using the percent of sales method. Interest expense is calculated based off of beginning borrowings or by using a computer program that can work around the circularity issues involved in forecasting interest expense. Income tax expense is calculated based off of the company's income tax rate.

Question 22

Answer: B

EBT = EBIT – Interest Expense = $230 - $50 = $180.

Question 23

Answer: A

All decreases in current liabilities should be subtracted from net income in order to get to operating cash flow.

Question 24

Answer: D

Retained earnings in 2015 = retained earnings in 2014 + projected net income in 2015 – projected dividends in 2015 = $22,000 + $5,500 - $2,100 = $25,400. Answer A was incorrectly calculated using 2013 retained earnings instead of 2014 retained earnings. Answer B simply assumed 2015 retained earnings would be the same as 2014 retained earnings. Answer C was incorrectly calculated using average retained earnings for 2013 and 2014.

Question 25

Answer: A, B

Cash increases by $2.50 because the customer paid cash to Acorns to purchase the muffin. Owners' equity increases by $2.50 because Acorns earned revenue from the purchase. Accounts payable was not affected by this transaction. Acorns does not owe additional money to any party as a result of this transaction.

Question 26

Answers: C,E

Cash would increase by $50 because Emily will pay FFS cash at the end of the month. In order to increase the asset cash, we would debit cash. The corresponding journal entry would be a decrease to accounts receivable to reflect that Emily no longer has the obligation to pay FFS. In order to decrease the asset accounts receivable, we would credit accounts receivable. Unearned revenue is not affected because FFS earned its revenue at the beginning of the month, when it delivered the products to Emily.

Question 27

Answer: B, D

LIFO stands for last in, first out. So, COGS under LIFO would be 10*$22 = $220. FIFO stands for first in, first out. So, COGS under FIFO would be 10*$20 = $200. The price that Pierre sold the paint for does not play a role in the calculation of COGS.

Question 28

Answer: C

The equity multiplier and debt to equity are measures of leverage. The equity multiplier and the debt to equity ratio show us how a company uses debt to finance its assets.

Question 29

Answers: A, C

The loan would increase cash by $50,000 and would increase loans payable by $50,000 to reflect Pizza Pizza's obligation to pay back the loan in the future. The loan would not increase accounts receivable by $50,000 because the loan payment would be immediate and in cash. The loan would not increase owners' equity by $50,000 because the owner's family is lending money, not making an investment in the company.

Question 30

Answers: B, C

Accounts receivable would increase by $50 to reflect that FFS will collect $50 from Emily at the end of the month. In order to increase the asset accounts receivable, we would debit the account. FFS also needs to recognize revenue it earned for delivering the products to Emily. In order to increase revenue, FFS would credit the account. Debits are on the left, and credits are on the right, so the t-accounts shown in answers B and C are correct.

Question 31

Answer: B

Gross Profit = Revenue – COGS = $400 - $120 = $280. Operating expenses and interest expense are not needed to calculate gross profit.

Question 32

Answer: C

This would be an example of an accrued expense. The company incurred the interest expense before it actually paid for it. Deferrals occur when a company delays recognizing revenue or expenses until a later point in time.

Question 33

Answer: B

To undo the effect of depreciation expense on net income, depreciation should be added back to net income in order to get to operating cash flow.

Question 34

Answer: A

Inventory turnover = COGS / average inventory. Company A sells through its inventory about 10 times per year whereas the industry average is to sell through inventory about 6 times per year. So, Company A sells through its inventory faster than others in the industry. It's not possible to tell how high Company A's average inventory is compared to others in the industry.

Question 35

Answer: A

The Gordon Growth Model is one way to determine the terminal value of a project. It is an approximate sum of the cash flows for the final years of a project. The model assumes that the growth rate will remain constant indefinitely and that margins will remain the same.

Question 36

Answer: B

Net Income = EBT – Taxes = $650 - $200 = $450.

Question 37

Answer: D

A company in a state of decline would likely have positive CFI because it does not need to invest in new equipment. It could also sell off its unnecessary assets, which would cause it to have positive CFI. Startups, growing companies, and mature companies often have negative CFI because they are investing in new equipment or making purchases to replace old equipment.

Question 38

Answer: C

In order to determine projected accounts receivable, we need to determine the historical relationship between revenues and accounts receivable by dividing accounts receivable in 2013 by revenues in 2013. Then we multiply this figure by 2015 projected revenues. So, 2013 accounts receivable / 2013 revenues = $3,000 / $20,000 = 15%. To determine 2015 projected revenues, we multiply $20,000*1.1*1.1 = $24,200. So, projected accounts receivable for 2015 = $24,200 * 15% = $3,630, so C is the correct answer.

Question 39

Answer: A

The conservatism principle states that companies should anticipate and record future losses but not gains. It is correct for Pizza Pizza to make a provision for $4,000 because it seems unlikely that Pizza Pizza will receive the money. It is incorrect for Pizza Pizza to record $8,000 in accounts receivable because it should not record future gains.

Question 40

Answers: A, D

Cash would increase by $50 because Emily will pay FFS cash at the end of the month. In order to increase the asset cash, we would debit cash. The corresponding journal entry would be a decrease to accounts receivable to reflect that Emily no longer has the obligation to pay FFS. In order to decrease the asset accounts receivable, we would credit accounts receivable. Debits are on the left, and credits are on the right, so the t-accounts shown in answers A and D are correct.

Question 41

Answer: B

The depreciation expense listed on the income statement would be $200,000. The formula for calculating depreciation expense using the straight line method is (gross book value - salvage value) / useful life. The useful life of the asset is 10 years (1/1/14 to 12/31/23), so the depreciation expense each year would be ($5 million - $3 million) / 10 years = $200,000.

Question 42

Answer: B

We need to calculate the profit margin for Company B in order to see which company appears more profitable. ROE = profit margin * asset turnover * leverage. For Company B, 10% = profit margin * 0.5 * 2.0, so profit margin = 10%. Since Company B has a higher profit margin than Company A (10% vs. 2%), Company B appears more profitable.

9

Glossary

Term	Definition	Chapter
Accelerated Depreciation	A depreciation method (such as the double-declining balance method) that recognizes more depreciation expense in the early years of an asset's life and less depreciation expense in the later years of an asset's life.	4
Accounting Equation	Assets = Liabilities + Owners' Equity. The fundamental equation of accounting is the basis for double entry accounting and requires that the total debits equal the total credits for each transaction.	1
Accounting Periods	The time frames for which financial results are reported; common accounting periods are a month, a quarter or a year.	1
Accounts Payable	A liability that represents money a company owes to its creditors for goods or services it received in the past.	1
Accounts Payable Turnover	Calculated by the formula: Credit Purchases / Average Accounts Payable. If no information about credit purchases is available, COGS may be used instead. AP Turnover is an efficiency ratio that measures how efficiently a business pays its vendors. It represents the number of times accounts payable turned over during the accounting period.	6
Accounts Receivable	An asset that represents money owed to a company by its customers for goods or services the company provided in the past.	1
Accounts Receivable Turnover	Calculated by the formula: Net Credit Sales / Average Accounts Receivable. If no information about credit sales is available, total sales may be used instead. Accounts receivable turnover is an efficiency ratio that measures how quickly a company can collect its receivables. The ratio represents the number of times per year that a company collects its receivables.	6
Accrual	A revenue amount that is recorded after the revenue is recognized but payment has not yet been received or an expense amount that is recorded after the expense has been incurred but payment has not yet been made. An accrual indicates the exchange of cash will occur at some point in the future after the initial revenue or expense is recognized.	5

Term	Definition	Chapter
Accrual Accounting Method	An accounting method that recognizes revenues when they are earned and expenses when they are incurred, not when cash exchanges hands. This method is followed by most companies and required under US GAAP and IFRS.	1
Accrued Expenses	Liability accounts that record expenses that have been recognized on the income statement but have not yet been paid. Examples include wages payable, accrued interest expense, accrued income taxes. At the time of the accrual, we debit the appropriate expense account (wage expense, interest expense, income tax expense) and credit the liability account titled accrued expenses, which will be paid at some point in the future. Note that accrued expenses is not an expense account but a liability account.	1
Accrued Liability	Liability accounts that record expenses that have been recognized on the income statement but have not yet been paid. Similar to accrued expenses.	4
Accrued Payroll	Also called accrued wages.	4
Accrued Revenue	An asset account that records revenue that has been earned and recognized on the income statement but not yet paid for by the customer. At the time of the accrual, we debit the receivable account and credit the appropriate accrued revenue account. When the cash transfer ultimately occurs, we debit the cash account and credit the receivable account.	4
Accumulated Depreciation	A contra-asset account on the balance sheet that shows the cumulative depreciation expense recognized against an asset. Accumulated depreciation typically has a credit balance which offsets the debit balance of the asset. It's shown on the asset side of the balance sheet as a subtraction from the corresponding assets.	4
Accumulated other comprehensive income	An equity account that consists of cumulative unrealized gains or losses on line items classified under other comprehensive income. It includes items such as unrealized gains or losses on investments available for sale, foreign currency gains or losses, and pension plan gains or losses.	3
Acid Test Ratio	Calculated by the formula: Highly Liquid Current Assets / Current Liabilities. The acid test ratio is a liquidity ratio that measures a company's ability to pay its short-term obligations. It is a more conservative estimate than the current ratio because it only includes highly liquid current assets. Also called the quick ratio.	6
Additional paid-in capital	Shareholder contributions that exceed a share's par value.	2
Adjusting Entries	Entries made to adjust the balances of accounts as a result of an implicit transaction or the passage of time. Recording depreciation expense, recording prepaid rent, and recording interest expense on a loan accrued but not yet paid are examples of adjusting entries.	4

Term	Definition	Chapter
Amortization	The method to allocate the cost of long-lived non-physical or intangible assets to different time periods. Items that are amortized include patents, copyrights, and brands.	4
Annuity	A fixed cash flow paid each period.	7
Asset Turnover	Calculated by the formula: Revenue / Average Total Assets. Asset turnover is an efficiency ratio that is used in the DuPont Framework.	6
Assets	Resources owned by a business that will provide an economic benefit in the future. A more formal definition states that an asset must: be purchased at a cost that is measurable, produce probable economic benefit in the future, result from a past event, be owned or controlled by the entity.	1
Average Collection Period	Calculated by the formula: Average Accounts Receivable / (Net Credit Sales / 365). Average collection period is an efficiency ratio that measures the average number of days it takes a business to collect cash from its customers. Also called days sales outstanding and days sales in receivables.	6
Balance Sheet	A financial statement that is a snapshot of a company's resources (assets) and how the resources were financed (liabilities and owners' equity) at a certain point in time.	1
Book Value of an Asset	Historical cost of an asset less accumulated depreciation or amortization on the asset.	4
Bond	A debt instrument issued by a government or corporation to an investor who borrows the funds for a defined period of time at a fixed interest rate.	4
CAGR	Compound Annual Growth Rate. The CAGR measures the rate of return of an investment over a certain period of time.	7
Capital	Financial resources available for use.	1
Capital Expenditures	Cash flows related to the purchase of fixed assets, such as property or equipment.	7
Capitalization	The practice of recording the cost of the purchase as an asset, rather than recording it as an expense when an item is purchased. For example, when a long-lived asset is purchased, such as a machine, the cost of the machine is said to be capitalized because it is recorded as an asset in the accounts. In contrast, something small and immaterial, such as pens and pencils, may be expensed immediately.	4
Cash Accounting Method	An accounting method where a company records revenues and expenses when cash exchanges hands (not necessarily when revenues are earned or expenses are incurred). This method is occasionally used by very small businesses but is not acceptable under IFRS or US GAAP.	1

Term	Definition	Chapter
Cash Conversion Cycle	Calculated by the formula: Days Inventory + Average Collection Period - Days Purchases Outstanding. The cash conversion cycle measures the length of the cycle that includes purchasing inventory on credit, keeping inventory on the shelf, selling it for credit, and collecting cash.	6
Chart of Accounts	A list of all the accounts (including asset, liability, equity, revenue, and expense accounts) of a business.	2
Circularity	An issue where two figures depend on the value of each other, making it challenging to calculate their values in a spreadsheet.	7
Common Stock	Shares that represent ownership in a business. This share class often includes the right to share proportionately in a business' profits and to vote on proposals and director elections.	3
Conservatism	An accounting principle that states businesses should anticipate and record future losses but not future gains. Businesses should also be conservative when recording assets and liabilities (recording the lower valuation for assets and the higher valuation for liabilities).	1
Consistency	An accounting principle that requires consistency across periods and states that businesses should record transactions in the same way from one period to the next.	1
Contra Account	An account for which the typical balance is the opposite of other accounts in its category. A contra account adjusts the net value of its related account. Accumulated depreciation is an example of a contra account.	4
Contra-Asset	An account that reduces the net value of an asset on the balance sheet. Assets typically have credit balances and contra-asset accounts typically have debit balances.	4
Contributed Capital	Money that an investor paid to buy stock directly from a company, also known as paid-in capital. Consists of the stated value (par value or face value) of the shares plus additional paid-in capital, the amount over the par value paid to a company.	2
Cost of Goods Sold (COGS)	An expense that corresponds to the cost of products sold to customers. Also called COGS or cost of sales.	2
Cost of Sales	An expense that corresponds to the cost of products sold to customers. Also called COGS or cost of sales.	2
Credit	An accounting entry that increases the balance in a liability, equity, or revenue account and decreases the account balance for an asset or expense account. Credits are shown on the right side in journal entries, t-accounts, and trial balances.	2

Term	Definition	Chapter
Credit Terms	Agreements between two or more companies that specify when the payment for goods or services purchased is due. The amount of time is often a certain number of days after the services were provided or the goods were delivered.	1
Current Asset	An asset that will be used or converted into cash within one year or one operating cycle, whichever is longer.	3
Current Liabilities	Liabilities that will come due within one year or one operating cycle, whichever is longer.	3
Current Ratio	Calculated by the formula current assets / current liabilities. The current ratio is a liquidity ratio that measures a company's ability to pay its short-term obligations.	6
Days Inventory	Calculated by the formula: 365 / Inventory Turnover. Days inventory is an efficiency ratio that tells us the average number of days inventory is held before being sold.	6
Days Purchases Outstanding	Calculated by the formula: Average Accounts Payable / (Annual Credit Purchases / 365). Days purchases outstanding measures the average number of days it takes a business to pay its vendors.	6
Days Sales in Receivables	Calculated by the formula: Average Accounts Receivable / (Net Credit Sales / 365). Days sales in receivables is an efficiency ratio that measures the average number of days it takes a business to collect cash from its customers. Also called days sales outstanding and average collection period.	6
Days Sales Outstanding	Calculated by the formula: Average Accounts Receivable / (Net Credit Sales / 365). Days sales outstanding is an efficiency ratio that measures the average number of days it takes a business to collect cash from its customers. Also called average collection period and days sales in receivables.	6
Debit	An accounting entry that increases the account balance in an asset or expense account and decreases the account balance for a liability, equity or revenue account. Debits are shown on the left side in journal entries, t-accounts, and trial balances.	2
Debt to Equity Ratio	Calculated by the formula Total Liabilities / Total Equity. Debt to equity is a leverage ratio that measures how much of a company's assets are financed by equity and how much are financed by debt.	6
Deductions	Tax term that refers to a company's expenses that are legally allowed to be subtracted from gross income for tax calculation purposes. Deductions differ from one geographic location to another based on the applicable tax codes.	4
Deferral	An amount that is recorded when the transfer of cash occurs before a company earns revenue or incurs an expense.	5

Term	Definition	Chapter
Deferred Expense	An asset account that records amounts paid towards expenses not yet recognized on the income statement. Note: Deferred expenses are not expenses, rather they are assets.	4
Deferred Revenue	A liability account that records revenue that have been received in advance from a customer but not yet earned or recognized on the income statement. It represents an obligation to provide goods or services in the future. Also called unearned revenue. Note: Deferred revenues are not revenues, rather they are liabilities.	2
Deferred Tax Assets	Assets that are used to decrease the amount of taxes a company will have to pay in the future. DTAs reflect that a company overpaid its taxes for the current period by prepaying taxes for income that will be reported in the future. DTAs occur when timing differences cause taxable income as per the tax returns for a period to be higher than reported income on the financial statements.	4
Deferred Tax Liability	A DTL is an obligation to pay taxes in the future on the income earned in the current period. DTLs reflect that a company paid less than its taxes for the current period and will have to pay more taxes in the future on the income it already reported. DTLs occur when timing differences cause taxable income for a period, as per the tax returns, to be lower than income reported on the financial statements.	4
Deferred Taxes	Deferred taxes arise from temporary timing differences between income reported on tax filings (taxable income) and income reported on financial statements (financial income).	4
Depreciation	The method to allocate expenses of long-lived physical assets over time to reflect the decrease in value of the asset over its useful life.	4
Depreciation Expense	A temporary account that shows the depreciation for the current accounting period. It's an expense reported on the income statement.	4
Direct Method	A method to report the cash flow from operating activities section on the cash flow statement. The direct method lists all cash collections and cash payments related to operating activities and simply subtracts the cash payments from the cash collections in order to get net cash flow from operating activities.	5
Discount Rate	A percentage rate determined by a company to calculate the present value of its future cash flows. The discount rate is determined based on the factors that influence the time value of money (such as inflation, risk and opportunity cost).	7
Discounted Cash Flow	Valuation methodology that takes a company's projected free cash flows and discounts them to arrive a present value.	7
Double Declining Balance Depreciation	A depreciation method that applies a constant rate of depreciation to the declining book value of an asset until the book value reaches the salvage value. This method recognizes more depreciation expense in the early years of an asset's life and less in the later years.	4

Term	Definition	Chapter
Double Entry Accounting	A system of accounting that requires transactions to be recorded using debits and credits and stipulates that the debits must equal the credits for each transaction.	2
DuPont Framework	A tool for analyzing a company's Return on Equity (ROE). Consists of three components: Profitability, Operating Efficiency, Financial Leverage. ROE = Profit Margin * Operating Efficiency * Leverage.	6
EBIAT	Earnings Before Interest After Taxes. A measure of how much income a business has earned without the effects of the capital structure of a business. Calculated as (1 - tax rate) * Earnings Before Interest and Taxes.	6
EBIT	Earnings Before Interest and Taxes. Income earned from a company's main operations, also known as operating profit and operating income. Calculated as Gross Profit - Operating Expenses. Can also be calculated by adding back interest and taxes to net income.	7
EBITDA	Earnings Before Interest Taxes Depreciation and Amortization. A measure sometimes used as a proxy for operating cash flows. EBITDA = EBIT + D + A	7
Employee Advances	Amounts paid to employees in advance of the employee earning the amount. Equivalent to a loan to the employee. These advances are made at the discretion of the management of the business and they are often repaid by deducting them from subsequent payroll amounts.	3
Entity Concept	An accounting principle that states that a business is a separately identifiable entity. The books of a business must be kept separately from the books of individuals, who own the company, even if there is only one owner of the company. In the case of large companies with subsidiaries or multinational companies, financial records should also be reported separately for each entity.	1
Equity Multiplier	Calculated by the formula Total Assets / Total Equity. Also called leverage.	6
Expenses	Costs associated with providing goods or services to customers which have been recognized as revenues, or costs incurred in a period whose benefits are expected to expire within the period. Additionally, assets that are not expected to produce future benefits would also be treated as expenses.	1
Explicit Transactions	Transactions that involve an activity or an exchange of resources between parties and have a clear event that triggers them.	4
Fair Market Value	The amount that an asset could be sold for on the market to a knowledgeable and willing buyer at a certain point in time.	4
FASB	FASB is an acronym for the Financial Accounting Standards Board, which is the accounting standard-setting body in the U.S. The rules and standards developed by FASB are referred to as Generally Accepted Accounting Principles, GAAP.	1

Term	Definition	Chapter
FIFO	First In First Out, a method of accounting for inventory invoked when inventory purchased or manufactured at different costs are on the books. It determines the value of inventory sold as if the first units sold are the oldest units remaining in inventory.	4
Financial Leverage	The degree to which a business uses debt to finance its assets. Measured using the leverage ratio or the debt to equity ratio.	6
Financing Section	The section of the cash flow statement that relates to a company's financing activities, such as when a company borrows cash, issues securities, repays borrowings, and retires stock.	5
Finished Goods	Items that have gone through the complete manufacturing process and are ready to be sold to customers.	4
Fiscal Year	The twelve month period over which a company reports its financial results. Many companies align their fiscal year with the calendar year, but they may choose to report over any twelve month period. Some companies use a 52/53 week period as their fiscal year.	3
Fixed Assets	Assets with a long-term useful life (over one year) that a business uses in its operations. Also known as tangible assets or property, plant and equipment (PP&E).	4
Free Cash Flows	Cash flows that are free, or available, to distribute to investors or to reinvest in the business after the business has covered all its expenses. FCF does not consider the impact of how a business is financed. Calculated by the formula: FCF = (1-t) * EBIT + Depreciation - Capital Expenditures - Change in Net Working Capital	7
Future Value	The value at a specific date in the future of an amount or a series of amounts invested at a certain interest rate.	7
GAAP	Generally Accepted Accounting Principles, the set of accounting standards issued by FASB and followed by most U.S. companies.	1
Gain	Arises when an asset is sold for greater than its book value. An increase in the value of an investment not yet sold is called an unrealized gain. Often related to an activity outside the normal operations of a business, such as selling a long-lived asset for more than its recorded value on the balance sheet.	4
General Ledger	A book that includes all of a company's transactions and the balances of all the accounts in the chart of accounts.	2
Going Concern	A company is a going concern if it is likely that a business will continue to operate for the foreseeable future and will be able to satisfy its obligations and realize the benefits of its assets.	1

Term	Definition	Chapter
Goods available for sale	In a retail business, goods available for sales can be calculated as beginning inventory plus purchases of additional inventory during the period. This calculation can be useful in determining cost of goods sold, because at the end of a period, the goods available for sale during the period will either remain in inventory or be moved to cost of goods sold, thus Cost of Goods Sold = Goods Available for Sale - Ending Inventory. This calculation is often used when using a periodic inventory system.	4
Goodwill	An intangible asset that arises during an acquisition; the amount the acquirer pays for the target less the fair market value of the target's net assets.	4
Gordon Growth Model	A method to calculate the terminal value of an indefinite stream of cash flows. Calculated by the following formula: Terminal Value = (Cash flows in the final year of the projection) / (Discount rate - Growth rate)	7
Gross Book Value	The price paid for an asset plus the extra expenses necessary to prepare the asset for service in the business. An asset is recorded at its gross book value in the financial books of a company. Also known as the original cost.	4
Gross Profit	Calculated by the formula: Sales - Cost of Goods Sold.	3
Gross Profit Margin	Calculated by the formula: Gross Profit / Sales. The gross profit margin is a measure of profitability that tells us the percentage of revenue available to cover other expenses once cost of goods sold has been removed. Also called gross profit percentage.	6
Historical Cost	The historical cost principle states that transactions should be recorded at the actual price paid at the time of the transaction. Assets should be recorded at their historical cost, not their current market value.	1
IASB	IASB is an acronym for the International Accounting Standards Board, which is an accounting standard-setting body outside the U.S. The rules and standards developed by IASB are referred to as International Financial Reporting Standards or IFRS. Many countries have adopted IFRS.	1
IFRS	International Financial Reporting Standards, the set of accounting standards followed by most companies outside of the U.S.	1
Impairment	A permanent decrease in the value of an asset below its carrying value.	4
Implicit Transactions	Transactions that do not have clear triggers that caused them. Implicit transactions often arise as a result of the passage of time, and they are typically recorded using adjusting journal entries. Examples of implicit transactions include depreciation, interest expense, and the amortization of a prepaid expense.	4
Income Before Taxes	Revenues and gains less all losses and expenses, except for tax expenses. Also called pretax income.	4

Term	Definition	Chapter
Income Statement	A financial statement that shows a company's revenues, expenses, and profits/losses over a given accounting period.	3
Income Tax Expense	Income taxes already paid or payable in the future corresponding to the pretax profit reported for the period.	4
Indirect Method	A method to report the cash flow from operating activities section on the cash flow statement. The indirect method starts with net income and adjusts for non-cash items and changes in current asset and current liability accounts in order to get net cash flow from operating activities.	5
Intangible Asset	A non-physical long-lived asset. Examples include patents and brands.	4
Interest Coverage Ratio	Calculated by the formula EBIT / Interest Expense. The interest coverage ratio measures a company's ability to make interest payments on its debt.	6
Inventory	Assets that are manufactured or purchased to be sold to customers.	4
Inventory Turnover	Calculated by the formula: COGS / Average Inventory. Inventory turnover is an efficiency ratio that represents how many times inventory turned over during an accounting period.	6
Investing Section	The section of the cash flow statement that relates to a company's investing activities. Includes cash flows related to long-lived assets, loans made to other parties, and investments in securities and in other entities.	5
Invoice	A document that itemizes goods sold or services provided along with their associated prices and the terms of the purchase.	4
IRR	IRR stands for the Internal Rate of Return, which is the discount rate that causes the NPV of all cash flows to be equal to zero.	7
Journal Entry	An entry made in the financial records of a business that lists the date, the account name that is debited (credited), and the amount by which it is debited (credited).	2
Last In First Out (LIFO)	Last In First Out, a method of accounting for inventory invoked when inventory purchased or manufactured at different costs are on the books. It determines the value of inventory sold as if the first units sold are the newest units placed in inventory.	4
Leasehold Improvements	Long-lived (multiple year) improvements made to a leased property by the tenant in order to make the property better serve the tenant's needs. The value of these improvements is treated as a long-lived asset (Property, Plant & Equipment, or PP&E) and is depreciated over the life of the asset or the life of the lease, whichever is shorter.	3
Ledgers	A ledger shows the transactions of one or more accounts. A sales ledger shows all sales transactions with customers. A general ledger shows transactions posted to asset, liability, income, and expense accounts.	2

Term	Definition	Chapter
Leverage	Calculated by the formula:Total Assets / Total Equity. Leverage is one of the components of the DuPont Framework. Also called the equity multiplier.	6
Liabilities	The obligations of a company. A more formal definition states that a liability must satisfy the following: it must impose a probable economic obligation on economic resources in the future, the obligation has to be to another entity, the event that created the obligation must have occurred in the past.	1
Liquidation	The process of winding down a company and selling its assets and discharging its liabilities.	2
Liquidity	Liquidity of an asset is the ease with which it can be converted into cash without losing value. The liquidity of a company is measured by the access it has to liquid assets.	3
Long-Lived Assets	Assets that are expected to provide a benefit to a company for more than one year. Can be physical or intangible. Also called fixed assets.	4
Loss	Arises when an asset is sold for less than its book value. A decrease in the value of an investment not yet sold is called an unrealized loss. Often related to an activity outside the normal operations of a business, such as selling a long-lived asset for less than its recorded value on the balance sheet.	4
Manufacturing Business	Businesses that manufacture products to sell to customers.	4
Mark to Market	An accounting act that occurs when a company writes the value of an asset up or down to its current market value, instead of its book value, even if the transaction does not take place. This type of accounting is also known as fair value accounting.	1
Matching Principle	An accounting principle that states that expenses should be recognized in the period in which the revenues they helped generate are recognized.	1
Materiality	An accounting principle that states that businesses are only required to report material items. A transaction is considered material if it is likely to influence the decision making of a reasonable user who is considering the accounting data or the financial reports.	1
Money Measurement Principle	An accounting principle that states that accounting records should only keep track of transactions that can be measured in monetary terms.	1
Net Book Value	Original cost of the asset (gross book value) less the accumulated depreciation or amortization. Also called book value or carrying value.	4
Net Earnings	Calculated by the formula Income before taxes - taxes. A company's total earnings. Also called net income, net profit, and the bottom line.	3
Net Income	Calculated by the formula Income before taxes - taxes. A company's total earnings. Also called net earnings, net profit, and the bottom line.	3
Net Profit	Calculated by the formula Income before taxes - taxes. A company's total earnings. Also called net earnings, net income, and the bottom line.	3

Term	Definition	Chapter
Net Revenue	A company's revenue less its contra-revenue accounts, such as sales returns or discounts on items.	1
Net Working Capital	Net Working Capital is defined as Current Assets - Current Liabilities.	7
Nominal Accounts	Accounts that show activity for a certain period of time and are reset to zero at the end of an accounting period. Nominal accounts are shown on the income statement, and the net balance of the accounts are moved to retained earnings at the end of an accounting period. Also called temporary accounts.	3
Non-Current Assets	Assets that a business will likely hold (or not consume) for more than a year or one operating cycle, whichever is longer.	3
Non-Current Liabilities	Liabilities that will come due in more than one year.	3
NPV	Net Present Value. The sum of the present value of cash inflows and cash outflows of a project or investment. The NPV is an estimate of what a project or investment is worth today.	7
On the Books	A phrase to indicate a transaction has been recorded in the financial records of a company.	1
Operating Cycle	The amount of time it takes a business to produce its goods, sell the goods, and receive the cash from its customers.	3
Operating Efficiency	A measure to determine how well a business runs its operations. For the DuPont Framework, operating efficiency is measured by the asset turnover ratio. Other measures of operating efficiency include inventory turnover, accounts receivable turnover, and accounts payable turnover.	6
Operating Expenses	Costs that a business incurs to fund its operations (excluding COGS, the costs directly associated with production). Includes items such as selling, general and administrative (SG&A) expenses and research and development (R&D) costs.	3
Operating Income	Calculated as Gross Profit - Operating Expenses. Income earned from a company's main operations. Also called EBIT (Earnings Before Interest and Taxes) and operating profit.	3
Operating Profit	Calculated as Gross Profit - Operating Expenses. Income earned from a company's main operations. Also called EBIT (Earnings Before Interest and Taxes) and operating income.	3
Operating Section	The section of the statement of cash flows that relates to a business' normal operations, which are the cash flows associated with producing and providing goods or services to customers.	5
Opportunity Cost	The lost opportunity of investing in one project as opposed to another. The opportunity cost of investing in one project is the amount that would have been earned by investing in the next best alternative project.	7

Term	Definition	Chapter
Original Cost	The price paid for an asset plus the extra expenses necessary to prepare the asset for service in the business. An asset is recorded at its original cost in the financial books of a company. Also known as gross book value.	4
Overhead	Costs incurred during the production process that cannot be traced directly to a particular unit. Some examples include utilities and rent expense for a factory building.	4
Owners' Equity	The residual interest in the assets of an entity that remains after deducting its liabilities. Owners' equity consists of two components: contributions (investments) made by owners of the business and earnings the business generates over time and retains in the business. Also called shareholders' equity, stockholders' equity, or equity.	1
Paid-In Capital	Paid-in capital consists of amounts that investors contributed to the business, and it is defined as the sum of a company's preferred stock, common stock, and additional paid-in capital.	3
Patents	Official documents issued by a government that give the document owner specific rights to an invention for a set period of time. A patent is classified as an intangible asset when it is purchased, and any costs related to developing a patent internally are expensed as research and development costs.	4
Payback Period	The number of years it would take for investors to recoup their money. The payback period is a useful way to determine the value of a potential investment, but it doesn't account for the time value of money or the additional money the project could generate after the original investment is recouped.	7
Period costs	Costs (excluding product costs) that are incurred every period while doing business, which cannot be capitalized into fixed assets, inventory, or pre-paid expenses.	4
Periodic Inventory System	An inventory system in which companies periodically determine the cost of goods sold by physically counting the inventory and subtracting the value of that inventory from the sum of the inventory it had at the beginning of the period and the inventory it purchased during that period.	4
Permanent accounts	Accounts that have a cumulative balance over time and are shown on the balance sheet. Also called real accounts.	3
Perpetual Inventory System	An inventory system in which inventory is expensed at the time the inventory is sold.	4
Preferred Stock	Shares that represent ownership of a business and rank above common stock. Preferred shares have a claim on earnings (and assets in the event of liquidation) before common stockholders.	3
Prepaid Expenses	An asset account that records expenses that have been paid in advance by a company but not yet expensed on the income statement. Prepaid expenses represent the right to receive goods or services in the future.	2

Term	Definition	Chapter
Present Value	The current value of an amount or series of amounts to be received in the future discounted by the discount rate. Calculated by the formula: $PV = FV / (1 /(1+r)^n)$ where: PV = present value, FV = future value, r = discount rate per period, n = number of periods.	7
Pretax income	Revenues and gains less all losses and expenses, except for tax expenses. Also called income before taxes.	4
Pro-formas	"As if" financial statements that forecast or prepare a firm's financial statements based on a series of assumptions. Also called financial forecasts or financial projections.	7
Product Costs	Costs of producing a good. These costs include materials, labor, and manufacturing overhead costs.	4
Profit Margin	Calculated by the formula: Net Income / Total Sales. Profit margin is a profitability ratio that is used in the DuPont Framework.	6
Profitability	The ability of a company to generate earnings above expenses and other costs incurred over a certain period of time. For the DuPont Framework, profitability is measured using the profit margin. Other measures of profitability include the gross profit margin.	6
Quick Ratio	Calculated by the formula: (Current Assets - Inventory) / Current Liabilities. The quick ratio is a liquidity ratio that measures a company's ability to pay its short-term obligations. It is a more conservative estimate than the current ratio because it only includes highly liquid current assets. Also called the acid test ratio.	6
Raw Materials	The items a manufacturing company uses to produce its inventory.	4
Real Accounts	Accounts which contain cumulative balances since the inception of the business. The balances in these accounts flow from one accounting period to the next. Real accounts include all asset, liability, and owners' equity accounts and may also be referred to as permanent accounts or Balance Sheet accounts.	3
Realization Principle	An accounting principle that states that revenues are recognized when they are earned and realized or realizable.	1
Realized Gain	Occurs when a company sells an asset for more than it bought it for.	1
Relevance	In accounting, information is relevant if it is useful to users of the financial statements and capable of influencing their decisions.	1
Relevant Cash Flows	The cash flows that will be generated specifically if, and only if, the project being evaluated is undertaken.	7
Reliability	In accounting, information is reliable if it is objective and unbiased, and accurately conveys the reality of the situation.	1
Repurchasing Stock	Occurs when a company buys back its own shares. Also called a stock buyback or share repurchase.	5

Term	Definition	Chapter
Retail Business	A retail business is one in which the company primarily purchases the products it sells and sells it to the end consumer.	4
Retained Earnings	An owners' equity account that reflects the profits a business generates and keeps for internal purposes, rather than distribute to shareholders.	3
Retiring Stock	Occurs when a company repurchases its own stock and then cancels the stock.	5
Return on Equity (ROE)	Calculated by the formula: Net Income / Total Owners' Equity. The return a company generates on the equity invested in the business by its owners.	6
Return on Investment (ROI)	ROI. Calculated by the formula: Profit related to investment / Investment amount. The return or profit earned by investing funds.	7
Revenue	Increase in a business's owner's equity as a result of providing goods or services related to its normal operations to its customers.	1
Revenue Recognition	A major principle behind accrual accounting that states that revenue should be recognized when it is earned and realized/realizable.	1
Salaries Payable	An accrued expense that represents money owed to employees for hours previously worked. Also called wages payable or accrued payroll.	1
Sales General and Administrative Expenses	The operating expenses of a company that relate to selling expenses and general and administrative expenses (such as rent, electricity, salaries of non-sales personnel). Also called SG&A.	3
Salvage Value	The amount the business believes the asset could be sold for after its useful life is over.	4
Seasonality	The fluctuations in a company's performances due to differences in the company's performance throughout the seasons.	6
Sensitivity Analysis	A method used to see how projected performance is affected by changes in assumptions.	7
Service Business	A service business is one which engages primarily in service activities to generate revenue rather than manufacture products.	4
Solvency	A company's ability to pay its debts as they come due.	5
Specific Identification	An inventory valuation method in which each specific inventory item is included in the inventory account at its specific cost. Not a common method because of the difficulties tracking specific inventory units. It tends to be most useful for businesses that sell a relatively small volume of unique, high value goods, such as car dealerships or expensive jewelry retailers.	4
Standard Cost	An inventory valuation method often used in manufacturing companies which values inventory and related cost of goods sold at a calculated standard cost of the units associated with the sale. Methods for calculating standard costs and methods for identifying and reporting variations from the standard are part of cost accounting and are outside the scope of this book.	4

Term	Definition	Chapter
Statement of Cash Flows	A financial statement that shows the cash generated and used by a company over a given accounting period. It includes three sections: cash flow from operating activities, cash flow from investing activities, and cash flow from financing activities.	5
Straight Line Depreciation	A method to calculate depreciation that spreads the depreciation expense evenly over an asset's life. Calculated by the formula: (Gross Book Value - Salvage Value) / Useful Life.	4
T-Account	T-accounts list all of the transactions that affect a particular account. They show the beginning balance, the debits and credits made to the account during that period, and the ending balance in the account. All debits are shown on the left side of the t-account and all credits are shown on the right side of the t-account.	2
Tangible Asset	Physical assets that one can touch and see.	4
Taxable Income	Gross income less all the company's tax deductions. Taxable income is found on a company's tax return, and it is the figure used to calculate taxes payable for an accounting period.	4
Taxes Payable	An amount calculated by multiplying a company's applicable income tax rate by its taxable income, which is found on the company's tax return.	4
Temporary Accounts	Accounts that show activity for a certain period of time, shown on the income statement. Also called nominal accounts. Typically includes revenue, expenses, gains and loss accounts.	3
Terminal Value	The present value of a steady stream of cash flows that extend indefinitely into the future or at a certain future date, or the value at which a business or asset can be sold at a future date.	7
Time Value of Money	The concept that a dollar received today is worth more than a dollar received a year from now. The further into the future the dollar is received, the less it is worth. This concept is true because of several factors: the opportunity cost of not investing the money in another profitable investment, inflation, and the potential risk of not receiving the money in the future.	7
Transactions	Events that impact the financial position of a business.	1
Treasury Stock	Stock that is repurchased by the issuing company. Treasury stock is shown in the equity section and has a debit balance because it is a reduction in the amount of stock.	3
Trial Balance	A list of all the accounts that have balances as of a certain date and the amount in each account. The total debits must equal the total credits.	2
Unearned Revenue	A liability account that records revenue that have been received in advance from a customer but not yet earned or recognized on the income statement. It represents an obligation to provide goods or services in the future. Also called deferred revenue.	2

Term	Definition	Chapter
Unrealized Gain	An increase in the value of an investment not yet sold.	1
Unrealized Loss	A decrease in the value of an investment not yet sold.	1
Useful Life	An estimate of how long an asset will provide a benefit to a company.	4
Variable Costs	Expenses that change with a company's production levels.	7
Wages Payable	An accrued expense that represents money owed to employees for hours previously worked. Also called accrued payroll or salaries payable.	1
Weighted Average Cost of Capital (WACC)	The discount rate that represents a company's cost of raising capital. Also called WACC. Many companies use the WACC in the NPV calculation.	7
Weighted Average Method	A method of accounting for inventory that uses the average cost of all the items in inventory to calculate COGS.	4
Work in Process (WIP) inventory	Inventory that is in production, or in between raw materials and finished goods.	4

About the Author

V.G. Narayanan

Thomas D. Casserly, Jr. Professor of Business Administration

Harvard Business School

Professor Narayanan is the Thomas D. Casserly, Jr. Professor of Business Administration at the Harvard Business School (HBS) and the Chair of the Elective Curriculum of the MBA program. He joined the HBS faculty in 1994 and has taught in several MBA, doctoral, and executive-education programs. He was the head of the Accounting and Management Unit at HBS from 2010 - 2015. In 2014, he developed the online accounting course in HBX CORe, and he continues to teach this course to thousands of students each year. His expertise is in corporate governance, executive compensation design, performance measurement, supply chain management, and cost accounting.

A recipient of several awards, Professor Narayanan has published articles and papers in several leading academic and practitioner-oriented journals, including the Harvard Business Review, Contemporary Accounting Research, Journal of Accounting and Economics, Journal of Accounting Research, Journal of Cost Management, Journal of Economics and Management Strategy, and the Management Science journal. He works with many companies in a variety of industries and locations all over the globe and has authored over seventy-five cases. Professor Narayanan has been interviewed and quoted by leading newspapers on issues relating to compensation, supply chain management, and accounting standards.

He is a member of the American Accounting Association, and the Institute of Chartered Accountants of India. He also serves on the board of directors of Leader Bank, Arlington, MA, the board of trustees of Fessenden School in Newton, MA, and the advisory board of SB International, Dallas, TX.

Professor Narayanan earned his Ph.D. in Business Administration, MA in Economics, and MS in Statistics at Stanford University. He received his Diploma in Management from the Indian Institute of Management (Ahmedabad). He is a Chartered Accountant from India.

CPSIA information can be obtained
at www.ICGtesting.com
Printed in the USA
LVHW061529171220
674450LV00011B/557